OUR *C*ONSTITUTION

LANDMARK

INTERPRETATIONS

OF AMERICA'S

GOVERNING

DOCUMENT

The FEDERALIST SOCIETY

EDITED BY

MICHAEL STOKES PAULSEN

BEAUFORT
BOOKS

Library of Congress Control Number: 2012942521
ISBN-13: 978-0-985-72150-3 (hardcover)
ISBN-13: 978-0-985-72151-0 (paperback)

For inquiries about volume orders, please contact:

Beaufort Books
27 West 20th Street, Suite 1102
New York, NY 10011
sales@beaufortbooks.com

Published in the United States by The Federalist Society

Distributed by Midpoint Trade Books
www.midpointtrade.com

Printed in the United States of America

Content design by Neuwirth & Associates, Inc.
Cover design by Oliver Munday

· OUR ·
CONSTITUTION

CONTENTS

ﻌﻠ

PREFACE

*T*he goal of this book is to provide readers with a concise, straightforward, and objective volume setting forth the text of the Constitution of the United States and the most important interpretations of that document by the U.S. Supreme Court and by other actors in our constitutional system.

The focus is on the most *important* interpretations of the Constitution—those that have shaped our understandings of the Constitution and have been of greatest historical consequence and enduring significance for the nation—*not* necessarily the "correct" or "best" interpretations of the document. Some of our nation's constitutional history has been shaped by what might charitably be called bad examples of constitutional interpretation. For example, the *Dred Scott* decision is almost universally regarded as an unsound, horrible interpretation of the Constitution, as is *Korematsu*, the case upholding the mass internment of Japanese Americans during World War II.

Because the emphasis is on what have proven to be important interpretations of the Constitution—those that have been foundational, historic, or enduring—the selections tilt slightly in the direction of *older* cases and materials. This is because they have proven themselves significant over time; their importance has endured. Where a modern case ventures a markedly new interpretation, it may be difficult to know if it will prove to be lastingly significant, for good or for ill. Today's landmarks might be tomorrow's discards. Thus, some well-known recent cases might not be included. An appendix offers a (debatable) list of the 101 most significant Supreme Court interpretations of the Constitution, including some notable recent decisions not presented in the main volume.

A vital caveat: This is not a work of commentary. It leaves *entirely to the reader* the task of evaluating the merits of the interpretations. The cases and other documents are presented here unadorned (and uncorrupted) by critical academic commentary. They are edited into as concise a form as possible, in order to make them accessible to general readers interested in America's Constitution and the most significant interpretations of that Constitution over time. The editing seeks to focus on the main propositions for which the cases are important or were important in their own time. The only editorial additions consist of short, descriptive introductions and some unavoidable notations necessary to make sense of the edits.

So let the reader beware. Not everything the Supreme Court has said about the Constitution—or that the authors of *The Federalist*, or the framing generation, or presidents in making veto statements or executive proclamations have said—is necessarily a sound, correct interpretation of the Constitution. The materials presented here simply lay out *what has been said* about the Constitution that has proved to be of enduring importance in shaping our understandings of the Constitution—for better or for worse.

The task of interpreting the interpretations—of evaluating these interpretations of the Constitution—is for you, the reader. In a sense, this reflects the faith of the framers of the Constitution, that "We the People of the United States" would be, and would remain, the masters of our own written constitution, fully capable of interpreting it for ourselves, doing so correctly, and applying it faithfully.

Michael Stokes Paulsen
The University of St. Thomas
Minneapolis, Minnesota
September 17, 2012

Acknowledgments

I have many people to thank (and no one to blame) for their help, support, and advice in producing this book.

Eugene Meyer, president of the Federalist Society, first suggested this project and enlisted me to do it. Gene found a publisher and offered comments, suggestions, and encouragement. He was truly the executive producer of the project. He was significantly assisted in this role by Dean Reuter, Vice President & Director of the Practice Groups.

Great thanks go to Scott and Cyan Banister, who first proposed this project to Gene and whose extraordinary generosity made it possible.

I could not have completed this project without the absolutely indispensable assistance of my son, Luke Paulsen (Princeton '14). Luke, my co-author on a different book project on the Constitution, was more than an assistant here. He was essentially my coeditor, working alongside me during the summers of 2011 and 2012. He assisted—or performed—the edits for every entry. His advice and judgment, uncorrupted by a law-school education, were always fresh and sound.

Nelson Lund, of George Mason University, reviewed the entire penultimate manuscript and offered invaluable comments, suggestions, and proposed additions, as did Gary Lawson of Boston University, who likewise contributed important comments and ideas.

Byron Millea (University of St. Thomas Law School '14) provided research assistance for the bibliography.

Finally, my thanks to the editorial and production staff at Midpoint Plus who worked on this project and saw it through to completion, especially Megan Trank, an uncommonly thoughtful, patient, and indulgent editor.

A Note on the Editing of Cases and Documents

Pruning these materials down to manageable size has meant deleting some content. Here are my rules: Where substantive material, other than footnotes or citations to other judicial opinions, has been deleted, it is marked with an ellipsis (". . ."). Footnotes, however, are deleted without notice. Where a case cites another case, or a treatise or article, as authority, such a reference is often deleted without an ellipsis. My thought is that a citation, without more, frequently does not help the reader understand an opinion's reasoning and is distracting and irritating to the general reader's eye. But so are too many ellipsis. Some case citations are retained where the precedent invoked is important, is already familiar, is quoted directly, or helps explain the citing court's reasoning.

Deletions shorten paragraphs. As a result, I have sometimes combined shortened paragraphs to save space and to create a better flow. I have not marked such changes, since they do not change content. Bracketed material ("[ ]") denotes an insertion, made either to make a deletion sensible, adjust grammar, or explain briefly what has been taken out. Entire concurring and dissenting opinions are often deleted, without ellipses. Concurrences are retained where they add significant points not contained in the majority opinion. Dissents are retained to highlight points of disagreement.

The editor's introductions provide vote counts for the cases, typically grouping all majority and concurring opinions together, and all dissents together. Sometimes this is misleading. A concurrence "in the judgment" sometimes rejects the reasoning of a majority or plurality opinion and is thus, in reality, something of a dissent. Sometimes an opinion is partly a concurrence and partly a dissent. Readers who desire a detailed understanding of the disagreements within the Court in any specific case should, of course, read the published opinions in their entirety.

The Constitution
of the
United States of America

PREAMBLE

We the People of the United States, in Order to form a more perfect Union, establish Justice, insure domestic Tranquility, provide for the common defence, promote the general Welfare, and secure the Blessings of Liberty to ourselves and our Posterity, do ordain and establish this Constitution for the United States of America.

ARTICLE I.

SECTION 1. All legislative Powers herein granted shall be vested in a Congress of the United States, which shall consist of a Senate and House of Representatives.

SECTION 2. The House of Representatives shall be composed of Members chosen every second Year by the People of the several States, and the Electors in each State shall have the Qualifications requisite for Electors of the most numerous Branch of the State Legislature.

No Person shall be a Representative who shall not have attained to the age of twenty five Years, and been seven Years a Citizen of the United States, and who shall not, when elected, be an Inhabitant of that State in which he shall be chosen.

Representatives and direct Taxes shall be apportioned among the several States which may be included within this Union, according to their respective Numbers, which shall be determined by adding to the whole Number of free Persons, including those bound to Service for a Term of Years, and excluding Indians not taxed, three fifths of all other Persons. The actual Enumeration shall be made within three Years after the first Meeting of the Congress of the United States, and within every subsequent Term of ten Years, in such Manner as they shall by Law direct. The Number of Representatives shall not exceed one for every thirty Thousand, but each State shall have at Least one Representative; and until such enumeration shall be made, the State of New Hampshire shall be entitled to chuse three, Massachusetts eight, Rhode-Island and Providence Plantations one, Connecticut five, New-York six, New Jersey four, Pennsylvania eight, Delaware one, Maryland six, Virginia ten, North Carolina five, South Carolina five, and Georgia three.

When vacancies happen in the Representation from any State, the Executive Authority thereof shall issue Writs of Election to fill such Vacancies.

The House of Representatives shall chuse their Speaker and other Officers; and shall have the sole Power of Impeachment.

SECTION 3. The Senate of the United States shall be composed of two Senators from each State, chosen by the Legislature thereof, for six Years; and each Senator shall have one Vote.

Immediately after they shall be assembled in Consequence of the first Election, they shall be divided as equally as may be into three Classes. The Seats of the Senators of the first Class shall be vacated at the Expiration of the second Year, of the second Class at the Expiration of the fourth Year, and of the third Class at the Expiration of the sixth Year, so that one third may be chosen every second Year; and if Vacancies happen by Resignation, or otherwise, during the Recess of the Legislature of any State, the Executive thereof may make temporary Appointments until the next Meeting of the Legislature, which shall then fill such Vacancies.

No Person shall be a Senator who shall not have attained to the Age of thirty Years, and been nine Years a Citizen of the United States, and who shall not, when elected, be an Inhabitant of that State for which he shall be chosen.

The Vice President of the United States shall be President of the Senate but shall have no Vote, unless they be equally divided.

The Senate shall chuse their other Officers, and also a President pro tempore, in the Absence of the Vice President, or when he shall exercise the Office of President of the United States.

The Senate shall have the sole Power to try all Impeachments. When sitting for that Purpose, they shall be on Oath or Affirmation. When the President of the United States is tried the Chief Justice shall preside: And no Person shall be convicted without the Concurrence of two thirds of the Members present.

Judgment in Cases of Impeachment shall not extend further than to removal from Office, and disqualification to hold and enjoy any Office of honor, Trust or Profit under the United States: but the Party convicted shall nevertheless be liable and subject to Indictment, Trial, Judgment and Punishment, according to Law.

SECTION 4. The Times, Places and Manner of holding Elections for Senators and Representatives, shall be prescribed in each State by the Legislature thereof; but the Congress may at any time by Law make or alter such Regulations, except as to the Places of chusing Senators.

The Congress shall assemble at least once in every Year, and such Meeting shall be on the first Monday in December, unless they shall by Law appoint a different Day.

SECTION 5. Each House shall be the Judge of the Elections, Returns and Qualifications of its own Members, and a Majority of each shall constitute a Quorum to do Business; but a smaller Number may adjourn from day to day, and may be authorized to compel the Attendance of absent Members, in such Manner, and under such Penalties as each House may provide.

Each House may determine the Rules of its Proceedings, punish its Members for disorderly Behaviour, and, with the Concurrence of two thirds, expel a Member.

Each House shall keep a Journal of its Proceedings, and from time to time publish the same, excepting such Parts as may in their Judgment require Secrecy; and the Yeas and Nays of the Members of either House on any question shall, at the Desire of one fifth of those Present, be entered on the Journal.

Neither House, during the Session of Congress, shall, without the Consent of the other, adjourn for more than three days, nor to any other Place than that in which the two Houses shall be sitting.

SECTION 6. The Senators and Representatives shall receive a

Compensation for their Services, to be ascertained by Law, and paid out of the Treasury of the United States. They shall in all Cases, except Treason, Felony and Breach of the Peace, be privileged from Arrest during their Attendance at the Session of their respective Houses, and in going to and returning from the same; and for any Speech or Debate in either House, they shall not be questioned in any other Place.

No Senator or Representative shall, during the Time for which he was elected, be appointed to any civil Office under the Authority of the United States, which shall have been created, or the Emoluments whereof shall have been encreased during such time; and no Person holding any Office under the United States, shall be a Member of either House during his Continuance in Office.

SECTION 7. All Bills for raising Revenue shall originate in the House of Representatives; but the Senate may propose or concur with amendments as on other Bills.

Every Bill which shall have passed the House of Representatives and the Senate, shall, before it become a law, be presented to the President of the United States: If he approve he shall sign it, but if not he shall return it, with his Objections to that House in which it shall have originated, who shall enter the Objections at large on their Journal, and proceed to reconsider it. If after such Reconsideration two thirds of that House shall agree to pass the Bill, it shall be sent, together with the Objections, to the other House, by which it shall likewise be reconsidered, and if approved by two thirds of that House, it shall become a Law. But in all such Cases the Votes of both Houses shall be determined by Yeas and Nays, and the Names of the Persons voting for and against the Bill shall be entered on the Journal of each House respectively. If any Bill shall not be returned by the President within ten Days (Sundays excepted) after it shall have been presented to him, the Same shall be a Law, in like Manner as if he had signed it, unless the Congress by their Adjournment prevent its Return, in which Case it shall not be a Law.

Every Order, Resolution, or Vote to which the Concurrence of the Senate and House of Representatives may be necessary (except on a question of Adjournment) shall be presented to the President of the United States; and before the Same shall take Effect, shall be approved by him, or being disapproved by him, shall be repassed by two thirds of the Senate and House of Representatives, according to the Rules and Limitations prescribed in the Case of a Bill.

SECTION 8. The Congress shall have Power To lay and collect Taxes, Duties, Imposts and Excises, to pay the Debts and provide for the common Defence and general Welfare of the United States; but all Duties, Imposts and Excises shall be uniform throughout the United States;

To borrow Money on the credit of the United States;

To regulate Commerce with foreign Nations, and among the several States, and with the Indian Tribes;

To establish an uniform Rule of Naturalization, and uniform Laws on the subject of Bankruptcies throughout the United States;

To coin Money, regulate the Value thereof, and of foreign Coin, and fix the Standard of Weights and Measures;

To provide for the Punishment of counterfeiting the Securities and current Coin of the United States;

To establish Post Offices and post Roads;

To promote the Progress of Science and useful Arts, by securing for limited Times to Authors and Inventors the exclusive Right to their respective Writings and Discoveries;

To constitute Tribunals inferior to the supreme Court;

To define and punish Piracies and Felonies committed on the high Seas, and Offences against the Law of Nations;

To declare War, grant Letters of Marque and Reprisal, and make Rules concerning Captures on Land and Water;

To raise and support Armies, but no Appropriation of Money to that Use shall be for a longer Term than two Years;

To provide and maintain a Navy;

To make Rules for the Government and Regulation of the land and naval Forces;

To provide for calling forth the Militia to execute the Laws of the Union, suppress Insurrections and repeal Invasions;

To provide for organizing, arming, and disciplining, the Militia, and for governing such Part of them as may be employed in the Service of the United States, reserving to the States respectively, the Appointment of the Officers, and the Authority of training the Militia according to the discipline prescribed by Congress;

To exercise exclusive Legislation in all Cases whatsoever, over such District (not exceeding ten Miles square) as may, by Cession of Particular States, and the Acceptance of Congress, become the Seat of the

Government of the United States, and to exercise like Authority over all Places purchased by the Consent of the Legislature of the State in which the Same shall be, for the Erection of Forts, Magazines, Arsenals, dock-Yards and other needful Buildings;—And

To make all Laws which shall be necessary and proper for carrying into Execution the foregoing Powers and all other Powers vested by this Constitution in the Government of the United States, or in any Department or Officer thereof.

SECTION 9. The Migration or Importation of such Persons as any of the States now existing shall think proper to admit, shall not be prohibited by the Congress prior to the Year one thousand eight hundred and eight, but a Tax or duty may be imposed on such Importation, not exceeding ten dollars for each Person.

The Privilege of the Writ of Habeas Corpus shall not be suspended, unless when in Cases or Rebellion or Invasion the public Safety may require it.

No Bill of Attainder or ex post facto Law shall be passed.

No Capitation, or other direct, Tax shall be laid, unless in Proportion to the Census of Enumeration herein before directed to be taken.

No Tax or Duty shall be laid on Articles exported from any State.

No Preference shall be given by any Regulation of Commerce or Revenue to the Ports of one State over those of another: nor shall Vessels bound to, or from, one State, be obliged to enter, clear or pay Duties in another.

No Money shall be drawn from the Treasury, but in Consequence of Appropriations made by Law; and a regular Statement and Account of the Receipts and Expenditures of all public Money shall be published from time to time.

No Title of Nobility shall be granted by the United States: And no Person holding any Office of Profit or Trust under them, shall, without the Consent of the Congress, accept of any present, Emolument, Office, or Title, of any kind whatever, from any King, Prince or foreign State.

SECTION 10. No State shall enter into any Treaty, Alliance, or Confederation; grant Letters of Marque and Reprisal; coin Money; emit Bills of Credit; make any Thing but gold and silver Coin a Tender in Payment of Debts; pass any Bill of Attainder, ex post facto Law, or Law impairing the Obligation of Contracts, or grant any Title of Nobility.

No State shall, without the Consent of the Congress, lay any Imposts or Duties on Imports or Exports, except what may be absolutely necessary for executing it's inspection Laws: and the net Produce of all Duties and Imposts, laid by any State on Imports or Exports, shall be for the Use of the Treasury of the United States; and all such Laws shall be subject to the Revision and Controul of the Congress.

No State shall, without the Consent of Congress, lay any Duty of Tonnage, keep Troops, or Ships of War in time of Peace, enter into any Agreement or Compact with another State, or with a foreign Power, or engage in War, unless actually invaded, or in such imminent Danger as will not admit of delay.

ARTICLE II.

SECTION 1. The executive Power shall be vested in a President of the United States of America. He shall hold his Office during the Term of four Years, and, together with the Vice President, chosen for the same Term, be elected, as follows:

Each State shall appoint, in such Manner as the Legislature thereof may direct, a Number of Electors, equal to the whole Number of Senators and Representatives to which the State may be entitled in the Congress: but no Senator or Representative, or Person holding an Office of Trust or Profit under the United States, shall be appointed an Elector.

The Electors shall meet in their respective States, and vote by Ballot for two Persons, of whom one at least shall not be an Inhabitant of the same State with themselves. And they shall make a List of all the Persons voted for, and of the Number of Votes for each; which List they shall sign and certify, and transmit sealed to the Seat of the Government of the United States, directed to the President of the Senate. The President of the Senate shall, in the Presence of the Senate and House of Representatives, open all the Certificates, and the Votes shall then be counted. The Person having the greatest Number of Votes shall be the President, if such Number be a Majority of the whole Number of Electors appointed; and if there be more than one who have such Majority, and have an equal Number of Votes, then the House of Representatives shall immediately chuse by Ballot one of them for President; and if no Person have a Majority, then from the five highest on the List the said House shall in like Manner chuse the President. But in chusing the President, the Votes shall be taken by States, the Representatives from each State having one Vote; a quorum for this Purpose shall consist of a Member or Members from two thirds of the States, and a Majority of all the States shall be necessary to a Choice. In every Case, after the Choice of the President, the Person having the greatest Number of Votes of the Electors shall be the Vice President. But if there should remain two or more who have equal Votes, the Senate shall chuse from them by Ballot the Vice President.

The Congress may determine the Time of chusing the Electors, and the Day on which they shall give their Votes; which Day shall be the same throughout the United States.

No Person except a natural born Citizen, or a Citizen of the United States, at the time of the Adoption of this Constitution, shall be eligible to the Office of President; neither shall any person be eligible to that Office who shall not have attained to the Age of thirty five Years, and been fourteen Years a Resident within the United States.

In Case of the Removal of the President from Office, or of his Death, Resignation, or Inability to discharge the Powers and Duties of the said Office, the Same shall devolve on the Vice President, and the Congress may by Law provide for the Case of Removal, Death, Resignation or Inability, both of the President and Vice President, declaring what Officer shall then act as President, and such Officer shall act accordingly, until the Disability be removed, or a President shall be elected.

The President shall, at stated Times, receive for his Services, a Compensation, which shall neither be encreased nor diminished during the Period for which he shall have been elected, and he shall not receive within that Period any other Emolument from the United States, or any of them.

Before he enter on the Execution of his Office, he shall take the following Oath or Affirmation:— "I do solemnly swear (or affirm) that I will faithfully execute the Office of President of the United States, and will to the best of my Ability, preserve, protect and defend the Constitution of the United States."

SECTION 2. The President shall be Commander in Chief of the Army and Navy of the United States, and of the Militia of the several States, when called into the actual Service of the United States; he may require the Opinion, in writing, of the principal Officer in each of the executive Departments, upon any Subject relating to the Duties of their respective Offices, and he shall have Power to Grant Reprieves and Pardons for Offences against the United States, except in Cases of Impeachment.

He shall have Power, by and with the Advice and Consent of the Senate, to make Treaties, provided two thirds of the Senators present concur; and he shall nominate, and by and with the Advice and Consent of the Senate, shall appoint Ambassadors, other public Ministers and Consuls, Judges of the supreme Court, and all other Officers of the United States, whose Appointments are not herein otherwise provided for, and which shall be established by Law: but the Congress may by Law vest the Appointment of such inferior Officers, as they think proper, in the President alone, in the Courts of Law, or in the Heads of Departments.

The President shall have Power to fill up all Vacancies that may happen during the Recess of the Senate, by granting Commissions which shall expire at the End of their next Session.

SECTION 3. He shall from time to time give to the Congress Information on the State of the Union, and recommend to their Consideration such Measures as he shall judge necessary and expedient; he may, on extraordinary Occasions, convene both Houses, or either of them, and in Case of Disagreement between them, with Respect to the Time of Adjournment, he may adjourn them to such Time as he shall think proper; he shall receive Ambassadors and other public Ministers; he shall take Care that the Laws be faithfully executed, and shall Commission all the Officers of the United States.

SECTION 4. The President, Vice President and all Civil Officers of the United States, shall be removed from Office on Impeachment for and Conviction of, Treason, Bribery, or other high Crimes and Misdemeanors.

ARTICLE III

SECTION 1. The judicial Power of the United States, shall be vested in one supreme Court, and in such inferior Courts as the Congress may from time to time ordain and establish. The Judges, both of the supreme and inferior Courts, shall hold their Offices during good Behaviour, and shall, at stated Times, receive for their Services, a Compensation, which shall not be diminished during their Continuance in Office.

SECTION 2. The judicial Power shall extend to all Cases, in Law and

Equity, arising under this Constitution, the Laws of the United States, and Treaties made, or which shall be made, under their Authority;—to all Cases affecting Ambassadors, other public ministers and Consuls;—to all Cases of admiralty and maritime Jurisdiction;—to Controversies to which the United States shall be a Party;—to Controversies between two or more States;—between a State and Citizens of another State;—between Citizens of different States;—between Citizens of the same State claiming Lands under Grants of different States, and between a State, or the Citizens thereof, and foreign States, Citizens or Subjects.

In all Cases affecting Ambassadors, other public Ministers and Consuls, and those in which a State shall be Party, the supreme Court shall have original Jurisdiction. In all the other Cases before mentioned, the supreme Court shall have appellate Jurisdiction, both as to Law and Fact, with such Exceptions, and under such Regulations as the Congress shall make.

The Trial of all Crimes, except in Cases of Impeachment, shall be by Jury; and such Trial shall be held in the State where the said Crimes shall have been committed; but when not committed within any State, the Trial shall be at such Place or Places as the Congress may by Law have directed.

SECTION 3. Treason against the United States, shall consist only in levying War against them, or in adhering to their Enemies, giving them Aid and Comfort. No Person shall be convicted of Treason unless on the Testimony of two Witnesses to the same overt Act, or on Confession in open Court.

The Congress shall have Power to declare the Punishment of Treason, but no Attainder of Treason shall work Corruption of Blood, or Forfeiture except during the Life of the Person attainted.

ARTICLE IV.

SECTION 1. Full Faith and Credit shall be given in each State to the public Acts, Records, and judicial Proceedings of every other State. And the Congress may by general Laws prescribe the Manner in which such Acts, Records and Proceedings shall be proved, and the Effect thereof.

SECTION 2. The Citizens of each State shall be entitled to all Privileges and Immunities of Citizens in the several States.

A Person charged in any State with Treason, Felony, or other Crime, who shall flee from Justice, and be found in another State, shall on Demand of the executive Authority of the State from which he fled, be delivered up, to be removed to the State having Jurisdiction of the Crime.

No Person held to Service or Labour in one State, under the Laws thereof, escaping into another, shall, in Consequence of any Law or Regulation therein, be discharged from such Service or Labour, but shall be delivered up on Claim of the Party to whom such Service or Labour may be due.

SECTION 3. New States may be admitted by the Congress into this Union; but no new State shall be formed or erected within the Jurisdiction of any other State; nor any State be formed by the Junction of two or more States, or Parts of States, without the Consent of the Legislatures of the States concerned as well as of the Congress.

The Congress shall have Power to dispose of and make all needful Rules and Regulations respecting the Territory or other Property belonging to the United States; and nothing in this Constitution shall be so construed as to Prejudice any Claims of the United States, or of any particular State.

SECTION 4. The United States shall guarantee to every State in this Union a Republican Form of Government, and shall protect each of them against Invasion; and on Application of the Legislature, or of the Executive (when the Legislature cannot be convened) against domestic Violence.

ARTICLE V.

The Congress, whenever two thirds of both Houses shall deem it necessary, shall propose Amendments to this Constitution, or, on the Application of the Legislatures of two thirds of the several States, shall call a Convention for proposing Amendments, which, in either Case, shall be valid to all Intents and Purposes, as Part of this Constitution, when ratified by the Legislatures of three fourths of the several States, or by Conventions in three fourths thereof, as the one or the other Mode of Ratification may be proposed by the Congress; Provided that no Amendment which may be made prior to the Year One thousand eight hundred and eight shall in any Manner affect the first and fourth Clauses in the Ninth Section of the first Article; and that no State, without its Consent, shall be deprived of its equal Suffrage in the Senate.

ARTICLE VI.

All Debts contracted and Engagements entered into, before the Adoption of this Constitution, shall be as valid against the United States under this Constitution, as under the Confederation.

This Constitution, and the Laws of the United States which shall be made in Pursuance thereof; and all Treaties made, or which shall be made, under the Authority of the United States, shall be the supreme Law of the Land; and the Judges in every State shall be bound thereby, any Thing in the Constitution or Laws of any state to the Contrary notwithstanding.

The Senators and Representatives before mentioned, and the Members of the several State Legislatures, and all executive and judicial Officers, both of the United States and of the several States, shall be bound by Oath or Affirmation, to support this Constitution; but no religious Test shall ever be required as a Qualification to any Office or public Trust under the United States.

ARTICLE VII.

The Ratification of the Conventions of nine States, shall be sufficient for the Establishment of this Constitution between the States so ratifying the same.

ARTICLES IN ADDITION TO, AND AMENDMENTS OF, THE CONSTITUTION OF THE UNITED STATES OF AMERICA, PROPOSED BY CONGRESS, AND RATIFIED BY THE LEGISLATURES OF THE SEVERAL STATES, PURSUANT TO THE FIFTH ARTICLE OF THE ORIGINAL CONSTITUTION

AMENDMENT I [1791].

Congress shall make no law respecting an establishment of religion, or prohibiting the free exercise thereof; or abridging the freedom of speech, or of the press; or the right of the people peaceably to assemble, and to petition the Government for a redress of grievances.

AMENDMENT II [1791].

A well regulated Militia, being necessary to the security of a free State, the right of the people to keep and bear Arms, shall not be infringed.

AMENDMENT III [1791].

No Soldier shall, in time of peace be quartered in any house, without the consent of the Owner, nor in time of war, but in a manner to be prescribed by law.

AMENDMENT IV [1791].

The right of the people to be secure in their persons, houses, papers, and effects, against unreasonable searches and seizures, shall not be violated, and no Warrants shall issue, but upon probable cause, supported by Oath or affirmation, and particularly describing the place to be searched, and the persons or things to be seized.

AMENDMENT V [1791].

No person shall be held to answer for a capital, or otherwise infamous crime, unless on a presentment or indictment of a Grand Jury, except in cases arising in the land or naval forces, or in the Militia, when in actual service in time of War or public danger; nor shall any person be subject for the same offence to be twice put in jeopardy of life or limb; nor shall be compelled in any criminal case to be a witness against himself, nor be deprived of life, liberty, or property, without due process of law; nor shall private property be taken for public use, without just compensation.

AMENDMENT VI [1791].

In all criminal prosecutions, the accused shall enjoy the right to a speedy and public trial, by an impartial jury of the State and district wherein the crime shall have been committed, which district shall have been previously ascertained by law, and to be informed of the nature and cause of the accusation; to be confronted with the witnesses against him; to have compulsory process for obtaining witnesses in his favor, and to have the Assistance of Counsel for his defence.

AMENDMENT VII [1791].

In Suits at common law, where the value in controversy shall exceed twenty dollars, the right of trial by jury shall be preserved, and no fact tried by a jury, shall be otherwise re-examined in any Court of the United States, than according to the rules of the common law.

AMENDMENT VIII [1791].

Excessive bail shall not be required, nor excessive fines imposed, nor cruel and unusual punishments inflicted.

AMENDMENT IX [1791].

The enumeration in the Constitution, of certain rights, shall not be construed to deny or disparage others retained by the people.

AMENDMENT X [1791].

The powers not delegated to the United States by the Constitution, nor prohibited by it to the States, are reserved to the States respectively, or to the people.

AMENDMENT XI [1798].

The Judicial power of the United States shall not be construed to extend to any suit in law or equity, commenced or prosecuted against one of the United States by Citizens of another State, or by Citizens or Subjects of any Foreign State.

AMENDMENT XII [1804].

The Electors shall meet in their respective states, and vote by ballot for President and Vice-President, one of whom, at least, shall not be an inhabitant of the same state with themselves; they shall name in their ballots the person voted for as President, and in distinct ballots the person voted for as Vice-President, and they shall make distinct lists of all persons voted for as President, and of all persons voted for as Vice-President, and of the number of votes for each, which lists they shall sign and certify, and transmit sealed to the seat of the government of the United States, directed to the President of the Senate;—The President of the Senate shall, in the presence of the Senate and House of Representatives, open all the certificates and the votes shall then be counted;—The person having the greatest number of votes for President, shall be the President, if such number be a majority of the whole number of Electors appointed; and if no person have such majority, then from the persons having the highest numbers not exceeding three on the list of those voted for as President, the House of Representatives shall choose immediately, by ballot, the President. But in choosing the President, the votes shall be taken by states, the representation from each state having one vote; a quorum for this purpose shall consist of a member or members from two-thirds of the states, and a majority of all the states shall be necessary to a choice. And if the House of Representatives shall not choose a President whenever the right of choice shall devolve upon them, before the fourth day of March next following, then the Vice-President shall act as President, as in the case of the death or other constitutional disability of the President.—The person having the greatest number of votes as Vice-President, shall be the Vice-President, if such number be a majority of the whole number of Electors appointed, and if no person have a majority, then from the two highest numbers on the list, the Senate shall choose the Vice-President; a quorum for the purpose shall consist of two-thirds of the whole number of Senators, and a majority of the whole number shall be necessary to a choice. But no person constitutionally ineligible to the office of President shall be eligible to that of Vice-President of the United States.

Amendment XIII [1865].

SECTION 1. Neither slavery nor involuntary servitude, except as a punishment for crime whereof the party shall have been duly convicted, shall exist within the United States, or any place subject to their jurisdiction.

SECTION 2. Congress shall have power to enforce this article by appropriate legislation.

AMENDMENT XIV [1868].

SECTION 1. All persons born or naturalized in the United States, and subject to the jurisdiction thereof, are citizens of the United States and of the State wherein they reside. No State shall make or enforce any law which shall abridge the privileges or immunities of citizens of the United States; nor shall any State deprive any person of life, liberty, or property, without due process of law; nor deny to any person within its jurisdiction the equal protection of the laws.

SECTION 2. Representatives shall be apportioned among the several States according to their respective numbers, counting the whole number of persons in each State, excluding Indians not taxed. But when the right to vote at any election for the choice of electors for President and Vice President of the United States, Representatives in Congress, the Executive and Judicial officers of a State, or the members of the Legislature thereof, is denied to any of the male inhabitants of such State, being twenty-one years of age, and citizens of the United States, or in any way abridged, except for participation in rebellion, or other crime, the basis of representation therein shall be reduced in the proportion which the number of such male citizens shall bear to the whole number of male citizens twenty-one years of age in such State.

SECTION 3. No person shall be a Senator or Representative in Congress, or elector of President and Vice President, or hold any office, civil or military, under the United States, or under any State, who, having previously taken an oath, as a member of Congress, or as an officer of the United States, or as a member of any State legislature, or as an executive or judicial officer of any State, to support the Constitution of the United States, shall have engaged in insurrection or rebellion against the same, or given aid or comfort to the enemies thereof. But Congress may by a vote of two-thirds of each House, remove such disability.

SECTION 4. The validity of the public debt of the United States, authorized by law, including debts incurred for payment of pensions and bounties for services in suppressing insurrection or rebellion, shall not be questioned. But neither the United States nor any State shall assume or pay any debt or obligation incurred in aid of insurrection or rebellion against the United States, or any claim for the loss or emancipation of any slave; but all such debts, obligations and claims shall be held illegal and void.

SECTION 5. The Congress shall have power to enforce, by appropriate legislation, the provisions of this article.

AMENDMENT XV [1870].

SECTION 1. The right of citizens of the United States to vote shall not be denied or abridged by the United States or by any State on account of race, color, or previous condition of servitude.

SECTION 2. The Congress shall have power to enforce this article by appropriate legislation.

AMENDMENT XVI [1913].

The Congress shall have power to lay and collect taxes on incomes, from whatever source derived, without apportionment among the several States, and without regard to any census or enumeration.

AMENDMENT XVII [1913].

The Senate of the United States shall be composed of two Senators from each State, elected by the people thereof, for six years; and each Senator shall have one vote. The electors in each State shall have the qualifications requisite for electors of the most numerous branch of the State legislatures.

When vacancies happen in the representation of any State in the Senate, the executive authority of such State shall issue writs of election to fill such vacancies: Provided, That the legislature of any State may empower the executive thereof to make temporary appointments until the people fill the vacancies by election as the legislature may direct.

This amendment shall not be so construed as to affect the election or term of any Senator chosen before it becomes valid as part of the Constitution.

AMENDMENT XVIII [1919].

SECTION 1. After one year from the ratification of this article the manufacture, sale, or transportation of intoxicating liquors within, the importation thereof into, or the exportation thereof from the United States and all territory subject to the jurisdiction thereof for beverage purposes is hereby prohibited.

SECTION 2. The Congress and the several States shall have concurrent power to enforce this article by appropriate legislation.

SECTION 3. This article shall be inoperative unless it shall have been ratified as an amendment to the Constitution by the legislatures of the several States, as provided in the Constitution, within seven years from the date of the submission hereof to the States by the Congress.

AMENDMENT XIX [1920].

The right of citizens of the United States to vote shall not be denied or abridged by the United States or by any State on account of sex.

Congress shall have power to enforce this article by appropriate legislation.

AMENDMENT XX [1933].

SECTION 1. The terms of the President and Vice President shall end at noon on the 20th day of January, and the terms of Senators and Representatives at noon on the 3d day of January, of the years in which such terms would have ended if this article had not been ratified; and the terms of their successors shall then begin.

SECTION 2. The Congress shall assemble at least once in every year, and such meeting shall begin at noon on the 3d day of January, unless they shall by law appoint a different day.

SECTION 3. If, at the time fixed for the beginning of the term of the President, the President elect shall have died, the Vice President elect shall become President. If a President shall not have been chosen before the time fixed for the beginning of his term, or if the President elect shall have failed to qualify, then the Vice President elect shall act as President until a President shall have qualified; and the Congress may by law provide for the case wherein neither a President elect nor a

Vice President elect shall have qualified, declaring who shall then act as President, or the manner in which one who is to act shall be selected, and such person shall act accordingly until a President or Vice President shall have qualified.

SECTION 4. The Congress may by law provide for the case of the death of any of the persons from whom the House of Representatives may choose a President whenever the right of choice shall have devolved upon them, and for the case of the death of any of the persons from whom the Senate may choose a Vice President whenever the right of choice shall have devolved upon them.

SECTION 5. Sections 1 and 2 shall take effect on the 15th day of October following the ratification of this article.

SECTION 6. This article shall be inoperative unless it shall have been ratified as an amendment to the Constitution by the legislatures of three-fourths of the several States within seven years from the date of its submission.

AMENDMENT XXI [1933].

SECTION 1. The eighteenth article of amendment to the Constitution of the United States is hereby repealed.

SECTION 2. The transportation or importation into any State, Territory, or possession of the United States for delivery or use therein of intoxicating liquors, in violation of the laws thereof, is hereby prohibited.

SECTION 3. This article shall be inoperative unless it shall have been ratified as an amendment to the Constitution by conventions in the several States, as provided in the Constitution, within seven years from the date of the submission hereof to the States by the Congress.

AMENDMENT XXII [1951].

SECTION 1. No person shall be elected to the office of the President more than twice, and no person who has held the office of President, or acted as President, for more than two years of a term to which some other person was elected President shall be elected to the office of the President more than once. But this article shall not apply to any person holding the office of President when this article was proposed by the Congress, and shall not prevent any person who may be holding the office of President, or acting as President, during the term within which this article becomes operative from holding the office of President or acting as President during the remainder of such term.

SECTION 2. This article shall be inoperative unless it shall have been ratified as an amendment to the Constitution by the legislatures of three-fourths of the several states within seven years from the date of its submission to the states by the Congress.

Amendment XXIII [1961].

SECTION 1. The District constituting the seat of government of the United States shall appoint in such manner as the Congress may direct:

A number of electors of President and Vice President equal to the whole number of Senators and Representatives in Congress to which the District would be entitled if it were a state, but in no event more than the least populous state; they shall be in addition to those appointed by the states, but they shall be considered, for the purposes of the election of President and Vice President, to be electors appointed by a state; and they shall meet in the District and perform such duties as provided by the twelfth article of amendment.

SECTION 2. The Congress shall have power to enforce this article by appropriate legislation.

Amendment XXIV [1964].

SECTION 1. The right of citizens of the United States to vote in any primary or other election for President or Vice President, for electors for President or Vice President, or for Senator or Representative in Congress, shall not be denied or abridged by the United States or any state by reason of failure to pay any poll tax or other tax.

SECTION 2. The Congress shall have power to enforce this article by appropriate legislation.

Amendment XXV [1967].

SECTION 1. In case of the removal of the President from office or of his death or resignation, the Vice President shall become President.

SECTION 2. Whenever there is a vacancy in the office of the Vice

President, the President shall nominate a Vice President who shall take office upon confirmation by a majority vote of both Houses of Congress.

SECTION 3. Whenever the President transmits to the President pro tempore of the Senate and the Speaker of the House of Representatives his written declaration that he is unable to discharge the powers and duties of his office, and until he transmits to them a written declaration to the contrary, such powers and duties shall be discharged by the Vice President as Acting President.

SECTION 4. Whenever the Vice President and a majority of either the principal officers of the executive departments or of such other body as Congress may by law provide, transmit to the President pro tempore of the Senate and the Speaker of the House of Representatives their written declaration that the President is unable to discharge the powers and duties of his office, the Vice President shall immediately assume the powers and duties of the office as Acting President.

Thereafter, when the President transmits to the President pro tempore of the Senate and the Speaker of the House of Representatives his written declaration that no inability exists, he shall resume the powers and duties of his office unless the Vice President and a majority of either the principal officers of the executive department or of such other body as Congress may by law provide, transmit within four days to the President pro tempore of the Senate and the Speaker of the House of Representatives their written declaration that the President is unable to discharge the powers and duties of his office. Thereupon Congress shall decide the issue, assembling within forty-eight hours for that purpose if not in session. If the Congress, within twenty-one days after receipt of the latter written declaration, or, if Congress is not in session, within twenty-one days after Congress is required to assemble, determines by two-thirds vote of both Houses that the President is unable to discharge the powers and duties of his office, the Vice President shall continue to discharge the same as Acting President; otherwise, the President shall resume the powers and duties of his office.

AMENDMENT XXVI [1971].

SECTION 1. The right of citizens of the United States, who are 18 years of age or older, to vote, shall not be denied or abridged by the United States or any state on account of age.

SECTION 2. The Congress shall have the power to enforce this article by appropriate legislation.

AMENDMENT XXVII [1992].

No law varying the compensation for the services of the Senators and Representatives shall take effect until an election of Representatives shall have intervened.

ON THE
NATURE AND
STRUCTURE
of the
NATIONAL
GOVERNMENT
(1787–1793)

EXCERPTS FROM
THE FEDERALIST

~⊙~

*T*he Constitutional Convention—the term now customarily used for the convention of states that met in Philadelphia in the spring and summer of 1787—was charged merely with proposing amendments to the Articles of Confederation, America's initial charter of joint governance among the several states. The Convention proposed an entirely new framework for national government, which the Confederation congress sent to the states for consideration.

The proposed "Constitution of the United States" provoked great debate. *The Federalist* was a series of newspaper essays by Alexander Hamilton, James Madison, and John Jay (all written under the pseudonym "Publius") urging ratification of the Constitution, justifying the actions of the convention, and explaining the Constitution's provisions. *The Federalist* remains today the most important work of constitutional interpretation and political theory in America's history.

The Federalist, No. 1 is Hamilton's introduction to the series and his invitation to serious, candid deliberation and choice over the proposed Constitution—noting that this was a unique opportunity in human history. No. 39 is Madison's concise description of the new system as "partly national" and "partly federal." Nos. 47, 48, and 51 sets forth his important description of the separation of powers. No. 78 is Hamilton's argument for judicial independence, including his defense of "judicial review" of the constitutionality of legislative acts.

✪

The Federalist, No. 1 (October 27, 1787)
ALEXANDER HAMILTON

•

TO THE PEOPLE OF THE STATE OF NEW YORK:

AFTER an unequivocal experience of the inefficacy of the subsisting federal government, you are called upon to deliberate on a new Constitution for the United States of America. The subject speaks its own importance; comprehending in its consequences nothing less than the existence of the UNION, the safety and welfare of the parts of which it is composed, the fate of an empire in many respects the most interesting in the world. It has been frequently remarked that it seems to have been reserved to the people of this country, by their conduct and example, to decide the important question, whether societies of men are really capable or not of establishing good government from reflection and choice, or whether they are forever destined to depend for their political constitutions on accident and force. If there be any truth in the remark, the crisis at which we are arrived may with propriety be regarded as the era in which that decision is to be made; and a wrong election of the part we shall act may, in this view, deserve to be considered as the general misfortune of mankind. . . .

I propose, in a series of papers, to discuss the following interesting particulars:—*The utility of the UNION to your political prosperity—The insufficiency of the present Confederation to preserve that Union—The necessity of a government at least equally energetic with the one proposed, to the attainment of this object—The conformity of the proposed Constitution to the true principles of republican government—Its analogy to your own State constitution—and lastly, the additional security which its adoption will afford to the preservation of that species of government, to liberty, and to property.* . . .

The Federalist, No. 39 (January 16, 1788)
JAMES MADISON

•

TO THE PEOPLE OF THE STATE OF NEW YORK:

THE last paper having concluded the observations which were meant to introduce a candid survey of the plan of government reported by the convention, we now proceed to the execution of that part of our undertaking.

The first question that offers itself is, whether the general form and aspect of the government be strictly republican. It is evident that no other form would be reconcilable with the genius of the people of America; with the fundamental principles of the Revolution; or with that honorable determination which animates every votary of freedom, to rest all our political experiments on the capacity of mankind for self-government. If the plan of the convention, therefore, be found to depart from the republican character, its advocates must abandon it as no longer defensible.

What, then, are the distinctive characters of the republican form? . . .

If we resort for a criterion to the different principles on which different forms of government are established, we may define a republic to be, or at least may bestow that name on, a government which derives all its powers directly or indirectly from the great body of the people, and is administered by persons holding their offices during pleasure, for a limited period, or during good behavior. It is *essential* to such a government that it be derived from the great body of the society, not from an inconsiderable proportion, or a favored class of it; otherwise a handful of tyrannical nobles, exercising their oppressions by a delegation of their powers, might aspire to the rank of republicans, and claim for their government the honorable title of republic. It is *sufficient* for such a government that the persons administering it be appointed, either directly or indirectly, by the people; and that they hold their appointments by either of the tenures just specified; otherwise every government in the United States, as well as every other popular government that has been or can be well organized or well executed, would be degraded from the republican character. . . .

. . . "[I]t was not sufficient," say the adversaries of the proposed

Constitution, "for the convention to adhere to the republican form. They ought, with equal care, to have preserved the *federal* form, which regards the Union as a *confederacy* of sovereign states; instead of which, they have framed a *national* government, which regards the Union as a *consolidation* of the States." . . .

In order to ascertain the real character of the government, it may be considered in relation to the foundation on which it is to be established; to the sources from which its ordinary powers are to be drawn; to the operation of those powers; to the extent of them; and to the authority by which future changes in the government are to be introduced.

On examining the first relation, it appears, on one hand, that the Constitution is to be founded on the assent and ratification of the people of America, given by deputies elected for the special purpose; but, on the other, that this assent and ratification is to be given by the people, not as individuals composing one entire nation, but as composing the distinct and independent States to which they respectively belong. It is to be the assent and ratification of the several States, derived from the supreme authority in each State—the authority of the people them-selves. The act, therefore, establishing the Constitution, will not be a national, but a federal act.

That it will be a federal and not a national act, as these terms are un-derstood by the objectors; the act of the people, as forming so many in-dependent States, not as forming one aggregate nation, is obvious from this single consideration, that it is to result neither from the decision of a *majority* of the people of the Union, nor from that of a *majority* of the States. It must result from the *unanimous* assent of the several States that are parties to it, differing no otherwise from their ordinary assent than in its being expressed, not by the legislative authority, but by that of the people themselves. Were the people regarded in this transaction as forming one nation, the will of the majority of the whole people of the United States would bind the minority, in the same manner as the majority in each State must bind the minority; and the will of the majority must be determined either by a comparison of the individual votes, or by considering the will of the majority of the States as evidence of the will of a majority of the people of the United States. Neither of these rules have been adopted. Each State, in ratifying the Constitu-tion, is considered as a sovereign body, independent of all others, and only to be bound by its own voluntary act. In this relation, then, the new Constitution will, if established, be a *federal*, and not a *national* constitution. . . .

The difference between a federal and national government, as it relates to the *operation of the Government*, is supposed to consist in this, that in the former the powers operate on the political bodies composing the Confederacy, in their political capacities; in the latter, on the individual citizens composing the nation, in their individual capacities. On trying the Constitution by this criterion, it falls under the national, not the federal character; though perhaps not so completely as has been understood. In several cases, and particularly in the trial of controversies to which States may be parties, they must be viewed and proceeded against in their collective and political capacities only. . . .

But if the government be national with regard to the *operation* of its powers, it changes its aspect again when we contemplate it in relation to the *extent* of its powers. The idea of a national government involves in it, not only an authority over the individual citizens, but an indefinite supremacy over all persons and things, so far as they are objects of lawful government. . . . In this relation, then, the proposed government cannot be deemed a *national* one; since its jurisdiction extends to certain enumerated objects only, and leaves to the several States a residuary and inviolable sovereignty over all other objects. It is true that in controversies relating to the boundary between the two jurisdictions, the tribunal which is ultimately to decide, is to be established under the general government. But this does not change the principle of the case. The decision is to be impartially made, according to the rules of the Constitution; and all the usual and most effectual precautions are taken to secure this impartiality. Some such tribunal is clearly essential to prevent an appeal to the sword and a dissolution of the compact; and that it ought to be established under the general rather than under the local governments, or, to speak more properly, that it could be safely established under the first alone, is a position not likely to be combated.

If we try the Constitution by its last relation to the authority by which amendments are to be made, we find it neither wholly *national* nor wholly *federal*. Were it wholly national, the supreme and ultimate authority would reside in the *majority* of the people of the Union; and this authority would be competent at all times, like that of a majority of every national society, to alter or abolish its established government. Were it wholly federal, on the other hand, the concurrence of each

State in the Union would be essential to every alteration that would be binding on all. The mode provided by the plan of the convention is not founded on either of these principles. In requiring more than a majority, and particularly in computing the proportion by *States*, not by *citizens*, it departs from the *national* and advances towards the *federal* character; in rendering the concurrence of less than the whole number of States sufficient, it loses again the *federal* and partakes of the *national* character.

The proposed Constitution, therefore, is, in strictness, neither a national nor a federal Constitution, but a composition of both. In its foundation it is federal, not national; in the sources from which the ordinary powers of the government are drawn, it is partly federal and partly national; in the operation of these powers, it is national, not federal; in the extent of them, again, it is federal, not national; and, finally, in the authoritative mode of introducing amendments, it is neither wholly federal, nor wholly national.

The Federalist, No. 47 (February 1, 1788)
JAMES MADISON

•

TO THE PEOPLE OF THE STATE OF NEW YORK:

HAVING reviewed the general form of the proposed government and the general mass of power allotted to it, I proceed to examine the particular structure of this government, and the distribution of this mass of power among its constituent parts.

One of the principal objections inculcated by the more respectable adversaries to the Constitution, is its supposed violation of the political maxim, that the legislative, executive, and judiciary departments ought to be separate and distinct. In the structure of the federal government, no regard, it is said, seems to have been paid to this essential precaution in favor of liberty. The several departments of power are distributed and blended in such a manner as at once to destroy all symmetry and beauty of form, and to expose some of the essential parts of the edifice to the danger of being crushed by the disproportionate weight of other parts.

No political truth is certainly of greater intrinsic value, or is stamped with the authority of more enlightened patrons of liberty, than that on which the objection is founded. The accumulation of all powers, legislative, executive, and judiciary, in the same hands, whether of one, a few, or many, and whether hereditary, self appointed, or elective, may justly be pronounced the very definition of tyranny. Were the federal Constitution, therefore, really chargeable with the accumulation of power, or with a mixture of powers, having a dangerous tendency to such an accumulation, no further arguments would be necessary to inspire a universal reprobation of the system. I persuade myself, however, that it will be made apparent to every one, that the charge cannot be supported, and that the maxim on which it relies has been totally misconceived and misapplied. In order to form correct ideas on this important subject, it will be proper to investigate the sense in which the preservation of liberty requires that the three great departments of power should be separate and distinct.

The oracle who is always consulted and cited on this subject is the celebrated Montesquieu. . . . The reasons on which Montesquieu grounds his maxim are a further demonstration of his meaning. "When the legislative and executive powers are united in the same person or body," says he, "there can be no liberty, because apprehensions may arise lest THE SAME monarch or senate should ENACT tyrannical laws to EXECUTE them in a tyrannical manner." Again: "Were the power of judging joined with the legislative, the life and liberty of the subject would be exposed to arbitrary control, for THE JUDGE would then be THE LEGISLATOR. Were it joined to the executive power, THE JUDGE might behave with all the violence of AN OPPRESSOR." Some of these reasons are more fully explained in other passages; but briefly stated as they are here, they sufficiently establish the meaning which we have put on this celebrated maxim of this celebrated author.

If we look into the constitutions of the several States, we find that, notwithstanding the emphatical and, in some instances, the unqualified terms in which this axiom has been laid down, there is not a single instance in which the several departments of power have been kept absolutely separate and distinct. . . .

The Federalist, No. 48 (February 1, 1788)
JAMES MADISON

•

IT WAS shown in the last paper that the political apothegm there examined does not require that the legislative, executive, and judiciary departments should be wholly unconnected with each other. I shall undertake, in the next place, to show that unless these departments be so far connected and blended as to give to each a constitutional control over the others, the degree of separation which the maxim requires, as essential to a free government, can never in practice be duly maintained.

It is agreed on all sides, that the powers properly belonging to one of the departments ought not to be directly and completely administered by either of the other departments. It is equally evident, that none of them ought to possess, directly or indirectly, an overruling influence over the others, in the administration of their respective powers. It will not be denied, that power is of an encroaching nature, and that it ought to be effectually restrained from passing the limits assigned to it. After discriminating, therefore, in theory, the several classes of power, as they may in their nature be legislative, executive, or judiciary, the next and most difficult task is to provide some practical security for each, against the invasion of the others. What this security ought to be, is the great problem to be solved.

Will it be sufficient to mark, with precision, the boundaries of these departments, in the constitution of the government, and to trust to these parchment barriers against the encroaching spirit of power? This is the security which appears to have been principally relied on by the compilers of most of the American constitutions. But experience assures us, that the efficacy of the provision has been greatly overrated; and that some more adequate defense is indispensably necessary for the more feeble, against the more powerful, members of the government. . . .

The conclusion which I am warranted in drawing from these observations is, that a mere demarcation on parchment of the constitutional limits of the several departments, is not a sufficient guard against those encroachments which lead to a tyrannical concentration of all the powers of government in the same hands.

The Federalist, No. 51 (February 8, 1788)
JAMES MADISON

•

TO WHAT expedient, then, shall we finally resort, for maintaining in practice the necessary partition of power among the several departments, as laid down in the Constitution? The only answer that can be given is, that as all these exterior provisions are found to be inadequate, the defect must be supplied, by so contriving the interior structure of the government as that its several constituent parts may, by their mutual relations, be the means of keeping each other in their proper places. . . .

In order to lay a due foundation for that separate and distinct exercise of the different powers of government, which to a certain extent is admitted on all hands to be essential to the preservation of liberty, it is evident that each department should have a will of its own; and consequently should be so constituted that the members of each should have as little agency as possible in the appointment of the members of the others. . . . [T]he members of each department should be as little dependent as possible on those of the others, for the emoluments annexed to their offices. Were the executive magistrate, or the judges, not independent of the legislature in this particular, their independence in every other would be merely nominal.

But the great security against a gradual concentration of the several powers in the same department, consists in giving to those who administer each department the necessary constitutional means and personal motives to resist encroachments of the others. The provision for defense must in this, as in all other cases, be made commensurate to the danger of attack. Ambition must be made to counteract ambition. The interest of the man must be connected with the constitutional rights of the place. It may be a reflection on human nature, that such devices should be necessary to control the abuses of government. But what is government itself, but the greatest of all reflections on human nature? If men were angels, no government would be necessary. If angels were to govern men, neither external nor internal controls on government would be necessary. In framing a government which is to be administered by men over men, the great difficulty lies in this: you must first enable the government to control the governed; and in the next place oblige it to control itself. A dependence on the people is, no doubt, the primary control on the government; but experience has taught mankind the necessity of auxiliary precautions.

This policy of supplying, by opposite and rival interests, the defect of better motives, might be traced through the whole system of human affairs, private as well as public. We see it particularly displayed in all the subordinate distributions of power, where the constant aim is to divide and arrange the several offices in such a manner as that each may be a check on the other, that the private interest of every individual may be a sentinel over the public rights. . . .

The Federalist, No. 78 (May 28, 1788)
ALEXANDER HAMILTON

•

TO THE PEOPLE OF THE STATE OF NEW YORK:

WE PROCEED now to an examination of the judiciary department of the proposed government. . . . In unfolding the defects of the existing Confederation, the utility and necessity of a federal judicature have been clearly pointed out. It is the less necessary to recapitulate the considerations there urged, as the propriety of the institution in the abstract is not disputed; the only questions which have been raised being relative to the manner of constituting it, and to its extent. To these points, therefore, our observations shall be confined. . . .

According to the plan of the convention, all judges who may be appointed by the United States are to hold their offices DURING GOOD BEHAVIOR . . . The standard of good behavior for the continuance in office of the judicial magistracy, is certainly one of the most valuable of the modern improvements in the practice of government. In a monarchy it is an excellent barrier to the despotism of the prince; in a republic it is a no less excellent barrier to the encroachments and oppressions of the representative body. And it is the best expedient which can be devised in any government, to secure a steady, upright, and impartial administration of the laws.

Whoever attentively considers the different departments of power must perceive, that, in a government in which they are separated from each other, the judiciary, from the nature of its functions, will always be the least dangerous to the political rights of the Constitution; because it will be least in a capacity to annoy or injure them. The Executive not only dispenses the honors, but holds the sword of the community. The legislature not only commands the purse, but prescribes the rules by which the duties and rights of every citizen are to be regulated. The judiciary, on the contrary, has no influence over either the sword or the purse; no direction either of the strength or of the wealth of the society; and can take no active resolution whatever. It may truly be said to have neither FORCE nor WILL, but merely judgment; and must ultimately depend upon the aid of the executive arm even for the efficacy of its judgments.

This simple view of the matter suggests several important consequences. It proves incontestably, that the judiciary is beyond comparison the weakest of the three departments of power; that it can never attack with success either of the other two; and that all possible care is requisite to enable it to defend itself against their attacks. It equally proves, that though individual oppression may now and then proceed from the courts of justice, the general liberty of the people can never be endangered from that quarter; I mean so long as the judiciary remains truly distinct from both the legislature and the Executive. For I agree, that "there is no liberty, if the power of judging be not separated from the legislative and executive powers." . . . And it proves, in the last place, that as liberty can have nothing to fear from the judiciary alone, but would have every thing to fear from its union with either of the other departments; that as all the effects of such a union must ensue from a dependence of the former on the latter, notwithstanding a nominal and apparent separation; that as, from the natural feebleness of the judiciary, it is in continual jeopardy of being overpowered, awed, or influenced by its co-ordinate branches; and that as nothing can contribute so much to its firmness and independence as permanency in office, this quality may therefore be justly regarded as an indispensable ingredient in its constitution, and, in a great measure, as the citadel of the public justice and the public security.

The complete independence of the courts of justice is peculiarly essential in a limited Constitution. By a limited Constitution, I understand one which contains certain specified exceptions to the legislative authority; such, for instance, as that it shall pass no bills of attainder, no ex-post-facto laws, and the like. Limitations of this kind can be preserved in practice no other way than through the medium of courts of justice, whose duty it must be to declare all acts contrary to the manifest tenor of the Constitution void. Without this, all the reservations of particular rights or privileges would amount to nothing.

Some perplexity respecting the rights of the courts to pronounce legislative acts void, because contrary to the Constitution, has arisen from an imagination that the doctrine would imply a superiority of the judiciary to the legislative power. It is urged that the authority which can declare the acts of another void, must necessarily be superior to the one whose acts may be declared void. As this doctrine is of great importance in all the American constitutions, a brief discussion of the ground on which it rests cannot be unacceptable.

There is no position which depends on clearer principles, than that every act of a delegated authority, contrary to the tenor of the commission under which it is exercised, is void. No legislative act, therefore, contrary to the Constitution, can be valid. To deny this, would be to affirm, that the deputy is greater than his principal; that the servant is above his master; that the representatives of the people are superior to the people themselves; that men acting by virtue of powers, may do not only what their powers do not authorize, but what they forbid.

If it be said that the legislative body are themselves the constitutional judges of their own powers, and that the construction they put upon them is conclusive upon the other departments, it may be answered, that this cannot be the natural presumption, where it is not to be collected from any particular provisions in the Constitution. It is not otherwise to be supposed, that the Constitution could intend to enable the representatives of the people to substitute their WILL to that of their constituents. It is far more rational to suppose, that the courts were designed to be an intermediate body between the people and the legislature, in order, among other things, to keep the latter within the limits assigned to their authority. The interpretation of the laws is the proper and peculiar province of the courts. A constitution is, in fact, and must be regarded by the judges, as a fundamental law. It therefore belongs to them to ascertain its meaning, as well as the meaning of any particular act proceeding from the legislative body. If there should happen to be an irreconcilable variance between the two, that which has the superior obligation and validity ought, of course, to be preferred; or, in other words, the Constitution ought to be preferred to the statute, the intention of the people to the intention of their agents.

Nor does this conclusion by any means suppose a superiority of the judicial to the legislative power. It only supposes that the power of the people is superior to both; and that where the will of the legislature, declared in its statutes, stands in opposition to that of the people, declared in the Constitution, the judges ought to be governed by the latter rather than the former. . . .

It can be of no weight to say that the courts, on the pretense of a repugnancy, may substitute their own pleasure to the constitutional intentions of the legislature. This might as well happen in the case of two contradictory statutes; or it might as well happen in every adjudication upon any single statute. The courts must declare the sense of the law; and if they should be disposed to exercise WILL instead of JUDGMENT, the consequence would equally be the substitution of their pleasure to that of the legislative body. The observation, if it prove any thing, would prove that there ought to be no judges distinct from that body.

If, then, the courts of justice are to be considered as the bulwarks of a limited Constitution against legislative encroachments, this consideration will afford a strong argument for the permanent tenure of judicial offices, since nothing will contribute so much as this to that independent spirit in the judges which must be essential to the faithful performance of so arduous a duty.

This independence of the judges is equally requisite to guard the Constitution and the rights of individuals from the effects of those ill humors, which the arts of designing men, or the influence of particular conjunctures, sometimes disseminate among the people themselves, and which, though they speedily give place to better information, and more deliberate reflection, have a tendency, in the meantime, to occasion dangerous innovations in the government, and serious oppressions of the minor party in the community. Though I trust the friends of the proposed Constitution will never concur with its enemies . . . in questioning that fundamental principle of republican government, which admits the right of the people to alter or abolish the established Constitution, whenever they find it inconsistent with their happiness, yet it is not to be inferred from this principle, that the representatives of the people, whenever a momentary inclination happens to lay hold of a majority of their constituents, incompatible with the provisions in the existing Constitution, would, on that account, be justifiable in a violation of those provisions; or that the courts would be under a greater obligation to connive at infractions in this shape, than when they had proceeded wholly from the cabals of the representative body. Until the people have, by some solemn and authoritative act, annulled or changed the established form, it is binding upon themselves collectively, as well as individually; and no presumption, or even knowledge, of their sentiments, can warrant their representatives in a departure from it, prior to such an act. But it is easy to see, that it would require an uncommon portion of fortitude in the judges to do their duty as faithful guardians of the Constitution, where legislative invasions of it had been instigated by the major voice of the community. . . .

That inflexible and uniform adherence to the rights of the Constitution, and of individuals, which we perceive to be indispensable in the courts of justice, can certainly not be expected from judges who hold their offices by a temporary commission. Periodical appointments, however regulated, or by whomsoever made, would, in some way or other, be fatal to their necessary independence. If the power of making them was committed either to the Executive or legislature, there would be danger of an improper complaisance to the branch which possessed it; if to both, there would be an unwillingness to hazard the displeasure of either; if to the people, or to persons chosen by them for the special purpose, there would be too great a disposition to consult popularity, to justify a reliance that nothing would be consulted but the Constitution and the laws. . . .

Upon the whole, there can be no room to doubt that the convention acted wisely in copying from the models of those constitutions which have established GOOD BEHAVIOR as the tenure of their judicial offices, in point of duration; and that so far from being blamable on this account, their plan would have been inexcusably defective, if it had wanted this important feature of good government. . . .

ON THE EXTENT OF "LEGISLATIVE POWERS HEREIN GRANTED"

⚓

O ne of the earliest, longest-running, and most enduringly difficult controversies under the Constitution has been the scope of Congress's enumerated powers. As early as 1791, a major dispute arose over whether the Constitution authorized Congress to create a "Bank of the United States." When Congress passed a bill establishing such a bank, two members of President George Washington's cabinet—Secretary of State Thomas Jefferson and Secretary of the Treasury Alexander Hamilton—presented him with dueling views on the subject. Jefferson's opinion is a classic formulation of the argument for a narrow reading of Congress's legislative powers; Hamilton's is a classic statement of the case for a broader reading—the position that Washington adopted by signing the bill into law.

✪

Opinion on the Constitutionality of a National Bank (1791)
THOMAS JEFFERSON

•

. . . I consider the foundation of the Constitution as laid on this ground: That "all powers not delegated to the United States, by the Constitution, nor prohibited by it to the States, are reserved to the States or to the people." To take a single step beyond the boundaries thus specially drawn around the powers of Congress, is to take possession of a boundless field of power, no longer susceptible of any definition.

The incorporation of a bank, and the powers assumed by this bill, have not, in my opinion, been delegated to the United States, by the Constitution.

I. THEY ARE NOT AMONG THE POWERS SPECIALLY ENUMERATED: FOR THESE ARE:

1st. A power to lay taxes for the purpose of paying the debts of the United States; but no debt is paid by this bill, nor any tax laid. . . .

2. "To borrow money." But this bill neither borrows money nor ensures the borrowing it. The proprietors of the bank will be just as free as any other money holders, to lend or not to lend their money to the public. . . .

3. To "regulate commerce with foreign nations, and among the States, and with the Indian tribes." To erect a bank, and to regulate commerce, are very different acts. He who erects a bank, creates a subject of commerce in its bills, so does he who makes a bushel of wheat, or digs a dollar out of the mines; yet neither of these persons regulates commerce thereby. To make a thing which may be bought and sold, is not to prescribe regulations for buying and selling. . . .

II. NOR ARE THEY WITHIN EITHER OF THE GENERAL PHRASES, WHICH ARE THE TWO FOLLOWING:

1. To lay taxes to provide for the general welfare of the United States, that is to say, "to lay taxes for *the purpose of* providing for the general welfare." For the laying of taxes is the *power*, and the general welfare the

purpose for which the power is to be exercised. They are not to lay taxes *ad libitum for any purpose they please*; but only *to pay the debts or provide for the welfare of the Union*. In like manner, they are not *to do anything they please* to provide for the general welfare, but only to *lay taxes* for that purpose. To consider the latter phrase, not as describing the purpose of the first, but as giving a distinct and independent power to do any act they please, which might be for the good of the Union, would render all the preceding and subsequent enumerations of power completely useless.

It would reduce the whole instrument to a single phrase, that of instituting a Congress with power to do whatever would be for the good of the United States; and, as they would be the sole judges of the good or evil, it would be also a power to do whatever evil they please.

It is an established rule of construction where a phrase will bear either of two meanings, to give it that which will allow some meaning to the other parts of the instrument, and not that which would render all the others useless. Certainly no such universal power was meant to be given them. It was intended to lace them up straitly within the enumerated powers, and those without which, as means, these powers could not be carried into effect. It is known that the very power now proposed *as a means* was rejected as *an end* by the Convention which formed the Constitution. A proposition was made to them to authorize Congress to open canals, and an amendatory one to empower them to incorporate. But the whole was rejected, and one of the reasons for rejection urged in debate was, that then they would have a power to erect a bank, which would render the great cities, where there were prejudices and jealousies on the subject, adverse to the reception of the Constitution.

2. The second general phrase is, "to make all laws *necessary* and proper for carrying into execution the enumerated powers." But they can all be carried into execution without a bank. A bank therefore is not *necessary*, and consequently not authorized by this phrase.

It has been urged that a bank will give great facility or convenience in the collection of taxes, Suppose this were true: yet the Constitution allows only the means which are "*necessary*," not those which are merely "convenient" for effecting the enumerated powers. If such a latitude of construction be allowed to this phrase as to give any non-enumerated power, it will go to everyone, for there is not one which ingenuity may not torture into a *convenience* in some instance *or other*, to *some one* of so long a list of enumerated powers. It would swallow up all the delegated powers, and reduce the whole to one power, as before observed. Therefore it was that the Constitution restrained them to the *necessary* means, that is to say, to those means without which the grant of power would be nugatory. . . .

The negative of the President is the shield provided by the Constitution to protect against the invasions of the legislature. . . The present is the case of a right remaining exclusively with the States, and consequently one of those intended by the Constitution to be placed under its protection. . . .

It must be added, however, that unless the President's mind on a view of everything which is urged for and against this bill, is tolerably clear that it is unauthorized by the Constitution; if the pro and the con hang so even as to balance his judgment, a just respect for the wisdom of the legislature would naturally decide the balance in favor of their opinion. It is chiefly for cases where they are clearly misled by error, ambition, or interest, that the Constitution has placed a check in the negative of the President.

Opinion on the Constitutionality of a National Bank (February 23, 1791), ALEXANDER HAMILTON

•

. . . [E]very power vested in a government is in its nature sovereign, and includes, by force of the term, a right to employ all the means requisite and fairly applicable to the attainment of the ends of such power, and which are not precluded by restrictions and exceptions specified in the Constitution, or not immoral, or not contrary to the essential ends of political society.

This principle, in its application to government in general, would be admitted as an axiom; and it will be incumbent upon those who may incline to deny it, to prove a distinction, and to show that a rule which, in the general system of things, is essential to the preservation of the social order, is inapplicable to the United States.

The circumstance that the powers of sovereignty are in this country divided between the National and State governments, does not afford the distinction required. It does not follow from this, that each of the portion of powers delegated to the one or to the other, is not sovereign with regard to its proper objects. It will only follow from it, that each has sovereign power as to certain things, and not as to other things. . . .

To this mode of reasoning respecting the right of employing all the means requisite to the execution of the specified powers of the government, it is objected, that none but necessary and proper means are to be employed; and the Secretary of State maintains, that no means are to be considered as necessary but those without which the grant of the power would be nugatory. . . .[N]either the grammatical nor popular sense of the term requires that construction. According to both, necessary often means no more than needful, requisite, incidental, useful, or conducive to. It is a common mode of expression to say, that it is necessary for a government or a person to do this or that thing, when nothing more is intended or understood, than that the interests of the government or person require, or will be promoted by, the doing of this or that thing. The imagination can be at no loss for exemplifications of the use of the word in this sense. And it is the true one in which it is to be understood as used in the Constitution. The whole turn of the clause containing it indicates, that it was the intent of the Convention, by that clause, to give a liberal latitude to the exercise of the specified powers. The expressions have peculiar comprehensiveness. They are thought to make all laws "necessary and proper for carrying into execution the foregoing powers, and all other powers vested by the Constitution in the government of the United States, or in any department or officer thereof."

To understand the word as the Secretary of State does, would be to depart from its obvious and popular sense, and to give it a restrictive operation, an idea never before entertained. It would be to give it the same force as if the word absolutely or indispensably had been prefixed to it.

Such a construction would beget endless uncertainty and embarrassment. The cases must be palpable and extreme, in which it could be pronounced, with certainty, that a measure was absolutely necessary, or one, without which, the exercise of a given power would be nugatory. There are few measures of any government which would stand so severe a test. To insist upon it, would be to make the criterion of the exercise of any implied power, a case of extreme necessity; which is rather a rule to justify the overleaping of the bounds of constitutional authority, than to govern the ordinary exercise of it. . . .

It is no valid objection to the doctrine to say, that it is calculated to extend the power of the government throughout the entire sphere of State legislation. . . . [D]ifficulties on this point are inherent in the nature of the Federal Constitution; they result inevitably from a division of the legislative power. The consequence of this division is, that there will be cases clearly within the power of the national government; others, clearly without its powers; and a third class, which will leave room for controversy and difference of opinion, and concerning which a reasonable latitude of judgment must be allowed.

But the doctrine which is contended for is not chargeable with the consequences imputed to it. It does not affirm that the national government is sovereign in all respects, but that it is sovereign to a certain extent; that is, to the extent of the objects of its specified powers.

It leaves, therefore, a criterion of what is constitutional, and of what is not so. This criterion is the end, to which the measure relates as a means. If the end be clearly comprehended within any of the specified powers, and if the measure have an obvious relation to that end, and is not forbidden by any particular provision of the Constitution, it may safely be deemed to come within the compass of the national authority. There is also this further criterion, which may materially assist the decision: Does the proposed measure abridge a pre-existing right of any State or of any individual? If it does not, there is a strong presumption in favor of its constitutionality, and slighter relations to any declared object of the Constitution may be permitted to turn the scale. . . .

A hope is entertained that it has, by this time, been made to appear, to the satisfaction of the President, that a bank has a natural relation to the power of collecting taxes; to that of regulating trade; to that of providing for the common defense; and that, as the bill under consideration contemplates the government in the light of a joint proprietor of the stock of the bank, it brings the case within the provision of the clause of the Constitution which immediately respects the property of the United States. . . .

ON THE NATURE OF
"THE EXECUTIVE POWER"

* உ*

Alexander Hamilton was the early republic's leading advocate of a broad view of the scope of executive power under the Constitution. In addition to writing *The Federalist* essays on the power of the president (numbers 70–77), Hamilton wrote a series of essays under the pseudonym "Pacificus" defending Washington's 1793 proclamation of American neutrality in the war between France and Great Britain. In the course of doing so, he provided an influential explanation of the president's power in foreign affairs, and of executive power generally, under the Constitution.

✪

Pacificus, No. 1 (June 29, 1793), ALEXANDER HAMILTON

•

. . . It will not be disputed that the management of the affairs of this country with foreign nations is confided to the Government of the UStates.

It can as little be disputed, that a Proclamation of Neutrality, where a Nation is at liberty to keep out of a War in which other Nations are engaged and means so to do, is a *usual* and a *proper* measure. *Its main object and effect are to prevent the Nation being immediately responsible for acts done by its citizens, without the privity or connivance of the Government, in contravention of the principles of neutrality.* . . .

The inquiry then is—what department of the Government of the UStates is the proper one to make a declaration of Neutrality in the cases in which the engagements of the Nation permit and its interests require such a declaration.

A correct and well informed mind will discern at once that it can belong neither to the Legislative nor Judicial Department and of course must belong to the Executive.

The Legislative Department is not the *organ* of intercourse between the UStates and foreign Nations. It is charged neither with *making* nor *interpreting* Treaties. It is therefore not naturally that Organ of the Government which is to pronounce the existing condition of the Nation, with regard to foreign Powers, or to admonish the Citizens of their obligations and duties as founded upon that condition of things. Still less is it charged with enforcing the execution and observance of these obligations and those duties.

It is equally obvious that the act in question is foreign to the Judiciary Department of the Government. The province of that Department is to decide litigations in particular cases. It is indeed charged with the interpretation of treaties; but it exercises this function only in the litigated cases; that is where contending parties bring before it a specific controversy. It has no concern with pronouncing upon the external political relations of Treaties between Government and Government. This position is too plain to need being insisted upon.

It must then of necessity belong to the Executive Department to exercise the function in Question—when a proper case for the exercise of it occurs.

It appears to be connected with that department in various capacities, as the *organ* of intercourse between the Nation and foreign Nations—as the interpreter of the National Treaties in those cases in which the Judiciary is not competent, that is in the cases between Government and Government—as that Power, which is charged with the Execution of the Laws, of which Treaties form a part—as that Power which is charged with the command and application of the Public Force.

This view of the subject is so natural and obvious—so analogous to general theory and practice—that no doubt can be entertained of its justness, unless such doubt can be deduced from particular provisions of the Constitution of the United States.

Let us see then if cause for such doubt is to be found in that constitution.

The second Article of the Constitution of the UStates, section 1st, establishes this general Proposition, That "The Executive Power shall be vested in a President of the United States of America."

The same article in a succeeding Section proceeds to designate particular cases of Executive Power. It declares among other things that the President shall be Commander in Chief of the army and navy of the UStates and of the Militia of the several states when called into the actual service of the UStates, that he shall have power by and with the advice of the senate to make treaties; that it shall be his duty to receive ambassadors and other public Ministers and to take care that the laws be faithfully executed. . . .

The general doctrine then of our constitution is, that the Executive Power of the Nation is vested in the President; subject only to the *exceptions* and *qualifications* which are expressed in the instrument.

Two of these have been already noticed—the participation of the Senate in the appointment of Officers and the making of Treaties. A third remains to be mentioned the right of the Legislature "to declare war and grant letters of marque and reprisal."

With these exceptions the Executive Power of the Union is completely lodged in the President. This mode of construing the Constitution has indeed been recognized by Congress in formal acts, upon full consideration and debate. The power of removal from office is an important instance.

And since upon general principles for reasons already given, the issuing of a proclamation of neutrality is merely an Executive Act; since also the general Executive Power of the Union is vested in the President, the conclusion is, that the step, which has been taken by him, is liable to no just exception on the score of authority.

It may be observed that this Inference would be just if the power of declaring war had not been vested in the Legislature, but that this power naturally includes the right of judging whether the Nation is under obligations to make war or not.

The answer to this is, that however true it may be . . . it will not follow that the Executive is in any case excluded from a similar right of Judgment, in the execution of its own functions.

If the Legislature have a right to make war on the one hand—it is on the other the duty of the Executive to preserve Peace till war is declared; and in fulfilling that duty, it must necessarily possess a right of judging what is the nature of the obligations which the treaties of the Country impose on the Government; and when in pursuance of this right it has concluded that there is nothing in them inconsistent with a *state* of neutrality, it becomes both its province and its duty to enforce the laws incident to that state of the Nation. The Executive is charged with the execution of all laws, the laws of Nations as well as the Municipal law, which recognises and adopts those laws. It is consequently bound, by faithfully executing the laws of neutrality, when that is the state of the Nation, to avoid giving a cause of war to foreign Powers. . . . In this distribution of powers the wisdom of our constitution is manifested. It is the province and duty of the Executive to preserve to the Nation the blessings of peace. The Legislature alone can interrupt those blessings, by placing the Nation in a state of War. . . .

The President is the constitutional Executor of the laws. Our Treaties and the laws of Nations form a part of the law of the land. He who is to execute the laws must first judge for himself of their meaning. In order to the observance of that conduct, which the laws of nations combined with our treaties prescribed to this country, in reference to the present War in Europe, it was necessary for the President to judge for himself whether there was any thing in our treaties incompatible with an ad-herence to neutrality. Having judged that there was not, he had a right, and if in his opinion the interests of the Nation required it, it was his duty, as Executor of the laws, to proclaim the neutrality of the Nation, to exhort all persons to observe it, and to warn them of the penalties which would attend its non observance.

ON THE
POWER OF
CONSTITUTIONAL
INTERPRETATION
and
"CONSTITUTIONAL
REVIEW"
(1798–1819)

THE VIRGINIA
AND KENTUCKY RESOLUTIONS

AND

THE 'REPORT OF 1800'

༄

*B*efore the Supreme Court first invoked the duty of judicial review of the constitutionality of acts of Congress (in *Marbury v. Madison* [1803], see p. 36), two states—Virginia and Kentucky—declared Congress's Alien and Sedition Acts, adopted in 1798, unconstitutional on the grounds that they exceeded the national government's enumerated power and also violated the First Amendment freedoms of speech and of the press. Virginia's and Kentucky's legislative resolutions, drafted by Madison and Jefferson respectively, pledged resistance to these allegedly unconstitutional federal laws.

Several other states condemned the Virginia and Kentucky Resolutions on the ground that only the courts had the power to interpret the Constitution. In 1800, James Madison's report for the Virginia legislature defended the view that all public officials, federal and state, have a responsibility to faithfully interpret the Constitution and to defend it against violations by other officials.

✪

The Virginia Resolutions of 1798
JAMES MADISON

•

RESOLVED, That the General Assembly of Virginia, doth unequivocally express a firm resolution to maintain and defend the Constitution of the United States, and the Constitution of this State, against every aggression either foreign or domestic, and that they will support the government of the United States in all measures warranted by the former.

That this assembly most solemnly declares a warm attachment to the Union of the States, to maintain which it pledges all its powers; and that for this end, it is their duty to watch over and oppose every infraction of those principles which constitute the only basis of that Union, because a faithful observance of them, can alone secure its existence and the public happiness.

That this Assembly doth explicitly and peremptorily declare, that it views the powers of the federal government, as resulting from the compact, to which the states are parties; as limited by the plain sense and intention of the instrument constituting the compact; as no further valid than they are authorized by the grants enumerated in that compact; and that in case of a deliberate, palpable, and dangerous exercise of other powers, not granted by the said compact, the states who are parties thereto, have the right, and are in duty bound, to interpose for arresting the progress of the evil, and for maintaining within their respective limits, the authorities, rights and liberties appertaining to them.

That the General Assembly doth also express its deep regret, that a spirit has in sundry instances, been manifested by the federal government, to enlarge its powers by forced constructions of the constitutional charter which defines them; and that implications have appeared of a design to expound certain general phrases (which having been copied from the very limited grant of power, in the former articles of confederation were the less liable to be misconstrued) so as to destroy the meaning and effect, of the particular enumeration which necessarily explains and limits the general phrases; and so as to consolidate the states by degrees, into one sovereignty, the obvious tendency and inevitable consequence of which would be, to transform the present republican system of the United States, into an absolute, or at best a mixed monarchy.

That the General Assembly doth particularly protest against the palpable and alarming infractions of the Constitution, in the two late cases of the "Alien and Sedition Acts" passed at the last session of Congress; the first of which exercises a power no where delegated to the federal government, and which by uniting legislative and judicial powers to those of executive, subverts the general principles of free government; as well as the particular organization, and positive provisions of the federal constitution; and the other of which acts, exercises in like manner, a power not delegated by the constitution, but on the contrary, expressly and positively forbidden by one of the amendments thererto; a power, which more than any other, ought to produce universal alarm, because it is leveled against that right of freely examining public characters and measures, and of free communication among the people thereon, which has ever been justly deemed, the only effectual guardian of every other right.

That this state having by its Convention, which ratified the federal Constitution, expressly declared, that among other essential rights, "the Liberty of Conscience and of the Press cannot be cancelled, abridged, restrained, or modified by any authority of the United States," and from its extreme anxiety to guard these rights from every possible attack of sophistry or ambition, having with other states, recommended an amendment for that purpose, which amendment was, in due time, annexed to the Constitution; it would mark a reproachable inconsistency, and criminal degeneracy, if an indifference were now shewn, to the most palpable violation of one of the Rights, thus declared and secured; and to the establishment of a precedent which may be fatal to the other.

That the good people of this commonwealth, having ever felt, and continuing to feel, the most sincere affection for their brethren of the other states; the truest anxiety for establishing and perpetuating the union of all; and the most scrupulous fidelity to that constitution, which is the pledge of mutual friendship, and the instrument of mutual happiness; the General Assembly doth solemnly appeal to the like dispositions of the other states, in confidence that they will concur with this commonwealth in declaring, as it does hereby declare, that the acts aforesaid, are unconstitutional; and that the necessary and proper measures will be taken by each, for co-operating with this state, in maintaining the Authorities, Rights, and Liberties, referred to the States respectively, or to the people. . . .

The Kentucky Resolutions of 1798: Original Draft
THOMAS JEFFERSON

•

1. *Resolved*, That the several States composing, the United States of America, are not united on the principle of unlimited submission to their general government; but that, by a compact under the style and title of a Constitution for the United States, and of amendments thereto, they constituted a general government for special purposes—delegated to that government certain definite powers, reserving, each State to itself, the residuary mass of right to their own self-government; and that whensoever the general government assumes undelegated powers, its acts are unauthoritative, void, and of no force: that to this compact each State acceded as a State, and is an integral part, its co-States forming, as to itself, the other party: that the government created by this compact was not made the exclusive or final judge of the extent of the powers delegated to itself; since that would have made its discretion, and not the Constitution, the measure of its powers; but that, as in all other cases of compact among powers having no common judge, each party has an equal right to judge for itself, as well of infractions as of the mode and measure of redress. . . .

7. *Resolved*, That the construction applied by the General Government (as is evidenced by sundry of their proceedings) to those parts of the Constitution of the United States which delegate to Congress a power "to lay and collect taxes, duties, imports, and excises, to pay the debts, and provide for the common defense and general welfare of the United States," and "to make all laws which shall be necessary and proper for carrying into execution, the powers vested by the Constitution in the government of the United States, or in any department or officer thereof," goes to the destruction of all limits prescribed to their powers by the Constitution: that words meant by the instrument to be subsidiary only to the execution of limited powers, ought not to be so construed as themselves to give unlimited powers, nor a part to be so taken as to destroy the whole residue of that instrument[.] . . .

8. *Resolved* . . . that therefore this commonwealth is determined, as it doubts not its co-States are, to submit to undelegated, and consequently unlimited powers in no man, or body of men on earth: that in cases of

an abuse of the delegated powers, the members of the general government, being chosen by the people, a change by the people would be the constitutional remedy; but, where powers are assumed which have not been delegated, a nullification of the act is the rightful remedy: that every State has a natural right in cases not within the compact . . . to nullify of their own authority all assumptions of power by others within their limits: that without this right, they would be under the dominion, absolute and unlimited, of whosoever might exercise this right of judgment for them: that nevertheless, this commonwealth, from motives of regard and respect for its co States, has wished to communicate with them on the subject: that with them alone it is proper to communicate, they alone being parties to the compact, and solely authorized to judge in the last resort of the powers exercised under it, Congress being not a party, but merely the creature of the compact, and subject as to its assumptions of power to the final judgment of those by whom, and for whose use itself and its powers were all created and modified. . . .

Report on the Virginia Resolutions: House of Delegates, Session of 1799–1800, JAMES MADISON

•

Report of the Committee to whom were referred the Communications of various States, relative to the Resolutions of the last General Assembly of this State, concerning the Alien and Sedition Laws

. . . It appears . . . to be a plain principle, founded in common sense, illustrated by common practice, and essential to the nature compacts, that, where resort can be had to no tribunal superior to the authority of the parties, the parties themselves must be the rightful judges, in the last resort, whether the bargain made has been pursued or violated. The Constitution of the United States was formed by the sanction of the states, given by each in its sovereign capacity. It adds to the stability and dignity, as well as to the authority, of the Constitution, that it rests on this legitimate and solid foundation. The states, then, being the parties to the constitutional compact, and in their sovereign capacity, it follows of necessity that there can be no tribunal, above their authority, to decide, in the last resort, whether the compact made by them be violated; and consequently, that, as the parties to it, they must themselves decide, in the last resort, such questions as may be of sufficient magnitude to require their interposition. . . .

But it is objected, that the judicial authority is to be regarded as the sole expositor of the Constitution in the last resort; and it may be asked for what reason the declaration by the General Assembly, supposing it to be theoretically true, could be required at the present day, and in so solemn a manner.

On this objection it might be observed, first, that there may be instances of usurped power, which the forms of the Constitution would never draw within the control of the judicial department; secondly, that, if the decision of the judiciary be raised above the authority of the sovereign parties to the Constitution, the decisions of the other departments, not carried by the forms of the Constitution before the judiciary, must be equally authoritative and final with the decisions of that department. But the proper answer to the objection is, that the resolution of the General Assembly relates to those great and extraordinary cases, in which all the forms of the Constitution may prove ineffectual against infractions dangerous to the essential rights of the parties to it. The resolution supposes that dangerous powers, not delegated, may not only be usurped and executed by the other departments, but that the judicial department, also, may exercise or sanction dangerous powers beyond the grant of the Constitution; and, consequently, that the ultimate right of the parties to the Constitution, to judge whether the compact has been dangerously violated, must extend to violations by one delegated authority as well as by another—by the judiciary as well as by the executive, or the legislature.

However true, therefore, it may be, that the judicial department is, in all questions submitted to it by the forms of the Constitution, to decide in the last resort, this resort must necessarily be deemed the last in relation to the authorities of the other departments of the government; not in relation to the rights of the parties to the constitutional compact, from which the judicial, as well as the other departments, hold their delegated trusts. On any other hypothesis, the delegation of judicial power would annul the authority delegating it; and the concurrence of this department with the others in usurped powers, might subvert forever, and beyond the possible reach of any rightful remedy, the very Constitution which all were instituted to preserve. . . .

It has been said that it belongs to the judiciary of the United States, and not the state legislatures, to declare the meaning of the Federal Constitution. But a declaration that proceedings of the federal government are not warranted by the Constitution, is a novelty neither among the citizens nor among the legislatures of the states; nor are the citizens or the legislature of Virginia singular in the example of it.

Nor can the declarations of either, whether affirming or denying the constitutionality of measures of the federal government, or whether made before or after judicial decisions thereon, be deemed, in any point of view, an assumption of the office of the judge. The declarations in such cases are expressions of opinion, unaccompanied with any other effect than what they may produce on opinion, by exciting reflection. The expositions of the judiciary, on the other hand, are carried into immediate effect by force. The former may lead to a change in the legislative expression of the general will—possibly to a change in the opinion of the judiciary; the latter enforces the general will, whilst that will and that opinion continue unchanged. . . .

Resolved, That the General Assembly, having carefully and respectfully attended to the proceedings of a number of the states, in answer to the resolutions of December 21, 1798, and having accurately and fully reexamined and reconsidered the latter, find it to be their indispensable duty to adhere to the same, as founded in truth, as consonant with the Constitution, and as conducive to its preservation; and more especially to be their duty to renew, as they do hereby renew, their PROTEST against Alien and Sedition Acts, as palpable and alarming infractions of the Constitution.

MARBURY v. MADISON

5 U.S. (1 CRANCH) 137 (1803)

arbury v. Madison is one of the Supreme Court's
most famous and most poorly understood
cases. In the waning hours of the Adams ad-
ministration, Secretary of State John Marshall failed to deliver a judicial
commission, signed by President Adams, to William Marbury. James
Madison, Marshall's successor and President Jefferson's new Secretary of
State, declined to give Marbury his commission. Marbury then brought
suit against Madison in the Supreme Court for a "writ of mandamus," a
court order that would compel Madison to make the delivery.

The Supreme Court, in a unanimous opinion by Chief Justice John
Marshall—the same man whose omission had led to the lawsuit—held
that the statute appearing to give the Court jurisdiction over Marbury's
suit was technically unconstitutional, in that it gave the Court "original"
rather than "appellate" jurisdiction. The Court therefore refused to exercise jurisdiction and ruled against Marbury. The case is noted today primarily for its exposition of the rationale for "judicial review," the power
of courts to decline to enforce laws they consider unconstitutional. The
Court's reasoning should be compared with that of Alexander Hamilton
in *The Federalist*, No. 78 (see p. 12).

✪

MR. CHIEF JUSTICE MARSHALL DELIVERED THE OPINION OF
THE COURT.

In the order in which the court has viewed this subject, the following
questions have been considered and decided. . . . 1st. Has the applicant
a right to the commission he demands? . . . 2d. If he has a right, and
that right has been violated, do the laws of his country afford him a
remedy? . . . 3d. If they do afford him a remedy, is it a mandamus issuing from this court? . . .

It is . . . the opinion of the Court . . . 1st. That by signing the commission of Mr. Marbury, the President of the United States appointed
him a justice of peace for the county of Washington, in the District of
Columbia; and that the seal of the United States, affixed thereto by the
Secretary of State, is conclusive testimony of the verity of the signature,
and of the completion of the appointment, and that the appointment
conferred on him a legal right to the office for the space of five years. . . .
2d. That, having this legal title to the office, he has a consequent right
to the commission; a refusal to deliver which is a plain violation of that
right, for which the laws of his country afford him a remedy. . . . It remains to be inquired whether . . . 3d. He is entitled to the remedy for
which he applies. . . .

The province of the court is, solely, to decide on the rights of individuals, not to inquire how the executive, or executive officers, perform duties in which they have a discretion. Questions in their nature
political, or which are, by the constitution and laws, submitted to the
executive, can never be made in this court. . . . But where [the head of a
department] is directed by law to do a certain act affecting the absolute
rights of individuals, in the performance of which he is not placed under
the particular direction of the President, and the performance of which
the President cannot lawfully forbid, and therefore is never presumed
to have forbidden; it is not perceived on what ground the courts of the
country are farther excused from the duty of giving judgment that right
be done to an injured individual, then if the same services were to be
performed by a person not the head of a department. . . .

The act to establish the judicial courts of the United States authorizes the Supreme Court "to issue writs of mandamus in cases warranted by the principles and usages of law, to any courts appointed, or persons holding office, under the authority of the United States." . . . The Secretary of State, being a person holding an office under the authority of the United States, is precisely within the letter of the description, and if this court is not authorized to issue a writ of mandamus to such an officer, it must be because the law is unconstitutional, and therefore absolutely incapable of conferring the authority, and assigning the duties which its words purport to confer and assign.

The constitution vests the whole judicial power of the United States in one Supreme Court, and such inferior courts as congress shall, from time to time, ordain and establish. This power is expressly extended to all cases arising under the laws of the United States; and, consequently, in some form, may be exercised over the present case; because the right claimed is given by a law of the United States. . . . In the distribution of this power it is declared that "the Supreme Court shall have original jurisdiction in all cases affecting ambassadors, other public ministers and consuls, and those in which a state shall be a party. In all other cases, the Supreme Court shall have appellate jurisdiction." . . . If it had been intended to leave it in the discretion of the legislature to apportion the judicial power between the supreme and inferior courts according to the will of that body, it would certainly have been useless to have proceeded further than to have defined the judicial power, and the tribunals in which it should be vested. . . .

When an instrument organizing fundamentally a judicial system, divides it into one supreme and so many inferior courts as the legislature may ordain and establish; then enumerates its powers, and proceeds so far to distribute them, as to define the jurisdiction of the Supreme Court by declaring the cases in which it shall take original jurisdiction, and that in others it shall take appellate jurisdiction; the plain import of the words seems to be, that in one class of cases its jurisdiction is original, and not appellate; in the other it is appellate, and not original. If any other construction would render the clause inoperative, that is an additional reason for rejecting such other construction and for adhering to their obvious meaning.

To enable this court, then, to issue a mandamus, it must be shown to be an exercise of appellate jurisdiction, or to be necessary to enable them to exercise appellate jurisdiction. . . . [T]o issue such a writ to an officer for the delivery of a paper is in effect the same as to sustain an original motion for that paper, and, therefore, seems not to belong to appellate but to original jurisdiction. . . . The authority, therefore, given to the Supreme Court, by the act establishing the judicial courts of the United States, to issue writs of mandamus to public officers, appears not to be warranted by the constitution and it becomes necessary to inquire whether a jurisdiction so conferred can be exercised.

The question, whether an act, repugnant to the constitution can become the law of the land is a question deeply interesting to the United States; but, happily, not of an intricacy proportioned to its interest. It seems only necessary to recognize certain principles, supposed to have been long and well established, to decide it.

That the people have an original right to establish for their future government, such principles, as, in their opinion, shall most conduce to their own happiness is the basis on which the whole American fabric has been erected. The exercise of this original right is a very great exertion; nor can it, nor ought it, to be frequently repeated. The principles, therefore, so established, are deemed fundamental. And as the authority from which they proceed is supreme, and can seldom act, they are designed to be permanent.

This original and supreme will organizes the government, and assigns to different departments their respective powers. It may either stop here, or establish certain limits not to be transcended by those departments.

The government of the United States is of the latter description. The powers of the legislature are defined and limited, and that those limits may not he mistaken, or forgotten, the constitution is written. To what purpose are powers limited, and to what purpose is that limitation committed to writing, if these limits may, at any time, be passed by those intended to be restrained? The distinction between a government with limited and unlimited powers is abolished, if those limits do not confine the persons on whom they are imposed, and if acts prohibited and acts allowed, are of equal obligation. It is a proposition too plain to be contested, that the constitution controls any legislative act repugnant to it; or, that the legislature may alter the constitution by an ordinary act.

Between these alternatives there is no middle ground. The constitution is either a superior paramount law, unchangeable by ordinary means, or it is on a level with ordinary legislative acts, and, like other acts, is alterable when the legislature shall please to alter it. . . . If the former part of the alternative be true then a legislative act contrary to the constitution is not law: if the latter part be true, then written constitutions are absurd attempts, on the part of the people, to limit a power in its own nature illimitable. . . .

Certainly all those who have framed written constitutions contemplate them as forming the fundamental and paramount law of the nation, and, consequently, the theory of every such government must be, that an act of the legislature, repugnant to the constitution, is void. . . . This theory is essentially attached to a written constitution, and, is consequently, to be considered, by this court, as one of the fundamental principles of our society. It is not therefore to be lost sight of in the further consideration of this subject.

If an act of the legislature, repugnant to the constitution, is void, does it, notwithstanding its invalidity, bind the courts, and oblige them to give it effect? Or, in other words, though it be not law, does it constitute a rule as operative as if it were a law? This would be to overthrow in fact what was established in theory; and would seem, at first view, an absurdity too gross to be insisted on. It shall, however, receive a more attentive consideration. . . . It is emphatically the province and duty of the judicial department to say what the law is. Those who apply the rule to particular cases, must of necessity expound and interpret that rule. If two laws conflict with each other the courts must decide on the operation of each. . . . So if a law be in opposition to the constitution; if both the law and the constitution apply to a particular case, so that the court must either decide that case conformably to the law, disregarding the constitution; or conformably to the constitution, disregarding the law; the court must determine which of these conflicting rules governs the case. This is of the very essence of judicial duty. . . . If, then, the courts are to regard the constitution, and the constitution is superior to any ordinary act of the legislature, the constitution, and not such ordinary act must govern the case to which they both apply.

Those, then, who controvert the principle that the constitution is to be considered, in court, as a paramount law are reduced to the necessity of maintaining that courts must close their eyes on the constitution, and see only the law. . . . This doctrine would subvert the very foundation of all written constitutions. It would declare that an act which according to the principles and theory of our government is entirely void, is yet, in practice, completely obligatory. It would declare that if the legislature shall do what is expressly forbidden, such act, notwithstanding the express prohibition, is in reality effectual. It would be giving to the legislature a practical and real omnipotence, with the same breath which professes to restrict their powers within narrow limits. It is prescribing limits and declaring that those limits may be passed at pleasure. . . . That it thus reduces to nothing what we have deemed the greatest improvement on political institutions, a written constitution, would of itself be sufficient, in America, where written constitutions have been viewed with so much reverence, for rejecting the construction. But the peculiar expressions of the constitution of the United States furnish additional arguments in favor of its rejection.

The judicial power of the United States is extended to all cases arising under the constitution. . . . Could it be the intention of those who gave this power to say that in using it the constitution should not be looked into? That a case arising under the constitution should be decided without examining the instrument under which it arises? . . . This is too extravagant to be maintained. . . . In some cases, then, the constitution must be looked into by the judges. And it they can open it at all, what part of it are they forbidden to read or to obey? . . . There are many other parts of the constitution which serve to illustrate this subject. . . . It is declared that "no tax or duty shall be laid on articles exported from any state." Suppose a duty on the export of cotton, of tobacco or of flour; and a suit instituted to recover it. Ought judgment to be rendered in such a case? Ought the judges to close their eyes on the constitution, and only see the law? . . . The constitution declares "that no bill of attainder or ex post facto law shall be passed." . . . If, however, such a bill should he passed and a person should be prosecuted under it; must the court condemn to death those victims whom the constitution endeavors to preserve? . . . "No person," says the constitution, "shall be convicted of treason unless on the testimony of two witnesses to the same overt act, or on confession in open court." . . . Here the language of the constitution is addressed especially to the courts. It prescribes directly for them, a rule of evidence not to be departed from. If the legislature should change that rule, and declare one witness, or a confession out of court, sufficient for conviction, must the constitutional principle yield to the legislative act?

From these, and many other selections which might be made, it is apparent, that the framers of the constitution contemplated that instrument as a rule for the government of courts, as well as of the legislature. Why otherwise does it direct the judges to take an oath to support it? This oath certainly applies in an especial manner, to their conduct in their official character. How immoral to impose it on them, if they were to be used as the instruments, and the knowing instruments, for violating what they swear to support! . . . The oath of office, too, imposed by the legislature, is completely demonstrative of the legislative opinion on this subject. It is in these words: "I do solemnly swear that I will administer justice without respect to persons, and do equal right to the poor and to the rich; and that I will faithfully and impartially discharge all the duties incumbent on me as, according to the best of my abilities and understanding agreeably to the constitution and laws of the United States." . . . Why does a judge swear to discharge his duties agreeably to the constitution of the United States if that constitution forms no rule for his government? if it is closed upon him, and cannot be inspected by him? . . . If such be the real state of things, this is worse than solemn mockery. To prescribe, or to take this oath, becomes equally a crime.

It is also not entirely unworthy of observation, that in declaring what shall be the supreme law of the land, the constitution itself is first mentioned; and not the laws of the United States generally, but those only which shall be made in pursuance of the constitution, have that rank. . . . Thus, the particular phraseology of the constitution of the United States confirms and strengthens the principle, supposed to be essential to all written constitutions, that a law repugnant to the constitution is void; and that courts, as well as other departments, are bound by that instrument. . . .

THOMAS JEFFERSON
ON THE EXECUTIVE POWER
OF CONSTITUTIONAL
INTERPRETATION

ـ، ۂ ـ

*T*homas Jefferson, the nation's third president, was a consistent critic of judicial interpretations of the Constitution and a fervent defender of the executive branch's power to interpret the Constitution independently of judicial interpretation and to act accordingly. As president, Jefferson allowed the Alien and Sedition acts to expire, ordered that prosecutions for past violations be ceased, and granted pardons to persons convicted under the acts during the administration of President John Adams. These two excerpts, from letters to his friends Abigail Adams (John's wife) and Spencer Roane, set forth his views on presidential and judicial powers in interpreting the Constitution.

✪

Letter to Abigail Adams (September 11, 1804)
THOMAS JEFFERSON

•

You seem to think it devolved on the judges to decide on the validity of the sedition law. But nothing in the Constitution has given them a right to decide for the Executive, more than to the Executive to decide for them. Both magistrates are equally independent in the sphere of action assigned to them. The judges, believing the law constitutional, had a right to pass a sentence of fine and imprisonment; because the power was placed in their hands by the Constitution. But the executive, believing the law to be unconstitutional, were bound to remit the execution of it; because that power has been confided to them by the Constitution. That instrument meant that its coordinate branches should be checks on each other. But the opinion which gives to the judges the right to decide what laws are constitutional, and what are not, not only for themselves in their own sphere of action, but for the legislature and executive also, in their spheres, would make the judiciary a despotic branch. . . .

Letter to Judge Spencer Roane (September 6, 1819)
THOMAS JEFFERSON

•

. . . In denying the right they [the judiciary] usurp of exclusively explaining the constitution, I go further than you do, if I understand rightly your quotation from the Federalist, of an opinion that "the judiciary is the last resort in relation to the other departments of the government, but not in relation to the rights of the parties to the compact under which the judiciary is derived." [The quotation was in fact from Madison's Report of 1800, not *The Federalist*. See p. 29.—Ed.] If this opinion be sound, then indeed is our constitution a complete *felo de se*. For intending to establish three departments, co-ordinate and independent, that they might check and balance one another, it has given, according to this opinion, to one of them alone, the right to prescribe rules for the government of the others, and to that one too, which is un-elected by, and independent of the nation. . . . The constitution, on this hypothesis, is a mere thing of wax in the hands of the judiciary, which they may twist, and shape into any form they please. It should be remembered, as an axiom of eternal truth in politics, that whatever power in any government is independent, is absolute also; in theory only, at first, while the spirit of the people is up, but in practice, as fast as that relaxes. Independence can be trusted nowhere but with the people in mass. They are inherently independent of all but moral law. My construction of the constitution is very different from that you quote. It is that each department is truly independent of the others, and has an equal right to decide for itself what is the meaning of the constitution in the cases submitted to its action; and especially, where it is to act ultimately and without appeal. I will explain myself by examples, which, having occurred while I was in office, are better known to me, and the principles which governed them.

A legislature had passed the sedition law. The federal courts had subjected certain individuals to its penalties of fine and imprisonment. On coming into office, I released these individuals by the power of pardon committed to executive discretion, which could never be more properly exercised than where citizens were suffering without the authority of law, or, which was equivalent, under a law unauthorized by the constitution, and therefore null. In the case of Marbury and Madison, the federal judges declared that commissions, signed and sealed by the President, were valid, although not delivered. I deemed delivery essential to complete a deed, which, as long as it remains in the hands of the party, is as yet no deed . . . and I withheld delivery of the commissions. . . .

These are examples of my position, that each of the three departments has equally the right to decide for itself what is its duty under the constitution, without any regard to what the others may have decided for themselves under a similar question. . . .

On the Powers of Government, of Government, the Rights of Individuals, *and* Federalism (1819–1833)

McCULLOCH v. MARYLAND

17 U.S. 316 (1819)

꧁

*M*cCulloch v. Maryland may be the most important, most foundational Supreme Court decision of the nation's early history. The case involved Maryland's attempt to impose a tax on deposits in a branch of the Bank of the United States located in that state. The Court unanimously held, first, that Congress had the power to create a national bank—embracing a broad, Hamiltonian view of national legislative power—and second, that states could not take actions interfering with the operation of valid national powers. The Court therefore struck down Maryland's tax. Both holdings became fundamental to understanding the relationship between federal and state power under the Constitution.

✪

MARSHALL, Ch. J., delivered the opinion of the court.

In the case now to be determined, the defendant, a sovereign state, denies the obligation of a law enacted by the legislature of the Union, and the plaintiff, on his part, contests the validity of an act which has been passed by the legislature of that state. The constitution of our country, in its most interesting and vital parts, is to be considered; the conflicting powers of the government of the Union and of its members, as marked in that constitution, are to be discussed; and an opinion given, which may essentially influence the great operations of the government. . . .

The first question made in the cause is—has congress power to incorporate a bank? It has been truly said, that this can scarcely be considered as an open question, entirely unprejudiced by the former proceedings of the nation respecting it. The principle now contested was introduced at a very early period of our history, has been recognised by many successive legislatures, and has been acted upon by the judicial department, in cases of peculiar delicacy, as a law of undoubted obligation.

It will not be denied, that a bold and daring usurpation might be resisted, after an acquiescence still longer and more complete than this. But it is conceived, that a doubtful question, one on which human reason may pause, and the human judgment be suspended, in the decision of which the great principles of liberty are not concerned, but the respective powers of those who are equally the representatives of the people, are to be adjusted; if not put at rest by the practice of the government, ought to receive a considerable impression from that practice. An exposition of the constitution, deliberately established by legislative acts, on the faith of which an immense property has been advanced, ought not to be lightly disregarded.

In discussing this question, the counsel for the state of Maryland have deemed it of some importance, in the construction of the constitution, to consider that instrument, not as emanating from the people, but as the act of sovereign and independent states. The powers of the general government, it has been said, are delegated by the states, who alone are truly sovereign; and must be exercised in subordination to the states, who alone possess supreme dominion. It would be difficult to sustain this proposition. The convention which framed the constitution was indeed elected by the state legislatures. But the instrument, when it came from their hands, was a mere proposal, without obligation, or pretensions to it. It was reported to the then existing congress of the United States, with a request that it might "be submitted to a convention of delegates, chosen in each state by the people thereof, under the recommendation of its legislature, for their assent and ratification." This mode of proceeding was adopted; and by the convention, by congress, and by the state legislatures, the instrument was submitted to the people. They acted upon it in the only manner in which they can act safely, effectively and wisely, on such a subject, by assembling in convention. It is true, they assembled in their several states—and where else should they have assembled? No political dreamer was ever wild enough to think of breaking down the lines which separate the states, and of compounding the American people into one common mass. Of consequence, when they act, they act in their states. But the measures they adopt do not, on that account, cease to be the measures of the people themselves, or become the measures of the state governments.

From these conventions, the constitution derives its whole authority. The government proceeds directly from the people; is 'ordained and established,' in the name of the people; and is declared to be ordained, 'in order to form a more perfect union, establish justice, insure domestic tranquility, and secure the blessings of liberty to themselves and to their posterity.' The assent of the states, in their sovereign capacity, is implied, in calling a convention, and thus submitting that instrument to the people. But the people were at perfect liberty to accept or reject it; and their act was final. It required not the affirmance, and could not be negatived, by the state governments. The constitution, when thus adopted, was of complete obligation, and bound the state sovereignties.

. . . The government of the Union, then (whatever may be the influence of this fact on the case), is, emphatically and truly, a government of the people. In form, and in substance, it emanates from them. Its powers are granted by them, and are to be exercised directly on them, and for their benefit.

This government is acknowledged by all, to be one of enumerated powers. The principle, that it can exercise only the powers granted to it, would seem too apparent, to have required to be enforced by all those arguments, which its enlightened friends, while it was depending before the people, found it necessary to urge; that principle is now universally admitted. But the question respecting the extent of the powers actually granted, is perpetually arising, and will probably continue to arise, so long as our system shall exist. In discussing these questions, the conflicting powers of the general and state governments must be brought into view, and the supremacy of their respective laws, when they are in opposition, must be settled.

If any one proposition could command the universal assent of mankind, we might expect it would be this—that the government of the Union, though limited in its powers, is supreme within its sphere of action. This would seem to result, necessarily, from its nature. It is the government of all; its powers are delegated by all; it represents all, and acts for all. Though any one state may be willing to control its operations, no state is willing to allow others to control them. The nation, on those subjects on which it can act, must necessarily bind its component parts. But this question is not left to mere reason: the people have, in express terms, decided it, by saying, 'this constitution, and the laws of the United States, which shall be made in pursuance thereof,' 'shall be the supreme law of the land,' and by requiring that the members of the state legislatures, and the officers of the executive and judicial departments of the states, shall take the oath of fidelity to it. The government of the United States, then, though limited in its powers, is supreme; and its laws, when made in pursuance of the constitution, form the supreme law of the land, 'anything in the constitution or laws of any state to the contrary notwithstanding.'

Among the enumerated powers, we do not find that of establishing a bank or creating a corporation. But there is no phrase in the instrument which, like the articles of confederation, excludes incidental or implied powers; and which requires that everything granted shall be expressly and minutely described. Even the 10th amendment, which was framed for the purpose of quieting the excessive jealousies which had been excited, omits the word 'expressly,' and declares only, that the powers 'not delegated to the United States, nor prohibited to the states, are reserved to the states or to the people;' thus leaving the question, whether the particular power which may become the subject of contest, has been delegated to the one government, or prohibited to the other, to depend on a fair construction of the whole instrument. The men who drew and adopted this amendment had experienced the embarrassments resulting from the insertion of this word in the articles of confederation, and probably omitted it, to avoid those embarrassments. A constitution, to contain an accurate detail of all the subdivisions of which its great powers will admit, and of all the means by which they may be carried into execution, would partake of the prolixity of a legal code, and could scarcely be embraced by the human mind. It would, probably, never be understood by the public. Its nature, therefore, requires, that only its great outlines should be marked, its important objects designated, and the minor ingredients which compose those objects, be deduced from the nature of the objects themselves. That this idea was entertained by the framers of the American constitution, is not only to be inferred from the nature of the instrument, but from the language. Why else were some of the limitations, found in the 9th section of the 1st article, introduced? It is also, in some degree, warranted, by their having omitted to use any restrictive term which might prevent its receiving a fair and just interpretation. In considering this question, then, we must never forget that it is a constitution we are expounding.

Although, among the enumerated powers of government, we do not find the word 'bank' or 'incorporation,' we find the great powers, to lay and collect taxes; to borrow money; to regulate commerce; to declare and conduct a war; and to raise and support armies and navies. The sword and the purse, all the external relations, and no inconsiderable portion of the industry of the nation, are entrusted to its government. It can never be pretended, that these vast powers draw after them others of inferior importance, merely because they are inferior. Such an idea can never be advanced. But it may with great reason be contended, that a government, intrusted with such ample powers, on the due execution of which the happiness and prosperity of the nation so vitally depends, must also be entrusted with ample means for their execution. . . . Can we adopt that construction (unless the words imperiously require it), which would impute to the framers of that instrument, when granting these powers for the public good, the intention of impeding their exercise, by withholding a choice of means? If, indeed, such be the mandate of the constitution, we have only to obey; but that instrument does not profess to enumerate the means by which the powers it confers may be executed; nor does it prohibit the creation of a corporation, if the existence of such a being be essential, to the beneficial exercise of those powers. It is, then, the subject of fair inquiry, how far such means may be employed.

It is not denied, that the powers given to the government imply the ordinary means of execution. That, for example, of raising revenue, and applying it to national purposes, is admitted to imply the power of conveying money from place to place, as the exigencies of the nation may require, and of employing the usual means of conveyance. But it is denied, that the government has its choice of means; or, that it may employ the most convenient means, if, to employ them, it be necessary to erect a corporation. On what foundation does this argument rest? On this alone: the power of creating a corporation, is one appertaining to sovereignty, and is not expressly conferred on congress. This is true. But all legislative powers appertain to sovereignty. . . . The power of creating a corporation is never used for its own sake, but for the purpose of effecting something else. No sufficient reason is, therefore, perceived, why it may not pass as incidental to those powers which are expressly given, if it be a direct mode of executing them.

But the constitution of the United States has not left the right of congress to employ the necessary means, for the execution of the powers conferred on the government, to general reasoning. To its enumeration of powers is added, that of making 'all laws which shall be necessary and proper, for carrying into execution the foregoing powers, and all other powers vested by this constitution, in the government of the United States, or in any department thereof.' The counsel for the state of Maryland have urged various arguments, to prove that this clause, though, in terms, a grant of power, is not so, in effect; but is really restrictive of the general right, which might otherwise be implied, of selecting means for executing the enumerated powers. . . . The word 'necessary' is considered as controlling the whole sentence, and as limiting the right to pass laws for the execution of the granted powers, to such as are indispensable, and without which the power would be nugatory. That it excludes the choice of means, and leaves to congress, in each case, that only which is most direct and simple.

Is it true, that this is the sense in which the word 'necessary' is always used? Does it always import an absolute physical necessity, so strong, that one thing to which another may be termed necessary, cannot exist without that other? We think it does not. If reference be had to its use, in the common affairs of the world, or in approved authors, we find that it frequently imports no more than that one thing is convenient, or useful, or essential to another. To employ the means necessary to an end, is generally understood as employing any means calculated to produce the end, and not as being confined to those single means, without which the end would be entirely unattainable. . . . It is essential to just construction, that many words which import something excessive, should be understood in a more mitigated sense—in that sense which common usage justifies. The word 'necessary' is of this description. It has not a fixed character, peculiar to itself. It admits of all degrees of comparison; and is often connected with other words, which increase or diminish the impression the mind receives of the urgency it imports. A thing may be necessary, very necessary, absolutely or indispensably necessary. To no mind would the same idea be conveyed by these several phrases. The comment on the word is well illustrated by the passage cited at the bar, from the 10th section of the 1st article of the constitution. It is, we think, impossible to compare the sentence which prohibits a state from laying 'imposts, or duties on imports or exports, except what may be absolutely necessary for executing its inspection laws,' with that which authorizes congress 'to make all laws which shall be necessary and proper for carrying into execution' the powers of the general government, without feeling a conviction, that the convention understood itself to change materially the meaning of the word 'necessary,' by prefixing the word 'absolutely.' This word, then, like others, is used in various senses; and, in its construction, the subject, the context, the intention of the person using them, are all to be taken into view.

Let this be done in the case under consideration. The subject is the execution of those great powers on which the welfare of a nation essentially depends. It must have been the intention of those who gave these powers, to insure, so far as human prudence could insure, their beneficial execution. This could not be done, by confiding the choice of means to such narrow limits as not to leave it in the power of congress to adopt any which might be appropriate, and which were conducive to the end. This provision is made in a constitution, intended to endure for ages to come, and consequently, to be adapted to the various crises of human affairs. To have prescribed the means by which government should, in all future time, execute its powers, would have been to change, entirely, the character of the instrument, and give it the properties of a legal code. It would have been an unwise attempt to provide, by immutable rules, for exigencies which, if foreseen at all, must have been seen dimly, and which can be best provided for as they occur. To have declared, that the best means shall not be used, but those alone, without which the power given would be nugatory, would have been to deprive the legislature of the capacity to avail itself of experience, to exercise its reason, and to accommodate its legislation to circumstances.

The baneful influence of this narrow construction on all the operations of the government, and the absolute impracticability of maintaining it, without rendering the government incompetent to its great objects, might be illustrated by numerous examples drawn from the constitution, and from our laws. The good sense of the public has pronounced, without hesitation, that the power of punishment appertains to sovereignty, and may be exercised, whenever the sovereign has a right to act, as incidental to his constitutional powers. It is a means for carrying into execution all sovereign powers, and may be used, although not indispensably necessary. It is a right incidental to the power, and conducive to its beneficial exercise.

But the argument which most conclusively demonstrates the error of the construction contended for by the counsel for the state of Maryland, is founded on the intention of the convention, as manifested in the whole clause. To waste time and argument in proving that, without it, congress might carry its powers into execution, would be not much less idle, than to hold a lighted taper to the sun. As little can it be required to prove, that in the absence of this clause, congress would have some choice of means. That it might employ those which, in its judgment, would most advantageously effect the object to be accomplished. That any means adapted to the end, any means which tended directly to the execution of the constitutional powers of the government, were in themselves constitutional. This clause, as construed by the state of Maryland, would abridge, and almost annihilate, this useful and necessary right of the legislature to select its means. That this could not be intended, is, we should think, had it not been already controverted, too apparent for controversy.

We think so for the following reasons: 1st. The clause is placed among the powers of congress, not among the limitations on those powers. 2d. Its terms purport to enlarge, not to diminish the powers vested in the government. It purports to be an additional power, not a restriction on those already granted. No reason has been, or can be assigned, for thus concealing an intention to narrow the discretion of the national legislature, under words which purport to enlarge it. . . . Had the intention been to make this clause restrictive, it would unquestionably have been so in form as well as in effect.

The result of the most careful and attentive consideration bestowed upon this clause is, that if it does not enlarge, it cannot be construed to restrain the powers of congress, or to impair the right of the legislature to exercise its best judgment in the selection of measures to carry into execution the constitutional powers of the government. If no other motive for its insertion can be suggested, a sufficient one is found in the desire to remove all doubts respecting the right to legislate on that vast mass of incidental powers which must be involved in the constitution, if that instrument be not a splendid bauble.

We admit, as all must admit, that the powers of the government are limited, and that its limits are not to be transcended. But we think the sound construction of the constitution must allow to the national legislature that discretion, with respect to the means by which the powers it confers are to be carried into execution, which will enable that body to perform the high duties assigned to it, in the manner most beneficial to the people. Let the end be legitimate, let it be within the scope of the constitution, and all means which are appropriate, which are plainly adapted to that end, which are not prohibited, but consist with the letter and spirit of the constitution, are constitutional. . . .

It being the opinion of the court, that the act incorporating the bank is constitutional; and that the power of establishing a branch in the state of Maryland might be properly exercised by the bank itself, we proceed to inquire—

2. Whether the state of Maryland may, without violating the constitution, tax that branch? That the power of taxation is one of vital importance; that it is retained by the states; that it is not abridged by the grant of a similar power to the government of the Union; that it is to be concurrently exercised by the two governments; are truths which have never been denied. But such is the paramount character of the constitution, that its capacity to withdraw any subject from the action of even this power, is admitted. The states are expressly forbidden to lay any duties on imports or exports, except what may be absolutely necessary for executing their inspection laws. If the obligation of this prohibition must be conceded—if it may restrain a state from the exercise of its taxing power on imports and exports—the same paramount character would seem to restrain, as it certainly may restrain, a state from such other exercise of this power, as is in its nature incompatible with, and repugnant to, the constitutional laws of the Union. A law, absolutely repugnant to another, as entirely repeals that other as if express terms of repeal were used.

On this ground, the counsel for the bank place its claim to be exempted from the power of a state to tax its operations. There is no express provision for the case, but the claim has been sustained on a principle which so entirely pervades the constitution, is so intermixed with the materials which compose it, so interwoven with its web, so blended with its texture, as to be incapable of being separated from it, without rending it into shreds. This great principle is, that the constitution and the laws made in pursuance thereof are supreme; that they control the constitution and laws of the respective states, and cannot be controlled by them. From this, which may be almost termed an axiom, other propositions are deduced as corollaries, on the truth or error of which, and on their application to this case, the cause has been supposed to depend. These are, 1st. That a power to create implies a power to preserve: 2d. That a power to destroy, if wielded by a different hand, is hostile to, and incompatible with these powers to create and to preserve: 3d. That where this repugnancy exists, that authority which is supreme must control, not yield to that over which it is supreme. . . .

The argument on the part of the state of Maryland, is, not that the states may directly resist a law of congress, but that they may exercise their acknowledged powers upon it, and that the constitution leaves them this right, in the confidence that they will not abuse it. Before we proceed to examine this argument, and to subject it to test of the constitution, we must be permitted to bestow a few considerations on the nature and extent of this original right of taxation, which is acknowledged to remain with the states. It is admitted, that the power of taxing the people and their property, is essential to the very existence of government, and may be legitimately exercised on the objects to which it is applicable, to the utmost extent to which the government may choose to carry it. The only security against the abuse of this power, is found in the structure of the government itself. In imposing a tax, the legislature acts upon its constituents. This is, in general, a sufficient security against erroneous and oppressive taxation. . . .

The sovereignty of a state extends to everything which exists by its own authority, or is introduced by its permission; but does it extend to those means which are employed by congress to carry into execution powers conferred on that body by the people of the United States? We think it demonstrable, that it does not. Those powers are not given by the people of a single state. They are given by the people of the United States, to a government whose laws, made in pursuance of the constitution, are declared to be supreme. Consequently, the people of a single state cannot confer a sovereignty which will extend over them. . . . We find, then, on just theory, a total failure of this original right to tax the means employed by the government of the Union, for the execution of its powers. . . .

But, waiving this theory for the present, let us resume the inquiry, whether this power can be exercised by the respective states, consistently with a fair construction of the constitution? That the power to tax involves the power to destroy; that the power to destroy may defeat and render useless the power to create; that there is a plain repugnance in conferring on one government a power to control the constitutional measures of another, which other, with respect to those very measures, is declared to be supreme over that which exerts the control, are propositions not to be denied. . . .

If we apply the principle for which the state of Maryland contends, to the constitution, generally, we shall find it capable of changing totally the character of that instrument. We shall find it capable of arresting all the measures of the government, and of prostrating it at the foot of the states. The American people have declared their constitution and the laws made in pursuance thereof, to be supreme; but this principle would transfer the supremacy, in fact, to the states. If the states may tax one instrument, employed by the government in the execution of its powers, they may tax any and every other instrument. They may tax the mail; they may tax the mint; they may tax patent-rights; they may tax the papers of the custom-house; they may tax judicial process; they may tax all the means employed by the government, to an excess which would defeat all the ends of government. This was not intended by the American people. They did not design to make their government dependent on the states. . . .

If the controlling power of the states be established; if their supremacy as to taxation be acknowledged; what is to restrain their exercising control in any shape they may please to give it? Their sovereignty is not confined to taxation; that is not the only mode in which it might be displayed. The question is, in truth, a question of supremacy; and if the right of the states to tax the means employed by the general government be conceded, the declaration that the constitution, and the laws made in pursuance thereof, shall be the supreme law of the land, is empty and unmeaning declamation. . . .

The court has bestowed on this subject its most deliberate consideration. The result is a conviction that the states have no power, by taxation or otherwise, to retard, impede, burden, or in any manner control, the operations of the constitutional laws enacted by congress to carry into execution the powers vested in the general government. This is, we think, the unavoidable consequence of that supremacy which the constitution has declared. We are unanimously of opinion, that the law passed by the legislature of Maryland, imposing a tax on the Bank of the United States, is unconstitutional and void.

ANDREW JACKSON'S BANK OF THE UNITED STATES VETO MESSAGE AND PROCLAMATION CONCERNING NULLIFICATION

*A*uthorization for the first Bank of the United States expired, and in 1832, President Andrew Jackson vetoed a bill to re-charter the Bank. Jackson considered the Bank unconstitutional, notwithstanding the Supreme Court's contrary decision in *McCulloch v. Maryland* in 1819 (see p. 49). President Jackson, like President Jefferson (see p. 44), interpreted the Constitution as giving the president—indeed, all officers of the national government—the independent power and duty to faithfully interpret the founding document, and held that no one branch of government bound the others.

That same year, President Jackson rebutted and condemned the assertion of Vice President John Calhoun and others, that states were sovereign and therefore possessed the ultimate power to "nullify" national laws. Calhoun's position—loosely extrapolated from Madison's and Jefferson's stance with respect to the Alien and Sedition Acts (see pp. 29–35)—threatened disunion. Jackson's Proclamation Concerning Nullification made the constitutional case for national supremacy in the Union as a whole, and against state powers of interposition and nullification—or secession. Jackson prevailed in the confrontation.

President Jackson's constitutional interpretations and actions had a major effect on the course of the nation, both in his own day and for the future. His positions greatly influenced Abraham Lincoln's own views and actions as president a quarter-century later.

✪

Veto Message (July 10, 1832)
ANDREW JACKSON

•

To the Senate:

The bill "to modify and continue" the act entitled "An act to incorporate the subscribers to the Bank of the United States" was presented to me on the 4th July instant. Having considered it with that solemn regard to the principles of the Constitution which the day was calculated to inspire, and come to the conclusion that it ought not to become a law, I herewith return it to the Senate, in which it originated, with my objections. . . .

It is maintained by the advocates of the bank that its constitutionality in all its features ought to be considered as settled by precedent and by the decision of the Supreme Court. To this conclusion I can not assent. Mere precedent is a dangerous source of authority, and should not be regarded as deciding questions of constitutional power except where the acquiescence of the people and the States can be considered as well settled. . . .

If the opinion of the Supreme Court covered the whole ground of this act, it ought not to control the coordinate authorities of this Government. The Congress, the Executive, and the Court must each for itself be guided by its own opinion of the Constitution. Each public officer who takes an oath to support the Constitution swears that he will support it as he understands it, and not as it is understood by others. It is as much the duty of the House of Representatives, of the Senate, and of the President to decide upon the constitutionality of any bill or resolution which may be presented to them for passage or approval as it is of the supreme judges when it may be brought before them for judicial decision. The opinion of the judges has no more authority over Congress than the opinion of Congress has over the judges, and on that point the President is independent of both. The authority of the Supreme Court must not, therefore, be permitted to control the Congress or the Executive when acting in their legislative capacities, but to have only such influence as the force of their reasoning may deserve. . . .

Proclamation Concerning Nullification (December 10, 1832)
ANDREW JACKSON

•

Whereas a convention, assembled in the State of South Carolina, have passed an ordinance, by which they declare "that the several acts and parts of acts of the Congress of the United States, purporting to be laws for the imposing of duties and imposts on the importation of foreign commodities . . . are unauthorized by the Constitution of the United States, and violate the true meaning and intent thereof, and are null and void, and no law," nor binding on the citizens of that State or its officers; and by the said ordinance it is further declared to be unlawful for any of the constituted authorities of the State, or of the United States, to enforce the payment of the duties imposed by the said acts within the same State, and that it is the duty of the legislature to pass such laws as may be necessary to give full effect to the said ordinances:

And whereas, by the said ordinance it is further ordained, that, in no case of law or equity, decided in the courts of said State, wherein shall be drawn in question the validity of the said ordinance, or of the acts of the legislature that may be passed to give it effect, or of the said laws of the United States, no appeal shall be allowed to the Supreme Court of the United States . . . and that any person attempting to take such appeal, shall be punished as for a contempt of court:

And, finally, the said ordinance declares that the people of South Carolina will maintain the said ordinance at every hazard; and that they will consider the passage of any act by Congress abolishing or closing the ports of the said State, or otherwise obstructing the free ingress or egress of vessels to and from the said ports, or any other act of the Federal Government to coerce the State, shut up her ports, destroy or harass her commerce, or to enforce the said acts otherwise than through the civil tribunals of the country, as inconsistent with the longer continuance of South Carolina in the Union; and that the people of the said State will thenceforth hold themselves absolved from all further obligation to maintain or preserve their political connection with the people of the other States, and will forthwith proceed to organize a separate government, and do all other acts and things which sovereign and independent States may of right do:

And whereas the said ordinance prescribes to the people of South Carolina a course of conduct in direct violation of their duty as citizens of the United States, contrary to the laws of their country, subversive of its Constitution, and having for its object the destruction of the Union . . . I, Andrew Jackson, President of the United States, have thought proper to issue this my Proclamation, stating my views of the Constitution and laws applicable to the measures adopted by the Convention of South Carolina, and to the reasons they have put forth to sustain them, declaring the course which duty will require me to pursue, and, appealing to the understanding and patriotism of the people, warn them of the consequences that must inevitably result from an observance of the dictates of the Convention.

Strict duty would require of me nothing more than the exercise of those powers with which I am now, or may hereafter be, invested, for preserving the Union, and for the execution of the laws. But the imposing aspect which opposition has assumed in this case, by clothing itself with State authority, and the deep interest which the people of the United States must all feel in preventing a resort to stronger measures, while there is a hope that anything will be yielded to reasoning and remonstrances, perhaps demand, and will certainly justify, a full exposition to South Carolina and the nation of the views I entertain of this important question, as well as a distinct enunciation of the course which my sense of duty will require me to pursue.

The ordinance is founded, not on the indefeasible right of resisting acts which are plainly unconstitutional, and too oppressive to be endured, but on the strange position that any one State may not only declare an act of Congress void, but prohibit its execution—that they may do this consistently with the Constitution—that the true construction of that instrument permits a State to retain its place in the Union, and yet be bound by no other of its laws than those it may choose to consider as constitutional. It is true they add, that to justify this abrogation of a law, it must be palpably contrary to the Constitution; but it is evident, that to give the right of resisting laws of that description, coupled with the uncontrolled right to decide what laws deserve that character, is to give the power of resisting all laws. For, as by the theory, there is no appeal, the reasons alleged by the State, good or bad, must prevail. If it should be said that public opinion is a sufficient check against the abuse of this power, it may be asked why it is not deemed a sufficient guard against the passage of an unconstitutional act by Congress. There is, however, a restraint in this last case, which makes the assumed power of a State more indefensible, and which does not exist in the other. There are two appeals from an unconstitutional act passed by Congress—one to the judiciary, the other to the people and the States. There is no appeal from the State decision in theory; and the practical illustration shows that the courts are closed against an application to review it, both judges and jurors being sworn to decide in its favor. But reasoning on this subject is superfluous, when our social compact in express terms declares, that the laws of the United States, its Constitution, and treaties made under it, are the supreme law of the land; and for greater caution adds, "that the judges in every State shall be bound thereby, anything in the Constitution or laws of any State to the contrary notwithstanding." And it may be asserted, without fear of refutation, that no federative government could exist without a similar provision. Look, for a moment, to the consequence. If South Carolina considers the revenue laws unconstitutional, and has a right to prevent their execution in the port of Charleston, there would be a clear constitutional objection to their collection in every other port, and no revenue could be collected anywhere; for all imposts must be equal. It is no answer to repeat that an unconstitutional law is no law, so long as the question of its legality is to be decided by the State itself . . .

If the doctrine of a State veto upon the laws of the Union carries with it internal evidence of its impracticable absurdity, our constitutional history will also afford abundant proof that it would have been repudiated with indignation had it been proposed to form a feature in our Government.

In our colonial state, although dependent on another power, we very early considered ourselves as connected by common interest with each other. . . . We declared ourselves a nation by a joint, not by several acts; and when the terms of our confederation were reduced to form, it was in that of a solemn league of several States, by which they agreed that they would, collectively, form one nation, for the purpose of conducting some certain domestic concerns, and all foreign relations. In the instrument forming that Union, is found an article which declares that "every State shall abide by the determinations of Congress on all questions which by that Confederation should be submitted to them."

Under the Confederation, then, no State could legally annul a decision of the Congress, or refuse to submit to its execution; but no provision was made to enforce these decisions. Congress made requisitions, but they were not complied with. The Government could not operate on individuals. They had no judiciary, no means of collecting revenue.

But the defects of the Confederation need not be detailed. Under its operation we could scarcely be called a nation. We had neither prosperity at home nor consideration abroad. This state of things could not be endured, and our present happy Constitution was formed, but formed in vain, if this fatal doctrine prevails. It was formed for important objects that are announced in the preamble made in the name and by the authority of the people of the United States, whose delegates framed, and whose conventions approved it.

The most important among these objects, that which is placed first in rank, on which all the others rest, is *"to form a more perfect Union."* Now, is it possible that, even if there were no express provision giving supremacy to the Constitution and laws of the United States over those of the States, it can be conceived that an instrument made for the purpose of *"forming a more perfect Union"* than that of the confederation, could be so constructed by the assembled wisdom of our country as to substitute for that confederation a form of government, dependent for its existence on the local interest, the party spirit of a State, or of a prevailing faction in a State? Every man, of plain, unsophisticated understanding, who hears the question, will give such an answer as will preserve the Union. Metaphysical subtlety, in pursuit of an impracticable theory, could alone have devised one that is calculated to destroy it.

I consider, then, the power to annul a law of the United States, assumed by one State, *incompatible with the existence of the Union, contradicted expressly by the letter of the Constitution, unauthorized by its spirit, inconsistent with every principle on which it was founded, and destructive of the great object for which it was formed.*

After this general view of the leading principle, we must examine the particular application of it which is made in the ordinance. [President Jackson then proceeded at length to refute the argument that the national tariff laws were unconstitutional. —Ed.] . . .

Every law . . . for raising revenue, according to the South Carolina ordinance, may be rightfully annulled, unless it be so framed as no law ever will or can be framed. Congress have a right to pass laws for raising revenue, and each State has a right to oppose their execution— two rights directly opposed to each other; and yet is this absurdity supposed to be contained in an instrument drawn for the express purpose of avoiding collisions between the States and the general government, by an assembly of the most enlightened statesmen and purest patriots ever embodied for a similar purpose. . . .

On such expositions and reasonings, the ordinance grounds not only an assertion of the right to annul the laws of which it complains, but to enforce it by a threat of seceding from the Union if any attempt is made to execute them.

This right to secede is deduced from the nature of the Constitution, which they say is a compact between sovereign States, who have preserved their whole sovereignty, and therefore are subject to no superior; that because they made the compact, they can break it when in their opinion it has been departed from by the other States. Fallacious as this course of reasoning is, it enlists State pride, and finds advocates in the honest prejudices of those who have not studied the nature of our government sufficiently to see the radical error on which it rests. . . .

The Constitution of the United States . . . forms a *government*, not a league, and whether it be formed by compact between the States, or in any other manner, its character is the same. It is a government in which all the people are represented, which operates directly on the people individually, not upon the States; they retained all the power they did not grant. But each State having expressly parted with so many powers as to constitute jointly with the other States a single nation, cannot from that period possess any right to secede, because such secession does not break a league, but destroys the unity of a nation, and any injury to that unity is not only a breach which would result from the contravention of a compact, but it is an offense against the whole Union. To say that any State may at pleasure secede from the Union, is to say that the United States are not a nation; because it would be a solecism to contend that any part of a nation might dissolve its connection with the other parts, to their injury or ruin, without committing any offense. Secession, like any other revolutionary act, may be morally justified by the extremity of oppression; but to call it a constitutional right, is confounding the meaning of terms, and can only be done through gross error, or to deceive those who are willing to assert a right, but would pause before they made a revolution, or incur the penalties consequent upon a failure.

Because the Union was formed by compact, it is said the parties to that compact may, when they feel themselves aggrieved, depart from it; but it is precisely because it is a compact that they cannot. A compact is an agreement or binding obligation. . . . A league between independent nations, generally, has no sanction other than a moral one; or if it should contain a penalty, as there is no common superior, it cannot be enforced. A government, on the contrary, always has a sanction, express or implied; and, in our case, it is both necessarily implied and expressly given. An attempt by force of arms to destroy a government is an offense, by whatever means the constitutional compact may have been formed; and such government has the right, by the law of self-defense, to pass acts for punishing the offender, unless that right is modified, restrained, or resumed by the constitutional act. In our system, although it is modified in the case of treason, yet authority is expressly given to pass all laws necessary to carry its powers into effect, and under this grant provision has been made for punishing acts which obstruct the due administration of the laws.

It would seem superfluous to add anything to show the nature of that union which connects us; but as erroneous opinions on this subject are the foundation of doctrines the most destructive to our peace, I must give some further development to my views on this subject. No one, fellow-citizens, has a higher reverence for the reserved rights of the States than the magistrate who now addresses you. No one would make greater personal sacrifices, or official exertions, to defend them from violation; but equal care must be taken to prevent, on their part, an improper interference with, or resumption of, the rights they have vested in the nation. The line has not been so distinctly drawn as to avoid doubts in some cases of the exercise of power. Men of the best intentions and soundest views may differ in their construction of some parts of the Constitution; but there are others on which dispassionate reflection can leave no doubt. Of this nature appears to be the assumed right of secession. It rests, as we have seen, on the alleged undivided sovereignty of the States, and on their having formed in this sovereign capacity a compact which is called the Constitution, from which, because they made it, they have the right to secede. Both of these positions are erroneous[.] . . .

The States severally have not retained their entire sovereignty. It has been shown that in becoming parts of a nation, not members of a league, they surrendered many of their essential parts of sovereignty. . . .

This, then, is the position in which we stand. A small majority of the citizens of one State in the Union have elected delegates to a State convention; that convention has ordained that all the revenue laws of the United States must be repealed, or that they are no longer a member of the Union. The governor of that State has recommended to the legislature the raising of an army to carry the secession into effect, and that he may be empowered to give clearances to vessels in the name of the State. No act of violent opposition to the laws has yet been committed, but such a state of things is hourly apprehended, and it is the intent of this instrument to Proclaim, not only that the duty imposed on me by the Constitution, "to take care that the laws be faithfully executed," shall be performed to the extent of the powers already vested in me by law, or of such others as the wisdom of Congress shall devise and intrust to me for that purpose; but to warn the citizens of South Carolina, who have been deluded into an opposition to the laws, of the danger they will incur by obedience to the illegal and disorganizing ordinance of the convention—to exhort those who have refused to support it to persevere in their determination to uphold the Constitution and laws of their country, and to point out to all the perilous situation into which the good people of that State have been led, and that the course they are urged to pursue is one of ruin and disgrace to the very State whose rights they affect to support.

Fellow-citizens of my native State! . . . Mark under what pretenses you have been led on to the brink of insurrection and treason on which you stand! . . . Eloquent appeals to your passions, to your State pride, to your native courage, to your sense of real injury, were used to prepare you for the period when the mask which concealed the hideous features of Disunion should be taken off.

. . . The laws of the United States must be executed. I have no discretionary power on the subject—my duty is emphatically pronounced in the Constitution. Those who told you that you might peaceably prevent their execution, deceived you—they could not have been de-ceived themselves. They know that a forcible opposition could alone prevent the execution of the laws, and they know that such opposi-tion must be repelled. Their object is disunion; but be not deceived by names; disunion, by armed force, is Treason. Are you really ready to incur its guilt? If you are, on the head of the instigators of the act be the dreadful consequences—on their heads be the dishonor, but on yours may fall the punishment—on your unhappy State will inevitably fall all the evils of the conflict you force upon the government of your country. It cannot accede to the mad project of disunion, of which you would be the first victims—its first magistrate cannot, if he would, avoid the performance of his duty[.] . . .

BARRON v. BALTIMORE

32 U.S. 243 (1833)

Τhe first ten amendments to the Constitution—commonly called the Bill of Rights—were adopted in 1791 to clarify some of the limits on the powers of the national government. *Barron v. Baltimore* rejected a claim that these provisions limited state governments as well. It was not until the enactment of the Fourteenth Amendment in 1868 following the Civil War that the states were constitutionally forbidden to abridge the "privileges or immunities of citizens of the United States," changing the rule of *Barron*. And it was not until much later that the Supreme Court began to apply the liberties of the Bill of Rights, as incorporated by the Fourteenth Amendment, to the states.

The *Barron* case involved the owner of a commercial wharf in Baltimore, who sued the city, claiming that its actions had rendered the water near the wharf too shallow for most ships, depriving him of his "private property" without compensation in violation of the Fifth Amendment.

✪

MR. CHIEF JUSTICE MARSHALL DELIVERED THE OPINION OF
THE COURT.

. . . The plaintiff in error contends that [this case] comes within that
clause in the fifth amendment to the constitution, which inhibits the
taking of private property for public use, without just compensation.
He insists that this amendment, being in favour of the liberty of the
citizen, ought to be so construed as to restrain the legislative power
of a state, as well as that of the United States. . . . The question thus
presented is, we think, of great importance, but not of much difficulty.

The constitution was ordained and established by the people of the
United States for themselves, for their own government, and not for the
government of the individual states. Each state established a constitution for itself, and, in that constitution, provided such limitations and
restrictions on the powers of its particular government as its judgment
dictated. The people of the United States framed such a government for
the United States as they supposed best adapted to their situation, and
best calculated to promote their interests. The powers they conferred on
this government were to be exercised by itself; and the limitations on
power, if expressed in general terms, are naturally, and, we think, necessarily applicable to the government created by the instrument. They
are limitations of power granted in the instrument itself; not of distinct
governments, framed by different persons and for different purposes.

If these propositions be correct, the fifth amendment must be understood as restraining the power of the general government, not as
applicable to the states. In their several constitutions they have imposed
such restrictions on their respective governments as their own wisdom
suggested; such as they deemed most proper for themselves. It is a subject on which they judge exclusively, and with which others interfere no
farther than they are supposed to have a common interest.

The counsel for the plaintiff in error insists that the constitution was
intended to secure the people of the several states against the undue exercise of power by their respective state governments; as well as against
that which might be attempted by their general government. In support of this argument he relies on the inhibitions contained in the tenth
section of the first article.

We think that section affords a strong if not a conclusive argument
in support of the opinion already indicated by the court.

The preceding section contains restrictions which are obviously intended for the exclusive purpose of restraining the exercise of power by the departments of the general government. Some of them use language applicable only to congress: others are expressed in general terms. The third clause, for example, declares that "no bill of attainder or ex post facto law shall be passed." No language can be more general; yet the demonstration is complete that it applies solely to the government of the United States. In addition to the general arguments furnished by the instrument itself, some of which have been already suggested, the succeeding section, the avowed purpose of which is to restrain state legislation, contains in terms the very prohibition. It declares that "no state shall pass any bill of attainder or ex post facto law." This provision, then, of the ninth section, however comprehensive its language, contains no restriction on state legislation.

The ninth section having enumerated, in the nature of a bill of rights, the limitations intended to be imposed on the powers of the general government, the tenth proceeds to enumerate those which were to operate on the state legislatures. These restrictions are brought together in the same section, and are by express words applied to the states. "No state shall enter into any treaty," &c. Perceiving that in a constitution framed by the people of the United States for the government of all, no limitation of the action of government on the people would apply to the state government, unless expressed in terms; the restrictions contained in the tenth section are in direct words so applied to the states.

It is worthy of remark, too, that these inhibitions generally restrain state legislation on subjects entrusted to the general government, or in which the people of all the states feel an interest.

A state is forbidden to enter into any treaty, alliance or confederation. If these compacts are with foreign nations, they interfere with the treaty making power which is conferred entirely on the general government; if with each other, for political purposes, they can scarcely fail to interfere with the general purpose and intent of the constitution. To grant letters of marque and reprisal, would lead directly to war; the power of declaring which is expressly given to congress. To coin money is also the exercise of a power conferred on congress. It would be tedious to recapitulate the several limitations on the powers of the states which are contained in this section. They will be found, generally, to restrain state legislation on subjects entrusted to the government of the union, in which the citizens of all the states are interested. In these alone were the whole people concerned. The question of their application to states is not left to construction. It is averred in positive words.

If the original constitution, in the ninth and tenth sections of the first article, draws this plain and marked line of discrimination between the limitations it imposes on the powers of the general government, and on those of the states; if in every inhibition intended to act on state power, words are employed which directly express that intent; some strong reason must be assigned for departing from this safe and judicious course in framing the amendments, before that departure can be assumed.

We search in vain for that reason. . . . Had the framers of these amendments intended them to be limitations on the powers of the state governments, they would have imitated the framers of the original constitution, and have expressed that intention. Had congress engaged in the extraordinary occupation of improving the constitutions of the several states by affording the people additional protection from the exercise of power by their own governments in matters which concerned themselves alone, they would have declared this purpose in plain and intelligible language.

But it is universally understood, it is a part of the history of the day, that the great revolution which established the constitution of the United States, was not effected without immense opposition. Serious fears were extensively entertained that those powers which the patriot statesmen, who then watched over the interests of our country, deemed essential to union, and to the attainment of those invaluable objects for which union was sought, might be exercised in a manner dangerous to liberty. In almost every convention by which the constitution was adopted, amendments to guard against the abuse of power were recommended. These amendments demanded security against the apprehended encroachments of the general government—not against those of the local governments.

In compliance with a sentiment thus generally expressed, to quiet fears thus extensively entertained, amendments were proposed by the required majority in congress, and adopted by the states. These amendments contain no expression indicating an intention to apply them to the state governments. This court cannot so apply them.

We are of opinion that the provision in the fifth amendment to the constitution, declaring that private property shall not be taken for public use without just compensation, is intended solely as a limitation on the exercise of power by the government of the United States, and is not applicable to the legislation of the states. We are therefore of opinion that there is no repugnancy between the several acts of the general assembly of Maryland, given in evidence by the defendants at the trial of this cause, in the court of that state, and the constitution of the United States. . . .

The Crisis:
Slavery,
Secession,
and
Civil War
(1857–1866)

DRED SCOTT v. SANDFORD
AND LINCOLN'S RESPONSE

ﾟﾟ

D *red Scott* is among the U.S. Supreme Court's most
famous and most severely criticized decisions and is of
enormous historical significance. The facts giving rise
to the case are as follows: Captain John Emerson, a doctor in the U.S.
Army, lived in Missouri, a slave state. When Captain Emerson was assigned to a military post in Illinois, a free state, he took his slave, Dred
Scott, with him. From there, Captain Emerson was assigned to Fort
Snelling, in Wisconsin Territory (present-day Minnesota), where slavery
was prohibited by the terms of an 1820 statute known as the Missouri
Compromise. He took Dred Scott with him there as well. While at Fort
Snelling, Scott married Harriet, a slave of another master. Dred and
Harriet Scott accompanied Captain Emerson in his travels, eventually
returning with him to Missouri. They had two children, Eliza—born
north of the Missouri Compromise line aboard a steamer in the Mississippi River—and Lizzie, who was born in Missouri. After Captain Emerson died, Dred Scott brought a series of lawsuits seeking to establish
his family's freedom based on the time he spent in Illinois, a free state,
and at Fort Snelling, in free federal territory.

With two justices dissenting, the Supreme Court dismissed Scott's
lawsuit. Those in the majority wrote several separate opinions, but Chief

Justice Taney's opinion was denominated that of the Court. Taney's opinion declared that blacks, whether free or slave, could not be citizens and had no rights under the Constitution—indeed, "no rights which the white man was bound to respect" at all—and thus could not bring suit in federal courts. Furthermore, according to Taney's opinion, Congress's prohibition of slavery in the territories unconstitutionally deprived slaveholders of their property, "without due process of law." The Court's decision threatened to make slavery national, rather than local, by requiring territories, and perhaps even free states, to accept slavery as an incident of the property rights of Southern slaveholders traveling in or moving to Northern states.

Dred Scott contributed to the sectional and political divisions leading to the Civil War. The decision provoked fury in the North among antislavery Republicans—and furious defenses of the decision, and of the Court, by Southerners and some Northern Democrats. In a speech at Springfield, Illinois in 1857, Abraham Lincoln criticized the *Dred Scott* decision as wrong in principle and set forth a theory of the limited force of judicial precedents. Both themes—the wrongness of *Dred Scott* and the question of whether citizens need regard the decision as absolutely binding—became prominent features of the famous series of debates between Lincoln and Senator Stephen Douglas in the 1858 Senate campaign. Lincoln lost the 1858 Senate election but defeated Douglas, and two other candidates, in the 1860 presidential election.

The *Dred Scott* decision was repudiated and ignored by President Lincoln's administration (1861–1865), was effectively overturned by the Civil War and Lincoln's Emancipation Proclamation (1863), and was permanently erased by the adoption of the Thirteenth Amendment, abolishing slavery (1865), and the Fourteenth Amendment, guaranteeing equal citizenship and equal rights (1868).

✪

Dred Scott v. Sandford
60 U.S. 393 (1857)

•

MR. CHIEF JUSTICE TANEY DELIVERED THE OPINION OF THE COURT. . . .

There are two leading questions presented by the record: 1. Had the Circuit Court of the United States jurisdiction to hear and determine the case between these parties? And 2. If it had jurisdiction, is the judgment it has given erroneous or not?

The plaintiff in error, was, with his wife and children, held as slaves by the defendant, in the State of Missouri; and he brought this action in the Circuit Court of the United States for that district, to assert the title of himself and his family to freedom. . . . The defendant pleaded in abatement to the jurisdiction of the court, that the plaintiff was not a citizen of the State of Missouri, as alleged in his declaration, being a negro of African descent, whose ancestors were of pure African blood, and who were brought into this country and sold as slaves. . . . The question is simply this: Can a negro, whose ancestors were imported into this country, and sold as slaves, become a member of the political community formed and brought into existence by the Constitution of the United States, and as such become entitled to all the rights, and privileges, and immunities, guarantied by that instrument to the citizen? One of which rights is the privilege of suing in a court of the United States in the cases specified in the Constitution. . . .

The words "people of the United States" and "citizens" are synonymous terms, and mean the same thing. They both describe the political body who, according to our republican institutions, form the sovereignty, and who hold the power and conduct the Government through their representatives. . . . The question before us is, whether [persons of African descent] compose a portion of this people, and are constituent members of this sovereignty? We think they are not, and that they are not included, and were not intended to be included, under the word "citizens" in the Constitution, and can therefore claim none of the rights and privileges which that instrument provides for and secures to citizens of the United States. On the contrary, they were at that time considered as a subordinate and inferior class of beings, who had been subjugated by the dominant race, and, whether emancipated or not, yet remained subject to their authority, and had no rights or privileges but such as those who held the power and the Government might choose to grant them. . . .

In discussing this question, we must not confound the rights of citizenship which a State may confer within its own limits, and the rights of citizenship as a member of the Union. It does not by any means follow, because he has all the rights and privileges of a citizen of a State, that he must be a citizen of the United States. He may have all of the rights and privileges of the citizen of a State, and yet not be entitled to the rights and privileges of a citizen in any other State. . . . Consequently, no State, since the adoption of the Constitution, can by naturalizing an alien invest him with the rights and privileges secured to a citizen of a State under the Federal Government, although, so far as the State alone was concerned, he would undoubtedly be entitled to the rights of a citizen, and clothed with all the rights and immunities which the Constitution and laws of the State attached to that character.

It is very clear, therefore, that no State can, by any act or law of its own, passed since the adoption of the Constitution, introduce a new member into the political community created by the Constitution of the United States. It cannot make him a member of this community by making him a member of its own. And for the same reason it cannot introduce any person, or description of persons, who were not intended to be embraced in this new political family, which the Constitution brought into existence, but were intended to be excluded from it.

The question then arises, whether the provisions of the Constitution, in relation to the personal rights and privileges to which the citizen of a State should be entitled, embraced the negro African race, at that time in this country, or who might afterwards be imported, who had then or should afterwards be made free in any State; and to put it in the power of a single State to make him a citizen of the United States, and endue him with the full rights of citizenship in every other State without their consent? Does the Constitution of the United States act upon him whenever he shall be made free under the laws of a State, and raised there to the rank of a citizen, and immediately cloth him with all the privileges of a citizen in every other State, and in its own courts?

The court think the affirmative of these propositions cannot be maintained. And if it cannot, the plaintiff in error could not be a citizen of the State of Missouri, within the meaning of the Constitution of the United States, and, consequently, was not entitled to sue in its courts. . . . In the opinion of the court, the legislation and histories of the times, and the language used in the Declaration of Independence, show, that neither the class of persons who had been imported as slaves, nor their descendants, whether they had become free or not, were then acknowledged as a part of the people, nor intended to be included in the general words used in that memorable instrument. . . .

They had for more than a century before been regarded as beings of an inferior order, and altogether unfit to associate with the white race, either in social or political relations; and so far inferior, that they had no rights which the white man was bound to respect; and that the negro might justly and lawfully be reduced to slavery for his benefit. He was bought and sold, and treated as an ordinary article of merchandise and traffic, whenever a profit could be made by it. This opinion was at that time fixed and universal in the civilized portion of the white race. It was regarded as an axiom in morals as well as in politics, which no one thought of disputing, or supposed to be open to dispute; and men in every grade and position in society daily and habitually acted upon it in their private pursuits, as well as in matters of public concern, without doubting for a moment the correctness of this opinion. . . .

The language of the Declaration of Independence is equally conclusive: . . . "We hold these truths to be self-evident: that all men are created equal; that they are endowed by their Creator with certain unalienable rights; that among them is life, liberty, and the pursuit of happiness; that to secure these rights, Governments are instituted, deriving their just powers from the consent of the governed."

The general words above quoted would seem to embrace the whole human family, and if they were used in a similar instrument at this day would be so understood. But it is too clear for dispute, that the enslaved African race were not intended to be included, and formed no part of the people who framed and adopted this declaration; for if the language, as understood in that day, would embrace them, the conduct of the distinguished men who framed the Declaration of Independence would have been utterly and flagrantly inconsistent with the principles they asserted; and instead of the sympathy of mankind, to which they so confidently appeared, they would have deserved and received universal rebuke and reprobation.

Yet the men who framed this declaration were great men—high in literary acquirements—high in their sense of honor, and incapable of asserting principles inconsistent with those on which they were acting. They perfectly understood the meaning of the language they used, and how it would be understood by others; and they knew that it would not in any part of the civilized world be supposed to embrace the negro race, which, by common consent, had been excluded from civilized Governments and the family of nations, and doomed to slavery. They spoke and acted according to the then established doctrines and principles, and in the ordinary language of the day, no one misunderstood them. The unhappy black race were separated from the white by indelible marks, and laws long before established, and were never thought of or spoken of except as property, and when the claims of the owner or the profit of the trader were supposed to need protection. . . .

The only two provisions [in the Constitution] which point to them and include them, treat them as property, and make it the duty of the Government to protect it; no other power, in relation to this race, is to be found in the Constitution; and as it is a Government of special, delegated, powers, no authority beyond these two provisions can be constitutionally exercised. The Government of the United States had no right to interfere for any other purpose but that of protecting the rights of the owner, leaving it altogether with the several States to deal with this race, whether emancipated or not, as each State may think justice, humanity, and the interests and safety of society, require. The States evidently intended to reserve this power exclusively to themselves.

No one, we presume, supposes that any change in public opinion or feeling, in relation to this unfortunate race, in the civilized nations of Europe or in this country, should induce the court to give to the words of the Constitution a more liberal construction in their favor than they were intended to bear when the instrument was framed and adopted. Such an argument would be altogether inadmissible in any tribunal called on to interpret it. . . . Any other rule of construction would abrogate the judicial character of this court, and make it the mere reflex of the popular opinion or passion of the day. . . . And upon a full and careful consideration of the subject, the court is of opinion, that, upon the facts stated in the plea in abatement, Dred Scott was not a citizen of

Missouri within the meaning of the Constitution of the United States, and not entitled as such to sue in its courts; and, consequently, that the Circuit Court had no jurisdiction of the case[.] . . .

It is true that the result either way, by dismissal or by a judgment for the defendant, makes very little, if any, difference in a pecuniary or personal point of view to either party. But the fact that the result would be very nearly the same to the parties in either form of judgment, would not justify this court in sanctioning an error in the judgment which is patent on the record, and which, if sanctioned, might be drawn into precedent, and lead to serious mischief and injustice in some future suit.

We proceed, therefore, to inquire whether the facts relied on by the plaintiff entitled him to his freedom. . . . The act of Congress, upon which the plaintiff relies, declares that slavery and involuntary servitude, except as a punishment for crime, shall be forever prohibited in all that part of the territory ceded by France, under the name of Louisiana, which lies north of thirty-six degrees thirty minutes north latitude, and not included within the limits of Missouri. And the difficulty which meets us at the threshold of this part of the inquiry is, whether Congress was authorized to pass this law under any of the powers granted to it by the Constitution; for if the authority is not given by that instrument, it is the duty of this court to declare it void and inoperative, and incapable of conferring freedom upon any one who is held as a slave under the laws of any one of the States. . . .

The power to expand the territory of the United States by the admission of new States is plainly given; and in the construction of this power by all the departments of the Government, it has been held to authorize the acquisition of territory, not fit for admission at the time, but to be admitted as soon as its population and situation would entitle it to admission. It is acquired to become a State, and not to be held as a colony and governed by Congress with absolute authority; and as the propriety of admitting a new State is committed to the sound discretion of Congress, the power to acquire territory for that purpose, to be held by the United States until it is in a suitable condition to become a State upon an equal footing with the other States, must rest upon the same discretion. . . . [I]t may be safely assumed that citizens of the United States who migrate to a Territory belonging to the people of the United States, cannot be ruled as mere colonists, dependent upon the will of the General Government, and to be governed by any laws it may think proper to impose. . . . [T]he Government and the citizen both enter it under the authority of the Constitution, with their respective rights defined and marked out; and the Federal Government can exercise no power over his person or property, beyond what that instrument confers, nor lawfully deny any right which it has reserved. . . .

For example, no one, we presume, will contend that Congress can make any law in a Territory respecting that establishment of religion, or the free exercise thereof, or abridging the freedom of speech or of the press, or the right of the people of the Territory peaceably to assemble, and to petition the Government for the redress of grievances. . . .

These powers, and others, in relation to rights of person, which it is not necessary here to enumerate, are, in express and positive terms, denied to the General Government; and the rights of private property have been guarded with equal care. Thus the rights of property are united with the rights of person, and placed on the same ground by the Fifth Amendment to the Constitution, which provides that no person shall be deprived of life, liberty, and property, without due process of law. And an act of Congress which deprives a citizen of the United States of his liberty or property, merely because he came himself or brought his property into a particular Territory of the United States, and who had committed no offence against the laws, could hardly be dignified with the name of due process of law. . . . And if Congress itself cannot do this—if it is beyond the powers conferred on the Federal Government—it will be admitted, we presume, that it could not authorize a Territorial Government to exercise them. It could confer no power on any local Government, established by its authority, to violate the provisions of the Constitution. . . .

Now, as we have already said in an earlier part of this opinion, upon a different point, the right of property in a slave is distinctly and expressly affirmed in the Constitution. The right to traffic in it, like an ordinary article of merchandise and property, was guarantied to the citizens of the United States, in every State that might desire it, for twenty years. And the Government in express terms is pledged to protect it in all future time, if the slave escapes from his owner. This is done in plain words—too plain to be misunderstood. And no word can be found in the Constitution which gives Congress a greater power over slave property, or which entitles property of that kind to less protection than property of any other description. The only power conferred is the power coupled with the duty of guarding and protecting the owner in his rights.

Upon these considerations, it is the opinion of the court that the act of Congress which prohibited a citizen from holding and owning property of this kind in the territory of the United States north of the line therein mentioned, is not warranted by the Constitution, and is therefore void; and that neither Dred Scott himself, nor any of his family, were made free by being carried into this territory; even if they had been carried there by the owner, with the intention of becoming a permanent resident. . . .

But there is another point in the case which depends on State power and State law. And it is contended, on the part of the plaintiff, that he is made free by being taken to Rock Island, in the State of Illinois, independently of his residence in the territory of the United States; and being so made free, he was not again reduced to a state of slavery by being brought back to Missouri.

Our notice of this part of the case will be very brief; for the principle on which it depends was decided . . . in the case of *Strader et al. v. Graham* [10 How. 82]. In that case, the slaves had been taken from Kentucky to Ohio, with the consent of the owner, and afterwards brought back to Kentucky. And this court held that their status or condition, as free or slave, depended upon the laws of Kentucky, when they were brought back into that State, and not of Ohio; and that this court had no jurisdiction to revise the judgment of a State court upon its own laws. . . . So in this case. As Scott was a slave when taken into the State of Illinois by his owner, and was there held as such, and brought back in that character, his status, as free or slave, depended on the laws of Missouri, and not of Illinois. . . .

MR. JUSTICE NELSON [CONCURRING].

. . . The question upon the merits, in general terms, is, whether or not the removal of the plaintiff, who was a slave, with his master, from the State of Missouri to the State of Illinois . . . works an emancipation. As appears from an agreed statement of facts, this question has been before the highest court of the State of Missouri, and a judgment rendered that this residence in the free State has no such effect; but, on the contrary, that his original condition continued unchanged. . . . The argument against these decisions is, that the laws of Illinois, forbidding slavery within her territory, had the effect to set the slave free while residing in that State, and to impress upon him the condition and status of a freeman; and that, by force of these laws, this status and condition accompanied him on his return to the slave State, and of consequence he could not be there held as a slave.

. . . Our opinion is, that the question is one which belongs to each State to decide for itself, either by its Legislature or courts of justice; and hence, in respect to the case before us, to the State of Missouri. . . . In other words, except in cases where the power is restrained by the Constitution of the United States, the law of the State is supreme over the subject of slavery within its jurisdiction. . . . And it is equally true, that no State or nation can affect or bind property out of its territory, or persons not residing within it. . . . [W]hatever force or effect the laws of one State or nation may have in the territories of another, must depend solely upon the laws and municipal regulations of the latter, upon its own jurisprudence and polity, and upon its own express or tacit consent. . . . These principles fully establish, that it belongs to the sovereign State of Missouri to determine by her laws the question of slavery within her jurisdiction, subject only to such limitations as may be found in the Federal Constitution; and, further, that the laws of other States . . . whether enacted by their Legislatures or expounded by their courts, can have no operation within her territory, or affect rights growing out of her own laws on the subject. . . .

In view of these principles, let us examine a little more closely the doctrine of those who maintain that the law of Missouri is not to govern the status and condition of the plaintiff. They insist that the removal and temporary residence with his master in Illinois, where slavery is inhibited, had the effect to set him free, and that the same effect is to be given to the law of Illinois, within the State of Missouri, after his return. Why was he set free in Illinois? Because the law of Missouri, under which he was held as a slave, had no operation by its own force extra-territorially; and the State of Illinois refused to recognize its effect within her limits, upon principles of comity, as a state of slavery was inconsistent with her laws, and contrary to her policy. But, how is the case different on the return of the plaintiff to the State of Missouri? Is she bound to recognize and enforce the law of Illinois? For, unless she is, the status and condition of the slave upon his return remains the same as originally existed. Has the law of Illinois any greater force within the jurisdiction of Missouri, than the laws of the latter within that of the former? Certainly not. They stand upon an equal footing. Neither has any force extra-territorially, except what may be voluntarily conceded to them. . . .

Our conclusion, therefore, is, upon this branch of the case, that the question involved is one depending solely upon the law of Missouri, and that the Federal court sitting in the State, and trying the case before us, was bound to follow it. . . .

MR. JUSTICE McLEAN, DISSENTING.

. . . In the great and leading case of *Prigg v. The State of Pennsylvania,* [41 U.S. (16 Pet.) 539 (1842)], this court say that, by the general law of nations, no nation is bound to recognize the state of slavery, as found within its territorial dominions, where it is in opposition to its own policy and institutions, in favor of the subjects of other nations where slavery is organized. . . .

By virtue of what law is it, that a master may take his slave into free territory, and exact from him the duties of a slave? The law of the Territory does not sanction it. No authority can be claimed under the Constitution of the United States, or any law of Congress. Will it be said that the slave is taken as property, the same as other property which the master may own? To this I answer, that colored persons are made property by the law of the State, and no such power has been given to Congress. Does the master carry with him the law of the State from which he removes into the Territory? . . . It is said the Territories are common property of the States, and that every man has a right to go there with his property. This is not controverted. But the courts say a slave is not property beyond the operation of the local law which makes him such. . . .

I [also] am not able to reconcile this result with the respect due to the State of Illinois. Having the same rights of sovereignty as the State of Missouri in adopting a Constitution, I can perceive no reason why the institutions of Illinois should not receive the same consideration as those of Missouri. . . .

[I]t seems to me the principle laid down will enable the people of a slave State to introduce slavery into a free State, for a longer or shorter time, as may suit their convenience; and by returning the slave to the State whence he was brought, by force or otherwise, the status of slavery attaches, and protects the rights of the master, and defies the sovereignty of the free State. There is no evidence before us that Dred Scott and his family returned to Missouri voluntarily. . . . It would be a mockery of law and an outrage on his rights to coerce his return, and then claim that it was voluntary, and on that ground that his former status of slavery attached. . . .

MR. JUSTICE CURTIS, DISSENTING.

I dissent from the opinion pronounced by the Chief Justice, and from the judgment which the majority of the court think it proper to render in this case. . . .

To determine whether any free persons, descended from Africans held in slavery, were citizens of the United States under the Confederation, and consequently at the time of the adoption of the Constitution of the United States, it is only necessary to know whether any such persons were citizens of either of the States under the Confederation, at the time of the adoption of the Constitution.

Of this there can be no doubt. At the time of the ratification of the Articles of Confederation, all free native-born inhabitants of the States of New Hampshire, Massachusetts, New York, New Jersey, and North Carolina, though descended from African slaves, were not only citizens of those States, but such of them as had the other necessary qualifications possessed the franchise of electors, on equal terms with other citizens. . . .

Did the Constitution of the United States deprive them or their descendants of citizenship? . . . I can find nothing in the Constitution which . . . deprives of their citizenship any class of persons who were citizens of the United States at the time of its adoption, or who should be native-born citizens of any State after its adoption; nor any power enabling Congress to disfranchise persons born on the soil of any State, and entitled to citizenship of such State by its Constitution and laws. And my opinion is, that, under the Constitution of the United States, every free person born on the soil of a State, who is a citizen of that State by force of its Constitution or laws, is also a citizen of the United States. . . .

It has been often asserted that the Constitution was made exclusively by and for the white race. It has already been shown that in five of the thirteen original States, colored persons then possessed the elective franchise, and were among those by whom the Constitution was ordained and established. If so, it is not true, in point of fact, that the Constitution was made exclusively by the white race. And that it was made exclusively for the white race is, in my opinion, not only an assumption not warranted by anything in the Constitution, but contradicted by its opening declaration, that it was ordained and established by the people of the United States, for themselves and their posterity. And as free colored persons were then citizens of at least five States, and so in every sense part of the people of the United States, they were among those for whom and whose posterity the Constitution was ordained and established. . . .

I dissent, therefore, from that part of the opinion of the majority of the court, in which it is held that a person of African descent cannot be a citizen of the United States; and I regret I must go further, and dissent both from what I deem their assumption of authority to examine the constitutionality of the act of Congress commonly called the Missouri compromise act, and the grounds and conclusions announced in their opinion. . . . The judgment of this court is, that the case is to be dismissed for want of jurisdiction, because the plaintiff was not a citizen of Missouri, as he alleged in his declaration. Into that judgment, according to the settled course of this court, nothing appearing after a plea to the merits can enter. A great question of constitutional law, deeply affecting the peace and welfare of the country, is not, in my opinion, a fit subject to be thus reached.

But as, in my opinion, the Circuit Court had jurisdiction, I am obliged to consider the question whether its judgment on the merits of the case should stand or be reversed.

. . . The Constitution declares that Congress shall have power to make "all needful rules and regulations" respecting the territory belonging to the United States. . . . There is nothing in the context which qualifies the grant of power. The regulations must be "respecting the territory." An enactment that slavery may or may not exist there, is a regulation respecting the territory. Regulations must be needful; but it is necessarily left to the legislative discretion to determine whether a law be needful. No other clause of the Constitution has been referred to at the bar, or has been seen by me, which imposes any restriction or makes any exception concerning the power of Congress to allow or prohibit slavery in the territory belonging to the United States. . . .

It appears, however, from what has taken place at the bar, that notwithstanding the language of the Constitution, and the long line of legislative and executive precedents under it, three different and opposite views are taken of the power of Congress respecting slavery in the Territories. One is, that though Congress can make a regulation prohibiting slavery in a Territory, they cannot make a regulation allowing it; another is, that it can neither be established nor prohibited by Congress, but that the people of a Territory, when organized by Congress, can establish or prohibit slavery; while the third is, that the Constitution itself secures to every citizen who holds slaves, under the laws of any State, the indefeasible right to carry them into any Territory, and there hold them as property.

No particular clause of the Constitution has been referred to at the bar in support of either of these views. . . . One or the other may be justly entitled to guide or control the legislative judgment upon what is a needful regulation. The question here is, whether they are sufficient to authorize this court to insert into this clause of the Constitution an exception of the exclusion or allowance of slavery, not found therein, nor in any other part of that instrument. . . . To allow this to be done with the Constitution, upon reasons purely political, renders its judicial interpretation impossible—because judicial tribunals, as such, cannot decide upon political considerations. Political reasons have not the requisite certainty to afford rules of juridical interpretation. They are different in different men. They are different in the same men at different times. And when a strict interpretation of the Constitution, according to the fixed rules which govern the interpretation of laws, is abandoned, and the theoretical opinions of individuals are allowed to control its meaning, we have no longer a Constitution; we are under the government of individual men, who for the time being have power to declare what the Constitution is, according to their own views of what it ought to mean. . . .

Looking at the power of Congress over the Territories as of the extent just described, what positive prohibition exists in the Constitution, which restrained Congress from enacting [the Missouri Compromise]? The only one suggested is that clause in the fifth article of the amendments of the Constitution which declares that no person shall be deprived of his life, liberty, or property, without due process of law. . . . Is it conceivable that the Constitution has conferred the right on every citizen to become a resident on the territory of the United States with his slaves, and there to hold them as such, but has neither made nor provided for any municipal regulations which are essential to the existence of slavery? . . . Nor, in my judgment, will the position, that a prohibition to bring slaves into a Territory deprives any one of his property without due process of law, bear examination. . . .

It was certainly understood by the Convention which framed the Constitution, and has been so understood ever since, that, under the power to regulate commerce, Congress could prohibit the importation of slaves; and the exercise of the power was restrained till 1808. A citizen of the United States owns slaves in Cuba, and brings them to the United States, where they are set free by the legislation of Congress. Does this legislation deprive him of his property without due process of law? If so, what becomes of the laws prohibiting the slave trade? If not, how can a similar regulation respecting a Territory violate the fifth amendment of the Constitution? . . .

For these reasons, I am of opinion that so much of the several acts of Congress as prohibited slavery and involuntary servitude within that part of the Territory of Wisconsin lying north of thirty-six degrees thirty minutes north latitude, and west of the river Mississippi, were constitutional and valid laws. . . .

Speech on the *Dred Scott* Decision
(June 26, 1857, Springfield, Illinois),
ABRAHAM LINCOLN

•

FELLOW CITIZENS: I am here to-night, partly by the invitation of some of you, and partly by my own inclination. Two weeks ago Judge Douglas spoke here on the several subjects of Kansas, the Dred Scott decision, and Utah. I listened to the speech at the time, and have read the report of it since. It was intended to controvert opinions which I think just, and to assail (politically, not personally,) those men who, in common with me, entertain those opinions. For this reason I wished then, and still wish, to make some answer to it, which I now take the opportunity of doing. . . .

And now as to the Dred Scott decision. That decision declares two propositions—first, that a negro cannot sue in the U.S. Courts; and secondly, that Congress cannot prohibit slavery in the Territories. It was made by a divided court-dividing differently on the different points. Judge Douglas does not discuss the merits of the decision; and, in that respect, I shall follow his example, believing I could no more improve on McLean and Curtis, than he could on Taney.

He denounces all who question the correctness of that decision, as offering violent resistance to it. But who resists it? Who has, in spite of the decision, declared Dred Scott free, and resisted the authority of his master over him?

Judicial decisions have two uses—first, to absolutely determine the case decided, and secondly, to indicate to the public how other similar cases will be decided when they arise. For the latter use, they are called "precedents" and "authorities."

We believe, as much as Judge Douglas, (perhaps more) in obedience to, and respect for the judicial department of government. We think its decisions on Constitutional questions, when fully settled, should control, not only the particular cases decided, but the general policy of the country, subject to be disturbed only by amendments of the Constitution as provided in that instrument itself. More than this would be revolution. But we think the Dred Scott decision is erroneous. We know the court that made it, has often over-ruled its own decisions, and we shall do what we can to have it to over-rule this. We offer no resistance to it.

Judicial decisions are of greater or less authority as precedents, according to circumstances. That this should be so, accords both with common sense, and the customary understanding of the legal profession.

If this important decision had been made by the unanimous concurrence of the judges, and without any apparent partisan bias, and in accordance with legal public expectation, and with the steady practice of the departments throughout our history, and had been in no part, based on assumed historical facts which are not really true; or, if wanting in some of these, it had been before the court more than once, and had there been affirmed and re-affirmed through a course of years, it then might be, perhaps would be, factious, nay, even revolutionary, to not acquiesce in it as a precedent.

But when, as it is true we find it wanting in all these claims to the public confidence, it is not resistance, it is not factious, it is not even disrespectful, to treat it as not having yet quite established a settled doctrine for the country—But Judge Douglas considers this view awful. Hear him:

"The courts are the tribunals prescribed by the Constitution and created by the authority of the people to determine, expound and enforce the law. Hence, whoever resists the final decision of the highest judicial tribunal, aims a deadly blow to our whole Republican system of government—a blow, which if successful would place all our rights and liberties at the mercy of passion, anarchy and violence. I repeat, therefore, that if resistance to the decisions of the Supreme Court of the United States, in a matter like the points decided in the Dred Scott case, clearly within their jurisdiction as defined by the Constitution, shall be forced upon the country as a political issue, it will become a distinct and naked issue between the friends and the enemies of the Constitution—the friends and the enemies of the supremacy of the laws."

Why this same Supreme court once decided a national bank to be constitutional; but Gen. Jackson, as President of the United States, disregarded the decision, and vetoed a bill for a re-charter, partly on constitutional ground, declaring that each public functionary must support the Constitution, "as he understands it."

Again and again have I heard Judge Douglas denounce that bank decision, and applaud Gen. Jackson for disregarding it. It would be interesting for him to look over his recent speech, and see how exactly his fierce philippics against us for resisting Supreme Court decisions, fall upon his own head. . . .

I have said, in substance, that the Dred Scott decision was, in part, based on assumed historical facts which were not really true; and I ought not to leave the subject without giving some reasons for saying this; I therefore give an instance or two, which I think fully sustain me. Chief Justice Taney, in delivering the opinion of the majority of the Court, insists at great length that negroes were no part of the people who made, or for whom was made, the Declaration of Independence, or the Constitution of the United States.

On the contrary, Judge Curtis, in his dissenting opinion, shows that in five of the then thirteen states, to wit, New Hampshire, Massachusetts, New York, New Jersey and North Carolina, free negroes were voters, and, in proportion to their numbers, had the same part in making the Constitution that the white people had. He shows this with so much particularity as to leave no doubt of its truth. . . .

There is a natural disgust in the minds of nearly all white people, to the idea of an indiscriminate amalgamation of the white and black races; and Judge Douglas evidently is basing his chief hope, upon the chances of being able to appropriate the benefit of this disgust to himself. . . . He finds the Republicans insisting that the Declaration of Independence includes ALL men, black as well as white; and forth-with he boldly denies that it includes negroes at all, and proceeds to argue gravely that all who contend it does, do so only because they want to vote, and eat, and sleep, and marry with negroes! He will have it that they cannot be consistent else. Now I protest against that counterfeit logic which concludes that, because I do not want a black woman for a slave I must necessarily want her for a wife. I need not have her for either, I can just leave her alone. In some respects she certainly is not my equal; but in her natural right to eat the bread she earns with her own hands without asking leave of any one else, she is my equal, and the equal of all others.

Chief Justice Taney, in his opinion in the Dred Scott case, admits that the language of the Declaration is broad enough to include the whole human family, but he and Judge Douglas argue that the authors of that instrument did not intend to include negroes, by the fact that they did not at once, actually place them on an equality with the whites. Now this grave argument comes to just nothing at all, by the other fact, that they did not at once, or ever afterwards, actually place all white people on an equality with one or another. And this is the staple argument of both the Chief Justice and the Senator, for doing this obvious violence to the plain unmistakable language of the Declaration. I think the authors of that notable instrument intended to include all men, but they did not intend to declare all men equal in all respects. They did not mean to say all were equal in color, size, intellect, moral developments, or social capacity. They defined with tolerable distinctness, in what respects they did consider all men created equal—equal in "certain inalienable rights, among which are life, liberty, and the pursuit of happiness." This they said, and this meant. They did not mean to assert the obvious untruth, that all were then actually enjoying that equality, nor yet, that they were about to confer it immediately upon them. In fact they had no power to confer such a boon. They meant simply to declare the right, so that the enforcement of it might follow as fast as circumstances should permit. They meant to set up a standard maxim for free society, which should be familiar to all, and revered by all; constantly looked to, constantly labored for, and even though never perfectly attained, constantly approximated, and thereby constantly spreading and deepening its influence, and augmenting the happiness and value of life to all people of all colors everywhere. The assertion that "all men are created equal" was of no practical use in effecting our separation from Great Britain; and it was placed in the Declaration, nor for that, but for future use. Its authors meant it to be, thank God, it is now proving itself, a stumbling block to those who in after times might seek to turn a free people back into the hateful paths of despotism. They knew the proneness of prosperity to breed tyrants, and they meant when such should re-appear in this fair land and commence their vocation they should find left for them at least one hard nut to crack.

JUDAH BENJAMIN'S SPEECH
IN CONGRESS
(DECEMBER 31, 1860)
JUDAH BENJAMIN

incoln's election to the presidency in 1860 led several Southern states to pass ordinances of secession declaring that they had left the union—months before Lincoln even took office. Louisiana Senator Judah Benjamin, who later served in three different cabinet posts in the Confederacy, was one prominent voice for the position that secession was constitutionally permitted as a remedy for alleged violation of Southern rights.

✪

In a great crisis like this, when the right asserted by a sovereign State is questioned, a decent respect for the opinions of mankind at least requires that those who maintain that right, and mean to act upon it, should state the reasons upon which they maintain it. . . .

From the time that this people declared its independence of Great Britain, the right of the people to self-government in its fullest and broadest extent has been a cardinal principal of American liberty. None deny it. And in that right, to use the language of the Declaration itself, is included the right whenever a form of government becomes destructive of their interests or their safety, "to alter or to abolish it, and to institute a new government, laying its foundation on such principles and organizing its powers in such form as to them shall seem most likely to effect that safety and happiness."

. . . . [T]he right of the people of one generation, in convention duly assembled, to alter the institutions bequeathed by their fathers, is inherent, inalienable, not susceptible of restriction . . . .. [I]t was precisely upon this principle that this Constitution was formed. . . . [T]he old Articles of Confederacy provided in express terms that they should be perpetual; that they should never be amended or altered without the consent of all the States. . . . [N]ine States of the Confederation seceded from the Confederation, and formed a new Government. They formed it upon the express ground that some of the States had violated their compact. . . .

[O]ne State may allege that the compact has been broken, and others may deny it; who is to judge? . . . [L]et us suppose a clear, palpable case of violation of the Constitution. Let us suppose that the State of South Carolina having sent two Senators to sit upon this floor, had been met by a resolution of the majority here that, according to her just weight in the Confederacy, one was enough, and that we had directed our Secretary to swear in but one, and to call but one name on our roll as the yeas and nays are called for voting. The Constitution says that each State shall be entitled to two Senators, and each Senator shall have one vote . . . [I]f, under these circumstances, the State of South Carolina had declared, "I entered into a Confederacy or a compact by which I was to have my rights guarantied by the constant presence of two Senators upon your floor; you allow me but one; you refuse to repair the injustice; I withdraw"; what man would dare say that that was a violation of the Constitution on the part of South Carolina? Who would say that that was a revolutionary remedy? Who would deny the plain and palpable proposition that it was the exercise of a right inherent in her under the very principles of the Constitution, and necessarily so inherent for self-defense?

Suppose this violation occurs under circumstances where it does not appear so plain to you, but where it does appear equally plain to South Carolina: then you are again brought back to the irrevocable point, who is to decide? South Carolina says "You forced me to the expenditure of my treasure, you forced me to the shedding of the blood of my people, by a majority vote, and with my aid you acquired territory; now I have a constitutional right to go into that territory with my property, and to be there secured by your laws against its loss." . . . [T]hat right is not put down in the Constitution in quite so clear terms as the right to have two Senators; but it is a right which she asserts with the concurrent opinion of the entire South. It is a right that she asserts . . . in accordance with the opinion expressed by the Supreme Court of the United States. . . . Is she without a remedy under the Constitution? . . .

These States, parties to the compact, have a right to withdraw from it, by virtue of its own provisions, when those provisions are violated by the other parties to the compact, when either powers not granted are usurped, or rights are refused that are especially granted to the States. . . .

LINCOLN'S FIRST INAUGURAL ADDRESS (March 4, 1861)

Abraham Lincoln

*P*resident Abraham Lincoln's First Inaugural Address is a systematic work of constitutional interpretation addressing the core issues dividing North and South: the legal status of slavery under the Constitution; the permanence of the Union and the resulting unconstitutionality of secession; the absence of just constitutional cause for secession or revolution; the non-authoritativeness of the Supreme Court's decision in *Dred Scott* as a political rule for the nation; and the president's duty to execute the laws and the Constitution faithfully throughout the nation. The address was delivered just over a month before South Carolina's assault on Fort Sumter, which started the Civil War. The First Inaugural Address represents the constitutional theory and justification for nearly every action Lincoln took in defending the Union and waging the war.

✪

Fellow citizens of the United States:

In compliance with a custom as old as the Government itself, I appear before you to address you briefly and to take in your presence the oath prescribed by the Constitution of the United States to be taken by the President "before he enters on the execution of this office."

I do not consider it necessary at present for me to discuss those matters of administration about which there is no special anxiety or excitement.

Apprehension seems to exist among the people of the Southern States that by the accession of a Republican Administration their property and their peace and personal security are to be endangered. There has never been any reasonable cause for such apprehension. Indeed, the most ample evidence to the contrary has all the while existed and been open to their inspection. It is found in nearly all the published speeches of him who now addresses you. I do but quote from one of those speeches when I declare that "I have no purpose, directly or indirectly, to inter-fere with the institution of slavery in the States where it exists. I believe I have no lawful right to do so, and I have no inclination to do so." Those who nominated and elected me did so with full knowledge that I had made this and many similar declarations and had never recanted them; and more than this, they placed in the platform for my accept-ance, and as a law to themselves and to me, the clear and emphatic resolution which I now read:

"*Resolved*, That the maintenance inviolate of the rights of the States, and especially the right of each State to order and control its own do-mestic institutions according to its own judgment exclusively, is essen-tial to that balance of power on which the perfection and endurance of our political fabric depend; and we denounce the lawless invasion by armed force of the soil of any State or Territory, no matter what pretext, as among the gravest of crimes."

I now reiterate these sentiments, and in doing so I only press upon the public attention the most conclusive evidence of which the case is susceptible that the property, peace, and security of no section are to be in any wise endangered by the now incoming Administration. I add, too, that all the protection which, consistently with the Constitution and the laws, can be given will be cheerfully given to all the States when lawfully demanded, for whatever cause—as cheerfully to one sec-tion as to another.

There is much controversy about the delivering up of fugitives from service or labor. The clause I now read is as plainly written in the Constitution as any other of its provisions:

"No person held to service or labor in one State, under the laws thereof, escaping into another, shall in consequence of any law or regulation therein be discharged from such service or labor, but shall be delivered up on claim of the party to whom such service or labor may be due."

It is scarcely questioned that this provision was intended by those who made it for the reclaiming of what we call fugitive slaves; and the intention of the lawgiver is the law. All members of Congress swear their support to the whole Constitution—to this provision as much as to any other. To the proposition, then, that slaves whose cases come within the terms of this clause "shall be delivered up" their oaths are unanimous. Now, if they would make the effort in good temper, could they not with nearly equal unanimity frame and pass a law by means of which to keep good that unanimous oath?

There is some difference of opinion whether this clause should be enforced by national or by State authority, but surely that difference is not a very material one. If the slave is to be surrendered, it can be of but little consequence to him or to others by which authority it is done. And should anyone in any case be content that his oath shall go unkept on a merely unsubstantial controversy as to *how* it shall be kept?

Again, in any law upon this subject ought not all the safeguards of liberty known in civilized and humane jurisprudence to be introduced, so that a free man be not in any case surrendered as a slave? And might it not be well at the same time to provide by law for the enforcement of that clause in the Constitution which guarantees that "the citizens of each State shall be entitled to all privileges and immunities of citizens in the several States"?

I take the official oath to-day with no mental reservations and with no purpose to construe the Constitution or laws by any hypercritical rules; and while I do not choose now to specify particular acts of Congress as proper to be enforced, I do suggest that it will be much safer for all, both in official and private stations, to conform to and abide by all those acts which stand unrepealed than to violate any of them trusting to find impunity in having them held to be unconstitutional.

It is seventy-two years since the first inauguration of a President under our National Constitution. During that period fifteen different and greatly distinguished citizens have in succession administered the executive branch of the Government. They have conducted it through many perils, and generally with great success. Yet, with all this scope of precedent, I now enter upon the same task for the brief constitutional term of four years under great and peculiar difficulty. A disruption of the Federal Union, heretofore only menaced, is now formidably attempted.

I hold that in contemplation of universal law and of the Constitution the Union of these States is perpetual. Perpetuity is implied, if not expressed, in the fundamental law of all national governments. It is safe to assert that no government proper ever had a provision in its organic law for its own termination. Continue to execute all the express provisions of our National Constitution, and the Union will endure forever, it being impossible to destroy it except by some action not provided for in the instrument itself.

Again, if the United States be not a government proper, but an association of States in the nature of contract merely, can it, as a contract, be peaceably unmade by less than all the parties who made it? One party to a contract may violate it—break it, so to speak—but does it not require all to lawfully rescind it?

Descending from these general principles, we find the proposition that in legal contemplation the Union is perpetual confirmed by the history of the Union itself. The Union is much older than the Constitution. It was formed, in fact, by the Articles of Association in 1774. It was matured and continued by the Declaration of Independence in 1776. It was further matured, and the faith of all the then thirteen States expressly plighted and engaged that it should be perpetual, by the Articles of Confederation in 1778. And finally, in 1787, one of the declared objects for ordaining and establishing the Constitution was *"to form a more perfect Union."*

But if destruction of the Union by one or by a part only of the States be lawfully possible, the Union is *less* perfect than before the Constitution, having lost the vital element of perpetuity.

It follows from these views that no State upon its own mere motion can lawfully get out of the Union; that *resolves* and *ordinances* to that effect are legally void, and that acts of violence within any State or States against the authority of the United States are insurrectionary or revolutionary, according to circumstances.

I therefore consider that in view of the Constitution and the laws the Union is unbroken, and to the extent of my ability, I shall take care, as the Constitution itself expressly enjoins upon me, that the laws of the Union be faithfully executed in all the States. Doing this I deem to be only a simple duty on my part, and I shall perform it so far as practicable unless my rightful masters, the American people, shall withhold the requisite means or in some authoritative manner direct the contrary. I trust this will not be regarded as a menace, but only as the declared purpose of the Union that it *will* constitutionally defend and maintain itself.

In doing this there needs to be no bloodshed or violence, and there shall be none unless it be forced upon the national authority. The power confided to me will be used to hold, occupy, and possess the property and places belonging to the Government and to collect the duties and imposts; but beyond what may be necessary for these objects, there will be no invasion, no using of force against or among the people anywhere. Where hostility to the United States in any interior locality shall be so great and universal as to prevent competent resident citizens from holding the Federal offices, there will be no attempt to force obnoxious strangers among the people for that object. While the strict legal right may exist in the Government to enforce the exercise of these offices, the attempt to do so would be so irritating and so nearly impracticable withal that I deem it better to forego for the time the uses of such offices.

The mails, unless repelled, will continue to be furnished in all parts of the Union. So far as possible the people everywhere shall have that sense of perfect security which is most favorable to calm thought and reflection. The course here indicated will be followed unless current events and experience shall show a modification or change to be proper, and in every case and exigency my best discretion will be exercised, according to circumstances actually existing and with a view and a hope of a peaceful solution of the national troubles and the restoration of fraternal sympathies and affections.

That there are persons in one section or another who seek to destroy the Union at all events and are glad of any pretext to do it I will neither affirm nor deny; but if there be such, I need address no word to them. To those, however, who really love the Union may I not speak?

Before entering upon so grave a matter as the destruction of our national fabric, with all its benefits, its memories, and its hopes, would it not be wise to ascertain precisely why we do it? Will you hazard so desperate a step while there is any possibility that any portion of the ills you fly from have no real existence? Will you, while the certain ills you fly to are greater than all the real ones you fly from, will you risk the commission of so fearful a mistake?

All profess to be content in the Union if all constitutional rights can be maintained. Is it true, then, that any right plainly written in the Constitution has been denied? I think not. Happily, the human mind is so constituted that no party can reach to the audacity of doing this. Think, if you can, of a single instance in which a plainly written provision of the Constitution has ever been denied. If by the mere force of numbers a majority should deprive a minority of any clearly written constitutional right, it might in a moral point of view justify revolution; certainly would if such right were a vital one. But such is not our case. All the vital rights of minorities and of individuals are so plainly assured to them by affirmations and negations, guaranties and prohibitions, in the Constitution that controversies never arise concerning them. But no organic law can ever be framed with a provision specifically applicable to every question which may occur in practical administration. No foresight can anticipate nor any document of reasonable length contain express provisions for all possible questions. Shall fugitives from labor be surrendered by national or by State authority? The Constitution does not expressly say. *May* Congress prohibit slavery in the Territories? The Constitution does not expressly say. *Must* Congress protect slavery in the Territories? The Constitution does not expressly say.

From questions of this class spring all our constitutional controversies, and we divide upon them into majorities and minorities. If the minority will not acquiesce, the majority must, or the Government must cease. There is no other alternative, for continuing the Government is acquiescence on one side or the other. If a minority in such case will secede rather than acquiesce, they make a precedent which in turn will divide and ruin them, for a minority of their own will secede from them whenever a majority refuses to be controlled by such minority. For instance, why may not any portion of a new confederacy a year or two hence arbitrarily secede again, precisely as portions of the present Union now claim to secede from it? All who cherish disunion sentiments are now being educated to the exact temper of doing this. Is there such perfect identity of interests among the States to compose a new union as to produce harmony only and prevent renewed secession?

Plainly the central idea of secession is the essence of anarchy. A majority held in restraint by constitutional checks and limitations, and always changing easily with deliberate changes of popular opinions and sentiments, is the only true sovereign of a free people. Whoever rejects it does of necessity fly to anarchy or to despotism. Unanimity is impossible. The rule of a minority, as a permanent arrangement, is wholly inadmissible; so that, rejecting the majority principle, anarchy or despotism in some form is all that is left.

I do not forget the position assumed by some that constitutional questions are to be decided by the Supreme Court, nor do I deny that such decisions must be binding in any case upon the parties to a suit as to the object of that suit, while they are also entitled to very high respect and consideration in all parallel cases by all other departments of the Government. And while it is obviously possible that such decision may be erroneous in any given case, still the evil effect following it, being limited to that particular case, with the chance that it may be overruled and never become a precedent for other cases, can better be borne than could the evils of a different practice. At the same time, the candid citizen must confess that if the policy of the Government upon vital questions affecting the whole people is to be irrevocably fixed by decisions of the Supreme Court, the instant they are made in ordinary litigation between parties in personal actions the people will have ceased to be their own rulers, having to that extent practically resigned their Government into the hands of that eminent tribunal. Nor is there in this view any assault upon the court or the judges. It is a duty from which they may not shrink to decide cases properly brought before them, and it is no fault of theirs if others seek to turn their decisions to political purposes.

One section of our country believes slavery is *right* and ought to be extended, while the other believes it is *wrong* and ought not to be extended. This is the only substantial dispute. The fugitive-slave clause of the Constitution and the law for the suppression of the foreign slave trade are each as well enforced, perhaps, as any law can ever be in a community where the moral sense of the people imperfectly supports the law itself. The great body of the people abide by the dry legal obligation in both cases, and a few break over in each. This, I think, can not be perfectly cured, and it would be worse in both cases *after* the separation of the sections than before. The foreign slave trade, now imperfectly suppressed, would be ultimately revived without restriction in one section, while fugitive slaves, now only partially surrendered, would not be surrendered at all by the other.

Physically speaking, we can not separate. We can not remove our respective sections from each other nor build an impassable wall between them. A husband and wife may be divorced and go out of the presence and beyond the reach of each other, but the different parts of our country can not do this. They can not but remain face to face, and intercourse, either amicable or hostile, must continue between them. Is it possible, then, to make that intercourse more advantageous or more satisfactory *after* separation than *before?* Can aliens make treaties easier than friends can make laws? Can treaties be more faithfully enforced between aliens than laws can among friends? Suppose you go to war, you can not fight always; and when, after much loss on both sides and no gain on either, you cease fighting, the identical old questions, as to terms of intercourse, are again upon you.

This country, with its institutions, belongs to the people who inhabit it. Whenever they shall grow weary of the existing Government, they can exercise their *constitutional* right of amending it or their *revolutionary* right to dismember or overthrow it. I can not be ignorant of the fact that many worthy and patriotic citizens are desirous of having the National Constitution amended. While I make no recommendation of amendments, I fully recognize the rightful authority of the people over the whole subject, to be exercised in either of the modes prescribed in the instrument itself; and I should, under existing circumstances, favor rather than oppose a fair opportunity being afforded the people to act upon it. I will venture to add that to me the convention mode seems preferable, in that it allows amendments to originate with the people themselves, instead of only permitting them to take or reject propositions originated by others, not especially chosen for the purpose, and which might not be precisely such as they would wish to either accept or refuse. I understand a proposed amendment to the Constitution— which amendment, however, I have not seen—has passed Congress, to the effect that the Federal Government shall never interfere with the domestic institutions of the States, including that of persons held to service. To avoid misconstruction of what I have said, I depart from my purpose not to speak of particular amendments so far as to say that, holding such a provision to now be implied constitutional law, I have no objection to its being made express and irrevocable.

The Chief Magistrate derives all his authority from the people, and they have referred none upon him to fix terms for the separation of the States. The people themselves can do this if also they choose, but the Executive as such has nothing to do with it. His duty is to administer the present Government as it came to his hands and to transmit it unimpaired by him to his successor.

Why should there not be a patient confidence in the ultimate justice of the people? Is there any better or equal hope in the world? In our present differences, is either party without faith of being in the right? If the Almighty Ruler of Nations, with His eternal truth and justice, be on your side of the North, or on yours of the South, that truth and that justice will surely prevail by the judgment of this great tribunal of the American people.

By the frame of the Government under which we live this same people have wisely given their public servants but little power for mischief, and have with equal wisdom provided for the return of that little to their own hands at very short intervals. While the people retain their virtue and vigilance no Administration by any extreme of wickedness or folly can very seriously injure the Government in the short space of four years.

My countrymen, one and all, think calmly and *well* upon this whole subject. Nothing valuable can be lost by taking time. If there be an object to *hurry* any of you in hot haste to a step which you would never take *deliberately*, that object will be frustrated by taking time; but no good object can be frustrated by it. Such of you as are now dissatisfied still have the old Constitution unimpaired, and, on the sensitive point, the laws of your own framing under it; while the new Administration will have no immediate power, if it would, to change either. If it were admitted that you who are dissatisfied hold the right side in the dispute, there still is no single good reason for precipitate action. Intelligence, patriotism, Christianity, and a firm reliance on Him who has never yet forsaken this favored land are still competent to adjust in the best way all our present difficulty.

In *your* hands, my dissatisfied fellow-countrymen, and not in *mine*, is the momentous issue of civil war. The Government will not assail *you*.

You can have no conflict without being yourselves the aggressors. *You* have no oath registered in heaven to destroy the Government, while I shall have the most solemn one to "preserve, protect, and defend it."

I am loath to close. We are not enemies, but friends. We must not be enemies. Though passion may have strained it must not break our bonds of affection. The mystic chords of memory, stretching from every battlefield and patriot grave to every living heart and hearthstone all over this broad land, will yet swell the chorus of the Union, when again touched, as surely they will be, by the better angels of our nature.

LINCOLN as COMMANDER in CHIEF
EXECUTIVE MILITARY ORDERS

∼

*L*incoln's military orders during the Civil War constitute important and controversial precedents for interpreting the scope of the president's constitutional power as commander in chief. At the outbreak of war in 1861, Lincoln, on his own authority, called up the militia, called for further troops, ordered a blockade of Southern ports, and suspended the writ of habeas corpus. In 1862, Lincoln issued a second order suspending habeas corpus and, further, authorized the military punishment of persons aiding the rebellion in any way—including by discouraging enlistments or the draft. In 1863, with Congress's authorization, Lincoln suspended habeas corpus throughout the United States with respect to any persons held by Union forces.

The most famous and important of Lincoln's wartime orders was the Emancipation Proclamation. On September 22, 1862, Lincoln issued the Preliminary Emancipation Proclamation, giving states in rebellion one hundred days to return to the Union or have their slaves deemed "forever free." The Final Emancipation Proclamation, of January 1, 1863, fulfilled this pledge, declaring all slaves in Confederate-controlled areas free. Lincoln further announced that the Union would receive liberated slaves into its armed forces.

The use of black troops infuriated the South, which established the policy that black Union soldiers would be enslaved or killed. Several massacres of black troops occurred. On July 30, 1863, Lincoln issued an "Order of Retaliation," authorizing the execution of captured Confederate prisoners in retribution, but no such executions ever took place.

✪

Letter to Winfield Scott (April 27, 1861)
ABRAHAM LINCOLN

•

To the Commanding General of the Army of the United States:

You are engaged in repressing an insurrection against the laws of the United States. If at any point on or in the vicinity of the military line, which is now used between the City of Philadelphia and the City of Washington, via Perryville, Annapolis City, and Annapolis Junction, you find resistance which renders it necessary to suspend the writ of Habeas Corpus for the public safety, you, personally or through the officer in command at the point where the resistance occurs, are authorized to suspend that writ. . . .

Proclamation Suspending the Writ of Habeas Corpus (September 24, 1862),
ABRAHAM LINCOLN

•

. . . Whereas, it has become necessary to call into service not only volunteers but also portions of the militia of the States by draft in order to suppress the insurrection existing in the United States, and disloyal persons are not adequately restrained by the ordinary processes of law from hindering this measure and from giving aid and comfort in various ways to the insurrection;

Now, therefore, be it ordered, first, that during the existing insurrection and as a necessary measure for suppressing the same, all Rebels and Insurgents, their aiders and abettors within the United States, and all persons discouraging volunteer enlistments, resisting militia drafts, or guilty of any disloyal practice, affording aid and comfort to Rebels against the authority of United States, shall be subject to martial law and liable to trial and punishment by courts-martial or military commission:

Second. That the Writ of Habeas Corpus is suspended in respect to all persons arrested, or who are now, or hereafter during the rebellion shall be, imprisoned in any fort, camp, arsenal, military prison, or other place of confinement by any military authority of by the sentence of any Court Martial or Military Commission. . . .

Proclamation Suspending the Writ of Habeas Corpus Throughout the United States (September 15, 1863)
ABRAHAM LINCOLN

•

Whereas the Constitution of the United States has ordained that the privilege of the writ of *habeas corpus* shall not be suspended unless when, in cases of rebellion or invasion, the public safety may require it; and

Whereas a rebellion was existing on the 3d day of March, 1863, which rebellion is still existing; and

Whereas by a statute which was approved on that day it was enacted by the Senate and House of Representatives of the United States in Congress assembled that during the present insurrection the President of the United States, whenever in his judgment the public safety may require, is authorized to suspend the privilege of the writ of *habeas corpus* in any case throughout the United States or any part thereof; and

Whereas, in the judgment of the President, the public safety does require that the privilege of the said writ shall now be suspended throughout the United States in the cases where, by the authority of the President of the United States, military, naval, and civil officers of the United States, or any of them, hold persons under their command or in their custody . . . as prisoners of war, spies, or alders or abettors of the enemy . . . or for any other offense against the military or naval service:

Now, therefore, I, Abraham Lincoln, President of the United States, do hereby proclaim and make known to all whom it may concern that the privilege of the writ of *habeas corpus* is suspended throughout the United States in the several cases before mentioned, and that this suspension will continue throughout the duration of the said rebellion or until this proclamation shall, by a subsequent one to be issued by the President of the United States, be modified or revoked. . . .

Emancipation Proclamation (January 1, 1863)
ABRAHAM LINCOLN

•

Whereas, on the twenty-second day of September, in the year of our Lord one thousand eight hundred and sixty-two, a proclamation was issued by the President of the United States, containing, among other things, the following, to wit:

"That on the first day of January, in the year of our Lord one thousand eight hundred and sixty-three, all persons held as slaves within any State or designated part of a State, the people whereof shall then be in rebellion against the United States, shall be then, thenceforward, and forever free; and the Executive Government of the United States, including the military and naval authority thereof, will recognize and maintain the freedom of such persons, and will do no act or acts to repress such persons, or any of them, in any efforts they may make for their actual freedom." . . .

Now, therefore I, Abraham Lincoln, President of the United States, by virtue of the power in me vested as Commander-in-Chief, of the Army and Navy of the United States in time of actual armed rebellion against the authority and government of the United States, and as a fit and necessary war measure for suppressing said rebellion, do, on this first day of January, in the year of our Lord one thousand eight hundred and sixty-three, and in accordance with my purpose so to do publicly proclaimed for the full period of one hundred days, from the day first above mentioned, order and designate as the States and parts of States wherein the people thereof respectively, are this day in rebellion against the United States, the following . . .

And by virtue of the power, and for the purpose aforesaid, I do order and declare that all persons held as slaves within said designated States, and parts of States, are, and henceforward shall be free; and that the Executive government of the United States, including the military and naval authorities thereof, will recognize and maintain the freedom of said persons.

And I hereby enjoin upon the people so declared to be free to abstain from all violence, unless in necessary self-defence; and I recommend to them that, in all cases when allowed, they labor faithfully for reasonable wages.

And I further declare and make known, that such persons of suitable condition, will be received into the armed service of the United States to garrison forts, positions, stations, and other places, and to man vessels of all sorts in said service.

And upon this act, sincerely believed to be an act of justice, warranted by the Constitution, upon military necessity, I invoke the considerate judgment of mankind, and the gracious favor of Almighty God. . . .

Order of Retaliation (July 30, 1863)
ABRAHAM LINCOLN

•

It is the duty of every government to give protection to its citizens, of whatever class, color, or condition, and especially to those who are duly organized as soldiers in the public service. The law of nations and the usages and customs of war as carried on by civilized powers, permit no distinction as to color in the treatment of prisoners of war as public enemies. To sell or enslave any captured person, on account of his color, and for no offence against the laws of war, is a relapse into barbarism and a crime against the civilization of the age.

The government of the United States will give the same protection to all its soldiers, and if the enemy shall sell or enslave anyone because of his color, the offense shall be punished by retaliation upon the enemy's prisoners in our possession.

It is therefore ordered that for every soldier of the United States killed in violation of the laws of war, a rebel soldier shall be executed; and for every one enslaved by the enemy or sold into slavery, a rebel soldier shall be placed at hard labor on the public works and continued at such labor until the other shall be released and receive the treatment due to a prisoner of war.

TANEY AND LINCOLN
ON THE SUSPENSION
of HABEAS CORPUS

و

*L*incoln's military orders did not go unchallenged. In the case of *Ex parte Merryman* (1861), Chief Justice Taney, acting as a single judge and not on behalf of the whole Supreme Court, declared Lincoln's April 1861 order suspending the writ of habeas corpus to be unconstitutional. Lincoln refused to comply with Taney's opinion and defended his actions as part of a special message to Congress.

✪

Ex parte Merryman
17 F. Cas. 144 (D. Md., April term 1861).

•

CIRCUIT JUSTICE TANEY.

The application in this case for a writ of habeas corpus is made to me under the 14th section of the judiciary act of 1789, which renders effectual for the citizen the constitutional privilege of the writ of habeas corpus. That act gives to the courts of the United States, as well as to each justice of the supreme court, and to every district judge, power to grant writs of habeas corpus for the purpose of an inquiry into the cause of commitment. . . . The petition presents the following case: The petitioner resides in Maryland, in Baltimore county; while peaceably in his own house, with his family, it was at two o'clock on the morning of the 25th of May 1861, entered by an armed force, professing to act under military orders; he was then compelled to rise from his bed, taken into custody, and conveyed to Fort McHenry, where he is imprisoned by the commanding officer, without warrant from any lawful authority. . . .

A copy of the warrant or order under which the prisoner was arrested was demanded by his counsel, and refused: and it is not alleged in the return, that any specific act, constituting any offence against the laws of the United States, has been charged against him upon oath, but he appears to have been arrested upon general charges of treason and rebellion, without proof, and without giving the names of the witnesses, or specifying the acts which, in the judgment of the military officer, constituted these crimes. Having the prisoner thus in custody upon these vague and unsupported accusations, he refuses to obey the writ of habeas corpus, upon the ground that he is duly authorized by the president to suspend it. . . .

As the case comes before me, therefore, I understand that the president not only claims the right to suspend the writ of habeas corpus himself, at his discretion, but to delegate that discretionary power to a military officer, and to leave it to him to determine whether he will or will not obey judicial process that may be served upon him. No official notice has been given to the courts of justice, or to the public, by proclamation or otherwise, that the president claimed this power, and had exercised it in the manner stated in the return. And I certainly listened to it with some surprise, for I had supposed it to be one of those points of constitutional law upon which there was no difference of opinion, and that it was admitted on all hands, that the privilege of the writ could not be suspended, except by act of congress. . . .

The clause of the constitution, which authorizes the suspension of the privilege of the writ of habeas corpus, is in the 9th section of the first article. This article is devoted to the legislative department of the United States, and has not the slightest reference to the executive department.

It begins by providing "that all legislative powers therein granted, shall be vested in a congress of the United States, which shall consist of a senate and house of representatives." And after prescribing the manner in which these two branches of the legislative department shall be chosen, it proceeds to enumerate specifically the legislative powers which it thereby grants . . .; and at the conclusion of this specification, a clause is inserted giving congress "the power to make all laws which shall be necessary and proper for carrying into execution the foregoing powers, and all other powers vested by this constitution in the government of the United States, or in any department or officer thereof."

The power of legislation granted by this latter clause is, by its words, carefully confined to the specific objects before enumerated. But as this limitation was unavoidably somewhat indefinite, it was deemed necessary to guard more effectually certain great cardinal principles, essential to the liberty of the citizen, and to the rights and equality of the states, by denying to congress, in express terms, any power of legislation over them. It was apprehended, it seems, that such legislation might be attempted, under the pretext that it was necessary and proper to carry into execution the powers granted; and it was determined, that there should be no room to doubt, where rights of such vital importance were concerned; and accordingly, this clause is immediately followed by an enumeration of certain subjects, to which the powers of legislation shall not extend. The great importance which the framers of the constitution attached to the privilege of the writ of habeas corpus, to protect the liberty of the citizen, is proved by the fact, that its suspension, except in cases of invasion or rebellion, is first in the list of prohibited powers; and even in these cases the power is denied, and its exercise prohibited, unless the public safety shall require it.

It is true, that in the cases mentioned, congress is, of necessity, the judge of whether the public safety does or does not require it; and their judgment is conclusive. But the introduction of these words is a standing admonition to the legislative body of the danger of suspending it, and of the extreme caution they should exercise, before they give the government of the United States such power over the liberty of a citizen.

It is the second article of the constitution that provides for the organization of the executive department, enumerates the powers conferred on it, and prescribes its duties. And if the high power over the liberty of the citizen now claimed, was intended to be conferred on the president, it would undoubtedly be found in plain words in this article; but there is not a word in it that can furnish the slightest ground to justify the exercise of the power. . . . [H]e is, from necessity, and the nature of his duties, the commander-in-chief of the army and navy, and of the militia, when called into actual service; but no appropriation for the support of the army can be made by congress for a longer term than two years, so that it is in the power of the succeeding house of representatives to withhold the appropriation for its support, and thus disband it, if, in their judgment, the president used, or designed to use it for improper purposes. And although the militia, when in actual service, is under his command, yet the appointment of the officers is reserved to the states, as a security against the use of the military power for purposes dangerous to the liberties of the people, or the rights of the states.

So too, his powers in relation to the civil duties and authority necessarily conferred on him are carefully restricted, as well as those belonging to his military character. . . . He is not empowered to arrest any one charged with an offence against the United States, and whom he may, from the evidence before him, believe to be guilty; nor can he authorize any officer, civil or military, to exercise this power, for the fifth article of the amendments to the constitution expressly provides that no person "shall be deprived of life, liberty or property, without due process of law"—that is, judicial process.

Even if the privilege of the writ of habeas corpus were suspended by act of congress, and a party not subject to the rules and articles of war were afterwards arrested and imprisoned by regular judicial process, he could not be detained in prison, or brought to trial before a military tribunal, for the article in the amendments to the constitution immediately following the one above referred to (that is, the sixth article) provides, that "in all criminal prosecutions, the accused shall enjoy the right to a speedy and public trial by an impartial jury of the state and district wherein the crime shall have been committed, which district shall have been previously ascertained by law; and to be informed of the nature and cause of the accusation; to be confronted with the witnesses against him; to have compulsory process for obtaining witnesses in his favor; and to have the assistance of counsel for his defence."

The only power, therefore, which the president possesses, where the "life, liberty or property" of a private citizen is concerned, is the power and duty prescribed in the third section of the second article, which requires "that he shall take care that the laws shall be faithfully exe-cuted." He is not authorized to execute them himself, or through agents or officers, civil or military, appointed by himself, but he is to take care that they be faithfully carried into execution, as they are expounded and adjudged by the co-ordinate branch of the government to which that duty is assigned by the constitution. It is thus made his duty to come in aid of the judicial authority, if it shall be resisted by a force too strong to be overcome without the assistance of the executive arm; but in exer-cising this power he acts in subordination to judicial authority, assisting it to execute its process and enforce its judgments.

With such provisions in the constitution, expressed in language too clear to be misunderstood by any one, I can see no ground whatever for supposing that the president, in any emergency, or in any state of things, can authorize the suspension of the privilege of the writ of habeas corpus, or the arrest of a citizen, except in aid of the judicial power. He certainly does not faithfully execute the laws, if he takes upon himself legislative power, by suspending the writ of habeas corpus, and the ju-dicial power also, by arresting and imprisoning a person without due process of law.

Nor can any argument be drawn from the nature of sovereignty, or the necessity of government, for self-defence in times of tumult and danger. The government of the United States is one of delegated and limited powers; it derives its existence and authority altogether from the constitution, and neither of its branches, executive, legislative or judicial, can exercise any of the powers of government beyond those specified and granted; for the tenth article of the amendments to the constitution, in express terms, provides that "the powers not delegated to the United States by the constitution, nor prohibited by it to the states, are reserved to the states, respectively, or to the people."

Indeed, the security against imprisonment by executive authority, provided for in the fifth article of the amendments to the constitution, which I have before quoted, is nothing more than a copy of a like pro-vision in the English constitution, which had been firmly established before the declaration of independence. Blackstone states it in the fol-lowing words: "To make imprisonment lawful, it must be either by process of law from the courts of judicature, or by warrant from some legal officer having authority to commit to prison." . . .

The right of the subject to the benefit of the writ of habeas corpus, it must be recollected, was one of the great points in controversy, during the long struggle in England between arbitrary government and free institutions, and must therefore have strongly attracted the attention of the statesmen engaged in framing a new and, as they supposed, a freer government than the one which they had thrown off by the revolution. . . . If the president of the United States may suspend the writ, then the constitution of the United States has conferred upon him more regal and absolute power over the liberty of the citizen, than the people of England have thought it safe to entrust to the crown; a power which the queen of England cannot exercise at this day, and which could not have been lawfully exercised by the sovereign even in the reign of Charles the First. . . .

But the documents before me show, that the military authority in this case has gone far beyond the mere suspension of the privilege of the writ of habeas corpus. It has, by force of arms, thrust aside the judicial authorities and officers to whom the constitution has confided the power and duty of interpreting and administering the laws, and substituted a military government in its place, to be administered and executed by military officers. For, at the time these proceedings were had against John Merryman, the district judge of Maryland, the commissioner appointed under the act of congress, the district attorney and the marshal, all resided in the city of Baltimore, a few miles only from the home of the prisoner. Up to that time, there had never been the slightest resistance or obstruction to the process of any court or judicial officer of the United States, in Maryland, except by the military authority. . . .

Yet, under these circumstances, a military officer, stationed in Pennsylvania, without giving any information to the district attorney, and without any application to the judicial authorities, assumes to himself the judicial power in the district of Maryland; undertakes to decide what constitutes the crime of treason or rebellion; what evidence (if indeed he required any) is sufficient to support the accusation and justify the commitment; and commits the party, without a hearing, even before himself, to close custody, in a strongly garrisoned fort, to be there held, it would seem, during the pleasure of those who committed him.

The constitution provides, as I have before said, that "no person shall be deprived of life, liberty or property, without due process of law." It declares that "the right of the people to be secure in their persons, houses, papers and effects, against unreasonable searches and seizures, shall not be violated; and no warrant shall issue, but upon probable cause, supported by oath or affirmation, and particularly describing the place to be searched, and the persons or things to be seized." It provides that the party accused shall be entitled to a speedy trial in a court of justice.

These great and fundamental laws, which congress itself could not suspend, have been disregarded and suspended, like the writ of habeas corpus, by a military order, supported by force of arms. Such is the case now before me, and I can only say that if the authority which the constitution has confided to the judiciary department and judicial officers, may thus, upon any pretext or under any circumstances, be usurped by the military power, at its discretion, the people of the United States are no longer living under a government of laws, but every citizen holds life, liberty and property at the will and pleasure of the army officer in whose military district he may happen to be found.

In such a case, my duty was too plain to be mistaken. I have exercised all the power which the constitution and laws confer upon me, but that power has been resisted by a force too strong for me to overcome. It is possible that the officer who has incurred this grave responsibility may have misunderstood his instructions, and exceeded the authority intended to be given him; I shall, therefore, order all the proceedings in this case, with my opinion, to be filed and recorded in the circuit court of the United States for the district of Maryland, and direct the clerk to transmit a copy, under seal, to the president of the United States. It will then remain for that high officer, in fulfillment of his constitutional obligation to "take care that the laws be faithfully executed," to determine what measures he will take to cause the civil process of the United States to be respected and enforced.

Special Message to Congress (July 4, 1861)
ABRAHAM LINCOLN

•

. . . Soon after the first call for militia, it was considered a duty to authorize the Commanding General, in proper cases, according to his discretion, to suspend the privilege of the writ of habeas corpus; or, in other words, to arrest, and detain, without resort to the ordinary processes and forms of law, such individuals as he might deem dangerous to the public safety. This authority has purposely been exercised but very sparingly. Nevertheless, the legality and propriety of what has been done under it, are questioned; and the attention of the country has been called to the proposition that one who is sworn to "take care that the laws be faithfully executed," should not himself violate them. Of course some consideration was given to the questions of power, and propriety, before this matter was acted upon. The whole of the laws which were required to be faithfully executed, were being resisted, and failing of execution, in nearly one-third of the States. Must they be allowed to finally fail of execution, even had it been perfectly clear, that by the use of the means necessary to their execution, some single law, made in such extreme tenderness of the citizen's liberty, that practically, it relieves more of the guilty, than of the innocent, should, to a very limited extent, be violated? To state the question more directly, are all the laws, *but one*, to go unexecuted, and the government itself go to pieces, lest that one be violated? Even in such a case, would not the official oath be broken, if the government should be overthrown, when it was believed that disregarding the single law, would tend to preserve it? But it was not believed that this question was presented. It was not believed that any law was violated. The provision of the Constitution that "The privilege of the writ of habeas corpus, shall not be suspended unless when, in cases of rebellion or invasion, the public safety may require it," is equivalent to a provision—is a provision—that such privilege may be suspended when, in cases of rebellion, or invasion, the public safety *does* require it. It was decided that we have a case of rebellion, and that the public safety does require the qualified suspension of the privilege of the writ which was authorized to be made. Now it is insisted that Congress, and not the Executive, is vested with this power. But the Constitution itself, is silent as to which, or who, is to exercise the power; and as the provision was plainly made for a dangerous emergency, it cannot be believed the framers of the instrument intended, that in every case, the danger should run its course, until Congress could be called together; the very assembling of which might be prevented, as was intended in this case, by the rebellion.

No more extended argument is now offered; as an opinion, at some length, will probably be presented by the Attorney General. Whether there shall be any legislation upon the subject, and if any, what, is submitted entirely to the better judgment of Congress. . . .

THE CONSTITUTIONAL DEBATE
ON THE EMANCIPATION
PROCLAMATION

لئے

*L*incoln's critics also challenged the constitutionality of the Emancipation Proclamation. Former Supreme Court Justice Benjamin Curtis, who had written an important dissent in *Dred Scott*, published a pamphlet called *Executive Power* in October 1862, which asserted the unconstitutionality of the proclamation. The issue never came before the courts for decision. Lincoln defended the lawfulness of the proclamation in several public letters explaining his constitutional views, including one addressed to James C. Conkling.

✪

Executive Power (October, 1862)
BENJAMIN R. CURTIS

•

. . . This proclamation, by then, an executive decree, proposes to repeal and annul valid State laws which regulate the domestic relations of their people. . . . [T]he President hereby assumes to himself the power to denounce it as a punishment against the entire people of a State, that the valid laws of that State which regulate the domestic condition of its inhabitants shall become null and void, at a certain future date, by reason of the criminal conduct of a governing majority of its people.

This penalty . . . is not to be inflicted on those persons who have been guilty of treason. The freedom of their slaves was already provided for by the act of Congress, recited in a subsequent part of the proclamation. It is not, therefore, as a punishment of guilty persons that the commander-in-chief decrees the freedom of slaves. . . . It is upon the slaves of loyal persons . . . that the proclamation is to operate, if at all; and it is to operate to set them free, in spite of the valid laws of their States. . . .

It has never been doubted that the power to abolish slavery within the States was not delegated to the United States by the Constitution, but was reserved to the States. If the President, as commander-in-chief of the army and navy in time of war, may, by an executive decree, exercise this power to abolish slavery in the States, because he is of the opinion that he may thus "best subdue the enemy," what other power, reserved to the States or to the people, may not be exercised by the President, for the same reason that he is of opinion he may thus best subdue the enemy? . . .

These conclusions concerning the powers of the President cannot be shaken by the assertion that "rebels have no rights." The assertion itself is not true, in reference either to the seceding States or their people.

It is not true of those States; for the Government of the United States has never admitted, and cannot admit, that as States, they are in rebellion. . . . [T]he Constitution is as much the supreme law of the land in Tennessee to-day, as it was before the void act of secession was attempted by a part of its people. Else the act was effectual, and the State is independent of the Government of the United States, and the war is a war of conquest and subjugation.

Nor is the assertion that "rebels have no rights" applicable to the people of these States. . . . [I]f public law and the Constitution and laws of the United States are now their rules of duty towards us, on what ground shall we deny that public law and the Constitution, and the laws made under it, are also our rules of duty towards them? . . .

Letter to James C. Conkling (August 26, 1863)
ABRAHAM LINCOLN

•

. . . There are those who are dissatisfied with me. . . . You dislike the emancipation proclamation; and, perhaps, would have it retracted. You say it is unconstitutional—I think differently. I think the constitution invests its commander-in-chief with the law of war, in time of war. The most that can be said, if so much, is, that slaves are property. Is there— has there ever been—any question that by the law of war, property, both of enemies and friends, may be taken when needed? And is it not needed whenever taking it, helps us, or hurts the enemy? Armies, the world over, destroy enemies' property when they can not use it and even destroy their own to keep it from the enemy. Civilized belligerents do all in their power to help themselves, or hurt the enemy, except a few things regarded as barbarous or cruel. Among the exceptions are the massacre of vanquished foes, and non-combatants, male and female. . . .

I thought that in your struggle for the Union, to whatever extent the negroes should cease helping the enemy, to that extent it weakened the enemy in his resistance to you. Do you think differently? I thought that whatever negroes can be got to do as soldiers, leaves just so much less for white soldiers to do, in saving the Union. . . .

THE *PRIZE CASES*

67 U.S. 635 (1863)

ﻌﻠﯩ

*T*his group of cases, decided together at the height of the Civil War, produced the Supreme Court's first major decision concerning presidential war powers under the Constitution. The cases concerned the legal status of neutral ships taken as "prizes" of war while attempting to evade President Lincoln's blockade of Southern ports.

The Court's decision upholding the blockade order embraced the understanding that the President constitutionally has power to respond with military measures to attacks on the nation, with or without awaiting congressional authorization; that no declaration of war was needed (or appropriate) in the case of civil war; that the powers of the President as Commander-in-Chief are triggered by the practical condition of actual military conflict, whether declared as war or not, and whether foreign or civil; that the President's power as Commander-in-Chief includes the choice of means to subdue and defeat an enemy force he thinks best, as well as the power to interpret and apply the customary laws of war to such end; and finally, that the power to conduct war includes the power to seize property in the possession of the enemy, including property of innocent owners and "neutral" parties of benefit to the enemy. Justice

Nelson's dissent took the view that the seizure was not legally valid until Congress ratified Lincoln's military actions.

The decision in the *Prize Cases* came several months after Lincoln had issued the Emancipation Proclamation and was not addressed to that issue. Nonetheless, the Court's reasoning supported Lincoln's position that he had constitutional power, as Commander-in-Chief, to proclaim emancipation as a military measure.

✪

Mr. Justice GRIER.

. . . Had the President a right to institute a blockade of ports in possession of persons in armed rebellion against the Government, on the principles of international law, as known and acknowledged among civilized States? . . . To legitimate the capture of a neutral vessel or property on the high seas, a war must exist de facto, and the neutral must have a knowledge or notice of the intention of one of the parties belligerent to use this mode of coercion against a port, city, or territory, in possession of the other. Let us enquire whether, at the time this blockade was instituted, a state of war existed which would justify a resort to these means of subduing the hostile force.

War has been well defined to be, "That state in which a nation prosecutes its right by force." The parties belligerent in a public war are independent nations. But it is not necessary to constitute war, that both parties should be acknowledged as independent nations or sovereign States. A war may exist where one of the belligerents, claims sovereign rights as against the other.

Insurrection against a government may or may not culminate in an organized rebellion, but a civil war always begins by insurrection against the lawful authority of the Government. A civil war is never solemnly declared; it becomes such by its accidents—the number, power, and organization of the persons who originate and carry it on. When the party in rebellion occupy and hold in a hostile manner a certain portion of territory; have declared their independence; have cast off their allegiance; have organized armies; have commenced hostilities against their former sovereign, the world acknowledges them as belligerents, and the contest a war. They claim to be in arms to establish their liberty and independence, in order to become a sovereign State, while the sovereign party treats them as insurgents and rebels who owe allegiance, and who should be punished with death for their treason. . . .

By the Constitution, Congress alone has the power to declare a national or foreign war. It cannot declare was against a State, or any number of States, by virtue of any clause in the Constitution. The Constitution confers on the President the whole Executive power. He is bound to take care that the laws be faithfully executed. He is Commander-in-chief of the Army and Navy of the United States, and of the militia of the several States when called into the actual service of the United States. He has no power to initiate or declare a war either against a foreign nation or a domestic State. But by the Acts of Congress of February 28th, 1795, and 3d of March, 1807, he is authorized to called out the militia and use the military and naval forces of the United States in case of invasion by foreign nations, and to suppress insurrection against the government of a State or of the United States.

If a war be made by invasion of a foreign nation, the President is not only authorized but bound to resist force by force. He does not initiate the war, but is bound to accept the challenge without waiting for any special legislative authority. And whether the hostile party be a foreign invader, or States organized in rebellion, it is none the less a war, although the declaration of it be "unilateral." . . .

This greatest of civil wars was not gradually developed by popular commotion, tumultuous assemblies, or local unorganized insurrections. However long may have been its previous conception, it nevertheless sprung forth suddenly from the parent brain, a Minerva in the full panoply of war. The President was bound to meet it in the shape it presented itself, without waiting for Congress to baptize it with a name; and no name given to it by him or them could change the fact.

It is not the less a civil war, with belligerent parties in hostile array, because it may be called an "insurrection" by one side, and the insurgents be considered as rebels or traitors. It is not necessary that the independence of the revolted province or State be acknowledged in order to constitute it a party belligerent in a war according to the law of nations. . . .

The law of nations is also called the law of nature; it is founded on the common consent as well as the common sense of the world. It contains no such anomalous doctrine as that which this Court are now for the first time desired to pronounce, to wit: That insurgents who have risen in rebellion against their sovereign, expelled her Courts, established a revolutionary government, organized armies, and commenced hostilities, are not enemies because they are traitors; and a war levied on the Government by traitors, in order to dismember and destroy it, is not a war because it is an "insurrection."

Whether the President in fulfilling his duties, as Commander-in-chief, in suppressing an insurrection, has met with such armed hostile resistance, and a civil war of such alarming proportions as will compel him to accord to them the character of belligerents, is a question to be decided by him, and this Court must be governed by the decisions and acts of the political department of the Government to which this power was entrusted. "He must determine what degree of force the crisis demands." The proclamation of blockade is itself official and conclusive evidence to the Court that a state of war existed which demanded and authorized a recourse to such a measure, under the circumstances peculiar to the case.

. . . If it were necessary to the technical existence of a war, that it should have a legislative sanction, we find it in almost every act passed at the extraordinary session of the Legislature of 1861, which was wholly employed in enacting laws to enable the Government to prosecute the war with vigor and efficiency. And finally, in 1861, we find Congress "*ex majore cautela*" and in anticipation of such astute objections, passing an act "approving, legalizing, and making valid all the acts, proclamations, and orders of the President, &c., as if they had been issued and done under the previous express authority and direction of the Congress of the United States." . . .

On this first question therefore we are of the opinion that the President had a right, *jure belli*, to institute a blockade of ports in possession of the States in rebellion, which neutrals are bound to regard. . . . We come now to the consideration of the second question. What is included in the term "enemies' property?" Is the property of all persons residing within the territory of the States now in rebellion, captured on the high seas, to be treated as "enemies' property" whether the owner be in arms against the Government or not?

The right of one belligerent not only to coerce the other by direct force, but also to cripple his resources by the seizure or destruction of his property, is a necessary result of a state of war. Money and wealth, the products of agriculture and commerce, are said to be the sinews of war, and as necessary in its conduct as numbers and physical force. Hence it is, that the laws of war recognize the right of a belligerent to cut these sinews of the power of the enemy, by capturing his property on the high seas.

The appellants contend that the term "enemy" is properly applicable to those only who are subjects or citizens of a foreign State at war with our own. . . .

They insist, moreover, that the President himself, in his proclamation, admits that great numbers of the persons residing within the territories in possession of the insurgent government, are loyal in their feelings, and forced by compulsion and the violence of the rebellious and revolutionary party and its "de facto government" to submit to their laws and assist in their scheme of revolution; that the acts of the usurping government cannot legally sever the bond of their allegiance; they have, therefore, a correlative right to claim the protection of the government for their persons and property, and to be treated as loyal citizens, till legally convicted of having renounced their allegiance and made war against the Government by treasonably resisting its laws.

They contend, also, that insurrection is the act of individuals and not of a government or sovereignty; that the individuals engaged are subjects of law. That confiscation of their property can be effected only under a municipal law. That by the law of the land such confiscation cannot take place without the conviction of the owner of some offence, and finally that the secession ordinances are nullities and ineffectual to release any citizen from his allegiance to the national Government, and consequently that the Constitution and Laws of the United States are still operative over persons in all the States for punishment as well as protection.

This argument rests on the assumption of two propositions, each of which is without foundation on the established law of nations. It assumes that where a civil war exists, the party belligerent claiming to be sovereign, cannot, for some unknown reason, exercise the rights of belligerents, although the revolutionary party may. Being sovereign, he can exercise only sovereign rights over the other party. The insurgent may be killed on the battle-field or by the executioner; his property on land may be confiscated under the municipal law; but the commerce on the ocean, which supplies the rebels with means to support the war, cannot be made the subject of capture under the laws of war, because it is "unconstitutional!!!" Now, it is a proposition never doubted, that the belligerent party who claims to be sovereign, may exercise both belligerent and sovereign rights, (see 4 Cr., 272.) Treating the other party as a belligerent and using only the milder modes of coercion which the law of nations has introduced to mitigate the rigors of war, cannot be a subject of complaint by the party to whom it is accorded as a grace or granted as a necessity. We have shown that a civil war such as that now waged between the Northern and Southern States is properly conducted according to the humane regulations of public law as regards capture on the ocean.

Under the very peculiar Constitution of this Government, although the citizens owe supreme allegiance to the Federal Government, they owe also a qualified allegiance to the State in which they are domiciled. Their persons and property are subject to its laws.

Hence, in organizing this rebellion, they have acted as States claiming to be sovereign over all persons and property within their respective limits, and asserting a right to absolve their citizens from their allegiance to the Federal Government. Several of these States have combined to form a new confederacy, claiming to be acknowledged by the world as a sovereign State. Their right to do so is now being decided by wager of battle. The ports and territory of each of these States are held in hostility to the General Government. It is no loose, unorganized insurrection, having no defined boundary or possession. It has a boundary marked by lines of bayonets, and which can be crossed only by force— south of this line is enemies' territory, because it is claimed and held in possession by an organized, hostile and belligerent power.

All persons residing within this territory whose property may be used to increase the revenues of the hostile power are, in this contest, liable to be treated as enemies, though not foreigners. They have cast off their allegiance and made war on their Government, and are none the less enemies because they are traitors. . . . Whether property be liable to capture as "enemies' property" does not in any manner depend on the personal allegiance of the owner. . . .

MILITARY ARRESTS, DETENTIONS, AND TRIALS DURING THE CIVIL WAR

ائﻟﮫ

*T*he Civil War saw the arrest and detention, even the military trial, of civilians in the North, without resort to civilian legal process. In one instance, a Union general in Ohio arrested, and tried before a military tribunal, a Northern congressman, Clement Vallandigham, who had made a scurrilous public speech denouncing emancipation (and blacks) and which arguably encouraged desertion from military service and resistance to the draft. The Supreme Court upheld military jurisdiction in *Ex parte Vallandigham* (1864), but this incident, and others, produced strong criticism of the Lincoln administration on civil liberties grounds. Lincoln defended the legality of such actions in a public letter in June 1863 ("Letter to Erastus Corning and Others").

After the war (and after Lincoln's death), the Supreme Court, in *Ex parte Milligan* (1866), struck down the use of a U.S. military tribunal in Indiana to try civilians for an alleged plot against the Union involving attempted seizure of Union arms, freeing of Confederate prisoners, and kidnapping of the governor. The Court was unanimous in result, but split 5–4 in its reasoning.

✪

Letter to Erastus Corning and Others (June 12, 1863)
ABRAHAM LINCOLN

•

Gentlemen: Your letter of May 19th inclosing the resolutions of a public meeting held at Albany, N.Y. on the 16th of the same month, was received several days ago. . . .

The resolutions promise to support me in every constitutional and lawful measure to suppress the rebellion; and I have not knowingly employed, nor shall knowingly employ, any other. But the meeting, by their resolutions, assert and argue, that certain military arrests and proceedings following them for which I am ultimately responsible, are unconstitutional. I think they are not. The resolutions quote from the constitution, the definition of treason; and also the limiting safe-guards and guarantees therein provided for the citizen, on trials for treason, and on his being held to answer for capital or otherwise infamous crimes, and, in criminal prosecutions, his right to a speedy and public trial by an impartial jury. . . . But these provisions of the constitution have no application to the case we have in hand, because the arrests complained of were not made for treason . . .; nor were the proceedings following, in any constitutional or legal sense, "criminal prosecutions." The arrests were made on totally different grounds, and the proceedings following, accorded with the grounds of the arrests. Let us consider the real case with which we are dealing, and apply to it the parts of the constitution plainly made for such cases. . . .

Ours is a case of Rebellion—so called by the resolutions before me— in fact, a clear, flagrant, and gigantic case of Rebellion; and the provision of the constitution that "The privilege of the writ of Habeas Corpus shall not be suspended, unless when in cases of Rebellion or Invasion, the public Safety may require it" is the provision which specially applies to our present case. This provision plainly attests the understanding of those who made the constitution that ordinary courts of justice are inadequate to "cases of Rebellion"—attests their purpose that in such cases, men may be held in custody whom the courts acting on ordinary rules, would discharge. Habeas Corpus does not discharge men who are proved to be guilty of defined crime; and its suspension is allowed by the constitution on purpose that, men may be arrested and held, who cannot be proved to be guilty of defined crime, "when, in cases of Rebellion or Invasion the public Safety may require it." This is precisely our present case—a case of Rebellion, wherein the public Safety does require the suspension. . . .

By the third resolution the meeting indicate their opinion that military arrests may be constitutional in localities where rebellion actually exists; but that such arrests are unconstitutional in localities where rebellion, or insurrection, does not actually exist. They insist that such arrests shall not be made "outside of the lines of necessary military occupation, and the scenes of insurrection." Inasmuch, however, as the constitution itself makes no such distinction, I am unable to believe that there is any such constitutional distinction. I concede that the class of arrests complained of, can be constitutional only when, in cases of Rebellion or Invasion, the public Safety may require them; and I insist that in such cases, they are constitutional wherever the public safety does require them—as well in places to which they may prevent the rebellion extending as in those where it may be already prevailing—as well where they may restrain mischievous interference with the raising and supplying of armies, to suppress the rebellion, as where the rebellion may actually be—as well where they may restrain the enticing men out of the army, as where they would prevent mutiny in the army—equally constitutional at all places where they will conduce to the public Safety, as against the dangers of Rebellion or Invasion.

Take the particular case mentioned by the meeting. They assert in substance that Mr. Vallandigham was by a military commander, seized and tried "for no other reason than words addressed to a public meeting, in criticism of the course of the administration, and in condemnation of the military orders of that general." Now, if there be no mistake about this—if this assertion is the truth and the whole truth—if there was no other reason for the arrest, then I concede that the arrest was wrong. But the arrest, as I understand, was made for a very different reason. Mr. Vallandigham avows his hostility to the war on the part of the Union; and his arrest was made because he was laboring, with some effect, to prevent the raising of troops, to encourage desertions from the army, and to leave the rebellion without an adequate military force to suppress it. He was not arrested because he was damaging the political prospects of the administration, or the personal interests of the commanding general; but because he was damaging the army, upon the existence, and vigor of which, the life of the nation depends. He was warring upon the military; and this gave the military constitutional jurisdiction to lay hands upon him. If Mr. Vallandigham was not damaging the military power of the country, then his arrest was made on mistake of fact, which I would be glad to correct, on reasonably satisfactory evidence.

I understand the meeting, whose resolutions I am considering, to be in favor of suppressing the rebellion by military force—by armies. Long experience has shown that armies can not be maintained unless desertion shall be punished by the severe penalty of death. The case requires, and the law and the constitution, sanction this punishment. Must I shoot a simple-minded soldier boy who deserts, while I must not touch a hair of a wily agitator who induces him to desert? This is none the less injurious when effected by getting a father, or brother, or friend, into a public meeting, and there working upon his feeling, till he is persuaded to write the soldier boy, that he is fighting in a bad cause, for a wicked administration of a contemptible government, too weak to arrest and punish him if he shall desert. I think that in such a case, to silence the agitator, and save the boy, is not only constitutional, but, withal, a great mercy.

If I be wrong on this question of constitutional power, my error lies in believing that certain proceedings are constitutional when, in cases of rebellion or Invasion, the public Safety requires them, which would not be constitutional when, in absence of rebellion or invasion, the public Safety does not require them—in other words, that the constitution is not in its application in all respects the same, in cases of Rebellion or invasion, involving the public Safety, as it is in times of profound peace and public security. The constitution itself makes the distinction; and I can no more be persuaded that the government can constitutionally take no strong measure in time of rebellion, because it can be shown that the same could not be lawfully taken in time of peace, than I can be persuaded that a particular drug is not good medicine for a sick man, because it can be shown to not be good food for a well one. . . .

And yet, let me say that in my own discretion, I do not know whether I would have ordered the arrest of Mr. V. . . . I have to say it gave me pain when I learned that Mr. V. had been arrested—that is, I was pained that there should have seemed to be a necessity for arresting him—and that it will afford me great pleasure to discharge him so soon as I can, by any means, believe the public safety will not suffer by it. . . .

Ex parte Milligan
71 U.S. 2 (1866)

•

MR. JUSTICE DAVIS DELIVERED THE OPINION OF THE COURT.

. . . The importance of the main question presented by this record cannot be overstated; for it involves the very framework of the government and the fundamental principles of American liberty. During the late wicked Rebellion, the temper of the times did not allow that calmness in deliberation and discussion so necessary to a correct conclusion of a purely judicial question. Then, considerations of safety were mingled with the exercise of power; and feelings and interests prevailed which are happily terminated. Now that the public safety is assured, this question, as well as all others, can be discussed and decided without passion or the admixture of any element not required to form a legal judgment. We approach the investigation of this case, fully sensible of the magnitude of the inquiry and the necessity of full and cautious deliberation.

The controlling question in the case is this: Upon the facts stated in Milligan's petition, and the exhibits filed, had the military commission mentioned in it jurisdiction, legally, to try and sentence him? Milligan, not a resident of one of the rebellious states, or a prisoner of war, but a citizen of Indiana for twenty years past, and never in the military or naval service, is, while at his home, arrested by the military power of the United States, imprisoned, and, on certain criminal charges preferred against him, tried, convicted, and sentenced to be hanged by a military commission, organized under the direction of the military commander of the military district of Indiana. Had this tribunal the legal power and authority to try and punish this man?

No graver question was ever considered by this court, nor one which more nearly concerns the rights of the whole people; for it is the birthright of every American citizen when charged with crime, to be tried and punished according to law.

. . . The Constitution of the United States is a law for rulers and people, equally in war and in peace, and covers with the shield of its protection all classes of men, at all times, and under all circumstances. No doctrine, involving more pernicious consequences, was ever invented by the wit of man than that any of its provisions can be suspended during any of the great exigencies of government. Such a doctrine leads directly to anarchy or despotism, but the theory of necessity on which it is based is false; for the government, within the Constitution, has all the powers granted to it, which are necessary to preserve its existence; as has been happily proved by the result of the great effort to throw off its just authority.

Have any of the rights guaranteed by the Constitution been violated in the case of Milligan? and if so, what are they?

Every trial involves the exercise of judicial power; and from what source did the military commission that tried him derive their authority? Certainly no part of judicial power of the country was conferred on them; because the Constitution expressly vests it "in one supreme court and such inferior courts as the Congress may from time to time ordain and establish," and it is not pretended that the commission was a court ordained and established by Congress. They cannot justify on the mandate of the President; because he is controlled by law, and has his appropriate sphere of duty, which is to execute, not to make, the laws; and there is 'no unwritten criminal code to which resort can be had as a source of jurisdiction.'

But it is said that the jurisdiction is complete under the 'laws and usages of war.'

It can serve no useful purpose to inquire what those laws and usages are, whence they originated, where found, and on whom they operate; they can never be applied to citizens in states which have upheld the authority of the government, and where the courts are open and their process unobstructed. This court has judicial knowledge that in Indiana the Federal authority was always unopposed, and its courts always open to hear criminal accusations and redress grievances; and no usage of war could sanction a military trial there for any offence whatever of a citizen in civil life, in nowise connected with the military service. Congress could grant no such power; and to the honor of our national legislature be it said, it has never been provoked by the state of the country even to attempt its exercise. One of the plainest constitutional provisions was, therefore, infringed when Milligan was tried by a court not ordained and established by Congress, and not composed of judges appointed during good behavior. . . .

Another guarantee of freedom was broken when Milligan was denied a trial by jury. . . . [T]his right—one of the most valuable in a free country—is preserved to every one accused of crime who is not attached to the army, or navy, or militia in actual service. . . .

The discipline necessary to the efficiency of the army and navy, required other and swifter modes of trial than are furnished by the common law courts; and, in pursuance of the power conferred by the Constitution, Congress has declared the kinds of trial, and the manner in which they shall be conducted, for offences committed while the party is in the military or naval service. . . . *All other persons*, citizens of states where the courts are open, if charged with crime, are guaranteed the inestimable privilege of trial by jury. This privilege is a vital principle, underlying the whole administration of criminal justice; it is not held by sufferance, and cannot be frittered away on any plea of state or political necessity. . . .

It is claimed that martial law covers with its broad mantle the proceedings of this military commission. The proposition is this: that in a time of war the commander of an armed force (if in his opinion the exigencies of the country demand it, and of which he is to judge), has the power, within the lines of his military district, to suspend all civil rights and their remedies, and subject citizens as well as soldiers to the rule of *his will*; and in the exercise of his lawful authority cannot be restrained, except by his superior officer or the President of the United States.

The statement of this proposition shows its importance; for, if true, republican government is a failure, and there is an end of liberty regulated by law. Martial law, established on such a basis, destroys every guarantee of the Constitution, and effectually renders the 'military independent of and superior to the civil power'—

the attempt to do which by the King of Great Britain was deemed by our fathers such an offence, that they assigned it to the world as one of the causes which impelled them to declare their independence. Civil liberty and this kind of martial law cannot endure together; the antagonism is irreconcilable; and, in the conflict, one or the other must perish. . . .

It follows, from what has been said on this subject, that there are occasions when martial rule can be properly applied. If, in foreign invasion or civil war, the courts are actually closed, and it is impossible to administer criminal justice according to law, *then*, on the theatre of active military operations, where war really prevails, there is a necessity to furnish a substitute for the civil authority, thus overthrown, to preserve the safety of the army and society; and as no power is left but the military, it is allowed to govern by martial rule until the laws can have their free course. As necessity creates the rule, so it limits its duration; for, if this government is continued *after* the courts are reinstated, it is a gross usurpation of power. Martial rule can never exist where the courts are open, and in the proper and unobstructed exercise of their jurisdiction. It is also confined to the locality of actual war. Because, during the late Rebellion it could have been enforced in Virginia, where the national authority was overturned and the courts driven out, it does not follow that it should obtain in Indiana, where that authority was never disputed, and justice was always administered. And so in the case of a foreign invasion, martial rule may become a necessity in one state, when, in another, it would be 'mere lawless violence.' . . .

THE CHIEF JUSTICE DELIVERED THE FOLLOWING OPINION.

Four members of the court, concurring with their brethren in the order heretofore made in this cause, but unable to concur in some important particulars with the opinion which has just been read, think it their duty to make a separate statement of their views of the whole case. . . . We think that Congress had power, though not exercised, to authorize the military commission which was held in Indiana. . . .

Congress has the power not only to raise and support and govern armies but to declare war. It has, therefore, the power to provide by law for carrying on war. This power necessarily extends to all legislation essential to the prosecution of war with vigor and success, except such as interferes with the command of the forces and the conduct of campaigns. That power and duty belong to the President as commander-in-chief. . . .

We by no means assert that Congress can establish and apply the laws of war where no war has been declared or exists. Where peace exists the laws of peace must prevail. What we do maintain is, that when the nation is involved in war, and some portions of the country are invaded, and all are exposed to invasion, it is within the power of Congress to determine in what states or district such great and imminent public danger exists as justifies the authorization of military tribunals for the trial of crimes and offences against the discipline or security of the army or against the public safety. . . .

THE
RECONSTRUCTION
AMENDMENTS
(1866–1883)

SPEECH INTRODUCING
THE PROPOSED FOURTEENTH
AMENDMENT
(*CONGRESSIONAL GLOBE*, MAY 23, 1866)
JACOB HOWARD

*T*he Civil War transformed the Constitution. It decisively repudiated the South's claim of state sovereignty and right to secession, and it produced three major constitutional amendments. In 1865, two months before the South's surrender at Appomattox, Congress proposed the Thirteenth Amendment abolishing slavery. The amendment was ratified by three-fourths of the states that year. The Fourteenth Amendment, proposed by Congress in 1866 and ratified in 1868, completed the nation's repudiation of *Dred Scott* by defining national and state citizenship, forbidding states from abridging the privileges and immunities of citizens or denying due process or equal protection of the laws to any person, and granting Congress broad legislative power to implement these commands. The Fifteenth Amendment, proposed in 1869 and ratified in 1870, prohibited racial discrimination in the right to vote.

The Fourteenth Amendment's general language has led to some of the most enduring disputes in modern constitutional law. One important historical source for its interpretation is Senator Jacob Howard's statement—on behalf of the Joint Committee for Reconstruction—introducing the draft of the amendment in the Senate and explaining its intended meaning and effect.

✪

The Senate, as in Committee of the Whole, proceeded to consider the joint resolution (H. R. No. 127) proposing an amendment to the Constitution of the United States, which was read as follows

ARTICLE—.

SEC. 1. No State shall make or enforce any law which shall abridge the privileges or immunities of citizens of the United States; nor shall any State deprive any person of life, liberty, or property, without due process of law; nor deny to any person within its jurisdiction the equal protection of the laws.

SEC. 2. Representatives shall be apportioned among the several States which may be included within the Union, according to their respective numbers, counting the whole number of persons in each State, excluding Indians not taxed. But whenever, in any State, the elective franchise shall be denied to any portion of its male citizens not less than twenty-one years of age, or in any way abridged, except for participation in rebellion or other crime, the basis of representation in such State shall be reduced in the proportion which the number of such male citizens shall bear to the whole number of male citizens not less than twenty-one years of age.

SEC. 3. Until the 4th day of July, in the year 1870, all persons who voluntarily adhered to the late insurrection, giving it aid and comfort, shall be excluded from the right to vote for Representatives in Congress and for electors for President and Vice President of the United States.

SEC. 4. Neither the United States {nor any State shall assume or pay any debt or obligation already incurred, or which may hereafter he incurred, in aid of insurrection or of war against the United States, or any claim for compensation for loss of involuntary service or labor.

SEC. 5. The Congress shall have power to enforce by appropriate legislation the provisions of this article.

Mr. HOWARD. Mr. President, I regret that the state of the health of the honorable Senator from Maine . . . who is chairman, on the part of the Senate, of the joint committee of fifteen, is such as to disable him from opening the discussion of this grave and important measure. . . . For myself, I can only promise to present to the Senate, in a very succinct way, the views and the motives which influenced that committee, so far as I understand those views and motives, in presenting the report which is now before us for consideration, and the ends it aims to accomplish.

The joint resolution creating that committee intrusted them with a very important inquiry, an inquiry involving a vast deal of attention and labor. They were instructed to inquire into the condition of the insurgent States, and authorized to report by bill or otherwise at their discretion. I believe that I do not overstate the truth when I say that no committee of Congress has ever proceeded with more fidelity and attention to the matter intrusted to them. . . . One result of their investigations has been the joint resolution for the amendment of the Constitution of the United States now under consideration. After most mature deliberation and discussion, reaching through weeks and even months, they came to the conclusion that it was necessary, in order to restore peace and quiet to the country and again to impart vigor and efficiency to the laws, and especially to obtain something in the shape of a security for the future against the recurrence of the enormous evils under which the country has labored for the last four years, that the Constitution of the United States ought to be amended; and the project which they have now submitted is the result of their deliberations upon that subject.

The first section of the amendment they have submitted for the consideration of the two Houses relates to the privileges and immunities of citizens of the several States, and to the rights and privileges of all persons, whether citizens or others, under the laws of the United States. It declares that—

No State shall make or enforce any law which shall abridge the privileges or immunities of citizens of the United States; nor shall any State deprive any person of life, liberty, or property without due process of law; nor deny to any person within its jurisdiction the equal protection of the laws.

It will be observed that this is a general prohibition upon all the States, as such, from abridging the privileges and immunities of the citizens of the United States. That is its first clause, and I regard it as very important. It also prohibits each one of the States from depriving any person of life, liberty, or property without due process of law, or denying to any person within the jurisdiction of the State the equal protection of its laws.

The first clause of this section relates to the privileges and immunities of citizens of the United States as such, and as distinguished from all other persons not citizens of the United States. . . . A citizen of the United States is held by the courts to be a person who was born within the limits of the United States and subject to their laws. Before the adoption of the Constitution of the United States, the citizens of each State were, in a qualified sense at least, aliens to one another, for the reason that the several States before that event were regarded by each other as independent Governments, each one possessing a sufficiency of sovereign power to enable it to claim the right of naturalization; and, undoubtedly, each one of them possessed for itself the right of naturalizing foreigners, and each one, also, if it had seen fit so to exercise its sovereign power, might have declared the citizens of every other State to be aliens in reference to itself. With a view to prevent such confusion and disorder, and to put the citizens of the several States on an equality with each other as to all fundamental rights, a clause was introduced in the Constitution declaring that "the citizens of each State shall be entitled to all privileges and immunities of citizens in the several States."

The effect of this clause was to constitute ipso facto the citizens of each one of the original States citizens of the United States. . . . Such persons were, therefore, citizens of the United States as were born in the country or were made such by naturalization; and the Constitution declares that they are entitled, as citizens, to all the privileges and immunities of citizens in the several States. They are, by constitutional right, entitled to these privileges and immunities, and may assert this right and these privileges and immunities, and ask for their enforcement whenever they go within the limits of the several States of the Union.

It would be a curious question to solve what are the privileges and immunities of citizens of each of the States in the several States. . . . [W]e may gather some intimation of what probably will be the opinion of the judiciary by referring to a case adjudged many years ago in one of the circuit courts of the United States by Judge Washington [*Corfield v. Coryell*, 6 Fed. Cas. 546 (C.C.E.D. Pa. 1823)]. . . .

Judge Washington says:

> ". . . *The inquiry is, what are the privileges and immunities of citizens in the several states? We feel no hesitation in confining these expressions to those privileges and immunities which are, in their nature, fundamental; which belong, of right, to the citizens of all free governments; and which have, at*

all times, been enjoyed by the citizens of the several states which compose this Union, from the time of their becoming free, independent, and sovereign. What these fundamental principles are, it would perhaps be more tedious than difficult to enumerate. They may, however, be all comprehended under the following general heads: Protection by the government; the enjoyment of life and liberty, with the right to acquire and possess property of every kind, and to pursue and obtain happiness and safety; subject nevertheless to such restraints as the government may justly prescribe for the general good of the whole.

The right of a citizen of one state to pass through, or to reside in any other state, for purposes of trade, agriculture, professional pursuits, or otherwise; to claim the benefit of the writ of habeas corpus; to institute and maintain actions of any kind in the courts of the state; to take, hold and dispose of property, either real or personal; and an exemption from higher taxes or impositions than are paid by the other citizens of the state; may be mentioned as some of the particular privileges and immunities of citizens, which are clearly embraced by the general description of privileges deemed to be fundamental: to which may be added, the elective franchise, as regulated and established by the laws or constitution of the state in which it is to be exercised. . . ."

Such is the character of the privileges and immunities spoken of in the second section of the fourth article of the Constitution. To these privileges and immunities, whatever they may be—for they are not and cannot be fully defined in their entire extent and precise nature—to these should be added the personal rights guarantied and secured by the first eight amendments of the Constitution; such as the freedom of speech and of the press; the right of the people peaceably to assemble and petition the Government for a redress of grievances, a right appertaining to each and all the people; the right to keep and to bear arms; the right to be exempted from the quartering of soldiers in a house without the consent of the owner; the right to be exempt from unreasonable searches and seizures, and from any search or seizure except by virtue of a warrant issued upon a formal oath or affidavit; the right of an accused person to be informed of the nature of the accusation against him, and his right to be tried by an impartial jury of the vicinage; and also the right to be secure against excessive bail and against cruel and unusual punishments.

Now, sir, here is a mass of privileges, immunities, and rights, some of them secured by the second section of the fourth article of the Constitution, which I have recited, some by the first eight amendments of the

Constitution; and it is a fact well worthy of attention that the course of decision of our courts and the present settled doctrine is, that all these immunities, privileges, rights, thus guarantied by the Constitution or recognized by it, are secured to the citizen solely as a citizen of the United States and as a party in their courts. They do not operate in the slightest degree as a restraint or prohibition upon State legislation. States are not affected by them, and it has been repeatedly held that the restriction contained in the Constitution against the taking of private property for public use without just compensation is not a restriction upon State legislation, but applies only to the legislation of Congress.

Now, sir, there is no power given in the Constitution to enforce and to carry out any of these guarantees. They are not powers granted by the Constitution to Congress, and of course do not come within the sweeping clause of the Constitution authorizing Congress to pass all laws necessary and proper for carrying out the foregoing or granted powers, but they stand simply as a bill of rights in the Constitution, without power on the part of Congress to give them full effect; while at the same time the States are not restrained from violating the principles embraced in them except by their own local constitutions, which may be altered from year to year. The great object of the first section of this amendment is, therefore, to restrain the power of the States and compel them at all times to respect these great fundamental guarantees. How will it be done under the present amendment? As I have remarked, they are not powers granted to Congress, and therefore it is necessary, if they are to be effectuated and enforced, as they assuredly ought to be, that additional power should be given to Congress to that end. This is done by the fifth section of this amendment, which declares that "the Congress shall have power to enforce by appropriate legislation the provisions of this article." Here is a direct affirmative delegation of power to Congress to carry out all the principles of all these guarantees, a power not found in the Constitution.

The last two clauses of the first section of the amendment disable a State from depriving not merely a citizen of the United States, but any person, whoever he may be, of life, liberty, or property without due process of law, or from denying to him the equal protection of the laws of the State. This abolishes all class legislation in the States and does away with the injustice of subjecting one caste of persons to a code not applicable to another. It prohibits the hanging of a black man for a crime for which the white man is not to be hanged. It protects the black man in his fundamental rights as a citizen with the same shield which it throws over the white man. Is it not time, Mr. President, that we extend to the black man, I had almost called it the poor privilege of the equal protection of the law? Ought not the time to be now passed when one measure of justice is to be meted out to a member of one caste while another and a different measure is meted out to the member of another caste, both castes being alike citizens of the United States, both bound to obey the same laws, to sustain the burdens of the same Government, and both equally responsible to justice and to God for the deeds done in the body?

But, sir, the first section of the proposed amendment does not give to either of these classes the right of voting. The right of suffrage is not, in law, one of the privileges or immunities thus secured by the Constitution. It is merely the creature of law. It has always been regarded in this country as the result of positive local law, not regarded as one of those fundamental rights lying at the basis of all society and without which a people cannot exist except as slaves, subject to a despotism.

As I have already remarked, section one is a restriction upon the States, and does not, of itself, confer any power upon Congress. The power which Congress has, under this amendment, is derived, not from that section, but from the fifth section, which gives it authority to pass laws which are appropriate to the attainment of the great object of the amendment. I look upon the first section, taken in connection with the fifth, as very important. It will, if adopted by the States, forever disable every one of them from passing laws trenching upon those fundamental rights and privileges which pertain to citizens of the United States, and to all persons who may happen to be within their jurisdiction. It establishes equality before the law, and it gives to the humblest, the poorest, the most despised of the race the same rights and the same protection before the law as it gives to the most powerful, the most wealthy, or the most haughty. That, sir, is republican government, as I understand it, and the only one which can claim the praise of a just Government. Without this principle of equal justice to all men and equal protection under the shield of the law, there is no republican government and none that is really worth maintaining.

[Senator Howard then read the second section of the proposed amendment, which eliminated the Three-fifths Clause, provided for representation based on population, and penalized states to the extent that they denied the vote to adult male citizens. —Ed.]

[T]his section of the amendment does not recognize the authority of the United States over the question of suffrage in the several States at all; nor does it recognize, much less secure, the right of suffrage to the colored race. . . . The committee were of opinion that the States are not yet prepared to sanction so fundamental a change as would be the concession of the right of suffrage to the colored race. . . . Formerly under the Constitution, while the free States were represented only according to their respective numbers of men, women, and children, all of course endowed with civil rights, the slave States had the advantage of being represented according to their number of the same free classes, increased by three fifths of the slaves whom they treated not as men but property. . . . [T]he advantage that was given to the slave States under the Constitution enabled them to send at least twenty one members to Congress in 1860, based entirely upon what they treated as property— a number sufficient to determine almost every contested measure that might come before the House of Representatives.

The three fifths principle has ceased in the destruction of slavery and in the enfranchisement of the colored race. . . . Shall the recently slave-holding States, while they exclude from the ballot the whole of their black population, be entitled to include the whole of that population in the basis of their representation, and thus to obtain an advantage which they did not possess before the rebellion and emancipation? In short, shall we permit it to take place that one of the results of emancipation and of the war is to increase the Representatives of the late slaveholding States? I object to this. I think they cannot . . . call upon us to grant them an additional number of Representatives simply because in consequence of their own misconduct they have lost the property which they once possessed, and which served as a basis in great part of their representation.

The committee thought this should no longer be permitted, and they thought it wiser to adopt a general principle applicable to all the States alike, namely, that where a State excludes any part of its male citizens from the elective franchise, it shall lose Representatives in proportion to the number so excluded[.] . . .

THE *SLAUGHTERHOUSE CASES*

83 U.S. 36 (1873)

T*he Slaughterhouse Cases* were the Supreme Court's first cases interpreting the new Thirteenth and Fourteenth Amendments. The Court recounted much of the history leading to the post–Civil War amendments, and their broad purpose of eliminating slavery and all racial discrimination by government. The Court then considered whether the amendments' broad terms could be construed to prevent a state (Louisiana) from granting an exclusive license to one company to operate an animal meat slaughterhouse within the city limits of New Orleans and prohibiting competing slaughterhouse businesses. The Court rejected such a construction, 5–4, as being beyond the amendment's intention and design.

❂

MR. JUSTICE MILLER DELIVERED THE OPINION OF THE COURT.

These cases . . . arise out of the efforts of the butchers of New Orleans to resist the Crescent City Live-Stock Landing and Slaughter-House Company in the exercise of certain powers conferred by the charter which created it, and which was granted by the legislature of that State. . . .

The first section forbids the landing or slaughtering of animals whose flesh is intended for food, within the city of New Orleans and other parishes and boundaries named and defined, or the keeping or establishing any slaughter-houses or abattoirs within those limits except by the corporation thereby created. . . . [T]he company . . . shall have the sole and exclusive privilege of conducting and carrying on the live-stock landing and slaughter-house business within the limits and privilege granted by the act, and that all such animals shall be landed at the stock-landings and slaughtered at the slaughter-houses of the company, and nowhere else. . . . This statute is denounced not only as creating a monopoly and conferring odious and exclusive privileges upon a small number of persons at the expense of the great body of the community of New Orleans, but it is asserted that it deprives a large and meritorious class of citizens—the whole of the butchers of the city—of the right to exercise their trade. . . .

The plaintiffs . . . allege that the statute is a violation of the Constitution of the United States in these several particulars:

That it creates an involuntary servitude forbidden by the thirteenth article of amendment;

That it abridges the privileges and immunities of citizens of the United States;

That it denies to the plaintiffs the equal protection of the laws; and,

That it deprives them of their property without due process of law, contrary to the provisions of the first section of the fourteenth article of amendment.

This court is thus called upon for the first time to give construction to these articles.

The most cursory glance at these articles discloses a unity of purpose, when taken in connection with the history of the times, which cannot fail to have an important bearing on any question of doubt concerning their true meaning. Nor can such doubts, when any reasonably exist, be safely and rationally solved without a reference to that history; for in it is found the occasion and the necessity for recurring again to the great source of power in this country, the people of the States, for additional guarantees of human rights; additional powers to the Federal government; additional restraints upon those of the States. Fortunately that history is fresh within the memory of us all, and its leading features, as they bear upon the matter before us, free from doubt.

The institution of African slavery, as it existed in about half the States of the Union, and the contests pervading the public mind for many years, between those who desired its curtailment and ultimate extinction and those who desired additional safeguards for its security and perpetuation, culminated in the effort, on the part of most of the States in which slavery existed, to separate from the Federal government, and to resist its authority. This constituted the war of the rebellion, and whatever auxiliary causes may have contributed to bring about this war, undoubtedly the overshadowing and efficient cause was African slavery.

In that struggle slavery, as a legalized social relation, perished. It perished as a necessity of the bitterness and force of the conflict. When the armies of freedom found themselves upon the soil of slavery they could do nothing less than free the poor victims whose enforced servitude was the foundation of the quarrel. And when hard pressed in the contest these men (for they proved them-selves men in that terrible crisis) offered their services and were accepted by thousands to aid in suppressing the unlawful rebellion, slavery was at an end wherever the Federal government succeeded in that purpose. The proclamation of President Lincoln expressed an accomplished fact as to a large portion of the insurrectionary districts, when he declared slavery abolished in them all. But the war being over, those who had succeeded in re-establishing the authority of the Federal government were not content to permit this great act of emancipation to rest on the actual results of the contest or the proclamation of the Executive, both of which might have been questioned in after times, and they determined to place this main and most valuable result in the Constitution of the restored Union as one of its fundamental articles. Hence the thirteenth article of amendment of that instrument. Its two short sections seem hardly to admit of construction, so vigorous is their expression and so appropriate to the purpose we have indicated.

1. Neither slavery nor involuntary servitude, except as a punishment for crime, whereof the party shall have been duly convicted, shall exist within the United States or any place subject to their jurisdiction.

2. Congress shall have power to enforce this article by appropriate legislation.

To withdraw the mind from the contemplation of this grand yet simple declaration of the personal freedom of all the human race within the jurisdiction of this government—a declaration designed to establish the freedom of four millions of slaves—and with a microscopic search endeavor to find in it a reference to servitudes, which may have been attached to property in certain localities, requires an effort, to say the least of it.

That a personal servitude was meant is proved by the use of the word "involuntary," which can only apply to human beings. The exception of servitude as a punishment for crime gives an idea of the class of servitude that is meant. The word servitude is of larger meaning than slavery, as the latter is popularly understood in this country, and the obvious purpose was to forbid all shades and conditions of African slavery. . . .

The process of restoring to their proper relations with the Federal government and with the other States those which had sided with the rebellion, undertaken under the proclamation of President Johnson in 1865, and before the assembling of Congress, developed the fact that, notwithstanding the formal recognition by those States of the abolition of slavery, the condition of the slave race would, without further protection of the Federal government, be almost as bad as it was before. Among the first acts of legislation adopted by several of the States in the legislative bodies which claimed to be in their normal relations with the Federal government, were laws which imposed upon the colored race onerous disabilities and burdens, and curtailed their rights in the pursuit of life, liberty, and property to such an extent that their freedom was of little value, while they had lost the protection which they had received from their former owners from motives both of interest and humanity.

They were in some States forbidden to appear in the towns in any other character than menial servants. They were required to reside on and cultivate the soil without the right to purchase or own it. They were excluded from many occupations of gain, and were not permitted to give testimony in the courts in any case where a white man was a party. It was said that their lives were at the mercy of bad men, either because the laws for their protection were insufficient or were not enforced.

These circumstances, whatever of falsehood or misconception may have been mingled with their presentation, forced upon the statesmen who had conducted the Federal government in safety through the crisis of the rebellion, and who supposed that by the thirteenth article of amendment they had secured the result of their labors, the conviction that something more was necessary in the way of constitutional protection to the unfortunate race who had suffered so much. They accordingly passed through Congress the proposition for the fourteenth amendment, and they declined to treat as restored to their full participation in the government of the Union the States which had been in insurrection, until they ratified that article. . . .

A few years' experience satisfied the thoughtful men who had been the authors of the other two amendments that, notwithstanding the restraints of those articles on the States, and the laws passed under the additional powers granted to Congress, these were inadequate for the protection of life, liberty, and property, without which freedom to the slave was no boon. They were in all those States denied the right of suffrage. The laws were administered by the white man alone. It was urged that a race of men distinctively marked as was the negro, living in the midst of another and dominant race, could never be fully secured in their person and their property without the right of suffrage.

Hence the fifteenth amendment, which declares that "the right of a citizen of the United States to vote shall not be denied or abridged by any State on account of race, color, or previous condition of servitude." The negro having, by the fourteenth amendment, been declared to be a citizen of the United States, is thus made a voter in every State of the Union.

We repeat, then, in the light of this recapitulation of events, almost too recent to be called history, but which are familiar to us all; and on the most casual examination of the language of these amendments, no one can fail to be impressed with the one pervading purpose found in them all . . . we mean the freedom of the slave race, the security and firm establishment of that freedom, and the protection of the newly-made freeman and citizen from the oppressions of those who had formerly exercised unlimited dominion over him. . . .

We do not say that no one else but the negro can share in this protection. Both the language and spirit of these articles are to have their fair and just weight in any question of construction. Undoubtedly while negro slavery alone was in the mind of the Congress which proposed the thirteenth article, it forbids any other kind of slavery, now or hereafter. If Mexican peonage or the Chinese coolie labor system shall develop slavery of the Mexican or Chinese race within our territory, this amendment may safely be trusted to make it void. And so if other rights are assailed by the States which properly and necessarily fall within the protection of these articles, that protection will apply, though the party interested may not be of African descent. But what we do say, and what we wish to be understood is, that in any fair and just construction of any section or phrase of these amendments, it is necessary to look to the purpose which we have said was the pervading spirit of them all, the evil which they were designed to remedy, and the process of continued addition to the Constitution, until that purpose was supposed to be accomplished, as far as constitutional law can accomplish it.

The first section of the fourteenth article, to which our attention is more specially invited, opens with a definition of citizenship—not only citizenship of the United States, but citizenship of the States. No such definition was previously found in the Constitution, nor had any attempt been made to define it by act of Congress. . . . But it had been held by this court, in the celebrated *Dred Scott* case, only a few years before the out-break of the civil war, that a man of African descent, whether a slave or not, was not and could not be a citizen of a State or of the United States. This decision, while it met the condemnation of some of the ablest statesmen and constitutional lawyers of the country, had never been overruled; and if it was to be accepted as a constitutional limitation of the right of citizenship, then all the negro race who had recently been made freemen, were still, not only not citizens, but were incapable of becoming so by anything short of an amendment to the Constitution.

To remove this difficulty primarily, and to establish a clear and comprehensive definition of citizenship which should declare what should constitute citizenship of the United States, and also citizenship of a State, the first clause of the first section was framed.

All persons born or naturalized in the United States, and subject to the jurisdiction thereof, are citizens of the United States and of the State wherein they reside.

[T]his clause . . . puts at rest both the questions which . . . have been the subject of differences of opinion. It declares that persons may be citizens of the United States without regard to their citizenship of a particular State, and it overturns the *Dred Scott* decision by making all persons born within the United States and subject to its jurisdiction citizens of the United States. . . .

[T]he distinction between citizenship of the United States and citizenship of a State is clearly recognized and established. . . . [T]here is a citizenship of the United States, and a citizenship of a State, which are distinct from each other, and which depend upon different characteristics or circumstances in the individual. . . . We think this distinction . . . of great weight in this argument, because the next paragraph of this same section . . . speaks only of privileges and immunities of citizens of the United States, and does not speak of those of citizens of the several States. The argument, however, in favor of the plaintiffs rests wholly on the assumption that the citizenship is the same, and the privileges and immunities guaranteed by the clause are the same.

The language is, "No State shall make or enforce any law which shall abridge the privileges or immunities of citizens of the United States." It is a little remarkable, if this clause was intended as a protection to the citizen of a State against the legislative power of his own State, that the word citizen of the State should be left out when it is so carefully used, and used in contradistinction to citizens of the United States, in the very sentence which precedes it. It is too clear for argument that the change in phraseology was adopted understandingly and with a purpose. . . .

If, then, there is a difference between the privileges and immunities belonging to a citizen of the United States as such, and those belonging to the citizen of the State as such the latter must rest for their security and protection where they have heretofore rested; for they are not embraced by this paragraph of the amendment. . . .

[The Court quoted and discussed the Privileges and Immunities Clause of Article IV, § 2—"The citizens of each State shall be entitled to all the privileges and immunities of citizens of the several States"—as well as prior judicial interpretation of that provision, including Justice Washington's opinion as a circuit judge, in *Corfield v. Coryell*. See p. 148. —Ed.] . . . [The] sole purpose [of this provision] was to declare to the several States, that whatever those rights, as you grant or establish them to your own citizens, or as you limit or qualify, or impose restrictions on their exercise, the same, neither more nor less, shall be the measure of the rights of citizens of other States within your jurisdiction. . . .

Was it the purpose of the fourteenth amendment, by the simple declaration that no State should make or enforce any law which shall abridge the privileges and immunities of citizens of the United States, to transfer the security and protection of all the civil rights which we have mentioned, from the States to the Federal government? And where it is declared that Congress shall have the power to enforce that article, was it intended to bring within the power of Congress the entire domain of civil rights heretofore belonging exclusively to the States?

All this and more must follow, if the proposition of the plaintiffs in error be sound. For not only are these rights subject to the control of Congress whenever in its discretion any of them are supposed to be abridged by State legislation, but that body may also pass laws in advance, limiting and restricting the exercise of legislative power by the States, in their most ordinary and usual functions, as in its judgment it may think proper on all such subjects. And still further, such a construction . . . would constitute this court a perpetual censor upon all legislation of the States, on the civil rights of their own citizens, with authority to nullify such as it did not approve as consistent with those rights, as they existed at the time of the adoption of this amendment. . . .

We are convinced that no such results were intended by the Congress which proposed these amendments, nor by the legislatures of the States which ratified them.

Having shown that the privileges and immunities relied on in the argument are those which belong to citizens of the States as such, and that they are left to the State governments for security and protection, and not by this article placed under the special care of the Federal government, we may hold ourselves excused from defining the privileges and immunities of citizens of the United States which no State can abridge, until some case involving those privileges may make it necessary to do so. . . .

The argument has not been much pressed in these cases that the defendant's charter deprives the plaintiffs of their property without due process of law, or that it denies to them the equal protection of the law. The first of these paragraphs has been in the Constitution since the adoption of the fifth amendment, as a restraint upon the Federal power. . . .[I]t is sufficient to say that under no construction of that provision that we have ever seen, or any that we deem admissible, can the restraint imposed by the State of Louisiana upon the exercise of their trade by the butchers of New Orleans be held to be a deprivation of property within the meaning of that provision.

Nor shall any State deny to any person within its jurisdiction the equal protection of the laws. In the light of the history of these amendments, and the pervading purpose of them, which we have already discussed, it is not difficult to give a meaning to this clause. The existence of laws in the States where the newly emancipated negroes resided, which discriminated with gross injustice and hardship against them as a class, was the evil to be remedied by this clause, and by it such laws are forbidden.

If, however, the States did not conform their laws to its requirements, then by the fifth section of the article of amendment Congress was authorized to enforce it by suitable legislation. We doubt very much whether any action of a State not directed by way of discrimination against the negroes as a class, or on account of their race, will ever be held to come within the purview of this provision. It is so clearly a provision for that race and that emergency, that a strong case would be necessary for its application to any other. . . .We find no such case in the one before us. . . .

MR. JUSTICE FIELD, DISSENTING.

 . . . The act of Louisiana presents the naked case, unaccompanied by any public considerations, where a right to pursue a lawful and necessary calling, previously enjoyed by every citizen, and in connection with which a thousand persons were daily employed, is taken away and vested exclusively for twenty-five years, for an extensive district and a large population, in a single corporation. . . .

The counsel for the plaintiffs in error have contended, with great force, that the act in question is . . . inhibited by the thirteenth amendment. That amendment prohibits slavery and involuntary servitude, except as a punishment for crime, but I have not supposed it was susceptible of a construction which would cover the enactment in question. I have been so accustomed to regard it as intended to meet that form of slavery which had previously prevailed in this country, and to which the recent civil war owed its existence, that I was not prepared, nor am I yet, to give to it the extent and force ascribed by counsel. Still it is evident that the language of the amendment is not used in a restrictive sense. It is not confined to African slavery alone. It is general and universal in its application. Slavery of white men as well as of black men is prohibited, and not merely slavery in the strict sense of the term, but involuntary servitude in every form. . . .

The abolition of slavery and involuntary servitude was intended to make every one born in this country a freeman, and as such to give to him the right to pursue the ordinary avocations of life without other restraint than such as affects all others, and to enjoy equally with them the fruits of his labor. A prohibition to him to pursue certain callings, open to others of the same age, condition, and sex, or to reside in places where others are permitted to live, would so far deprive him of the rights of a freeman, and would place him, as respects others, in a condition of servitude. A person allowed to pursue only one trade or calling, and only in one locality of the country, would not be, in the strict sense of the term, in a condition of slavery, but probably none would deny that he would be in a condition of servitude. He certainly would not possess the liberties nor enjoy the privileges of a freeman. The compulsion which would force him to labor even for his own benefit only in one direction, or in one place, would be almost as oppressive and nearly as great an invasion of his liberty as the compulsion which would force him to labor for the benefit or pleasure of another, and would equally constitute an element of servitude. . . .

It is not necessary, however . . . to rest my objections to the act in question upon the terms and meaning of the thirteenth amendment. The provisions of the fourteenth amendment, which is properly a supplement to the thirteenth, cover, in my judgment, the case before us . . . The first clause of this amendment determines who are citizens of the United States, and how their citizenship is created. . . . A citizen of a State is now only a citizen of the United States residing in that State. The fundamental rights, privileges, and immunities which belong to him as a free man and a free citizen, now belong to him as a citizen of the United States, and are not dependent upon his citizenship of any State. . . .

The amendment does not attempt to confer any new privileges or immunities upon citizens, or to enumerate or define those already existing. It assumes that there are such privileges and immunities which belong of right to citizens as such, and ordains that they shall not be abridged by State legislation. If this inhibition . . . only refers, as held by the majority of the court in their opinion, to such privileges and immunities as were before its adoption specially designated in the Constitution or necessarily implied as belonging to citizens of the United States, it was a vain and idle enactment, which accomplished nothing, and most unnecessarily excited Congress and the people on its passage. . . . The supremacy of the Constitution and the laws of the United States always, controlled any State legislation of that character. But if the amendment refers to the natural and inalienable rights which belong to all citizens, the inhibition has a profound significance and consequence.

What, then, are the privileges and immunities which are secured against abridgment by State legislation?

In the first section of the Civil Rights Act [of 1866] Congress has given its interpretation to these terms, or at least has stated some of the rights which, in its judgment, these terms include; it has there declared that they include the right "to make and enforce contracts, to sue, be parties and give evidence, to inherit, purchase, lease, sell, hold, and convey real and personal property, and to full and equal benefit of all laws and proceedings for the security of person and property." That act, it is true, was passed before the fourteenth amendment, but the amendment was adopted . . . to obviate objections to legislation of a similar character, extending the protection of the National government over the common rights of all citizens of the United States. Accordingly, after its ratification, Congress reenacted the act under the belief that whatever doubts may have previously existed of its validity, they were removed by the amendment.

The terms, privileges and immunities, are not new in the amendment; they were in the Constitution before the amendment was adopted. They are found in the second section of the fourth article, which declares that "the citizens of each State shall be entitled to all privileges and immunities of citizens in the several States," and they have been the subject of frequent consideration in judicial decisions. . . . The privileges and immunities designated are those which of right belong to the citizens of all free governments. Clearly among these must be placed the right to pursue a lawful employment in a lawful manner, without other restraint than such as equally affects all persons. . . .

What the clause in question did for the protection of the citizens of one State against hostile and discriminating legislation of other States, the fourteenth amendment does for the protection of every citizen of the United States against hostile and discriminating legislation against him in favor of others, whether they reside in the same or in different States. If under the fourth article of the Constitution equality of privileges and immunities is secured between citizens of different States, under the fourteenth amendment the same equality is secured between citizens of the United States.

It will not be pretended that under the fourth article of the Constitution any State could create a monopoly in any known trade or manufacture in favor of her own citizens, or any portion of them, which would exclude an equal participation in the trade or manufacture monopolized by citizens of other States. . . . [W]hat the clause in question does for the protection of citizens of one State against the creation of monopolies in favor of citizens of other States, the fourteenth amendment does for the protection of every citizen of the United States against the creation of any monopoly whatever. . . .

BRADWELL v. ILLINOIS
AND MINOR v. HAPPERSETT

*B*radwell v. Illinois upheld an Illinois Supreme Court decision denying Myra Bradwell a license to practice law
because of her sex. The majority rejected the claim that
this deprived Mrs. Bradwell of one of the "privileges or immunities" of
citizens, citing its decision in The *Slaughterhouse Cases* the previous day.
Three justices concurred on different grounds, and Chief Justice Chase
dissented. The Court did not focus on whether the Equal Protection
Clause of the Fourteenth Amendment might forbid state governmental
discrimination on the basis of sex. *Bradwell's* tolerance of sex discrimination endured for nearly a century, until the Supreme Court, beginning in the 1970s, held that the Fourteenth Amendment bars most
state laws classifying persons on the basis of sex without true biological
justification.

   Minor v. Happersett, decided the next year, held unanimously that the
Fourteenth Amendment did not confer upon women the right to vote in
state elections. It was not until the adoption of the Nineteenth Amendment, in 1920, that women obtained the constitutional right to vote in
national and state elections.

✪

Bradwell v. Illinois
83 U.S. 130 (1873)

•

MR. JUSTICE MILLER DELIVERED THE OPINION OF THE COURT.

The record in this case is not very perfect, but it may be fairly taken that the plaintiff asserted her right to a license on the grounds, among others, that she was a citizen of the United States, and that having been a citizen of Vermont at one time, she was, in the State of Illinois, entitled to any right granted to citizens of the latter State. . . .

As regards the provision of the Constitution that citizens of each State shall be entitled to all the privileges and immunities of citizens in the several States [Article IV, § 2] the plaintiff in her affidavit has stated very clearly a case to which it is inapplicable.

The protection designed by that clause, as has been repeatedly held, has no application to a citizen of the State whose laws are complained of. If the plaintiff was a citizen of the State of Illinois, that provision of the Constitution gave her no protection against its courts or its legislation. . . .

In regard to [the Fourteenth Amendment,] counsel for the plaintiff in this court truly says that there are certain privileges and immunities which belong to a citizen of the United States as such; otherwise it would be nonsense for the fourteenth amendment to prohibit a State from abridging them, and he proceeds to argue that admission to the bar of a State of a person who possesses the requisite learning and character is one of those which a State may not deny.

In this latter proposition we are not able to concur with counsel. We agree with him that there are privileges and immunities belonging to citizens of the United States, in that relation and character, and that it is these and these alone which a State is forbidden to abridge. But the right to admission to practice in the courts of a State is not one of them. This right in no sense depends on citizenship of the United States. It has not, as far as we know, ever been made in any State, or in any case, to depend on citizenship at all. Certainly many prominent and distinguished lawyers have been admitted to practice, both in the State and Federal courts, who were not citizens of the United States or of any State. But, on whatever basis this right may be placed, so far as it can have any relation to citizenship at all, it would seem that, as to the courts of a State, it would relate to citizenship of the State, and as to Federal courts, it would relate to citizenship of the United States.

The opinion just delivered in the Slaughter-House Cases renders elaborate argument in the present case unnecessary; for, unless we are wholly and radically mistaken in the principles on which those cases are decided, the right to control and regulate the granting of license to practice law in the courts of a State is one of those powers which are not transferred for its protection to the Federal government, and its exercise is in no manner governed or controlled by citizenship of the United States in the party seeking such license. . . .

MR. JUSTICE BRADLEY [CONCURRING]:

I concur in the judgment of the court in this case, by which the judgment of the Supreme Court of Illinois is affirmed, but not for the reasons specified in the opinion just read. . . . [T]he civil law, as well as nature herself, has always recognized a wide difference in the respective spheres and destinies of man and woman. Man is, or should be, woman's protector and defender. The natural and proper timidity and delicacy which belongs to the female sex evidently unfits it for many of the occupations of civil life. The constitution of the family organization, which is founded in the divine ordinance, as well as in the nature of things, indicates the domestic sphere as that which properly belongs to the domain and functions of womanhood. The harmony, not to say identity, of interest and views which belong, or should belong, to the family institution is repugnant to the idea of a woman adopting a distinct and independent career from that of her husband. So firmly fixed was this sentiment in the founders of the common law that it became a maxim of that system of jurisprudence that a woman had no legal existence separate from her husband, who was regarded as her head and representative in the social state; and, notwithstanding some recent modifications of this civil status, many of the special rules of law flowing from and dependent upon this cardinal principle still exist in full force in most States. One of these is, that a married woman is incapable, without her husband's consent, of making contracts which shall be binding on her or him. This very incapacity was one circumstance which the Supreme Court of Illinois deemed important in rendering a married woman incompetent fully to perform the duties and trusts that belong to the office of an attorney and counsellor.

It is true that many women are unmarried and not affected by any of the duties, complications, and incapacities arising out of the married state, but these are exceptions to the general rule. The paramount destiny and mission of woman are to fulfil the noble and benign offices of wife and mother. This is the law of the Creator. And the rules of civil society must be adapted to the general constitution of things, and cannot be based upon exceptional cases.

The humane movements of modern society, which have for their object the multiplication of avenues for woman's advancement, and of occupations adapted to her condition and sex, have my heartiest concurrence. But I am not prepared to say that it is one of her fundamental rights and privileges to be admitted into every office and position, including those which require highly special qualifications and demanding special responsibilities. . . .

Minor v. Happersett
88 U.S. 162 (1874)

•

THE CHIEF JUSTICE DELIVERED THE OPINION OF THE COURT.

The question is presented in this case, whether, since the adoption of the fourteenth amendment, a woman, who is a citizen of the United States and of the State of Missouri, is a voter in that State, notwithstanding the provision of the constitution and laws of the State, which confine the right of suffrage to men alone. . . .

It is contended that the provisions of the constitution and laws of the State of Missouri which confine the right of suffrage and registration therefor to men, are in violation of the Constitution of the United States, and therefore void. The argument is, that as a woman, born or naturalized in the United States and subject to the jurisdiction thereof, is a citizen of the United States and of the State in which she resides, she has the right of suffrage as one of the privileges and immunities of her citizenship, which the State cannot by its laws or constitution abridge.

There is no doubt that women may be citizens. They are persons, and by the fourteenth amendment "all persons born or naturalized in the United States and subject to the jurisdiction thereof" are expressly declared to be "citizens of the United States and of the State wherein they reside." But, in our opinion, it did not need this amendment to give them that position. . . . [S]ex has never been made one of the elements of citizenship in the United States. In this respect men have never had an advantage over women. The same laws precisely apply to both. The fourteenth amendment did not affect the citizenship of women any more than it did of men. In this particular, therefore, the rights of Mrs. Minor do not depend upon the amendment. She has always been a citizen from her birth, and entitled to all the privileges and immunities of citizenship. . . .

If the right of suffrage is one of the necessary privileges of a citizen of the United States, then the constitution and laws of Missouri confining it to men are in violation of the Constitution of the United States, as amended, and consequently void. The direct question is, therefore, presented whether all citizens are necessarily voters.

The Constitution does not define the privileges and immunities of citizens. For that definition we must look elsewhere. In this case we need not determine what they are, but only whether suffrage is necessarily one of them.

It certainly is nowhere made so in express terms. The United States has no voters in the States of its own creation. The elective officers of the United States are all elected directly or indirectly by State voters. The members of the House of Representatives are to be chosen by the people of the States, and the electors in each State must have the qualifications requisite for electors of the most numerous branch of the State legislature. Senators are to be chosen by the legislatures of the States, and necessarily the members of the legislature required to make the choice are elected by the voters of the State. . . .

The amendment did not add to the privileges and immunities of a citizen. It simply furnished an additional guaranty for the protection of such as he already had. No new voters were necessarily made by it.

Indirectly it may have had that effect, because it may have increased the number of citizens entitled to suffrage under the constitution and laws of the States, but it operates for this purpose, if at all, through the States and the State laws, and not directly upon the citizen.

It is clear, therefore, we think, that the Constitution has not added the right of suffrage to the privileges and immunities of citizenship as they existed at the time it was adopted. This makes it proper to inquire whether suffrage was coextensive with the citizenship of the States at the time of its adoption. If it was, then it may with force be argued that suffrage was one of the rights which belonged to citizenship, and in the enjoyment of which every citizen must be protected. But if it was not, the contrary may with propriety be assumed. . . .

Upon an examination of [state] constitutions [at the time the U.S. Constitution was adopted,] we find that in no State were all citizens permitted to vote. Each State determined for itself who should have that power. . . . In this condition of the law in respect to suffrage in the several States it cannot for a moment be doubted that if it had been intended to make all citizens of the United States voters, the framers of the Constitution would not have left it to implication. So important a change in the condition of citizenship as it actually existed, if intended, would have been expressly declared.

But if further proof is necessary to show that no such change was intended, it can easily be found both in and out of the Constitution. . . . [B]y the very terms of the amendment we have been considering, "Representatives shall be apportioned among the several States according to their respective numbers, counting the whole number of persons in each State, excluding Indians not taxed. But when the right to vote at any election for the choice of electors for President and Vice-President of the United States, representatives in Congress, the executive and judicial officers of a State, or the members of the legislature thereof, is denied to any of the male inhabitants of such State, being twenty-one years of age and citizens of the United States, or in any way abridged, except for participation in the rebellion, or other crimes, the basis of representation therein shall be reduced in the proportion which the number of such male citizens shall bear to the whole number of male citizens twenty-one years of age in such State." Why this, if it was not in the power of the legislature to deny the right of suffrage to some male inhabitants? And if suffrage was necessarily one of the absolute rights of citizenship, why confine the operation of the limitation to male inhabitants? Women and children are, as we have seen, "persons." They are counted in the enumeration upon which the apportionment is to be made, but if they were necessarily voters because of their citizenship unless clearly excluded, why inflict the penalty for the exclusion of males alone? Clearly, no such form of words would have been selected to express the idea here indicated if suffrage was the absolute right of all citizens.

And still again, after the adoption of the fourteenth amendment, it was deemed necessary to adopt a fifteenth, as follows: "The right of citizens of the United States to vote shall not be denied or abridged by the United States, or by any State, on account of race, color, or previous condition of servitude." The fourteenth amendment had already provided that no State should make or enforce any law which should abridge the privileges or immunities of citizens of the United States. If suffrage was one of these privileges or immunities, why amend the Constitution to prevent its being denied on account of race, &c.? . . .

We have given this case the careful consideration its importance demands. If the law is wrong, it ought to be changed; but the power for that is not with us. The arguments addressed to us bearing upon such a view of the subject may perhaps be sufficient to induce those having the power, to make the alteration, but they ought not to be permitted to influence our judgment in determining the present rights of the parties now litigating before us. No argument as to woman's need of suffrage can be considered. We can only act upon her rights as they exist. It is not for us to look at the hardship of withholding. Our duty is at an end if we find it is within the power of a State to withhold.

Being unanimously of the opinion that the Constitution of the United States does not confer the right of suffrage upon any one, and that the constitutions and laws of the several States which commit that important trust to men alone are not necessarily void, we AFFIRM THE JUDGMENT.

STRAUDER v. WEST VIRGINIA

100 U.S. 303 (1880)

الله

*S*trauder v. West Virginia, one of the Supreme Court's earliest cases interpreting the Fourteenth Amendment, concluded by a vote of 7–2 that the Equal Protection Clause forbids state discrimination on the basis of race in the content and administration of its laws. A decade and a half later, in *Plessy v. Ferguson* (1896), the Court would retreat from *Strauder*'s categorical statement of principle and would instead uphold laws mandating racial segregation. (See p. 192.) The Court would not return to *Strauder*'s vision for nearly sixty years, until *Brown v. Board of Education* in 1954. (See p. 268.)

✪

MR. JUSTICE STRONG DELIVERED THE OPINION OF THE COURT.

The plaintiff in error, a colored man, was indicted for murder in the Circuit Court of Ohio County, in West Virginia, on the 20th of October, 1874, and upon trial was convicted and sentenced. . . . [I]t is now, in substance, averred that at the trial in the State court the defendant (now plaintiff in error) was denied rights to which he was entitled under the Constitution and laws of the United States.

In the Circuit Court of the State, before the trial of the indictment was commenced, the defendant presented his petition, verified by his oath, praying for a removal of the cause into the Circuit Court of the United States, assigning, as ground for the removal, that "by virtue of the laws of the State of West Virginia no colored man was eligible to be a member of the grand jury or to serve on a petit jury in the State; that white men are so eligible, and that by reason of his being a colored man and having been a slave, he had reason to believe, and did believe, he could not have the full and equal benefit of all laws and proceedings in the State of West Virginia for the security of his person as is enjoyed by white citizens, and that he had less chance of enforcing in the courts of the State his rights on the prosecution, as a citizen of the United States, and that the probabilities of a denial of them to him as such citizen on every trial which might take place on the indictment in the courts of the State were much more enhanced than if he was a white man." This petition was denied by the State court, and the cause was forced to trial. . . .

In this court, several errors have been assigned, and the controlling questions underlying them all are, first, whether, by the Constitution and laws of the United States, every citizen of the United States has a right to a trial of an indictment against him by a jury selected and impanelled without discrimination against his race or color, because of race or color; and, second, if he has such a right, and is denied its enjoyment by the State in which he is indicted, may he cause the case to be removed into the Circuit Court of the United States?

It is to be observed that the first of these questions is not whether a colored man, when an indictment has been preferred against him, has a right to a grand or a petit jury composed in whole or in part of persons of his own race or color, but it is whether, in the composition or selection of jurors by whom he is to be indicted or tried, all persons of his race or color may be excluded by law, solely because of their race or color, so that by no possibility can any colored man sit upon the jury.

The questions are important, for they demand a construction of the recent amendments of the Constitution. . . . The Fourteenth Amendment . . . is one of a series of constitutional provisions having a common purpose; namely, securing to a race recently emancipated, a race that through many generations had been held in slavery, all the civil rights that the superior race enjoy. . . .

If this is the spirit and meaning of the amendment, whether it means more or not, it is to be construed liberally to carry out the purposes of its framers. It ordains that no State shall make or enforce any laws which shall abridge the privileges or immunities of citizens of the United States (evidently referring to the newly made citizens, who, being citizens of the United States, are declared to be also citizens of the State in which they reside). It ordains that no State shall deprive any person of life, liberty, or property, without due process of law, or deny to any person within its jurisdiction the equal protection of the laws. What is this but declaring that the law in the States shall be the same for the black as for the white; that all persons, whether colored or white, shall stand equal before the laws of the States, and, in regard to the colored race, for whose protection the amendment was primarily designed, that no discrimination shall be made against them by law because of their color? The words of the amendment, it is true, are prohibitory, but they contain a necessary implication of a positive immunity, or right, most valuable to the colored race, the right to exemption from unfriendly legislation against them distinctively as colored, exemption from legal discriminations, implying inferiority in civil society, lessening the security of their enjoyment of the rights which others enjoy, and discriminations which are steps towards reducing them to the condition of a subject race.

That the West Virginia statute respecting juries . . . is such a discrimination ought not to be doubted. Nor would it be if the persons excluded by it were white men. If in those States where the colored people constitute a majority of the entire population a law should be enacted excluding all white men from jury service, thus denying to them the privilege of participating equally with the blacks in the administration of justice, we apprehend no one would be heard to claim that it would not be a denial to white men of the equal protection of the laws. Nor if a law should be passed excluding all naturalized Celtic Irishmen, would there be any doubt of its inconsistency with the spirit of the amendment. The very fact that colored people are singled out and expressly denied by a statute all right to participate in the administration of the law, as jurors, because of their color, though they are citizens, and may be in other respects fully qualified, is practically a brand upon them, affixed by the law, an assertion of their inferiority, and a stimulant to that race prejudice which is an impediment to securing to individuals of the race that equal justice which the law aims to secure to all others.

The right to a trial by jury is guaranteed to every citizen of West

Virginia by the Constitution of that State, and the constitution of juries is a very essential part of the protection such a mode of trial is intended to secure. The very idea of a jury is a body of men composed of the peers or equals of the person whose rights it is selected or summoned to determine; that is, of his neighbors, fellows, associates, persons having the same legal status in society as that which he holds. . . . It is well known that prejudices often exist against particular classes in the community, which sway the judgment of jurors, and which, therefore, operate in some cases to deny to persons of those classes the full enjoyment of that protection which others enjoy. . . . In view of these considerations, it is hard to see why the statute of West Virginia should not be regarded as discriminating against a colored man when he is put upon trial for an alleged criminal offence against the State. . . . [H]ow can it be maintained that compelling a colored man to submit to a trial for his life by a jury drawn from a panel from which the State has expressly excluded every man of his race, because of color alone, however well qualified in other respects, is not a denial to him of equal legal protection? . . .

This act puts in the form of a statute what had been substantially ordained by the constitutional amendment. It was a step towards enforcing the constitutional provisions . . . fully warranted, we think, by the fifth section of the Fourteenth Amendment.

THE *CIVIL RIGHTS CASES*
109 U.S. 3 (1883)

ﷺ

T he *Civil Rights Cases* held that Congress lacked the power to directly prohibit discrimination by railroads, innkeepers, and places of public amusement, as it had done in the Civil Rights Act of 1875. The Court held: (1) that the Thirteenth Amendment's ban on slavery did not permit Congress to prohibit discrimination by private parties, (2) that the Fourteenth Amendment's ban on discrimination applied only to actions by state-government actors, and (3) that Congress's power to enforce the Fourteenth Amendment did not permit it to ban discrimination by private businesses. Justice John Marshall Harlan (grandfather of a future Supreme Court justice of the same name) issued a solo dissent challenging these holdings.

The *Civil Rights Cases* were foundational for much subsequent interpretation of the Thirteenth and Fourteenth amendments, both for the "state action" requirement and for the scope of Congress's enforcement powers. The Civil Rights Act of 1964, prohibiting discrimination in much commercial activity (such as in restaurants, inns, and in employment), rested on Congress's power to regulate interstate commerce because The *Civil Rights Cases* had foreclosed relying on the Fourteenth Amendment for such power.

✪

Mr. Justice BRADLEY DELIVERED THE OPINION OF THE
COURT.

. . . [T]he primary and important question in all the cases is the
constitutionality of the law [the Civil Rights Act of 1875]: for if the law
is unconstitutional, none of the prosecutions can stand. The sections of
the law referred to provide . . . [that] colored citizens, whether formerly
slaves or not, and citizens of other races, shall have the same accommodations and privileges in all inns, public conveyances, and places of
amusement, as are enjoyed by white citizens[.] . . .

Has congress constitutional power to make such a law? Of course, no
one will contend that the power to pass it was contained in the constitution before the adoption of the last three amendments. The power is
sought, first, in the Fourteenth Amendment[.] . . .

Individual invasion of individual rights is not the subject-matter
of the amendment. It has a deeper and broader scope. It nullifies and
makes void all state legislation, and state action of every kind, which
impairs the privileges and immunities of citizens of the United States,
or which injures them in life, liberty, or property without due process
of law, or which denies to any of them the equal protection of the laws.
It not only does this, but, in order that the national will, thus declared,
may not be a mere *brutum fulmen*, the last section of the amendment
invests congress with power to enforce it by appropriate legislation. To
enforce what? To enforce the prohibition. To adopt appropriate legislation for correcting the effects of such prohibited state law and state acts,
and thus to render them effectually null, void, and innocuous. This is
the legislative power conferred upon congress, and this is the whole
of it. It does not invest congress with power to legislate upon subjects
which are within the domain of state legislation; but to provide modes
of relief against state legislation, or state action, of the kind referred to.
It does not authorize congress to create a code of municipal law for the
regulation of private rights; but to provide modes of redress against the
operation of state laws, and the action of state officers, executive or judicial, when these are subversive of the fundamental rights specified in
the amendment. Positive rights and privileges are undoubtedly secured
by the fourteenth amendment; but they are secured by way of prohibition against state laws and state proceedings affecting those rights and
privileges, and by power given to congress to legislate for the purpose of

carrying such prohibition into effect; and such legislation must necessarily be predicated upon such supposed state laws or state proceedings, and be directed to the correction of their operation and effect. . . .

And so in the present case, until some state law has been passed, or some state action through its officers or agents has been taken, adverse to the rights of citizens sought to be protected by the fourteenth amendment, no legislation of the United States under said amendment, nor any proceeding under such legislation, can be called into activity, for the prohibitions of the amendment are against state laws and acts done under state authority.

. . . An inspection of the law shows that it makes no reference whatever to any supposed or apprehended violation of the fourteenth amendment on the part of the states. It is not predicated on any such view. It proceeds *ex directo* to declare that certain acts committed by individuals shall be deemed offenses, and shall be prosecuted and punished by proceedings in the courts of the United States. It does not profess to be corrective of any constitutional wrong committed by the states; it does not make its operation to depend upon any such wrong committed. . . .

In this connection, it is proper to state that civil rights, such as are guarantied by the constitution against state aggression, cannot be impaired by the wrongful acts of individuals, unsupported by state authority in the shape of laws, customs, or judicial or executive proceedings. The wrongful act of an individual, unsupported by any such authority, is simply a private wrong, or a crime of that individual; an invasion of the rights of the injured party, it is true, whether they affect his person, his property, or his reputation; but if not sanctioned in some way by the state, or not done under state authority, his rights remain in full force, and may presumably be vindicated by resort to the laws of the state for redress. . . .

The law in question, without any reference to adverse state legislation on the subject, declares that all persons shall be entitled to equal accommodation and privileges of inns, public conveyances, and places of public amusement, and imposes a penalty upon any individual who shall deny to any citizen such equal accommodations and privileges. This is not corrective legislation; it is primary and direct; it takes immediate and absolute possession of the subject of the right of admission to inns, public conveyances, and places of amusement. It supersedes and displaces state legislation on the same subject, or only allows it permissive force. It ignores such legislation, and assumes that the matter is one that belongs to the domain of national regulation. Whether it would not have been a more effective protection of the rights of citizens to have clothed congress with plenary power over the whole subject, is not now the question. What we have to decide is, whether such plenary power has been conferred upon congress by the fourteenth amendment, and, in our judgment, it has not. . . .

But the power of congress to adopt direct and primary, as distinguished from corrective, legislation on the subject in hand, is sought, in the second place, from the thirteenth amendment, which abolishes slavery. This amendment declares 'that neither slavery, nor involuntary servitude, except as a punishment for crime, whereof the party shall have been duly convicted, shall exist within the United States, or any place subject to their jurisdiction;' and it gives Congress power to enforce the amendment by appropriate legislation. . . . [S]uch legislation may be primary and direct in its character; for the amendment is not a mere prohibition of state laws establishing or upholding slavery, but an absolute declaration that slavery or involuntary servitude shall not exist in any part of the United States.

It is true that slavery cannot exist without law, any more than property in lands and goods can exist without law, and, therefore, the Thirteenth Amendment may be regarded as nullifying all State laws which establish or uphold slavery. But it has a reflex character also, establishing and decreeing universal civil and political freedom throughout the United States, and it is assumed that the power vested in congress to enforce the article by appropriate legislation, clothes congress with power to pass all laws necessary and proper for abolishing all badges and incidents of slavery in the United States; and upon this assumption it is claimed that this is sufficient authority for declaring by law that all persons shall have equal accommodations and privileges in all inns, public conveyances, and places of public amusement; the argument being that the denial of such equal accommodations and privileges is in itself a subjection to a species of servitude within the meaning of the amendment. Conceding the major proposition to be true, that that congress has a right to enact all necessary and proper laws for the obliteration and prevention of slavery, with all its badges and incidents, is the minor proposition also true, that the denial to any person of admission to the accommodations and privileges of an inn, a public conveyance, or a theater, does subject that person to any form of servitude, or tend to fasten upon him any badge of slavery? . . .

We must not forget that the province and scope of the thirteenth and fourteenth amendments are different: the former simply abolished slavery: the latter prohibited the states from abridging the privileges or immunities of citizens of the United States, from depriving them of life, liberty, or property without due process of law, and from denying to any the equal protection of the laws. The amendments are different, and the powers of congress under them are different. What congress has power to do under one, it may not have power to do under the other. . . . Under the thirteenth amendment the legislation, so far as necessary or proper to eradicate all forms and incidents of slavery and involuntary servitude, may be direct and primary, operating upon the acts of individuals, whether sanctioned by state legislation or not; under the fourteenth, as we have already shown, it must necessarily be, and can only be, corrective in its character, addressed to counteract and afford relief against state regulations or proceedings.

The only question under the present head, therefore, is, whether the refusal to any persons of the accommodations of an inn, or a public conveyance, or a place of public amusement, by an individual, and without any sanction or support from any state law or regulation, does inflict upon such persons any manner of servitude, or form of slavery, as those terms are understood in this country? Many wrongs may be obnoxious to the prohibitions of the fourteenth amendment which are not, in any just sense, incidents or elements of slavery. Such, for example, would be the taking of private property without due process of law; or allowing persons who have committed certain crimes (horse-stealing, for example) to be seized and hung by the *posse comitatus* without regular trial; or denying to any person, or class of persons, the right to pursue any peaceful avocations allowed to others. What is called class legislation would belong to this category, and would be obnoxious to the prohibitions of the fourteenth amendment, but would not to the prohibitions of the fourteenth when not involving the idea of any subjection of one man to another. The thirteenth amendment has respect, not to distinctions of race, or class, or color, but to slavery. The fourteenth amendment extends its protection to races and classes, and prohibits any state legislation which has the effect of denying to any race or class, or to any individual, the equal protection of the laws. . . .

After giving to these questions all the consideration which their importance demands, we are forced to the conclusion that such an act of refusal has nothing to do with slavery or involuntary servitude, and that if it is violative of any right of the party, his redress is to be sought under the laws of the state; or, if those laws are adverse to his rights and do not protect him, his remedy will be found in the corrective legislation which congress has adopted, or may adopt, for counteracting the effect of state laws, or state action, prohibited by the fourteenth amendment. It would be running the slavery argument into the ground to make it apply to every act of discrimination which a person may see fit to make as to the guests he will entertain, or as to the people he will take into his coach or cab or car, or admit to his concert or theater, or deal with in other matters of intercourse or business. . . . If the laws themselves make any unjust discrimination, amenable to the prohibitions of the fourteenth amendment, congress has full power to afford a remedy under that amendment and in accordance with it.

When a man has emerged from slavery, and by the aid of beneficent legislation has shaken off the inseparable concomitants of that state, there must be some stage in the progress of his elevation when he takes the rank of a mere citizen, and ceases to be the special favorite of the laws, and when his rights as a citizen, or a man, are to be protected in the ordinary modes by which other men's rights are protected. . . .

On the whole, we are of opinion that no countenance of authority for the passage of the law in question can be found in either the thirteenth or fourteenth amendment of the constitution; and no other ground of authority for its passage being suggested, it must necessarily be declared void, at least so far as its operation in the several states is concerned. . . .

HARLAN, J., DISSENTING.

The opinion in these case proceeds, as it seems to me, upon grounds entirely too narrow and artificial. I cannot resist the conclusion that the substance and spirit of the recent amendments of the constitution have been sacrificed by a subtle and ingenious verbal criticism. . . .

The Thirteenth Amendment, it is conceded, did something more than to prohibit slavery as an institution, resting upon distinctions of race, and upheld by positive law. My brethren admit that it established and decreed universal civil freedom throughout the United States. But did the freedom thus established involve nothing more than exemption from actual slavery? Was nothing more intended than to forbid one man from owning another as property? Was it the purpose of the nation simply to destroy the institution, and then remit the race, theretofore held in bondage, to the several states for such protection, in their civil rights, necessarily growing out of freedom, as those states, in their discretion, choose to provide? Were the states, against whose solemn protest the institution was destroyed, to be left perfectly free, so far as national interference was concerned, to make or allow discriminations against that race, as such, in the enjoyment of those fundamental rights that inhere in a state of freedom? . . .

That there are burdens and disabilities which constitute badges of slavery and servitude, and that the express power delegated to congress to enforce, by appropriate legislation, the thirteenth amendment, may be exerted by legislation of a direct and primary character, for the eradication, not simply of the institution, but of its badges and incidents, are propositions which ought to be deemed indisputable. They lie at the very foundation of the civil rights act of 1866. . . . Congress, by the act of 1866, passed in view of the thirteenth amendment, before the fourteenth was adopted, undertook to remove certain burdens and disabilities, the necessary incidents of slavery, and to secure to all citizens of every race and color, and without regard to previous servitude, those fundamental rights which are the essence of civil freedom, namely, the same right to make and enforce contracts, to sue, be parties, give evidence, and to inherit, purchase, lease, sell, and convey property as is enjoyed by white citizens.

. . . I do not contend that the thirteenth amendment invests congress with authority, by legislation, to regulate the entire body of the civil rights which citizens enjoy, or may enjoy, in the several states. But I do hold that since slavery, as the court has repeatedly declared, was the moving or principal cause of the adoption of that amendment, and since that institution rested wholly upon the inferiority, as a race, of those held in bondage, their freedom necessarily involved immunity from, and protection against, all discrimination against them, because of their race, in respect of such civil rights as belong to freemen of other races. Congress, therefore, under its express power to enforce that amendment, by appropriate legislation, may enact laws to protect that people against the deprivation, on account of their race, of any civil rights enjoyed by other freemen in the same state; and such legislation may be of a direct and primary character, operating upon states, their officers and agents, and also upon, at least, such individuals and corporations as exercise public functions and wield power and authority under the state. . . .

I am of the opinion that such discrimination practiced by corporations and individuals in the exercise of their public or quasi-public functions is a badge of servitude, the imposition of which congress may prevent under its power, by appropriate legislation, to enforce the thirteenth amendment; and consequently, without reference to its enlarged power under the fourteenth amendment, the act of March 1, 1875, is not, in my judgment, repugnant to the constitution.

It remains now to consider these cases with reference to the power congress has possessed since the adoption of the fourteenth amendment. . . . The assumption that this amendment consists wholly of prohibitions upon state laws and state proceedings in hostility to its provisions, is unauthorized by its language. The first clause of the first section—"all persons born or naturalized in the United States, and subject to the jurisdiction thereof, are citizens of the United States, and of the state wherein they reside"—is of a distinctly affirmative character. . . .

It is, therefore, an essential inquiry what, if any, right, privilege, or immunity was given by the nation to colored persons when they were made citizens of the state in which they reside? . . . That they became entitled, upon the adoption of the fourteenth amendment, "to all privileges and immunities of citizens in the several states," within the meaning of section 2 of article 4 of the constitution, no one, I suppose, will for a moment question. . . . But what was secured to colored citizens of the United States—as between them and their respective states—by the grant to them of state citizenship? With what rights, privileges, or immunities did this grant from the nation invest them? There is one, if there be no others—exemption from race discrimination in respect of any civil right belonging to citizens of the white race in the same state. That, surely, is their constitutional privilege when within the jurisdiction of other states. And such must be their constitutional right, in their own state, unless the recent amendments be "splendid baubles," thrown out to delude those who deserved fair and generous treatment at the hands of the nation. Citizenship in this country necessarily imports equality of civil rights among citizens of every race in the same state. . . .

But if it were conceded that the power of congress could not be brought into activity until the rights specified in the act of 1875 had been abridged or denied by some state law or state action, I maintain that the decision of the court is erroneous. There has been adverse state action within the fourteenth amendment. . . . In every material sense applicable to the practical enforcement of the fourteenth amendment, railroad corporations, keepers of inns, and managers of places of public amusement are agents of the state, because amenable, in respect of their public duties and functions, to public regulation. It seems to me that . . . a denial by these instrumentalities of the state to the citizen, because of his race, of that equality of civil rights secured to him by law, is a denial by the state within the meaning of the fourteenth amendment. . . .

It is, I submit, scarcely just to say that the colored race has been the special favorite of the laws. What the nation, through congress, has sought to accomplish in reference to that race is, what had already been done in every state in the Union for the white race, to secure and protect rights belonging to them as freemen and citizens; nothing more. The one underlying purpose of congressional legislation has been to enable the black race to take the rank of mere citizens. The difficulty has been to compel a recognition of their legal right to take that rank, and to secure the enjoyment of privileges belonging, under the law, to them as a component part of the people for whose welfare and happiness government is ordained. . . . The supreme law of the land has decreed that no authority shall be exercised in this country upon the basis of discrimination, in respect of civil rights, against freemen and citizens because of their race, color, or previous condition of servitude. To that decree—for the due enforcement of which, by appropriate legislation, congress has been invested with express power—every one must bow, whatever may have been, or whatever now are, his individual views as to the wisdom or policy, either of the recent changes in the fundamental law, or of the legislation which has been enacted to give them effect. . . .

From Reconstruction *to the* New Deal (1879–1919)

REYNOLDS *v.* UNITED STATES

98 U.S. 145 (1879)

~Ω~

*T*he Supreme Court's first major interpretation of the religious freedom provisions of the First Amendment did not occur until 1879, when it took up the case of George Reynolds, a Mormon charged with the federal crime of polygamy in Utah territory. Reynolds defended on the ground that the practice was part of the exercise of his religious convictions and thus protected by the First Amendment. The Court unanimously rejected the argument, adopting a narrow view of protected religious freedom under the Free Exercise Clause.

✪

MR. CHIEF JUSTICE WAITE DELIVERED THE OPINION OF THE COURT.

. . . On the trial, the plaintiff in error, the accused, proved that at the time of his alleged second marriage he was, and for many years before had been, a member of the Church of Jesus Christ of Latter-Day Saints, commonly called the Mormon Church, and a believer in its doctrines; that it was an accepted doctrine of that church 'that it was the duty of male members of said church, circumstances permitting, to practise polygamy; . . . that this duty was enjoined by different books which the members of said church believed to be of divine origin, and among others the Holy Bible, and also that the members of the church believed that the practice of polygamy was directly enjoined upon the male members thereof by the Almighty God, in a revelation to Joseph Smith, the founder and prophet of said church; that the failing or refusing to practise polygamy by such male members of said church, when circumstances would admit, would be punished, and that the penalty for such failure and refusal would be damnation in the life to come.' . . .

Upon this proof he asked the court to instruct the jury that if they found from the evidence that he 'was married as charged—if he was married—in pursuance of and in conformity with what he believed at the time to be a religious duty, that the verdict must be 'not guilty.'" This request was refused. . . .

Upon this . . . refusal to charge the question is raised, whether religious belief can be accepted as a justification of an overt act made criminal by the law of the land. The inquiry is not as to the power of Congress to prescribe criminal laws for the Territories, but as to the guilt of one who knowingly violates a law which has been properly enacted, if he entertains a religious belief that the law is wrong.

Congress cannot pass a law for the government of the Territories which shall prohibit the free exercise of religion. The first amendment to the Constitution expressly forbids such legislation. Religious freedom is guaranteed everywhere throughout the United States, so far as congressional interference is concerned. The question to be determined is, whether the law now under consideration comes within this prohibition.

The word 'religion' is not defined in the Constitution. We must go elsewhere, therefore, to ascertain its meaning, and nowhere more appropriately, we think, than to the history of the times in the midst of which the provision was adopted. The precise point of the inquiry is, what is the religious freedom which has been guaranteed.

Before the adoption of the Constitution, attempts were made in some of the colonies and States to legislate not only in respect to the establishment of religion, but in respect to its doctrines and precepts as well. The people were taxed, against their will, for the support of religion, and sometimes for the support of particular sects to whose tenets they could not and did not subscribe. Punishments were prescribed for a failure to attend upon public worship, and sometimes for entertaining heretical opinions. The controversy upon this general subject was animated in many of the States, but seemed at last to culminate in Virginia. In 1784, the House of Delegates of that State having under consideration 'a bill establishing provision for teachers of the Christian religion,' postponed it until the next session, and directed that the bill should be published and distributed, and that the people be requested 'to signify their opinion respecting the adoption of such a bill at the next session of assembly.'

This brought out a determined opposition. Amongst others, Mr. Madison prepared a 'Memorial and Remonstrance,' which was widely circulated and signed, and in which he demonstrated 'that religion, or the duty we owe the Creator,' was not within the cognizance of civil government. At the next session the proposed bill was not only defeated, but another, 'for establishing religious freedom,' drafted by Mr. Jefferson, was passed. In the preamble of this act religious freedom is defined; and after a recital 'that to suffer the civil magistrate to intrude his powers into the field of opinion, and to restrain the profession or propagation of principles on supposition of their ill tendency, is a dangerous fallacy which at once destroys all religious liberty,' it is declared 'that it is time enough for the rightful purposes of civil government for its officers to interfere when principles break out into overt acts against peace and good order.' In these two sentences is found the true distinction between what properly belongs to the church and what to the State. . . .

. . . [A]t the first session of the first Congress the amendment now under consideration was proposed with others by Mr. Madison. It met the views of the advocates of religious freedom, and was adopted. Mr. Jefferson afterwards, in reply to an address to him by a committee of the Danbury Baptist Association, took occasion to say: 'Believing with you that religion is a matter which lies solely between man and his God; that he owes account to none other for his faith or his worship; that the legislative powers of the government reach actions only, and not opinions—I contemplate with sovereign reverence that act of the whole American people which declared that their legislature should 'make no law respecting an establishment of religion or prohibiting the free exercise thereof,' thus building a wall of separation between church and State. Adhering to this expression of the supreme will of the nation in behalf of the rights of conscience, I shall see with sincere satisfaction the progress of those sentiments which tend to restore man to all his natural rights, convinced he has no natural right in opposition to his social duties.' Coming as this does from an acknowledged leader of the advocates of the measure, it may be accepted almost as an authoritative declaration of the scope and effect of the amendment thus secured. Congress was deprived of all legislative power over mere opinion, but was left free to reach actions which were in violation of social duties or subversive of good order.

Polygamy has always been odious among the northern and western nations of Europe, and, until the establishment of the Mormon Church, was almost exclusively a feature of the life of Asiatic and of African people. At common law, the second marriage was always void, and from the earliest history of England polygamy has been treated as an offence against society.... Marriage, while from its very nature a sacred obligation, is nevertheless, in most civilized nations, a civil contract, and usually regulated by law. Upon it society may be said to be built, and out of its fruits spring social relations and social obligations and duties, with which government is necessarily required to deal. In fact, according as monogamous or polygamous marriages are allowed, do we find the principles on which the government of the people, to a greater or less extent, rests. Professor Lieber says, polygamy leads to the patriarchal principle, and which, when applied to large communities, fetters the people in stationary despotism, while that principle cannot long exist in connection with monogamy. . . . [T]here cannot be a doubt that, unless restricted by some form of constitution, it is within the legitimate scope of the power of every civil government to determine whether polygamy or monogamy shall be the law of social life under its dominion.

In our opinion, the statute immediately under consideration is within the legislative power of Congress. It is constitutional and valid as prescribing a rule of action for all those residing in the Territories, and in places over which the United States have exclusive control. This being so, the only question which remains is, whether those who make polygamy a part of their religion are excepted from the operation of the statute. If they are, then those who do not make polygamy a part of their religious belief may be found guilty and punished, while those who do, must be acquitted and go free. This would be introducing a new element into criminal law. Laws are made for the government of actions, and while they cannot interfere with mere religious belief and opinions, they may with practices. Suppose one believed that human sacrifices were a necessary part of religious worship, would it be seriously contended that the civil government under which he lived could not interfere to prevent a sacrifice? Or if a wife religiously believed it was her duty to burn herself upon the funeral pyre of her dead husband, would it be beyond the power of the civil government to prevent her carrying her belief into practice?

So here, as a law of the organization of society under the exclusive dominion of the United States, it is provided that plural marriages shall not be allowed. Can a man excuse his practices to the contrary because of his religious belief? To permit this would be to make the professed doctrines of religious belief superior to the law of the land, and in effect to permit every citizen to become a law unto himself. Government could exist only in name under such circumstances. . . .

PLESSY v. FERGUSON
163 U.S. 537 (1896)

lessy v. Ferguson is the most famous of a series of post–Reconstruction era cases upholding laws or practices requiring racial segregation. The case arose from a challenge to a Louisiana law requiring segregation of the races in railroad passenger cars. The Court held that "separate but equal" treatment of different races did not violate the Constitution. Justice Harlan was the only dissenter. *Plessy* reigned for nearly sixty years, until *Brown v. Board of Education* (1954) repudiated the "separate but equal" doctrine in the context of public education, leading quickly to the doctrine's complete demise (see pp. 267–268).

✪

MR. JUSTICE BROWN DELIVERED THE OPINION OF THE COURT

The constitutionality of this act is attacked upon the ground that it conflicts both with the thirteenth amendment of the constitution, abolishing slavery, and the fourteenth amendment, which prohibits certain restrictive legislation on the part of the states. . . . That it does not conflict with the thirteenth amendment, which abolished slavery and involuntary servitude, except as a punishment for crime, is too clear for argument. . . . A statute which implies merely a legal distinction between the white and colored races—a distinction which is founded in the color of the two races, and which must always exist so long as white men are distinguished from the other race by color—has no tendency to destroy the legal equality of the two races, or re-establish a state of involuntary servitude. . . .

The object of the [Fourteenth] Amendment was undoubtedly to enforce the absolute equality of the two races before the law, but, in the nature of things, it could not have been intended to abolish distinctions based upon color, or to enforce social, as distinguished from political, equality, or a commingling of the two races upon terms unsatisfactory to either. Laws permitting, and even requiring, their separation, in places where they are liable to be brought into contact, do not necessarily imply the inferiority of either race to the other, and have been generally, if not universally, recognized as within the competency of the state legislatures in the exercise of their police power. The most common instance of this is connected with the establishment of separate schools for white and colored children, which have been held to be a valid exercise of the legislative power even by courts of states where the political rights of the colored race have been longest and most earnestly enforced. . . .

. . . [W]e think the enforced separation of the races, as applied to the internal commerce of the state, neither abridges the privileges or immunities of the colored man, deprives him of his property without due process of law, nor denies him the equal protection of the laws, within the meaning of the fourteenth amendment. . . .

In this connection, it is also suggested by the learned counsel for the plaintiff in error that the same argument that will justify the state legislature in requiring . . . colored people to walk upon one side of the street, and white people upon the other, or requiring white men's houses to be painted white, and colored men's black, or their vehicles or business signs to be of different colors, upon the theory that one side of the street is as good as the other, or that a house or vehicle of one color is as good as one of another color. The reply to all this is that every exercise of the police power must be reasonable, and extend only to such laws as are enacted in good faith for the promotion of the public good, and not for the annoyance or oppression of a particular class. . . .

So far, then, as a conflict with the fourteenth amendment is concerned, the case reduces itself to the question whether the statute of Louisiana is a reasonable regulation, and with respect to this there must necessarily be a large discretion on the part of the legislature. In determining the question of reasonableness, it is at liberty to act with reference to the established usages, customs, and traditions of the people, and with a view to the promotion of their comfort, and the preservation of the public peace and good order. Gauged by this standard, we cannot say that a law which authorizes or even requires the separation of the two races in public conveyances is unreasonable, or . . . obnoxious to the fourteenth amendment. . . .

We consider the underlying fallacy of the plaintiff's argument to consist in the assumption that the enforced separation of the two races stamps the colored race with a badge of inferiority. If this be so, it is not by reason of anything found in the act, but solely because the colored race chooses to put that construction upon it. The argument necessarily assumes that if . . . the colored race should become the dominant power in the state legislature, and should enact a law in precisely similar terms, it would thereby relegate the white race to an inferior position. We imagine that the white race, at least, would not acquiesce in this assumption. The argument also assumes that social prejudices may be overcome by legislation, and that equal rights cannot be secured to the negro except by an enforced commingling of the two races. We cannot accept this proposition. If the two races are to meet upon terms of social equality, it must be the result of natural affinities, a mutual appreciation of each other's merits, and a voluntary consent of individuals. . . . Legislation is powerless to eradicate racial instincts, or to abolish distinctions based upon physical differences, and the attempt to do so can only result in accentuating the difficulties of the present situation. If the civil and political rights of both races be equal, one cannot be inferior to the other civilly or politically. If one race be inferior to the other socially, the constitution of the United States cannot put them upon the same plane. . . .

MR. JUSTICE HARLAN DISSENTING.

By the Louisiana statute . . . the managers of the railroad . . . are required to assign each passenger to some coach or compartment set apart for the exclusive use of his race. . . . Thus, the state regulates the use of a public highway by citizens of the United States solely upon the basis of race . . . I deny that any legislative body or judicial tribunal may have regard to the race of citizens when the civil rights of those citizens are involved. . . .

It was said in argument that the statute of Louisiana does not discriminate against either race, but prescribes a rule applicable alike to white and colored citizens. But this argument does not meet the difficulty. Every one knows that the statute in question had its origin in the purpose, not so much to exclude white persons from railroad cars occupied by blacks, as to exclude colored people from coaches occupied by or assigned to white persons. . . . The thing to accomplish was, under the guise of giving equal accommodation for whites and blacks, to compel the latter to keep to themselves while traveling in railroad passenger coaches. No one would be so wanting in candor as to assert the contrary. . . .

If a state can prescribe, as a rule of civil conduct, that whites and blacks shall not travel as passengers in the same railroad coach, why may it not so regulate the use of the streets of its cities and towns as to compel white citizens to keep on one side of a street, and black citizens to keep on the other? Why may it not, upon like grounds, punish whites and blacks who ride together in street cars or in open vehicles on a public road or street? Why may it not require sheriffs to assign whites to one side of a court room, and blacks to the other? And why may it not also prohibit the commingling of the two races in the galleries of legislative halls or in public assemblages convened for the consideration of the political questions of the day? Further, if this statute of Louisiana is consistent with the personal liberty of citizens, why may not the state require the separation in railroad coaches of native and naturalized citizens of the United States, or of Protestants and Roman Catholics? . . . The white race deems itself to be the dominant race in this country. And so it is, in prestige, in achievements, in education, in wealth, and in power. So, I doubt not, it will continue to be for all time, if it remains true to its great heritage, and holds fast to the principles of constitutional liberty. But in view of the constitution, in the eye of the law, there is in this country no superior, dominant, ruling class of citizens. There is no caste here. Our constitution is color-blind, and neither knows nor tolerates classes among citizens. In respect of civil rights, all citizens are equal before the law. The humblest is the peer of the most powerful.

The law regards man as man, and takes no account of his surroundings or of his color when his civil rights as guaranteed by the supreme law of the land are involved. . . .

In my opinion, the judgment this day rendered will, in time, prove to be quite as pernicious as the decision made by this tribunal in the *Dred Scott* Case.

It was adjudged in that case that the descendants of Africans who were imported into this country, and sold as slaves, were not included nor intended to be included under the word "citizens" in the constitution, and could not claim any of the rights and privileges which that instrument provided for and secured to citizens of the United States; that, at time of the adoption of the constitution, they were "considered as a subordinate and inferior class of beings, who had been subjugated by the dominant race, and, whether emancipated or not, yet remained subject to their authority, and had no rights or privileges but such as those who held the power and the government might choose to grant them." The recent amendments of the constitution, it was supposed, had eradicated these principles from our institutions. But it seems that we have yet, in some of the states, a dominant race—a superior class of citizens—which assumes to regulate the enjoyment of civil rights, common to all citizens, upon the basis of race. The present decision, it may well be apprehended, will not only stimulate aggressions, more or less brutal and irritating, upon the admitted rights of colored citizens, but will encourage the belief that it is possible, by means of state enactments, to defeat the beneficent purposes which the people of the United States had in view when they adopted the recent amendments of the constitution, by one of which the blacks of this country were made citizens of the United States and of the states in which they respectively reside, and whose privileges and immunities, as citizens, the states are forbidden to abridge. . . . The destinies of the two races, in this country, are indissolubly linked together, and the interests of both require that the common government of all shall not permit the seeds of race hate to be planted under the sanction of law. What can more certainly arouse race hate, what more certainly create and perpetuate a feeling of distrust between these races, than state enactments which, in fact, proceed on the ground that colored citizens are so inferior and degraded that they cannot be allowed to sit in public coaches occupied by white citizens? That, as all will admit, is the real meaning of such legislation as was enacted in Louisiana.

The sure guaranty of the peace and security of each race is the clear, distinct, unconditional recognition by our governments, national and state, of every right that inheres in civil freedom, and of the equality before the law of all citizens of the United States, without regard to race. State enactments regulating the enjoyment of civil rights upon the basis of race, and cunningly devised to defeat legitimate results of the war, under the pretense of recognizing equality of rights, can have no other result than to render permanent peace impossible, and to keep alive a conflict of races, the continuance of which must do harm to all concerned. . . .

It is scarcely just to say that a colored citizen should not object to occupying a public coach assigned to his own race. He does not object, nor, perhaps, would he object to separate coaches for his race if his rights under the law were recognized. But he does object, and he ought never to cease objecting, that citizens of the white and black races can be adjudged criminals because they sit, or claim the right to sit, in the same public coach on a public highway.

The arbitrary separation of citizens, on the basis of race, while they are on a public highway, is a badge of servitude wholly inconsistent with the civil freedom and the equality before the law established by the constitution. It cannot be justified upon any legal grounds.

If evils will result from the commingling of the two races upon public highways established for the benefit of all, they will be infinitely less than those that will surely come from state legislation regulating the enjoyment of civil rights upon the basis of race. We boast of the freedom enjoyed by our people above all other peoples. But it is difficult to reconcile that boast with a state of the law which, practically, puts the brand of servitude and degradation upon a large class of our fellow citizens—our equals before the law. The thin disguise of "equal" accommodations for passengers in railroad coaches will not mislead any one, nor atone for the wrong this day done.

LOCHNER v. NEW YORK

198 U.S. 44 (1905)

ochner is the signature decision of its era, the roughly forty years (ca. 1897–1937) during which the Supreme Court invalidated nearly 200 state and federal economic and social regulations that it considered violations of "liberty" under the Due Process Clauses of the Fifth and Fourteenth amendments. In *Lochner* itself, the Court struck down, by a vote of 5–4, a New York law providing that bakers could work no more than sixty hours a week. The *Lochner* approach, known as "substantive due process," was eventually repudiated in 1937 in *West Coast Hotel v. Parrish* (see p. 210) and in subsequent cases.

❂

MR. JUSTICE PECKHAM DELIVERED THE OPINION OF THE COURT:

The indictment, it will be seen, charges that the plaintiff in error violated . . . the labor law of the state of New York, in that he wrongfully and unlawfully required and permitted an employee working for him to work more than sixty hours in one week. . . . The mandate of the statute, that 'no employee shall be required or permitted to work,' is the substantial equivalent of an enactment that 'no employee shall contract or agree to work,' more than ten hours per day; and, as there is no provision for special emergencies, the statute is mandatory in all cases. . . .

The statute necessarily interferes with the right of contract between the employer and employees, concerning the number of hours in which the latter may labor in the bakery of the employer. The general right to make a contract in relation to his business is part of the liberty of the individual protected by the 14th Amendment of the Federal Constitution. Under that provision no state can deprive any person of life, liberty, or property without due process of law. The right to purchase or to sell labor is part of the liberty protected by this amendment, unless there are circumstances which exclude the right. There are, however, certain powers, existing in the sovereignty of each state in the Union, somewhat vaguely termed police powers, the exact description and limitation of which have not been attempted by the courts. Those powers, broadly stated, and without, at present, any attempt at a more specific limitation, relate to the safety, health, morals, and general welfare of the public. Both property and liberty are held on such reasonable conditions as may be imposed by the governing power of the state in the exercise of those powers, and with such conditions the 14th Amendment was not designed to interfere. . . .

It must, of course, be conceded that there is a limit to the valued exercise of the police power by the state. There is no dispute concerning this general proposition. Otherwise the 14th Amendment would have no efficacy and the legislatures of the states would have unbounded power, and it would be enough to say that any piece of legislation was enacted to conserve the morals, the health, or the safety of the people; such legislation would be valid, no matter how absolutely without foundation the claim might be. . . . In every case that comes before this court, therefore, where legislation of this character is concerned, and where the protection of the Federal Constitution is sought, the question necessarily arises: Is this a fair, reasonable, and appropriate exercise of the police power of the state, or is it an unreasonable, unnecessary, and arbitrary interference with the right of the individual to his personal liberty, or to enter into those contracts in relation to labor which may seem to him appropriate or necessary for the support of himself and his family? . . .

There is no reasonable ground for interfering with the liberty of person or the right of free contract, by determining the hours of labor, in the occupation of a baker. . . . We think the limit of the police power has been reached and passed in this case. There is, in our judgment, no reasonable foundation for holding this to be necessary or appropriate as a health law to safeguard the public health, or the health of the individuals who are following the trade of a baker. If this statute be valid . . . there would seem to be no length to which legislation of this nature might not go. . . . It is unfortunately true that labor, even in any department, may possibly carry with it the seeds of unhealthiness. But are we all, on that account, at the mercy of legislative majorities? A printer, a tinsmith, a locksmith, a carpenter, a cabinetmaker, a dry goods clerk, a bank's, a lawyer's, or a physician's clerk, or a clerk in almost any kind of business, would all come under the power of the legislature, on this assumption. No trade, no occupation, no mode of earning one's living, could escape this all-pervading power, and the acts of the legislature in limiting the hours of labor in all employments would be valid, although such limitation might seriously cripple the ability of the laborer to support himself and his family. . . .

It is manifest to us that the limitation of the hours of labor as provided for in this section of the statute under which the indictment was found, and the plaintiff in error convicted, has no such direct relation to, and no such substantial effect upon, the health of the employee, as to justify us in regarding the section as really a health law. It seems to us that the real object and purpose were simply to regulate the hours of labor between the master and his employees . . . in a private business, not dangerous in any degree to morals, or in any real and substantial degree to the health of the employees. Under such circumstances the freedom of master and employee to contract with each other in relation to their employment, and in defining the same, cannot be prohibited or interfered with, without violating the Federal Constitution. . . .

MR. JUSTICE HOLMES, DISSENTING.

. . . This case is decided upon an economic theory which a large part of the country does not entertain. If it were a question whether I agreed with that theory, I should desire to study it further and long before making up my mind. But I do not conceive that to be my duty, because

I strongly believe that my agreement or disagreement has nothing to do with the right of a majority to embody their opinions in law. It is settled by various decisions of this court that state constitutions and state laws may regulate life in many ways which we as legislators might think as injudicious, or if you like as tyrannical, as this, and which, equally with this, interfere with the liberty to contract. Sunday laws and usury laws are ancient examples. A more modern one is the prohibition of lotteries. The liberty of the citizen to do as he likes so long as he does not interfere with the liberty of others to do the same, which has been a shibboleth for some well-known writers, is interfered with by school laws, by the Post office, by every state or municipal institution which takes his money for purposes thought desirable, whether he likes it or not. The 14th Amendment does not enact Mr. Herbert Spencer's Social Statics. . . . A Constitution is not intended to embody a particular economic theory, whether of paternalism and the organic relation of the citizen to the state or of *laissez faire*. It is made for people of fundamentally differing views, and the accident of our finding certain opinions natural and familiar, or novel, and even shocking, ought not to conclude our judgment upon the question whether statutes embodying them conflict with the Constitution of the United States.

. . . I think that the word 'liberty,' in the 14th Amendment, is perverted when it is held to prevent the natural outcome of a dominant opinion, unless it can be said that a rational and fair man necessarily would admit that the statute proposed would infringe fundamental principles as they have been understood by the traditions of our people and our law. It does not need research to show that no such sweeping condemnation can be passed upon the statute before us. . . .

SCHENCK *v.* UNITED STATES

AND

UNITED STATES *v.* DEBS

ᶜℓ

*I*n a group of cases in 1919, the Supreme Court upheld convictions obtained in prosecutions by the administration of President Woodrow Wilson for anti-war, anti-draft, or general anti-government advocacy, alleged to have violated the Sedition Act. The Court rejected First Amendment defenses, using what became known as the "clear and present danger" test, which prevailed for nearly fifty years. The lead case, *Schenck v. United States*, upheld a conviction for the distribution of a pamphlet arguing that the draft was unconstitutional and urging people to assert their rights. A week later, in *United States v. Debs*, the Court upheld the conviction of Socialist former presidential candidate Eugene V. Debs for anti-war advocacy. Both decisions were unanimous.

✪

Schenck v. United States
249 U.S. 47 (1919)

•

MR. JUSTICE HOLMES DELIVERED THE OPINION OF THE COURT:
This is an indictment in three counts. The first charges a conspiracy to violate the Espionage Act of June 15, 1917 by causing and attempting to cause insubordination, &c., in the military and naval forces
of the United States, and to obstruct the recruiting and enlistment service of the United States, when the United States was at war with the
German Empire, to-wit, that the defendants willfully conspired to have
printed and circulated to men who had been called and accepted for
military service . . . a document set forth and alleged to be calculated
to cause such insubordination and obstruction. The count alleges overt
acts in pursuance of the conspiracy, ending in the distribution of the
document set forth. The second count alleges a conspiracy to commit
an offence against the United States, to-wit, to use the mails for the
transmission of matter declared to be non-mailable by Title XII, § 2, of
the Act of June 15, 1917[.] . . . The third count charges an unlawful use
of the mails for the transmission of the same matter and otherwise as
above. The defendants were found guilty on all the counts. They set up
the First Amendment to the Constitution forbidding Congress to make
any law abridging the freedom of speech, or of the press[.] . . .

The document in question, upon its first printed side, recited the first
section of the Thirteenth Amendment, said that the idea embodied in it
was violated by the Conscription Act, and that a conscript is little better
than a convict. In impassioned language, it intimated that conscription
was despotism in its worst form, and a monstrous wrong against humanity
in the interest of Wall Street's chosen few. It said "Do not submit to in-
timidation," but in form, at least, confined itself to peaceful measures such
as a petition for the repeal of the act. The other and later printed side of
the sheet was headed "Assert Your Rights." It stated reasons for alleging
that anyone violated the Constitution when he refused to recognize "your
right to assert your opposition to the draft," and went on, "If you do not
assert and support your rights, you are helping to deny or disparage rights
which it is the solemn duty of all citizens and residents of the United States
to retain." It described the arguments on the other side as coming from

cunning politicians and a mercenary capitalist press, and even silent consent to the conscription law as helping to support an infamous conspiracy. It denied the power to send our citizens away to foreign shores to shoot up the people of other lands, and added that words could not express the condemnation such cold-blooded ruthlessness deserves, &c., &c., winding up, "You must do your share to maintain, support and uphold the rights of the people of this country." Of course, the document would not have been sent unless it had been intended to have some effect, and we do not see what effect it could be expected to have upon persons subject to the draft except to influence them to obstruct the carrying of it out. The defendants do not deny that the jury might find against them on this point.

But it is said, suppose that that was the tendency of this circular, it is protected by the First Amendment to the Constitution. . . . We admit that, in many places and in ordinary times, the defendants, in saying all that was said in the circular, would have been within their constitutional rights. But the character of every act depends upon the circumstances in which it is done. The most stringent protection of free speech would not protect a man in falsely shouting fire in a theatre and causing a panic. It does not even protect a man from an injunction against uttering words that may have all the effect of force. The question in every case is whether the words used are used in such circumstances and are of such a nature as to create a clear and present danger that they will bring about the substantive evils that Congress has a right to prevent. It is a question of proximity and degree. When a nation is at war, many things that might be said in time of peace are such a hindrance to its effort that their utterance will not be endured so long as men fight, and that no Court could regard them as protected by any constitutional right.

United States v. Debs
249 U.S. 211 (1919)

•

JUSTICE HOLMES DELIVERED THE OPINION OF THE COURT.

This is an indictment under the Espionage Act of June 15, 1917[.] . . . It has been cut down to two counts[.] . . . The former of these alleges that on or about June 16, 1918, at Canton, Ohio, the defendant caused and incited and attempted to cause and incite insubordination, disloyalty, mutiny and refusal of duty in the military and naval forces of the United States and with intent so to do delivered, to an assembly of people, a public speech, set forth. The [latter] count alleges that he obstructed and attempted to obstruct the recruiting and enlistment service of the United States and to that end and with that intent delivered the same speech, again set forth. . . . The defendant was found guilty and was sentenced to ten years' imprisonment on each of the two counts[.] . . .

The main theme of the speech was Socialism, its growth, and a prophecy of its ultimate success. . . . [I]f a part or the manifest intent of the more general utterances was to encourage those present to obstruct the recruiting service and if in passages such encouragement was directly given, the immunity of the general theme may not be enough to protect the speech. The speaker began by saying that he had just returned from a visit to the workhouse in the neighborhood where three of their most loyal comrades were paying the penalty for their devotion to the working class—these being Wagenknecht, Baker and Ruthenberg, who had been convicted of aiding and abetting another in failing to register for the draft. He said that he had to be prudent and might not be able to say all that he thought, thus intimating to his hearers that they might infer that he meant more, but he did say that those persons were paying the penalty for standing erect and for seeking to pave the way to better conditions for all mankind. Later he added further eulogies and said that he was proud of them. He then expressed opposition to Prussian militarism in a way that naturally might have been thought to be intended to include the mode of proceeding in the United States.

The defendant . . . said that the master class has always declared the war and the subject class has always fought the battles—that the subject class has had nothing to gain and all to lose, including their lives; that the working class, who furnish the corpses, have never yet had a voice in declaring war and never yet had a voice in declaring peace. 'You have your lives to lose; you certainly ought to have the right to declare war if you consider a war necessary.'

There followed personal experiences and illustrations of the growth of Socialism, a glorification of minorities, and a prophecy of the success of the international Socialist crusade, with the interjection that 'you need to know that you are fit for something better than slavery and cannon fodder.' The rest of the discourse had only the indirect though not necessarily ineffective bearing on the offences alleged that is to be found in the usual contrasts between capitalists and laboring men, sneers at the advice to cultivate war gardens, attribution to plutocrats of the high price of coal, &c., with the implication running through it all that the working men are not concerned in the war, and a final exhortation, 'Don't worry about the charge of treason to your masters; but be concerned about the treason that involves yourselves.' The defendant addressed the jury himself, and while contending that his speech did not warrant the charges said, 'I have been accused of obstructing the war. I admit it. Gentlemen, I abhor war. I would oppose the war if I stood alone.' The statement was not necessary to warrant the jury in finding that one purpose of the speech, whether incidental or not does not matter, was to oppose not only war in general but this war, and that the opposition was so expressed that its natural and intended effect would be to obstruct recruiting. If that was intended and if, in all the circumstances, that would be its probable effect, it would not be protected by reason of its being part of a general program and expressions of a general and conscientious belief.

The chief defences upon which the defendant seemed willing to rely were the denial that we have dealt with and that based upon the First Amendment to the Constitution, disposed of in *Schenck v. United States*, 249 U. S. 47. . . . [W]e are of opinion that the verdict . . . for obstructing and attempting to obstruct the recruiting service of the United States must be sustained. . . .

THE
NEW DEAL,
WORLD WAR II,
and the
COLD WAR
(1937–1952)

THE NEW DEAL "REVOLUTION"

⌇

*B*eginning in 1937, the Supreme Court repudiated earlier decisions narrowly interpreting Congress's power to
regulate business and labor practices and increasingly
began to uphold New Deal economic policies. *West Coast Hotel v. Parrish* (1937) marked a crucial turning point. By a 5–4 vote, the Court
rejected the substantive due process approach of *Lochner* and other
cases and overruled a case that had applied *Lochner* to invalidate state
minimum wage laws.

In another 5–4 decision two weeks later, *National Labor Relations
Board v. Jones & Laughlin Steel* (1937) became the first in a series of decisions in which the Court, abandoning earlier precedents, adopted a
broad interpretation of Congress's legislative power under the Commerce Clause. The Court held that the power to regulate interstate
commerce, along with the Necessary and Proper Clause, included the
power to regulate labor practices in connection with the manufacture of
goods for sale in commerce. In *United States v. Darby* (1941), the Court
unanimously upheld a ban on interstate commerce in goods manufactured in violation of federal child labor restrictions. Finally, in *Wickard
v. Filburn* (1942), the Court unanimously upheld national marketing
quotas on agricultural production, even as applied to wheat grown

purely for home consumption—the broadest interpretation of the Commerce Clause yet. This trio of decisions—*Jones & Laughlin*, *Darby*, and *Wickard*—transformed interpretation of the Commerce Clause and the Necessary and Proper Clause and permitted the exercise of broad national legislative power over economic activity.

✪

West Coast Hotel Company v. Parrish
300 U.S. 379 (1937)

•

JUSTICE HUGHES DELIVERED THE OPINION OF THE COURT.

This case presents the question of the constitutional validity of the minimum wage law of the state of Washington. The act, entitled 'Minimum Wages for Women,' authorizes the fixing of minimum wages for women and minors. . . .

The appellant relies upon the decision of this Court in *Adkins v. Children's Hospital*, 261 U.S. 525, which held invalid the District of Columbia Minimum Wage Act which was attacked under the due process clause of the Fifth Amendment. On the argument at bar, counsel for the appellees attempted to distinguish the *Adkins* Case upon the ground that the appellee was employed in a hotel and that the business of an innkeeper was affected with a public interest. That effort at distinction is obviously futile, as it appears that in one of the cases ruled by the *Adkins* opinion the employee was a woman employed as an elevator operator in a hotel. . . .

The principle which must control our decision is not in doubt. The constitutional provision invoked is the due process clause of the Fourteenth Amendment governing the states, as the due process clause invoked in the *Adkins* Case governed Congress. In each case the violation alleged by those attacking minimum wage regulation for women is deprivation of freedom of contract. What is this freedom? The Constitution does not speak of freedom of contract. It speaks of liberty and prohibits the deprivation of liberty without due process of law. In prohibiting that deprivation, the Constitution does not recognize an absolute and uncontrollable liberty. Liberty in each of its phases has its history and connotation. But the liberty safeguarded is liberty in a social organization which requires the protection of law against the evils which menace the health, safety, morals, and welfare of the people. Liberty under the Constitution is thus necessarily subject to the restraints of due process, and regulation which is reasonable in relation to its subject and is adopted in the interests of the community is due process. . . .

'The guaranty of liberty does not withdraw from legislative supervision that wide department of activity which consists of the making of contracts, or deny to government the power to provide restrictive safeguards. Liberty implies the absence of arbitrary restraint, not immunity from reasonable regulations and prohibitions imposed in the interests of the community.' . . .

We think . . . that the decision in the *Adkins* Case was a departure from the true application of the principles governing the regulation by the state of the relation of employer and employed. Those principles have been reenforced by our subsequent decisions. . . .

Our conclusion is that the case of *Adkins v. Children's Hospital*, supra, should be, and it is, overruled. The judgment of the Supreme Court of the state of Washington is affirmed.

National Labor Relations Board v. Jones & Laughlin Steel Corporation, 301 U.S. 1 (1937)

•

JUSTICE HUGHES DELIVERED THE OPINION OF THE COURT.

In a proceeding under the National Labor Relations Act of 1935 the National Labor Relations Board found that the respondent, Jones & Laughlin Steel Corporation, had violated the act by engaging in unfair labor practices affecting commerce. . . . The unfair labor practices charged were that the corporation was discriminating against members of the union with regard to hire and tenure of employment, and was coercing and intimidating its employees in order to interfere with their self-organization. The discriminatory and coercive action alleged was the discharge of certain employees. . . .

Contesting the ruling of the Board, the respondent argues (1) that the act is in reality a regulation of labor relations and not of interstate commerce; (2) that the act can have no application to the respondent's relations with its production employees because they are not subject to regulation by the federal government; and (3) that the provisions of the act violate section 2 of article 3 and the Fifth and Seventh Amendments of the Constitution of the United States. . . . We turn to the questions of law which respondent urges in contesting the validity and application of the act.

First. The Scope of the Act. The act is challenged in its entirety as an attempt to regulate all industry, thus invading the reserved powers of the States over their local concerns. It is asserted that the references in the act to interstate and foreign commerce are colorable at best; that the act is not a true regulation of such commerce or of matters which directly affect it, but on the contrary has the fundamental object of placing under the compulsory supervision of the federal government all industrial labor relations within the nation. The argument seeks support in the broad words of the preamble . . . and in the sweep of the provisions of the act, and it is further insisted that its legislative history shows an essential universal purpose in the light of which its scope cannot be limited by either construction or by the application of the separability clause.

If this conception of terms, intent and consequent inseparability were sound, the act would necessarily fall by reason of the limitation upon the federal power which inheres in the constitutional grant, as well as because of the explicit reservation of the Tenth Amendment. . . . The authority of the federal government may not be pushed to such an extreme as to destroy the distinction, which the commerce clause itself establishes, between commerce 'among the several States' and the internal concerns of a state. That distinction between what is national and what is local in the activities of commerce is vital to the maintenance of our federal system. . . .

We think it clear that the National Labor Relations Act may be construed so as to operate within the sphere of constitutional authority. . . . The grant of authority to the Board does not purport to extend to the relationship between all industrial employees and employers. Its terms do not impose collective bargaining upon all industry regardless of effects upon interstate or foreign commerce. It purports to reach only what may be deemed to burden or obstruct that commerce and, thus qualified, it must be construed as contemplating the exercise of control within constitutional bounds. It is a familiar principle that acts which directly burden or obstruct interstate or foreign commerce, or its free flow, are within the reach of the congressional power. Acts having that effect are not rendered immune because they grow out of labor disputes. . . . Whether or not particular action does affect commerce in such a close and intimate fashion as to be subject to federal control, and hence to lie within the authority conferred upon the Board, is left by the statute to be determined as individual cases arise. We are thus to inquire whether in the instant case the constitutional boundary has been passed.

Second. The Unfair Labor Practices in Question. . . .

[I]n its present application, the statute goes no further than to safeguard the right of employees to self-organization and to select representatives of their own choosing for collective bargaining or other mutual protection without restraint or coercion by their employer.

That is a fundamental right. Employees have as clear a right to organize and select their representatives for lawful purposes as the respondent has to organize its business and select its own officers and agents. Discrimination and coercion to prevent the free exercise of the right of employees to self-organization and representation is a proper subject for condemnation by competent legislative authority. . . .

Third. The application of the Act to Employees Engaged in Production. . . . Respondent says that, whatever may be said of employees engaged in interstate commerce, the industrial relations and activities in the manufacturing department of respondent's enterprise are not subject to federal regulation. The argument rests upon the proposition that manufacturing in itself is not commerce. . . .

That intrastate activities, by reason of close and intimate relation to interstate commerce, may fall within federal control is demonstrated in the case of carriers who are engaged in both interstate and intrastate transportation. There federal control has been found essential to secure the freedom of interstate traffic from interference or unjust discrimination and to promote the efficiency of the interstate service. . . . The close and intimate effect which brings the subject within the reach of federal power may be due to activities in relation to productive industry although the industry when separately viewed is local. . . . It is thus apparent that the fact that the employees here concerned were engaged in production is not determinative. The question remains as to the effect upon interstate commerce of the labor practice involved. . . .

Fourth. Effects of the Unfair Labor Practice in Respondent's Enterprise. Giving full weight to respondent's contention with respect to a break in the complete continuity of the "stream of commerce" by reason of respondent's manufacturing operations, the fact remains that the stoppage of those operations by industrial strife would have a most serious effect upon interstate commerce. In view of respondent's far-flung activities, it is idle to say that the effect would be indirect or remote. It is obvious that it would be immediate and might be catastrophic. We are asked to shut our eyes to the plainest facts of our national life and to deal with the question of direct and indirect effects in an intellectual vacuum. Because there may be but indirect and remote effects upon interstate commerce in connection with a host of local enterprises throughout the country, it does not follow that other industrial activities do not have such a close and intimate relation to interstate commerce as to make the presence of industrial strife a matter of the most urgent national concern. When industries organize themselves on a national scale, making their relation to interstate commerce the dominant factor in their activities, how can it be maintained that their industrial labor relations constitute a forbidden field into which Congress may not enter when it is necessary to protect interstate commerce from the paralyzing consequences of industrial war? We have often said that interstate commerce itself is a practical conception. It is equally true that interferences with that commerce must be appraised by a judgment that does not ignore actual experience. . . .

It is not necessary again to detail the facts as to respondent's enterprise. Instead of being beyond the pale, we think that it presents in a most striking way the close and intimate relation which a manufacturing industry may have to interstate commerce and we have no doubt that Congress had constitutional authority to safeguard the right of respondent's employees to self-organization and freedom in the choice of representatives for collective bargaining.

Fifth. The Means Which the Act Employs.—Questions under the Due Process Clause and Other Constitutional Restrictions.—Respondent asserts its right to conduct its business in an orderly manner without being subjected to arbitrary restraints. What we have said points to the fallacy in the argument. Employees have their correlative right to organize for the purpose of securing the redress of grievances and to promote agreements with employers relating to rates of pay and conditions of work. . . . Restraint for the purpose of preventing an unjust interference with that right cannot be considered arbitrary or capricious. . . .

The act has been criticized as one-sided in its application; that it subjects the employer to supervision and restraint and leaves untouched the abuses for which employees may be responsible; that it fails to provide a more comprehensive plan, with better assurances of fairness to both sides and with increased chances of success in bringing about, if not compelling, equitable solutions of industrial disputes affecting interstate commerce. But we are dealing with the power of Congress, not with a particular policy or with the extent to which policy should go. We have frequently said that the legislative authority, exerted within its proper field, need not embrace all the evils within its reach. . . .

Our conclusion is that the order of the Board was within its competency and that the act is valid as here applied. . . .

United States v. Darby
310 U.S. 100 (1941)

•

MR. JUSTICE STONE DELIVERED THE OPINION OF THE COURT.

The two principal questions raised by the record in this case are, first, whether Congress has constitutional power to prohibit the shipment in interstate commerce of lumber manufactured by employees whose wages are less than a prescribed minimum or whose weekly hours of labor at that wage are greater than a prescribed maximum, and, second, whether it has power to prohibit the employment of workmen in the production of goods "for interstate commerce" at other than prescribed wages and hours. . . .

The Fair Labor Standards Act set up a comprehensive legislative scheme for preventing the shipment in interstate commerce of certain products and commodities produced in the United States under labor conditions as respects wages and hours which fail to conform to standards set up by the Act. . . .

While manufacture is not, of itself, interstate commerce, the shipment of manufactured goods interstate is such commerce, and the prohibition of such shipment by Congress is indubitably a regulation of the commerce. The power to regulate commerce is the power "to prescribe the rule by which commerce is to be governed." *Gibbons v. Ogden* 1824]. It extends not only to those regulations which aid, foster and protect the commerce, but embraces those which prohibit it. . . .

But it is said that the present prohibition falls within the scope of none of these categories; that, while the prohibition is nominally a regulation of the commerce, its motive or purpose is regulation of wages and hours of persons engaged in manufacture, the control of which has been reserved to the states and upon which Georgia and some of the states of destination have placed no restriction; that the effect of the present statute is not to exclude the proscribed articles from interstate commerce in aid of state regulation, . . . but instead, under the guise of a regulation of interstate commerce, it undertakes to regulate wages and hours within the state contrary to the policy of the state which has elected to leave them unregulated.

The power of Congress over interstate commerce "is complete in itself, may be exercised to its utmost extent, and acknowledges no limitations other than are prescribed in the Constitution." [*Gibbons v. Ogden*] That power can neither be enlarged nor diminished by the exercise or non-exercise of state power. Such regulation is not a forbidden invasion of state power merely because either its motive or its consequence is to restrict the use of articles of commerce within the states of destination, and is not prohibited unless by other Constitutional provisions. It is no objection to the assertion of the power to regulate interstate commerce that its exercise is attended by the same incidents which attend the exercise of the police power of the states. . . .

The motive and purpose of the present regulation are plainly to make effective the Congressional conception of public policy that interstate commerce should not be made the instrument of competition in the distribution of goods produced under substandard labor conditions, which competition is injurious to the commerce and to the states from and to which the commerce flows. The motive and purpose of a regulation of interstate commerce are matters for the legislative judgment upon the exercise of which the Constitution places no restriction, and over which the courts are given no control. . . . Whatever their motive and purpose, regulations of commerce which do not infringe some constitutional prohibition are within the plenary power conferred on Congress by the Commerce Clause. Subject only to that limitation, presently to be considered, we conclude that the prohibition of the shipment interstate of goods produced under the forbidden substandard labor conditions is within the constitutional authority of Congress.

In the more than a century which has elapsed since the decision of *Gibbons v. Ogden*, these principles of constitutional interpretation have been so long and repeatedly recognized by this Court as applicable to the Commerce Clause that there would be little occasion for repeating them now were it not for the decision of this Court twenty-two years ago in *Hammer v. Dagenhart*, 247 U.S. 251 [1918]. In that case, it was held by a bare majority of the Court, over the powerful and now classic dissent of Mr. Justice Holmes setting forth the fundamental issues involved, that Congress was without power to exclude the products of child labor from interstate commerce. The reasoning and conclusion of the Court's opinion there cannot be reconciled with the conclusion which we have reached, that the power of Congress under the Commerce Clause is plenary to exclude any article from interstate commerce subject only to the specific prohibitions of the Constitution.

Hammer v. Dagenhart has not been followed. The distinction on which the decision was rested, that Congressional power to prohibit interstate commerce is limited to articles which in themselves have some harmful or deleterious property—a distinction which was novel when made and unsupported by any provision of the Constitution—has long since been abandoned. The thesis of the opinion—that the motive of the prohibition or its effect to control in some measure the use or production within the states of the article thus excluded from the commerce can operate to deprive the regulation of its constitutional authority—has long since ceased to have force. . . . The conclusion is inescapable that *Hammer v. Dagenhart* was a departure from the principles which have prevailed in the interpretation of the Commerce Clause both before and since the decision, and that such vitality, as a precedent, as it then had, has long since been exhausted. It should be, and now is, overruled. . . .

There remains the question whether such restriction on the production of goods for commerce is a permissible exercise of the commerce power. The power of Congress over interstate commerce is not confined to the regulation of commerce among the states. It extends to those activities intrastate which so affect interstate commerce or the exercise of the power of Congress over it as to make regulation of them appropriate means to the attainment of a legitimate end, the exercise of the granted power of Congress to regulate interstate commerce. See *McCulloch v. Maryland* (1819). . . .

Congress having by the present Act adopted the policy of excluding from interstate commerce all goods produced for the commerce which do not conform to the specified labor standards, it may choose the means reasonably adapted to the attainment of the permitted end even though they involve control of intrastate activities. Such legislation has often been sustained with respect to powers other than the commerce power granted to the national government when the means chosen, although not themselves within the granted power, were nevertheless deemed appropriate aids to the accomplishment of some purpose within an admitted power of the national government. . . .

As we have said, the evils aimed at by the Act are the spread of substandard labor conditions through the use of the facilities of interstate commerce for competition by the goods so produced with those produced under the prescribed or better labor conditions, and the consequent dislocation of the commerce itself caused by the impairment or destruction of local businesses by competition made effective through interstate commerce. The Act is thus directed at the suppression of a method or kind of competition in interstate commerce which it has, in effect, condemned as "unfair," as the Clayton Act has condemned other "unfair methods of competition" made effective through interstate commerce.

Our conclusion is unaffected by the Tenth Amendment, which provides:

The powers not delegated to the United States by the Constitution, nor prohibited by it to the States, are reserved to the States respectively, or to the people.

The amendment states but a truism that all is retained which has not been surrendered. There is nothing in the history of its adoption to suggest that it was more than declaratory of the relationship between the national and state governments as it had been established by the Constitution before the amendment, or that its purpose was other than to allay fears that the new national government might seek to exercise powers not granted, and that the states might not be able to exercise fully their reserved powers. . . . From the beginning and for many years, the amendment has been construed as not depriving the national government of authority to resort to all means for the exercise of a granted power which are appropriate and plainly adapted to the permitted end. . . .

Wickard v. Filburn
317 U.S. 111 (1942)

•

Mr. Justice JACKSON delivered the opinion of the Court.

The appellee . . . sought to enjoin enforcement against himself of the marketing penalty imposed by the amendment of May 26, 1941, to the Agricultural Adjustment Act of 1938, upon that part of his 1941 wheat crop which was available for marketing in excess of the marketing quota established for his farm. He also sought a declaratory judgment that the wheat marketing quota provisions of the Act as amended and applicable to him were unconstitutional because not sustainable under the Commerce Clause or consistent with the Due Process Clause of the Fifth Amendment. . . .

The appellee for many years past has owned and operated a small farm in Montgomery County, Ohio, maintaining a herd of dairy cattle, selling milk, raising poultry, and selling poultry and eggs. It has been his practice to raise a small acreage of winter wheat, sown in the Fall and harvested in the following July; to sell a portion of the crop; to feed part to poultry and livestock on the farm, some of which is sold; to use some in making flour for home consumption; and to keep the rest for the following seeding. The intended disposition of the crop here involved has not been expressly stated.

In July of 1940, pursuant to the Agricultural Adjustment Act of 1938, as then amended, there were established for the appellee's 1941 crop a wheat acreage allotment of 11.1 acres and a normal yield of 20.1 bushels of wheat an acre. He was given notice of such allotment in July of 1940 before the Fall planting of his 1941 crop of wheat, and again in July of 1941, before it was harvested. He sowed, however, 23 acres, and harvested from his 11.9 acres of excess acreage 239 bushels, which under the terms of the Act as amended on May 26, 1941, constituted farm marketing excess, subject to a penalty of 49 cents a bushel, or $117.11 in all. The appellee has not paid the penalty and he has not postponed or avoided it by storing the excess under regulations of the Secretary of Agriculture, or by delivering it up to the Secretary. The Committee, therefore, refused him a marketing card, which was, under the terms of Regulations promulgated by the Secretary, necessary to protect a buyer from liability to the penalty and upon its protecting lien.

The general scheme of the Agricultural Adjustment Act of 1938 as related to wheat is to control the volume moving in interstate and foreign commerce in order to avoid surpluses and shortages and the consequent abnormally low or high wheat prices and obstructions to commerce. Within prescribed limits and by prescribed standards the Secretary of Agriculture is directed to ascertain and proclaim each year a national acreage allotment for the next crop of wheat, which is then apportioned to the states and their counties, and is eventually broken up into allotments for individual farms. Loans and payments to wheat farmers are authorized in stated circumstances.

The Act provides further that whenever it appears that the total supply of wheat as of the beginning of any marketing year, beginning July 1, will exceed a normal year's domestic consumption and export by more than 35 per cent, the Secretary shall so proclaim not later than May 15 prior to the beginning of such marketing year; and that during the marketing year a compulsory national marketing quota shall be in effect with respect to the marketing of wheat. . . .

It is urged that under the Commerce Clause of the Constitution, Article I, §8, clause 3, Congress does not possess the power it has in this instance sought to exercise. The question would merit little consideration since our decision in *United States v. Darby*, sustaining the federal power to regulate production of goods for commerce except for the fact that this Act extends federal regulation to production not intended in any part for commerce but wholly for consumption on the farm. The Act includes a definition of 'market' and its derivatives so that as related to wheat in addition to its conventional meaning it also means to dispose of 'by feeding (in any form) to poultry or livestock which, or the products of which, are sold, bartered, or exchanged, or to be so disposed of.' Hence, marketing quotas not only embrace all that may be sold without penalty but also what may be consumed on the premises. . . .

Appellee says that this is a regulation of production and consumption of wheat. Such activities are, he urges, beyond the reach of Congressional power under the Commerce Clause, since they are local in character, and their effects upon interstate commerce are at most 'indirect.' In answer the Government argues that the statute regulates neither production nor consumption, but only marketing; and, in the alternative, that if the Act does go beyond the regulation of marketing it is sustainable as a 'necessary and proper' implementation of the power of Congress over interstate commerce.

The Government's concern lest the Act be held to be a regulation of production or consumption rather than of marketing is attributable to a few dicta and decisions of this Court which might be understood to lay it down that activities such as 'production,' 'manufacturing,' and 'mining' are strictly 'local' and, except in special circumstances which are not present here, cannot be regulated under the commerce power because their effects upon interstate commerce are, as matter of law, only 'indirect.' Even today, when this power has been held to have great latitude, there is no decision of this Court that such activities may be regulated where no part of the product is intended for interstate commerce or intermingled with the subjects thereof. We believe that a review of the course of decision under the Commerce Clause will make plain, however, that questions of the power of Congress are not to be decided by reference to any formula which would give controlling force to nomenclature such as 'production' and 'indirect' and foreclose consideration of the actual effects of the activity in question upon interstate commerce.

At the beginning Chief Justice Marshall described the Federal commerce power with a breadth never yet exceeded [*Gibbons v. Ogden* (1824)]. He made emphatic the embracing and penetrating nature of this power by warning that effective restraints on its exercise must proceed from political rather than from judicial processes. . . .

It was not until 1887 with the enactment of the Interstate Commerce Act that the interstate commerce power began to exert positive influence in American law and life. This first important federal resort to the commerce power was followed in 1890 by the Sherman Anti-Trust

Act and, thereafter, mainly after 1903, by many others. These statutes ushered in new phases of adjudication, which required the Court to approach the interpretation of the Commerce Clause in the light of an actual exercise by Congress of its power thereunder. . . .

The Court's recognition of the relevance of the economic effects in the application of the Commerce Clause . . . has made the mechanical application of legal formulas no longer feasible. Once an economic measure of the reach of the power granted to Congress in the Commerce Clause is accepted, questions of federal power cannot be decided simply by finding the activity in question to be 'production' nor can consideration of its economic effects be foreclosed by calling them 'indirect.' . . .

Whether the subject of the regulation in question was 'production,' 'consumption,' or 'marketing' is, therefore, not material for purposes of deciding the question of federal power before us. That an activity is of local character may help in a doubtful case to determine whether Congress intended to reach it. The same consideration might help in determining whether in the absence of Congressional action it would be permissible for the state to exert its power on the subject matter, even though in so doing it to some degree affected interstate commerce. But even if appellee's activity be local and though it may not be regarded as commerce, it may still, whatever its nature, be reached by Congress if it exerts a substantial economic effect on interstate commerce and this irrespective of whether such effect is what might at some earlier time have been defined as 'direct' or 'indirect.' . . .

The effect of consumption of homegrown wheat on interstate commerce is due to the fact that it constitutes the most variable factor in the disappearance of the wheat crop. Consumption on the farm where grown appears to vary in an amount greater than 20 per cent of average production. The total amount of wheat consumed as food varies but relatively little, and use as seed is relatively constant.

The maintenance by government regulation of a price for wheat undoubtedly can be accomplished as effectively by sustaining or increasing the demand as by limiting the supply. The effect of the statute before us is to restrict the amount which may be produced for market and the extent as well to which one may forestall resort to the market by producing to meet his own needs. That appellee's own contribution to the demand for wheat may be trivial by itself is not enough to remove him from the scope of federal regulation where, as here, his contribution, taken together with that of many others similarly situated, is far from trivial. . . .

It is well established by decisions of this Court that the power to regulate commerce includes the power to regulate the prices at which commodities in that commerce are dealt in and practices affecting such prices. One of the primary purposes of the Act in question was to increase the market price of wheat and to that end to limit the volume thereof that could affect the market. It can hardly be denied that a factor of such volume and variability as home-consumed wheat would have a substantial influence on price and market conditions. This may arise because being in marketable condition such wheat overhangs the market and if induced by rising prices tends to flow into the market and check price increases. But if we assume that it is never marketed, it supplies a need of the man who grew it which would otherwise be reflected by purchases in the open market. Home-grown wheat in this sense competes with wheat in commerce. The stimulation of commerce is a use of the regulatory function quite as definitely as prohibitions or restrictions thereon. This record leaves us in no doubt that Congress may properly have considered that wheat consumed on the farm where grown if wholly outside the scheme of regulation would have a substantial effect in defeating and obstructing its purpose to stimulate trade therein at increased prices.

It is said, however, that this Act, forcing some farmers into the market to buy what they could provide for themselves, is an unfair promotion of the markets and prices of specializing wheat growers. It is of the essence of regulation that it lays a restraining hand on the self-interest of the regulated and that advantages from the regulation commonly fall to others. The conflicts of economic interest between the regulated and those who advantage by it are wisely left under our system to resolution by the Congress under its more flexible and responsible legislative process. Such conflicts rarely lend themselves to judicial determination. And with the wisdom, workability, or fairness, of the plan of regulation we have nothing to do. . . .

UNITED STATES v.
CAROLENE PRODUCTS CO.

304 U.S. 144 (1938)

*U*nited States v. Carolene Products Co. is famous chiefly for a footnote—"Footnote Four" of the opinion. The straightforward holding of the case was that Congress may regulate milk products under the Commerce Clause and that such regulation does not violate any substantive due process or equal protection right to be free from government regulation. Footnote Four stated that judicial scrutiny of legislation may be stricter when laws infringe specific constitutional freedoms, interfere with the political process, or discriminate against minorities.

✪

MR. JUSTICE STONE DELIVERED THE OPINION OF THE COURT.

The question for decision is whether the 'Filled Milk Act' of Congress . . . which prohibits the shipment in interstate commerce of skimmed milk compounded with any fat or oil other than milk fat, so as to resemble milk or cream, transcends the power of Congress to regulate interstate commerce or infringes the Fifth Amendment. . . .

Appellee assails the statute as beyond the power of Congress over interstate commerce, and hence an invasion of a field of action said to be reserved to the states by the Tenth Amendment. Appellee also complains that the statute denies to it equal protection of the laws, and in violation of the Fifth Amendment, deprives it of its property without due process of law, particularly in that the statute purports to make binding and conclusive upon appellee the legislative declaration that appellee's product 'is an adulterated article of food, injurious to the public health, and its sale constitutes a fraud on the public.'

First. The power to regulate commerce is the power 'to prescribe the rule by which commerce is to be governed,' and extends to the prohibition of shipments in such commerce. The power 'is complete in itself, may be exercised to its utmost extent, and acknowledges no limitations, other than are prescribed in the Constitution.' *Gibbons v. Ogden.* Hence Congress is free to exclude from interstate commerce articles whose use in the states for which they are destined it may reasonably conceive to be injurious to the public health, morals, or welfare, or which contravene the policy of the state of their destination. Such regulation is not a forbidden invasion of state power either because its motive or its consequence is to restrict the use of articles of commerce within the states of destination, and is not prohibited unless by the due process clause of the Fifth Amendment. And it is no objection to the exertion of the power to regulate interstate commerce that its exercise is attended by the same incidents which attend the exercise of the police power of the states. The prohibition of the shipment of filled milk in interstate commerce is a permissible regulation of commerce, subject only to the restrictions of the Fifth Amendment.

Second. The prohibition of shipment of appellee's product in interstate commerce does not infringe the Fifth Amendment. . . . Appellee raises no valid objection to the present statute by arguing that its prohibition has not been extended to oleomargarine or other butter substitutes in which vegetable fats or oils are substituted for butter fat. The Fifth Amendment has no equal protection clause, and even that of the Fourteenth, applicable only to the states, does not compel their Legislatures to prohibit all like evils, or none. A Legislature may hit at an abuse which it has found, even though it has failed to strike at another.

Third. We may assume . . . that a statute would deny due process which precluded the disproof in judicial proceedings of all facts which would show or tend to show that a statute depriving the suitor of life, liberty, or property had a rational basis. . . . [R]egulatory legislation affecting ordinary commercial transactions is not to be pronounced unconstitutional unless in the light of the facts made known or generally assumed it is of such a character as to preclude the assumption that it rests upon some rational basis within the knowledge and experience of the legislators.[4] . . . The prohibition of shipment in interstate commerce of appellee's product, as described in the indictment, is a constitutional exercise of the power to regulate interstate commerce. . . .

4 There may be narrower scope for operation of the presumption of constitutionality when legislation appears on its face to be within a specific prohibition of the Constitution, such as those of the first ten Amendments, which are deemed equally specific when held to be embraced within the Fourteenth.

It is unnecessary to consider now whether legislation which restricts those political processes which can ordinarily be expected to bring about repeal of undesirable legislation, is to be subjected to more exacting judicial scrutiny under the general prohibitions of the Fourteenth Amendment than are most other types of legislation. . . .

Nor need we enquire whether similar considerations enter into the review of statutes directed at particular religious, or national, or racial minorities; whether prejudice against discrete and insular minorities may be a special condition, which tends seriously to curtail the operation of those political processes ordinarily to be relied upon to protect minorities, and which may call for a correspondingly more searching judicial inquiry.

MINERSVILLE SCHOOL DISTRICT *v.* GOBITIS

AND

WEST VIRGINIA STATE BOARD OF EDUCATION *v.* BARNETTE

꙳

*T*hese two cases—both decided during World War II—involved constitutional challenges to a rule compelling children to salute the U.S. flag and recite the Pledge of Allegiance, or be expelled from public school. In *Minersville School District v. Gobitis* (1940), the Supreme Court rejected, 8–1, the argument that such a requirement violated the right to the free exercise of religion and to freedom of speech, upholding the expulsion from school of Jehovah's Witnesses for whom recitation of the pledge conflicted with religious conscience. In *West Virginia State Board of Education v. Barnette* (1943), the Court overruled *Gobitis*, 6–3, on freedom of speech grounds. The Court in *Barnette* did not separately address the freedom of religion argument.

✪

Minersville School District v. Gobitis
310 U.S. 586 (1940)

•

MR. JUSTICE FRANKFURTER DELIVERED THE OPINION OF
THE COURT.

A grave responsibility confronts this Court whenever in course of litigation it must reconcile the conflicting claims of liberty and authority.
But when the liberty invoked is liberty of conscience, and the authority
is authority to safeguard the nation's fellowship, judicial conscience is
put to its severest test. Of such a nature is the present controversy.

Lillian Gobitis, aged twelve, and her brother William, aged ten, were
expelled from the public schools of Minersville, Pennsylvania, for refusing
to salute the national flag as part of a daily school exercise. The local
Board of Education required both teachers and pupils to participate in
this ceremony. . . . The Gobitis family are affiliated with 'Jehovah's Witnesses', for whom the Bible as the Word of God is the supreme authority.
The children had been brought up conscientiously to believe that such
a gesture of respect for the flag was forbidden by command of scripture.

The Gobitis children were of an age for which Pennsylvania makes
school attendance compulsory. Thus they were denied a free education
and their parents had to put them into private schools. To be relieved
of the financial burden thereby entailed, their father, on behalf of the
children and in his own behalf, brought this suit. He sought to enjoin
the authorities from continuing to exact participation in the flag-salute
ceremony as a condition of his children's attendance at the Minersville
school. . . .

Centuries of strife over the erection of particular dogmas as exclusive or all-comprehending faiths led to the inclusion of a guarantee for
religious freedom in the Bill of Rights. The First Amendment, and the
Fourteenth through its absorption of the First, sought to guard against
repetition of those bitter religious struggles by prohibiting the establishment of a state religion and by securing to every sect the free exercise of its faith. So pervasive is the acceptance of this precious right that
its scope is brought into question, as here, only when the conscience of
individuals collides with the felt necessities of society.

Certainly the affirmative pursuit of one's convictions about the ultimate mystery of the universe and man's relation to it is placed beyond
the reach of law. Government may not interfere with organized or individual expression of belief or disbelief. Propagation of belief—or even
of disbelief in the supernatural—is protected, whether in church or
chapel, mosque or synagogue, tabernacle or meetinghouse. . . .

But the manifold character of man's relations may bring his conception of religious duty into conflict with the secular interests of his
fellow-men. When does the constitutional guarantee compel exemption
from doing what society thinks necessary for the promotion of some
great common end, or from a penalty for conduct which appears dangerous to the general good? To state the problem is to recall the truth
that no single principle can answer all of life's complexities. The right to
freedom of religious belief, however dissident and however obnoxious to
the cherished beliefs of others—even of a majority—is itself the denial
of an absolute. But to affirm that the freedom to follow conscience has
itself no limits in the life of a society would deny that very plurality of
principles which, as a matter of history, underlies protection of religious
toleration. . . .

The religious liberty which the Constitution protects has never excluded legislation of general scope not directed against doctrinal loyalties of particular sects. Judicial nullification of legislation cannot be
justified by attributing to the framers of the Bill of Rights views for
which there is no historic warrant. Conscientious scruples have not, in
the course of the long struggle for religious toleration, relieved the individual from obedience to a general law not aimed at the promotion or
restriction of religious beliefs. The mere possession of religious convictions which contradict the relevant concerns of a political society does
not relieve the citizen from the discharge of political responsibilities.
The necessity for this adjustment has again and again been recognized.
In a number of situations the exertion of political authority has been
sustained, while basic considerations of religious freedom have been
left inviolate. *Reynolds v. United States*, 98 U.S. 145. . . . In all these
cases the general laws in question, upheld in their application to those
who refused obedience from religious conviction, were manifestations
of specific powers of government deemed by the legislature essential
to secure and maintain that orderly, tranquil, and free society without
which religious toleration itself is unattainable. Nor does the freedom

of speech . . . move in a more absolute circle of immunity than that enjoyed by religious freedom. Even if it were assumed that freedom of speech goes beyond the historic concept of full opportunity to utter and to disseminate views, however heretical or offensive to dominant opinion, and includes freedom from conveying what may be deemed an implied but rejected affirmation, the question remains whether school children, like the Gobitis children, must be excused from conduct required of all the other children in the promotion of national cohesion. We are dealing with an interest inferior to none in the hierarchy of legal values. National unity is the basis of national security. To deny the legislature the right to select appropriate means for its attainment presents a totally different order of problem from that of the propriety of subordinating the possible ugliness of littered streets to the free expression of opinion through distribution of handbills. . . .

Unlike the instances we have cited, the case before us is not concerned with an exertion of legislative power for the promotion of some specific need or interest of secular society—the protection of the family, the promotion of health, the common defense, the raising of public revenues to defray the cost of government. But all these specific activities of government presuppose the existence of an organized political society. The ultimate foundation of a free society is the binding tie of cohesive sentiment. Such a sentiment is fostered by all those agencies of the mind and spirit which may serve to gather up the traditions of a people, transmit them from generation to generation, and thereby create that continuity of a treasured common life which constitutes a civilization. 'We live by symbols.' The flag is the symbol of our national unity, transcending all internal differences, however large, within the framework of the Constitution. . . .

The precise issue, then, for us to decide is whether the legislatures of the various states and the authorities in a thousand counties and school districts of this country are barred from determining the appropriateness of various means to evoke that unifying sentiment without which there can ultimately be no liberties, civil or religious. To stigmatize legislative judgment in providing for this universal gesture of respect for the symbol of our national life in the setting of the common school as a lawless inroad on that freedom of conscience which the Constitution protects, would amount to no less than the pronouncement of pedagogical and psychological dogma in a field where courts possess no marked and certainly no controlling competence. . . .

The wisdom of training children in patriotic impulses by those compulsions which necessarily pervade so much of the educational process is not for our independent judgment. . . . It is not our province to choose among competing considerations in the subtle process of securing effective loyalty to the traditional ideals of democracy, while respecting at the same time individual idiosyncracies among a people so diversified in racial origins and religious allegiances. So to hold would in effect make us the school board for the country. That authority has not been given to this Court, nor should we assume it. . . .

What the school authorities are really asserting is the right to awaken in the child's mind considerations as to the significance of the flag contrary to those implanted by the parent. In such an attempt the state is normally at a disadvantage in competing with the parent's authority, so long—and this is the vital aspect of religious toleration—as parents are unmolested in their right to counteract by their own persuasiveness the wisdom and rightness of those loyalties which the state's educational system is seeking to promote. Except where the transgression of constitutional liberty is too plain for argument, personal freedom is best maintained—so long as the remedial channels of the democratic process remain open and unobstructed—when it is ingrained in a people's habits and not enforced against popular policy by the coercion of adjudicated law. That the flag salute is an allowable portion of a school program for those who do not invoke conscientious scruples is surely not debatable. But for us to insist that, though the ceremony may be required, exceptional immunity must be given to dissidents, is to maintain that there is no basis for a legislative judgment that such an exemption might introduce elements of difficulty into the school discipline, might cast doubts in the minds of the other children which would themselves weaken the effect of the exercise.

The preciousness of the family relation, the authority and independence which give dignity to parenthood, indeed the enjoyment of all freedom, presuppose the kind of ordered society which is summarized by our flag. A society which is dedicated to the preservation of these ultimate values of civilization may in self-protection utilize the educational process for inculcating those almost unconscious feelings which bind men together in a comprehending loyalty, whatever may be their lesser differences and difficulties. . . .

West Virginia State Board of Education v. Barnette
319 U.S. 624 (1943)

•

MR. JUSTICE JACKSON DELIVERED THE OPINION OF THE COURT.

Following the decision by this Court on June 3, 1940, in *Minersville School District v. Gobitis*, 310 U.S. 586, the West Virginia legislature amended its statutes to require all schools therein to conduct courses of instruction in history, civics, and in the Constitutions of the United States and of the State 'for the purpose of teaching, fostering and perpetuating the ideals, principles and spirit of Americanism, and increasing the knowledge of the organization and machinery of the government.' . . . The Act made it the duty of private, parochial and denominational schools to prescribe courses of study 'similar to those required for the public schools.'

The Board of Education on January 9, 1942, adopted a resolution containing recitals taken largely from the Court's *Gobitis* opinion and ordering that the salute to the flag become 'a regular part of the program of activities in the public schools,' that all teachers and pupils 'shall be required to participate in the salute honoring the Nation represented by the Flag; provided, however, that refusal to salute the Flag be regarded as an Act of insubordination, and shall be dealt with accordingly. . . . Failure to conform is 'insubordination' dealt with by expulsion. Readmission is denied by statute until compliance. Meanwhile the expelled child is 'unlawfully absent and may be proceeded against as a delinquent. His parents or guardians are liable to prosecution, and if convicted are subject to fine not exceeding $50 and jail term not exceeding thirty days. . . .

This case calls upon us to reconsider a precedent decision, as the Court throughout its history often has been required to do. Before turning to the *Gobitis* case, however, it is desirable to notice certain characteristics by which this controversy is distinguished. The freedom asserted by these appellees does not bring them into collision with rights asserted by any other individual. It is such conflicts which most frequently require intervention of the State to determine where the rights of one end

and those of another begin. But the refusal of these persons to participate in the ceremony does not interfere with or deny rights of others to
do so. Nor is there any question in this case that their behavior is peace-
able and orderly. The sole conflict is between authority and rights of the
individual. The State asserts power to condition access to public education on making a prescribed sign and profession and at the same time
to coerce attendance by punishing both parent and child. The latter
stand on a right of self-determination in matters that touch individual
opinion and personal attitude. . . .

There is no doubt that, in connection with the pledges, the flag
salute is a form of utterance. Symbolism is a primitive but effective way
of communicating ideas. The use of an emblem or flag to symbolize
some system, idea, institution, or personality, is a short cut from mind
to mind. Causes and nations, political parties, lodges and ecclesiastical
groups seek to knit the loyalty of their followings to a flag or banner,
a color or design. . . . Here it is the State that employs a flag as a
symbol of adherence to government as presently organized. It requires
the individual to communicate by word and sign his acceptance of the
political ideas it thus bespeaks. Objection to this form of communication when coerced is an old one, well known to the framers of the Bill
of Rights.

It is also to be noted that the compulsory flag salute and pledge
requires affirmation of a belief and an attitude of mind. . . . It is now
a commonplace that censorship or suppression of expression of opinion
is tolerated by our Constitution only when the expression presents a
clear and present danger of action of a kind the State is empowered to
prevent and punish. It would seem that involuntary affirmation could
be commanded only on even more immediate and urgent grounds than
silence. . . . To sustain the compulsory flag salute we are required to say
that a Bill of Rights which guards the individual's right to speak his
own mind, left it open to public authorities to compel him to utter what
is not in his mind.

Whether the First Amendment to the Constitution will permit officials to order observance of ritual of this nature does not depend upon
whether as a voluntary exercise we would think it to be good, bad or
merely innocuous. . . . [V]alidity of the asserted power to force an
American citizen publicly to profess any statement of belief or to engage
in any ceremony of assent to one presents questions of power that must

be considered independently of any idea we may have as to the utility of the ceremony in question.

Nor does the issue, as we see it, turn on one's possession of particular religious views or the sincerity with which they are held. . . . It is not necessary to inquire whether non-conformist beliefs will exempt from the duty to salute unless we first find power to make the salute a legal duty.

The *Gobitis* decision, however, assumed . . . that power exists in the State to impose the flag salute discipline upon school children in general. The Court only examined and rejected a claim based on religious beliefs of immunity from an unquestioned general rule. The question which underlies the flag salute controversy is whether such a ceremony so touching matters of opinion and political attitude may be imposed upon the individual by official authority under powers committed to any political organization under our Constitution. We examine rather than assume existence of this power and, against this broader definition of issues in this case, re-examine specific grounds assigned for the *Gobitis* decision.

1. It was said that the flag-salute controversy confronted the Court with 'the problem which Lincoln cast in memorable dilemma: 'Must a government of necessity be too strong for the liberties of its people, or too weak to maintain its own existence?'' and that the answer must be in favor of strength. . . . It may be doubted whether Mr. Lincoln would have thought that the strength of government to maintain itself would be impressively vindicated by our confirming power of the state to expel a handful of children from school. Such oversimplification, so handy in political debate, often lacks the precision necessary to postulates of judicial reasoning. If validly applied to this problem, the utterance cited would resolve every issue of power in favor of those in authority and would require us to override every liberty thought to weaken or delay execution of their policies.

Government of limited power need not be anemic government. Assurance that rights are secure tends to diminish fear and jealousy of strong government, and by making us feel safe to live under it makes for its better support. Without promise of a limiting Bill of Rights it is doubtful if our Constitution could have mustered enough strength to enable its ratification. To enforce those rights today is not to choose weak government over strong government. It is only to adhere as a means of strength to individual freedom of mind in preference to officially disciplined uniformity for which history indicates a disappointing and disastrous end. . . . Observance of the limitations of the Constitution will not weaken government in the field appropriate for its exercise.

2. It was also considered in the *Gobitis* case that functions of educational officers in states, counties and school districts were such that to interfere with their authority 'would in effect make us the school board for the country.'

The Fourteenth Amendment, as now applied to the States, protects the citizen against the State itself and all of its creatures—Boards of Education not excepted. These have, of course, important, delicate, and highly discretionary functions, but none that they may not perform within the limits of the Bill of Rights. That they are educating the young for citizenship is reason for scrupulous protection of Constitutional freedoms of the individual, if we are not to strangle the free mind at its source and teach youth to discount important principles of our government as mere platitudes. . . .

3. The *Gobitis* opinion reasoned that this is a field 'where courts possess no marked and certainly no controlling competence,' that it is committed to the legislatures as well as the courts to guard cherished liberties and that it is constitutionally appropriate to 'fight out the wise use of legislative authority in the forum of public opinion and before legislative assemblies rather than to transfer such a contest to the judicial arena,' since all the 'effective means of inducing political changes are left free.' . . . The very purpose of a Bill of Rights was to withdraw certain subjects from the vicissitudes of political controversy, to place them beyond the reach of majorities and officials and to establish them as legal principles to be applied by the courts. One's right to life, liberty, and property, to free speech, a free press, freedom of worship and assembly, and other fundamental rights may not be submitted to vote; they . . . are susceptible of restriction only to prevent grave and immediate danger to interests which the state may lawfully protect. . . .

4. Lastly, and this is the very heart of the *Gobitis* opinion, it reasons that 'National unity is the basis of national security,' that the authorities have 'the right to select appropriate means for its attainment,' and hence reaches the conclusion that such compulsory measures toward 'national unity' are constitutional. . . . Upon the verity of this assumption depends our answer in this case. National unity as an end which officials

may foster by persuasion and example is not in question. The problem is whether under our Constitution compulsion as here employed is a permissible means for its achievement.

Struggles to coerce uniformity of sentiment in support of some end thought essential to their time and country have been waged by many good as well as by evil men. Nationalism is a relatively recent phenomenon but at other times and places the ends have been racial or territorial security, support of a dynasty or regime, and particular plans for saving souls. As first and moderate methods to attain unity have failed, those bent on its accomplishment must resort to an ever-increasing severity. As governmental pressure toward unity becomes greater, so strife becomes more bitter as to whose unity it shall be. Probably no deeper division of our people could proceed from any provocation than from finding it necessary to choose what doctrine and whose program public educational officials shall compel youth to unite in embracing. Ultimate futility of such attempts to compel coherence is the lesson of every such effort from the Roman drive to stamp out Christianity as a disturber of its pagan unity, the Inquisition as a means to religious and dynastic unity, the Siberian exiles as a means to Russian unity, down to the fast failing efforts of our present totalitarian enemies. Those who begin coercive elimination of dissent soon find themselves exterminating dissenters. Compulsory unification of opinion achieves only the unanimity of the graveyard.

It seems trite but necessary to say that the First Amendment to our Constitution was designed to avoid these ends by avoiding these beginnings. There is no mysticism in the American concept of the State or of the nature or origin of its authority. We set up government by consent of the governed, and the Bill of Rights denies those in power any legal opportunity to coerce that consent. Authority here is to be controlled by public opinion, not public opinion by authority.

The case is made difficult not because the principles of its decision are obscure but because the flag involved is our own. Nevertheless, we apply the limitations of the Constitution with no fear that freedom to be intellectually and spiritually diverse or even contrary will disintegrate the social organization. To believe that patriotism will not flourish if patriotic ceremonies are voluntary and spontaneous instead of a compulsory routine is to make an unflattering estimate of the appeal of our institutions to free minds. We can have intellectual individualism and the rich cultural diversities that we owe to exceptional minds only at the price of occasional eccentricity and abnormal attitudes. When they are so harmless to others or to the State as those we deal with here, the price is not too great. But freedom to differ is not limited to things that do not matter much. That would be a mere shadow of freedom. The test of its substance is the right to differ as to things that touch the heart of the existing order.

If there is any fixed star in our constitutional constellation, it is that no official, high or petty, can prescribe what shall be orthodox in politics, nationalism, religion, or other matters of opinion or force citizens to confess by word or act their faith therein. If there are any circumstances which permit an exception, they do not now occur to us. . . . We think the action of the local authorities in compelling the flag salute and pledge transcends constitutional limitations on their power and invades the sphere of intellect and spirit which it is the purpose of the First Amendment to our Constitution to reserve from all official control. . . .

EX PARTE QUIRIN

AND

KOREMATSU v. UNITED STATES

࣭ࣹ࣭

World War II produced significant cases concerning the rights of captured Nazi enemy spies and saboteurs and—in sharp contrast—the lawfulness of the detention and internment of civilians lawfully resident in the United States, based on Japanese ethnicity. *Ex parte Quirin* (1942) unanimously upheld the authority of the U.S. government to use military commissions rather than civilian courts to try unlawful enemy combatants (including U.S. citizens) for alleged violations of the laws of war. *Korematsu v. United States* upheld, 6–3, the constitutionality of the mass internment of innocent Japanese-American civilians during the war—many of whom were U.S. citizens—without specific evidence that any individual was disloyal. *Korematsu* has been repudiated in subsequent Supreme Court opinions and is today considered a regrettable departure from the principle that no one's liberty should be abridged on the basis of race or ethnicity alone and that the war power to hold prisoners must distinguish enemy combatants from members of civilian populations.

✪

Ex parte Quirin
323 U.S. 214 (1942)

•

MR. CHIEF JUSTICE STONE DELIVERED THE OPINION OF THE
COURT.

. . . The question for decision is whether the detention of petitioners
by respondent for trial by Military Commission, appointed by Order of
the President of July 2, 1942, on charges preferred against them purporting to set out their violations of the law of war and of the Articles of
War, is in conformity to the laws and Constitution of the United States.

. . . All the petitioners were born in Germany; all have lived in the
United States. All returned to Germany between 1933 and 1941. All
except petitioner Haupt are admittedly citizens of the German Reich,
with which the United States is at war. . . .

After the declaration of war between the United States and the
German Reich, petitioners received training at a sabotage school near
Berlin, Germany, where they were instructed in the use of explosives
and in methods of secret writing. Thereafter petitioners, with a German
citizen, Dasch, proceeded from Germany to a seaport in Occupied
France, where petitioners Burger, Heinck and Quirin, together with
Dasch, boarded a German submarine which proceeded across the Atlantic to Amagansett Beach on Long Island, New York. The four were
there landed from the submarine in the hours of darkness, on or about
June 13, 1942, carrying with them a supply of explosives, fuses and in-
cendiary and timing devices. While landing they wore German Marine
Infantry uniforms or parts of uniforms. Immediately after landing they
buried their uniforms and the other articles mentioned and proceeded
in civilian dress to New York City.

The remaining four petitioners at the same French port boarded an-
other German submarine, which carried them across the Atlantic to
Ponte Vedra Beach, Florida. . . . All were taken into custody in New
York or Chicago by agents of the Federal Bureau of Investigation. All
had received instructions in Germany from an officer of the German
High Command to destroy war industries and war facilities in the
United States, for which they or their relatives in Germany were to

receive salary payments from the German Government. They also had been paid by the German Government during their course of training at the sabotage school and had received substantial sums in United States currency, which were in their possession when arrested. . . .

The President, as President and Commander in Chief of the Army and Navy, by Order of July 2, 1942, appointed a Military Commission and directed it to try petitioners for offenses against the law of war and the Articles of War, and prescribed regulations for the procedure on the trial and for review of the record of the trial and of any judgment or sentence of the Commission. . . .

Petitioners' main contention is that the President is without any statutory or constitutional authority to order the petitioners to be tried by military tribunal for offenses with which they are charged; that in consequence they are entitled to be tried in the civil courts with the safeguards, including trial by jury, which the Fifth and Sixth Amendments guarantee to all persons charged in such courts with criminal offenses. . . .

We are not here concerned with any question of the guilt or innocence of petitioners. Constitutional safeguards for the protection of all who are charged with offenses are not to be disregarded in order to inflict merited punishment on some who are guilty. . . . But the detention and trial of petitioners—ordered by the President in the declared exercise of his powers as Commander in Chief of the Army in time of war and of grave public danger—are not to be set aside by the courts without the clear conviction that they are in conflict with the Constitution or laws of Congress constitutionally enacted.

Congress and the President, like the courts, possess no power not derived from the Constitution. But one of the objects of the Constitution, as declared by its preamble, is to 'provide for the common defence'. As a means to that end the Constitution gives to Congress the power to 'provide for the common Defence', 'To raise and support Armies', 'To provide and maintain a Navy'; and 'To make Rules for the Government and Regulation of the land and naval Forces'. Congress is given authority 'To declare War, grant Letters of Marque and Reprisal, and make Rules concerning Captures on Land and Water'; and 'To define and punish Piracies and Felonies committed on the high Seas, and Offenses against the Law of Nations'. And finally the Constitution authorizes Congress 'To make all Laws which shall be necessary and proper for carrying into Execution the foregoing Powers, and all other Powers vested by this Constitution in the Government of the United States, or in any Department or Officer thereof.'

The Constitution confers on the President the 'executive Power' and imposes on him the duty to 'take Care that the Laws be faithfully executed'. It makes him the Commander in Chief of the Army and Navy, and empowers him to appoint and commission officers of the United States. The Constitution thus invests the President as Commander in Chief with the power to wage war which Congress has declared, and to carry into effect all laws passed by Congress for the conduct of war and for the government and regulation of the Armed Forces, and all laws defining and punishing offences against the law of nations, including those which pertain to the conduct of war. . . .

From the very beginning of its history this Court has recognized and applied the law of war as including that part of the law of nations which prescribes, for the conduct of war, the status, rights and duties of enemy nations as well as of enemy individuals. By the Articles of War, and especially Article 15, Congress has explicitly provided, so far as it may constitutionally do so, that military tribunals shall have jurisdiction to try offenders or offenses against the law of war in appropriate cases. Congress, in addition to making rules for the government of our Armed Forces, has thus exercised its authority to define and punish offenses against the law of nations by sanctioning, within constitutional limitations, the jurisdiction of military commissions to try persons for offenses which, according to the rules and precepts of the law of nations, and more particularly the law of war, are cognizable by such tribunals. And the President, as Commander in Chief, by his Proclamation in time of war his invoked that law. By his Order creating the present Commission he has undertaken to exercise the authority conferred upon him by Congress, and also such authority as the Constitution itself gives the Commander in Chief, to direct the performance of those functions which may constitutionally be performed by the military arm of the nation in time of war.

An important incident to the conduct of war is the adoption of measures by the military command not only to repel and defeat the enemy, but to seize and subject to disciplinary measures those enemies who in their attempt to thwart or impede our military effort have violated the law of war. It is unnecessary for present purposes to determine to what extent the President as Commander in Chief has constitutional power to create military commissions without the support of Congressional legislation. For here Congress has authorized trial of offenses against the law of war before such commissions. We are concerned only with the question whether it is within the constitutional power of the national government to place petitioners upon trial before a military commission for the offenses with which they are charged. . . .

By universal agreement and practice the law of war draws a distinction between the armed forces and the peaceful populations of belligerent nations and also between those who are lawful and unlawful combatants. Lawful combatants are subject to capture and detention as prisoners of war by opposing military forces. Unlawful combatants are likewise subject to capture and detention, but in addition they are subject to trial and punishment by military tribunals for acts which render their belligerency unlawful. The spy who secretly and without uniform passes the military lines of a belligerent in time of war, seeking to gather military information and communicate it to the enemy, or an enemy combatant who without uniform comes secretly through the lines for the purpose of waging war by destruction of life or property, are familiar examples of belligerents who are generally deemed not to be entitled to the status of prisoners of war, but to be offenders against the law of war subject to trial and punishment by military tribunals. . . .

By a long course of practical administrative construction by its military authorities, our Government has . . . recognized that those who during time of war pass surreptitiously from enemy territory into our own, discarding their uniforms upon entry, for the commission of hostile acts involving destruction of life or property, have the status of unlawful combatants punishable as such by military commission. This precept of the law of war has been so recognized in practice both here and abroad, and has so generally been accepted as valid by authorities on international law that we think it must be regarded as a rule or principle of the law of war recognized by this Government by its enactment of the Fifteenth Article of War. . . .

Modern warfare is directed at the destruction of enemy war supplies and the implements of their production and transportation quite as much as at the armed forces. Every consideration which makes the unlawful belligerent punishable is equally applicable whether his objective is the one or the other. The law of war cannot rightly treat those agents of enemy armies who enter our territory, armed with explosives intended for the destruction of war industries and supplies, as any the less belligerent enemies than are agents similarly entering for the purpose of destroying fortified places or our Armed Forces. By passing our boundaries for such purposes without uniform or other emblem signifying their belligerent status, or by discarding that means of identification after entry, such enemies become unlawful belligerents subject to trial and punishment.

Citizenship in the United States of an enemy belligerent does not relieve him from the consequences of a belligerency which is unlawful because in violation of the law of war. Citizens who associate themselves with the military arm of the enemy government, and with its aid, guidance and direction enter this country bent on hostile acts are enemy belligerents within the meaning of the Hague Convention and the law of war. . . . It is as an enemy belligerent that petitioner Haupt is charged with entering the United States, and unlawful belligerency is the gravamen of the offense of which he is accused. . . .

But petitioners insist that even if the offenses with which they are charged are offenses against the law of war, their trial is subject to the requirement of the Fifth Amendment that no person shall be held to answer for a capital or otherwise infamous crime unless on a presentment or indictment of a grand jury, and that such trials by Article III, §2, and the Sixth Amendment must be by jury in a civil court. . . .

Presentment by a grand jury and trial by a jury of the vicinage where the crime was committed were at the time of the adoption of the Constitution familiar parts of the machinery for criminal trials in the civil courts. But they were procedures unknown to military tribunals, which are not courts in the sense of the Judiciary Article . . . and which in the natural course of events are usually called upon to function under conditions precluding resort to such procedures. As this Court has often recognized, it was not the purpose or effect of § 2 of Article III, read in the light of the common law, to enlarge the then existing right to a jury trial. The object was to preserve unimpaired trial by jury in all those cases in which it had been recognized by the common law and in all cases of a like nature as they might arise in the future . . . but not to bring within the sweep of the guaranty those cases in which it was then well understood that a jury trial could not be demanded as of right.

The Fifth and Sixth Amendments, while guaranteeing the continuance of certain incidents of trial by jury which Article III, § 2 had left unmentioned, did not enlarge the right to jury trial as it had been established by that Article. . . . In the light of this long-continued and consistent interpretation we must conclude that § 2 of Article III and the Fifth and Sixth Amendments cannot be taken to have extended the right to demand a jury to trials by military commission, or to have required that offenses against the law of war not triable by jury at common law be tried only in the civil courts. . . .

Petitioners, and especially petitioner Haupt, stress the pronounce- ment of this Court in the Milligan case [*Ex parte Milligan*, 71 U.S. (4 Wall.) 2 (1866)], that the law of war "can never be applied to citizens in states which have upheld the authority of the government, and where the courts are open and their process unobstructed". Elsewhere in its opinion, the Court was at pains to point out that Milligan, a citizen twenty years resident in Indiana, who had never been a resident of any of the states in rebellion, was not an enemy belligerent either entitled to the status of a prisoner of war or subject to the penalties imposed upon unlawful belligerents. We construe the Court's statement as to the inapplicability of the law of war to Milligan's case as having particular reference to the facts before it. . . .

The Court's opinion is inapplicable to the case presented by the pre- sent record. We have no occasion now to define with meticulous care the ultimate boundaries of the jurisdiction of military tribunals to try per- sons according to the law of war. It is enough that petitioners here, upon the conceded facts, were plainly within those boundaries, and were held in good faith for trial by military commission, charged with being en- emies who, with the purpose of destroying war materials and utilities, entered or after entry remained in our territory without uniform—an offense against the law of war. . . .

Korematsu v. United States
323 U.S. 214 (1944)

•

MR. JUSTICE BLACK DELIVERED THE OPINION OF THE COURT.

The petitioner, an American citizen of Japanese descent, was convicted in a federal district court for remaining in San Leandro, California, a

"Military Area," contrary to Civilian Exclusion Order No. 34 of the Commanding General of the Western Command, U.S. Army, which directed that after May 9, 1942, all persons of Japanese ancestry should be excluded from that area. No question was raised as to petitioner's loyalty to the United States. . . .

It should be noted, to begin with, that all legal restrictions which curtail the civil rights of a single racial group are immediately suspect. That is not to say that all such restrictions are unconstitutional. It is to say that courts must subject them to the most rigid scrutiny. Pressing public necessity may sometimes justify the existence of such restrictions; racial antagonism never can. . . .

[A] curfew order, which like the exclusion order here was promulgated pursuant to Executive Order 9066, subjected all persons of Japanese ancestry in prescribed West Coast military areas to remain in their residences from 8 p.m. to 6 a.m. As is the case with the exclusion order here, that prior curfew order was designed as a "protection against espionage and against sabotage." In *Hirabayashi v. United States* [1943] we sustained a conviction obtained for violation of the curfew order. The *Hirabayashi* conviction and this one thus rest on the same 1942 Congressional Act and the same basic executive and military orders, all of which orders were aimed at the twin dangers of espionage and sabotage. . . .

In the light of the principles we announced in the *Hirabayashi* case, we are unable to conclude that it was beyond the war power of Congress and the Executive to exclude those of Japanese ancestry from the West Coast war area at the time they did. True, exclusion from the area in which one's home is located is a far greater deprivation than constant confinement to the home from 8 p.m. to 6 a.m. Nothing short of apprehension by the proper military authorities of the gravest imminent danger to the public safety can constitutionally justify either. But exclusion from a threatened area, no less than curfew, has a definite and close relationship to the prevention of espionage and sabotage. The military authorities, charged with the primary responsibility of defending our shores, concluded that curfew provided inadequate protection and ordered exclusion. They did so, as pointed out in our Hirabayashi opinion, in accordance with Congressional authority to the military to say who should, and who should not, remain in the threatened areas.

Here, as in the Hirabayashi case, ". . . we cannot reject as unfounded the judgment of the military authorities and of Congress that there were disloyal members of that population, whose number and strength could not be precisely and quickly ascertained. We cannot say that the war-making branches of the Government did not have ground for believing that in a critical hour such persons could not readily be isolated and separately dealt with, and constituted a menace to the national defense and safety, which demanded that prompt and adequate measures be taken to guard against it."

Like curfew, exclusion of those of Japanese origin was deemed necessary because of the presence of an unascertained number of disloyal members of the group, most of whom we have no doubt were loyal to this country. It was because we could not reject the finding of the military authorities that it was impossible to bring about an immediate segregation of the disloyal from the loyal that we sustained the validity of the curfew order as applying to the whole group. In the instant case, temporary exclusion of the entire group was rested by the military on the same ground. The judgment that exclusion of the whole group was for the same reason a military imperative answers the contention that the exclusion was in the nature of group punishment based on antagonism to those of Japanese origin. That there were members of the group who retained loyalties to Japan has been confirmed by investigations made subsequent to the exclusion. Approximately five thousand American citizens of Japanese ancestry refused to swear unqualified allegiance to the United States and to renounce allegiance to the Japanese Emperor, and several thousand evacuees requested repatriation to Japan.

We uphold the exclusion order as of the time it was made and when the petitioner violated it. In doing so, we are not unmindful of the hardships imposed by it upon a large group of American citizens. But hardships are part of war, and war is an aggregation of hardships. All citizens alike, both in and out of uniform, feel the impact of war in greater or lesser measure. Citizenship has its responsibilities as well as its privileges, and in time of war the burden is always heavier. Compulsory exclusion of large groups of citizens from their homes, except under circumstances of direst emergency and peril, is inconsistent with our basic governmental institutions. But when under conditions of modern warfare our shores are threatened by hostile forces, the power to protect must be commensurate with the threatened danger. . . .

It is said that we are dealing here with the case of imprisonment of a citizen in a concentration camp solely because of his ancestry, without evidence or inquiry concerning his loyalty and good disposition towards the United States. Our task would be simple, our duty clear, were this a case involving the imprisonment of a loyal citizen in a concentration camp because of racial prejudice. Regardless of the true nature of the assembly and relocation centers—and we deem it unjustifiable to call them concentration camps with all the ugly connotations that term implies—we are dealing specifically with nothing but an exclusion order. To cast this case into outlines of racial prejudice, without reference to the real military dangers which were presented, merely confuses the issue. Korematsu was not excluded from the Military Area because of hostility to him or his race. He was excluded because we are at war with the Japanese Empire, because the properly constituted military authorities feared an invasion of our West Coast and felt constrained to take proper security measures, because they decided that the military urgency of the situation demanded that all citizens of Japanese ancestry be segregated from the West Coast temporarily, and finally, because Congress, reposing its confidence in this time of war in our military leaders—as inevitably it must—determined that they should have the power to do just this. There was evidence of disloyalty on the part of some, the military authorities considered that the need for action was great, and time was short. We cannot—by availing ourselves of the calm perspective of hindsight—now say that at that time these actions were unjustified.

MR. JUSTICE MURPHY, DISSENTING.

. . . In dealing with matters relating to the prosecution and progress of a war, we must accord great respect and consideration to the judgments of the military authorities who are on the scene and who have full knowledge of the military facts. The scope of their discretion must, as a matter of necessity and common sense, be wide. And their judgments ought not to be overruled lightly by those whose training and duties ill-equip them to deal intelligently with matters so vital to the physical security of the nation.

At the same time, however, it is essential that there be definite limits to military discretion, especially where martial law has not been declared. Individuals must not be left impoverished of their constitutional rights on a plea of military necessity that has neither substance nor support. . . . The judicial test of whether the Government, on a plea of military necessity, can validly deprive an individual of any of his constitutional rights is whether the deprivation is reasonably related to a public danger that is so "immediate, imminent, and impending" as not to admit of delay and not to permit the intervention of ordinary constitutional processes to alleviate the danger. Civilian Exclusion Order No. 34, banishing from a prescribed area of the Pacific Coast "all persons of Japanese ancestry, both alien and non-alien," clearly does not meet that test. Being an obvious racial discrimination, the order deprives all those within its scope of the equal protection of the laws as guaranteed by the Fifth Amendment. . . . Yet no reasonable relation to an "immediate, imminent, and impending" public danger is evident to support this racial restriction which is one of the most sweeping and complete deprivations of constitutional rights in the history of this nation in the absence of martial law.

It must be conceded that the military and naval situation in the spring of 1942 was such as to generate a very real fear of invasion of the Pacific Coast, accompanied by fears of sabotage and espionage in that area. The military command was therefore justified in adopting all reasonable means necessary to combat these dangers. In adjudging the military action taken in light of the then apparent dangers, we must not erect too high or too meticulous standards; it is necessary only that the action have some reasonable relation to the removal of the dangers of invasion, sabotage and espionage. But the exclusion, either temporarily or permanently, of all persons with Japanese blood in their veins has no such reasonable relation. And that relation is lacking because the exclusion order necessarily must rely for its reasonableness upon the assumption that all persons of Japanese ancestry may have a dangerous tendency to commit sabotage and espionage and to aid our Japanese enemy in other ways. It is difficult to believe that reason, logic or experience could be marshalled in support of such an assumption.

That this forced exclusion was the result in good measure of this erroneous assumption of racial guilt rather than bona fide military necessity is evidenced by the Commanding General's Final Report on the evacuation from the Pacific Coast area. In it he refers to all individuals of Japanese descent as "subversive," as belonging to "an enemy race" whose "racial strains are undiluted," and as constituting "over 112,000 potential enemies . . . at large today" along the Pacific Coast. In support of this blanket condemnation of all persons of Japanese descent, however, no reliable evidence is cited to show that such individuals were generally disloyal, or had generally so conducted themselves in this area as to constitute a special menace to defense installations or war industries, or had otherwise by their behavior furnished reasonable ground for their exclusion as a group.

Justification for the exclusion is sought, instead, mainly upon questionable racial and sociological grounds not ordinarily within the realm of expert military judgment, supplemented by certain semi-military conclusions drawn from an unwarranted use of circumstantial evidence. Individuals of Japanese ancestry are condemned because they are said to be "a large, unassimilated, tightly knit racial group, bound to an enemy nation by strong ties of race, culture, custom and religion." They are claimed to be given to "emperor worshipping ceremonies" and to "dual citizenship." Japanese language schools and allegedly pro-Japanese organizations are cited as evidence of possible group disloyalty, together with facts as to certain persons being educated and residing at length in Japan. It is intimated that many of these individuals deliberately resided "adjacent to strategic points," thus enabling them "to carry into execution a tremendous program of sabotage on a mass scale should any considerable number of them have been inclined to do so." . . .

The main reasons relied upon by those responsible for the forced evacuation . . . do not prove a reasonable relation between the group characteristics of Japanese Americans and the dangers of invasion, sabotage and espionage. The reasons appear, instead, to be largely an accumulation of much of the misinformation, half-truths and insinuations that for years have been directed against Japanese Americans by people with racial and economic prejudices—the same people who have been among the foremost advocates of the evacuation. A military judgment based upon such racial and sociological considerations is not entitled to the great weight ordinarily given the judgments based upon strictly military considerations. . . .

. . . No adequate reason is given for the failure to treat these Japanese Americans on an individual basis by holding investigations and hearings to separate the loyal from the disloyal, as was done in the case of persons of German and Italian ancestry. It is asserted merely that the loyalties of this group "were unknown and time was of the essence." Yet nearly four months elapsed after Pearl Harbor before the first exclusion order was issued; nearly eight months went by until the last order was issued; and the last of these "subversive" persons was not actually re-moved until almost eleven months had elapsed. . . .

It seems incredible that under these circumstances it would have been impossible to hold loyalty hearings for the mere 112,000 persons involved—or at least for the 70,000 American citizens—especially when a large part of this number represented children and elderly men and women. Any inconvenience that may have accompanied an attempt to conform to procedural due process cannot be said to justify violations of constitutional rights of individuals.

I dissent, therefore, from this legalization of racism. Racial discrimi-nation in any form and in any degree has no justifiable part whatever in our democratic way of life. It is unattractive in any setting but it is utterly revolting among a free people who have embraced the principles set forth in the Constitution of the United States. All residents of this nation are kin in some way by blood or culture to a foreign land. Yet they are primarily and necessarily a part of the new and distinct civiliza-tion of the United States. They must accordingly be treated at all times as the heirs of the American experiment and as entitled to all the rights and freedoms guaranteed by the Constitution.

MR. JUSTICE JACKSON, DISSENTING.

Korematsu was born on our soil, of parents born in Japan. The Con-stitution makes him a citizen of the United States by nativity and a cit-izen of California by residence. No claim is made that he is not loyal to this country. There is no suggestion that apart from the matter involved here he is not law-abiding and well disposed. Korematsu, however, has been convicted of an act not commonly a crime. It consists merely of being present in the state whereof he is a citizen, near the place where he was born, and where all his life he has lived. . . .

A citizen's presence in the locality, however, was made a crime only if his parents were of Japanese birth. Had Korematsu been one of four—the others being, say, a German alien enemy, an Italian alien enemy, and a citizen of American-born ancestors, convicted of treason but out on parole—only Korematsu's presence would have violated the order. The difference between their innocence and his crime would result, not from anything he did, said, or thought, different than they, but only in that he was born of different racial stock.

Now, if any fundamental assumption underlies our system, it is that guilt is personal and not inheritable. Even if all of one's antecedents had been convicted of treason, the Constitution forbids its penalties to be visited upon him, for it provides that "no attainder of treason shall work corruption of blood, or forfeiture except during the life of the person attainted." But here is an attempt to make an otherwise innocent act a crime merely because this prisoner is the son of parents as to whom he had no choice, and belongs to a race from which there is no way to resign. If Congress in peace-time legislation should enact such a criminal law, I should suppose this Court would refuse to enforce it.

But the "law" which this prisoner is convicted of disregarding is not found in an act of Congress, but in a military order. Neither the Act of Congress nor the Executive Order of the President, nor both together, would afford a basis for this conviction. It rests on the orders of General DeWitt. And it is said that if the military commander had reasonable military grounds for promulgating the orders, they are constitutional and become law, and the Court is required to enforce them. There are several reasons why I cannot subscribe to this doctrine.

It would be impracticable and dangerous idealism to expect or insist that each specific military command in an area of probable operations will conform to conventional tests of constitutionality. When an area is so beset that it must be put under military control at all, the paramount consideration is that its measures be successful, rather than legal. The armed services must protect a society, not merely its Constitution. The very essence of the military job is to marshal physical force, to remove every obstacle to its effectiveness, to give it every strategic advantage. Defense measures will not, and often should not, be held within the limits that bind civil authority in peace. No court can require such a commander in such circumstances to act as a reasonable man; he may be unreasonably cautious and exacting. Perhaps he should be. But a commander in temporarily focusing the life of a community on defense is carrying out a military program; he is not making law in the sense the courts know the term. He issues orders, and they may have a certain authority as military commands, although they may be very bad as constitutional law.

But if we cannot confine military expedients by the Constitution, neither would I distort the Constitution to approve all that the military may deem expedient. That is what the Court appears to be doing, whether consciously or not. I cannot say, from any evidence before me, that the orders of General DeWitt were not reasonably expedient military precautions, nor could I say that they were. But even if they were permissible military procedures, I deny that it follows that they are constitutional. If, as the Court holds, it does follow, then we may as well say that any military order will be constitutional and have done with it.

The limitation under which courts always will labor in examining the necessity for a military order are illustrated by this case. How does the Court know that these orders have a reasonable basis in necessity? No evidence whatever on that subject has been taken by this or any other court. There is sharp controversy as to the credibility of the DeWitt report. So the Court, having no real evidence before it, has no choice but to accept General DeWitt's own unsworn, self-serving statement, untested by any cross-examination, that what he did was reasonable. And thus it will always be when courts try to look into the reasonableness of a military order. . . .

Much is said of the danger to liberty from the Army program for deporting and detaining these citizens of Japanese extraction. But a judicial construction of the due process clause that will sustain this order is a far more subtle blow to liberty than the promulgation of the order itself. A military order, however unconstitutional, is not apt to last longer than the military emergency. Even during that period a succeeding commander may revoke it all. But once a judicial opinion rationalizes such an order to show that it conforms to the Constitution, or rather rationalizes the Constitution to show that the Constitution sanctions such an order, the Court for all time has validated the principle of racial discrimination in criminal procedure and of transplanting American citizens. The principle then lies about like a loaded weapon ready for the hand of any authority that can bring forward a plausible claim of an urgent need. . . . A military commander may overstep the bounds of constitutionality, and it is an incident. But if we review and approve, that passing incident becomes the doctrine of the Constitution. There it has a generative power of its own, and all that it creates will be in its own image. Nothing better illustrates this danger than does the Court's opinion in this case.

It argues that we are bound to uphold the conviction of Korematsu because we upheld one in *Hirabayashi v. United States*, when we sustained these orders in so far as they applied a curfew requirement to a citizen of Japanese ancestry. I think we should learn something from that experience.

In that case we were urged to consider only the curfew feature, that being all that technically was involved, because it was the only count necessary to sustain Hirabayashi's conviction and sentence. We yielded, and the Chief Justice guarded the opinion as carefully as language will do. . . . However, in spite of our limiting words we did validate a discrimination on the basis of ancestry for mild and temporary deprivation of liberty. Now the principle of racial discrimination is pushed from support of mild measures to very harsh ones, and from temporary deprivations to indeterminate ones. And the precedent which it is said requires us to do so is *Hirabayashi*. . . . Because we said that these citizens could be made to stay in their homes during the hours of dark, it is said we must require them to leave home entirely; and if that, we are told they may also be taken into custody for deportation; and if that, it is argued they may also be held for some undetermined time in detention camps. How far the principle of this case would be extended before plausible reasons would play out, I do not know.

I should hold that a civil court cannot be made to enforce an order which violates constitutional limitations even if it is a reasonable exercise of military authority. The courts can exercise only the judicial power, can apply only law, and must abide by the Constitution, or they cease to be civil courts and become instruments of military policy.

. . . My duties as a justice as I see them do not require me to make a military judgment as to whether General DeWitt's evacuation and detention program was a reasonable military necessity. I do not suggest that the courts should have attempted to interfere with the Army in carrying out its task. But I do not think they may be asked to execute a military expedient that has no place in law under the Constitution. I would reverse the judgment and discharge the prisoner.

YOUNGSTOWN SHEET & TUBE CO.
v. SAWYER
343 U.S. 579 (1952)

oungstown Sheet & Tube Co. v. Sawyer, sometimes called the Steel Seizure Case, involved a challenge to President Harry S. Truman's seizure of the nation's steel mills in order to avert a strike during the Korean War. By a vote of 6–3, the Court declared the seizure unconstitutional. The case reached the Court with extraordinary speed—it was decided less than two months after Truman's order—and it produced seminal judicial opinions concerning the scope of presidential versus legislative power under the Constitution. Justice Jackson's concurrence, in particular, has been cited many times in subsequent cases. *Youngstown* is regarded as one of the most important modern cases on the separation of powers generally, and of war and foreign affairs powers specifically.

✪

MR. JUSTICE BLACK DELIVERED THE OPINION OF THE COURT.

We are asked to decide whether the President was acting within his constitutional power when he issued an order directing the Secretary of Commerce to take possession of and operate most of the Nation's steel mills. The mill owners argue that the President's order amounts to lawmaking, a legislative function which the Constitution has expressly confided to the Congress and not to the President. The Government's position is that the order was made on findings of the President that his action was necessary to avert a national catastrophe which would inevitably result from a stoppage of steel production, and that in meeting this grave emergency the President was acting within the aggregate of his constitutional powers as the Nation's Chief Executive and the Commander in Chief of the Armed Forces of the United States. The issue emerges here from the following series of events:

In the latter part of 1951, a dispute arose between the steel companies and their employees over terms and conditions that should be included in new collective bargaining agreements. Long-continued conferences failed to resolve the dispute. . . . On April 4, 1952, the Union gave notice of a nation-wide strike called to begin at 12:01 A.M. April 9. The indispensability of steel as a component of substantially all weapons and other war materials led the President to believe that the proposed work stoppage would immediately jeopardize our national defense and that governmental seizure of the steel mills was necessary in order to assure the continued availability of steel. Reciting these considerations for his action, the President, a few hours before the strike was to begin, issued Executive Order 10340. . . . The order directed the Secretary of Commerce to take possession of most of the steel mills and keep them running. The Secretary immediately issued his own possessory orders[.] . . . The next morning the President sent a message to Congress reporting his action. Twelve days later he sent a second message.

Obeying the Secretary's orders under protest, the companies brought proceedings against him in the District Court. . . . [T]he District Court on April 30 issued a preliminary injunction restraining the Secretary from 'continuing the seizure and possession of the plant . . . and from acting under the purported authority of Executive Order No. 10340.' . . . On the same day the Court of Appeals stayed the District Court's injunction. . . . Deeming it best that the issues raised be promptly decided by this Court, we granted certiorari on May 3 and set the cause for argument on May 12. . . .

The President's power, if any, to issue the order must stem either from an act of Congress or from the Constitution itself. There is no statute that expressly authorizes the President to take possession of property as he did here. Nor is there any act of Congress to which our attention has been directed from which such a power can fairly be implied. . . . Moreover, the use of the seizure technique to solve labor disputes in order to prevent work stoppages was not only unauthorized by any congressional enactment; prior to this controversy, Congress had refused to adopt that method of settling labor disputes. When the Taft-Hartley Act was under consideration in 1947, Congress rejected an amendment which would have authorized such governmental seizures in cases of emergency. . . .

It is clear that if the President had authority to issue the order he did, it must be found in some provisions of the Constitution. And it is not claimed that express constitutional language grants this power to the President. The contention is that presidential power should be implied from the aggregate of his powers under the Constitution. Particular reliance is placed on provisions in Article II which say that 'the executive Power shall be vested in a President. . . ; that 'he shall take Care that the Laws be faithfully executed'; and that he 'shall be Commander in Chief of the Army and Navy of the United States.'

The order cannot properly be sustained as an exercise of the President's military power as Commander in Chief of the Armed Forces. . . . [W]e cannot with faithfulness to our constitutional system hold that the Commander in Chief of the Armed Forces has the ultimate power as such to take possession of private property in order to keep labor disputes from stopping production. This is a job for the Nation's lawmakers, not for its military authorities.

Nor can the seizure order be sustained because of the several constitutional provisions that grant executive power to the President. In the framework of our Constitution, the President's power to see that the laws are faithfully executed refutes the idea that he is to be a lawmaker. The Constitution limits his functions in the lawmaking process to the recommending of laws he thinks wise and the vetoing of laws he thinks bad. And the Constitution is neither silent nor equivocal about who shall make laws which the President is to execute. The first section of the first article says that 'All legislative Powers herein granted shall be vested in a Congress of the United States. . . .' After granting many powers to the Congress, Article I goes on to provide that Congress may 'make all Laws which shall be necessary and proper for carrying into Execution the foregoing Powers and all other Powers vested by this Constitution in the Government of the United States, or in any Department or Officer thereof.'

The President's order does not direct that a congressional policy be executed in a manner prescribed by Congress—it directs that a presidential policy be executed in a manner prescribed by the President. . . . The power of Congress to adopt such public policies as those proclaimed by the order is beyond question. It can authorize the taking of private property for public use. It can makes laws regulating the relationships between employers and employees, prescribing rules designed to settle labor disputes, and fixing wages and working conditions in certain fields of our economy. The Constitution did not subject this law-making power of Congress to presidential or military supervision or control.

It is said that other Presidents without congressional authority have taken possession of private business enterprises in order to settle labor disputes. But even if this be true, Congress has not thereby lost its exclusive constitutional authority to make laws necessary and proper to carry out the powers vested by the Constitution 'in the Government of the United States, or in any Department or Officer thereof.' . . . The Founders of this Nation entrusted the law making power to the Congress alone in both good and bad times. It would do no good to recall the historical events, the fears of power and the hopes for freedom that lay behind their choice. Such a review would but confirm our holding that this seizure order cannot stand. . . . Affirmed.

MR. JUSTICE JACKSON, CONCURRING IN THE JUDGMENT AND OPINION OF THE COURT.

That comprehensive and undefined presidential powers hold both practical advantages and grave dangers for the country will impress anyone who has served as legal adviser to a President in time of transition and public anxiety. While an interval of detached reflection may temper teachings of that experience, they probably are a more realistic influence on my views than the conventional materials of judicial decision which seem unduly to accentuate doctrine and legal fiction. . . .

A judge, like an executive adviser, may be surprised at the poverty of really useful and unambiguous authority applicable to concrete problems of executive power as they actually present themselves. Just what our forefathers did envision, or would have envisioned had they foreseen modern conditions, must be divined from materials almost as enigmatic as the dreams Joseph was called upon to interpret for Pharaoh. A century and a half of partisan debate and scholarly speculation yields no net result but only supplies more or less apt quotations from respected sources on each side of any question. They largely cancel each other. And court decisions are indecisive because of the judicial practice of dealing with the largest questions in the most narrow way.

The actual art of governing under our Constitution does not and cannot conform to judicial definitions of the power of any of its branches based on isolated clauses or even single Articles torn from context. While the Constitution diffuses power the better to secure liberty, it also contemplates that practice will integrate the dispersed powers into a workable government. It enjoins upon its branches separateness but interdependence, autonomy but reciprocity. Presidential powers are not fixed but fluctuate, depending upon their disjunction or conjunction with those of Congress. We may well begin by a somewhat over-simplified grouping of practical situations in which a President may doubt, or others may challenge, his powers, and by distinguishing roughly the legal consequences of this factor of relativity.

1. When the President acts pursuant to an express or implied authorization of Congress, his authority is at its maximum, for it includes all that he possesses in his own right plus all that Congress can delegate. In these circumstances, and in these only, may he be said (for what it may be worth), to personify the federal sovereignty. If his act is held unconstitutional under these circumstances, it usually means that the Federal Government as an undivided whole lacks power. A seizure executed by the President pursuant to an Act of Congress would be supported by the strongest of presumptions and the widest latitude of judicial interpretation, and the burden of persuasion would rest heavily upon any who might attack it.

2. When the President acts in absence of either a congressional grant or denial of authority, he can only rely upon his own independent powers, but there is a zone of twilight in which he and Congress may have concurrent authority, or in which its distribution is uncertain. Therefore, congressional inertia, indifference or quiescence may sometimes, at least as a practical matter, enable, if not invite, measures on independent presidential responsibility. In this area, any actual test of power is likely to depend on the imperatives of events and contemporary imponderables rather than on abstract theories of law.

3. When the President takes measures incompatible with the expressed or implied will of Congress, his power is at its lowest ebb, for

then he can rely only upon his own constitutional powers minus any constitutional powers of Congress over the matter. Courts can sustain exclusive Presidential control in such a case only be disabling the Congress from acting upon the subject. Presidential claim to a power at once so conclusive and preclusive must be scrutinized with caution, for what is at stake is the equilibrium established by our constitutional system.

Into which of these classifications does this executive seizure of the steel industry fit? It is eliminated from the first by admission, for it is conceded that no congressional authorization exists for this seizure. . . . Can it then be defended under flexible tests available to the second category? It seems clearly eliminated from that class because Congress has not left seizure of private property an open field but has covered it by three statutory policies inconsistent with this seizure. . . .

This leaves the current seizure to be justified only by the severe tests under the third grouping, where it can be supported only by any remainder of executive power after subtraction of such powers as Congress may have over the subject. In short, we can sustain the President only by holding that seizure of such strike-bound industries is within his domain and beyond control by Congress. . . .

I did not suppose, and I am not persuaded, that history leaves it open to question, at least in the courts, that the executive branch, like the Federal Government as a whole, possesses only delegated powers. The purpose of the Constitution was not only to grant power, but to keep it from getting out of hand. However, because the President does not enjoy unmentioned powers does not mean that the mentioned ones should be narrowed by a niggardly construction. Some clauses could be made almost unworkable, as well as immutable, by refusal to indulge some latitude of interpretation for changing times. I have heretofore, and do now, give to the enumerated powers the scope and elasticity afforded by what seem to be reasonable practical implications instead of the rigidity dictated by a doctrinaire textualism.

The Solicitor General seeks the power of seizure in three clauses of the Executive Article, the first reading, 'The executive Power shall be vested in a President of the United States of America.' Lest I be thought to exaggerate, I quote the interpretation which his brief puts upon it: 'In our view, this clause constitutes a grant of all the executive powers of which the Government is capable.' If that be true, it is difficult to see why the forefathers bothered to add several specific items, including some trifling ones.

. . . The example of such unlimited executive power that must have most impressed the forefathers was the prerogative exercised by George III, and the description of its evils in the Declaration of Independence leads me to doubt that they were creating their new Executive in his image. . . . I cannot accept the view that this clause is a grant in bulk of all conceivable executive power but regard it as an allocation to the presidential office of the generic powers thereafter stated.

The clause on which the Government next relies is that 'The President shall be Commander in Chief of the Army and Navy of the United States. . . .' These cryptic words have given rise to some of the most persistent controversies in our constitutional history. Of course, they imply something more than an empty title. But just what authority goes with the name has plagued Presidential advisers who would not waive or narrow it by nonassertion yet cannot say where it begins or ends. It undoubtedly puts the Nation's armed forces under Presidential command. Hence, this loose appellation is sometimes advanced as support for any Presidential action, internal or external, involving use of force, the idea being that it vests power to do anything, anywhere, that can be done with an army or navy.

That seems to be the logic of an argument tendered at our bar—that the President having, on his own responsibility, sent American troops abroad derives from that act 'affirmative power' to seize the means of producing a supply of steel for them. . . . I cannot foresee all that it might entail if the Court should indorse this argument. Nothing in our Constitution is plainer than that declaration of a war is entrusted only to Congress. Of course, a state of war may in fact exist without a formal declaration. But no doctrine that the Court could promulgate would seem to me more sinister and alarming than that a President whose conduct of foreign affairs is so largely uncontrolled, and often even is unknown, can vastly enlarge his mastery over the internal affairs of the country by his own commitment of the Nation's armed forces to some foreign venture. I do not, however, find it necessary or appropriate to consider the legal status of the Korean enterprise to discountenance argument based on it.

Assuming that we are in a war *de facto*, whether it is or is not a war *de jure*, does that empower the Commander-in-Chief to seize industries he thinks necessary to supply our army? The Constitution expressly places in Congress power 'to raise and *support* Armies' and 'to *provide* and *maintain* a Navy.' (Emphasis supplied.) This certainly lays upon Congress primary responsibility for supplying the armed forces. Congress alone controls the raising of revenues and their appropriation and may determine in what manner and by what means they shall be spent for military and naval procurement. . . .

There are indications that the Constitution did not contemplate that the title Commander-in-Chief of the Army and Navy will constitute him also Commander-in-Chief of the country, its industries and its inhabitants. He has no monopoly of "war powers," whatever they are. While Congress cannot deprive the President of the command of the army and navy, only Congress can provide him an army or navy to command. . . .

The third clause in which the Solicitor General finds seizure powers is that 'he shall take Care that the Laws be faithfully executed. . . .' That authority must be matched against words of the Fifth Amendment that 'No person shall be . . . deprived of life, liberty, or property, without due process of law. . . .' One gives a governmental authority that reaches so far as there is law, the other gives a private right that authority shall go no farther. These signify about all there is of the principle that ours is a government of laws, not of men, and that we submit ourselves to rulers only if under rules.

The Solicitor General lastly grounds support of the seizure upon nebulous, inherent powers never expressly granted but said to have accrued to the office from the customs and claims of preceding administrations. The plea is for a resulting power to deal with a crisis or an emergency according to the necessities of the case, the unarticulated assumption being that necessity knows no law. . . .

The appeal . . . that we declare the existence of inherent powers *ex necessitate* to meet an emergency asks us to do what many think would be wise, although it is something the forefathers omitted. They knew what emergencies were, knew the pressures they engender for authoritative action, knew, too, how they afford a ready pretext for usurpation. We may also suspect that they suspected that emergency powers would tend to kindle emergencies. Aside from suspension of the privilege of the writ of habeas corpus in time of rebellion or invasion, when the public safety may require it, they made no express provision for exercise of extraordinary authority because of a crisis. I do not think we rightfully may so amend their work, and, if we could, I am not convinced it would be wise to do so[.] . . .

In view of the ease, expedition and safety with which Congress can grant and has granted large emergency powers, certainly ample to embrace this crisis, I am quite unimpressed with the argument that we should affirm possession of them without statute. Such power either has no beginning or it has no end. If it exists, it need submit to no legal restraint. I am not alarmed that it would plunge us straightway into dictatorship, but it is at least a step in that wrong direction. . . .

The Executive, except for recommendation and veto, has no legislative power. The executive action we have here originates in the individual will of the President and represents an exercise of authority without law. . . . With all its defects, delays and inconveniences, men have discovered no technique for long preserving free government except that the Executive be under the law, and that the law be made by parliamentary deliberations. . . . Such institutions may be destined to pass away. But it is the duty of the Court to be last, not first, to give them up.

MR. CHIEF JUSTICE VINSON, WITH WHOM MR. JUSTICE REED AND MR. JUSTICE MINTON JOIN, DISSENTING.

. . . Those who suggest that this is a case involving extraordinary powers should be mindful that these are extraordinary times. A world not yet recovered from the devastation of World War II has been forced to face the threat of another and more terrifying global conflict. . . .

In 1950, when the United Nations called upon member nations "to render every assistance" to repel aggression in Korea, the United States furnished its vigorous support. For almost two full years, our armed forces have been fighting in Korea, suffering casualties of over 108,000 men. Hostilities have not abated. . . . Congressional support of the action in Korea has been manifested by provisions for increased military manpower and equipment and for economic stabilization, as hereinafter described. . . .

The President has the duty to execute the foregoing legislative programs. Their successful execution depends upon continued production of steel and stabilized prices for steel. Accordingly, when the collective bargaining agreements between the Nation's steel producers and their employees, represented by the United Steel Workers, were due to expire on December 31, 1951, and a strike shutting down the entire basic steel industry was threatened, the President acted to avert a complete shutdown of steel production. . . .

A review of executive action demonstrates that our Presidents have on many occasions exhibited the leadership contemplated by the Framers when they made the President Commander in Chief, and imposed upon him the trust to 'take Care that the Laws be faithfully executed.' With or without explicit statutory authorization, Presidents have at such times dealt with national emergencies by acting promptly and resolutely to enforce legislative programs, at least to save those programs until Congress could act. Congress and the courts have responded to such executive initiative with consistent approval. . . . Presidents have taken prompt action to enforce the laws and protect the country whether or not Congress happened to provide in advance for the particular method of execution. . . . [T]he fact that Congress and the courts have consistently recognized and given their support to such executive action indicates that . . . a power of seizure has been accepted throughout our history.

. . . Whatever the extent of Presidential power on more tranquil occasions, and whatever the right of the President to execute legislative programs as he sees fit without reporting the mode of execution to Congress, the single Presidential purpose disclosed on this record is to faithfully execute the laws by acting in an emergency to maintain the status quo, thereby preventing collapse of the legislative programs until Congress could act. The President's action served the same purposes as a judicial stay entered to maintain the status quo in order to preserve the jurisdiction of a court. In his Message to Congress immediately following the seizure, the President . . . expressed his desire to cooperate with any legislative proposals approving, regulating or rejecting the seizure of the steel mills. Consequently, there is no evidence whatever of any Presidential purpose to defy Congress or act in any way inconsistent with the legislative will. . . . There is no cause to fear Executive tyranny so long as the laws of Congress are being faithfully executed. Certainly there is no basis for fear of dictatorship when the Executive acts, as he did in this case, only to save the situation until Congress could act. . . .

The broad executive power granted by Article II to an officer on duty 365 days a year cannot, it is said, be invoked to avert disaster. Instead, the President must confine himself to sending a message to Congress recommending action. Under this messenger-boy concept of the Office, the President cannot even act to preserve legislative programs from destruction so that Congress will have something left to act upon. . . . No basis for claims of arbitrary action, unlimited powers or dictatorial usurpation of congressional power appears from the facts of this case. On the contrary, judicial, legislative and executive precedents throughout our history demonstrate that in this case the President acted in full conformity with his duties under the Constitution. . . .

THE
MODERN ERA
(1954–2012)

RACE AND SEX

❧

*B*rown v. Board of Education (1954) was a landmark decision. The Court unanimously repudiated the "separate
but equal" doctrine of *Plessy v. Ferguson* (1896) in the area
of education, holding that segregation on the basis of race is unconstitutional. Over the next several years, the Court ordered desegregation
of public schools and applied the principle of *Brown* to invalidate other
laws segregating or discriminating on the basis of race.

In *Loving v. Virginia* (1967), the Court unanimously struck down
state laws forbidding interracial marriage, holding that racial classifications designed to segregate or treat persons differently on account of
race were unconstitutional.

✪

Brown v. Board of Education
347 U.S. 483 (1954)

•

MR. CHIEF JUSTICE WARREN DELIVERED THE OPINION OF THE COURT.

These cases come to us from the States of Kansas, South Carolina, Virginia, and Delaware. They are premised on different facts and different local conditions, but a common legal question justifies their consideration together in this consolidated opinion.

In each of the cases, minors of the Negro race, through their legal representatives, seek the aid of the courts in obtaining admission to the public schools of their community on a nonsegregated basis. In each instance, they have been denied admission to schools attended by white children under laws requiring or permitting segregation according to race. This segregation was alleged to deprive the plaintiffs of the equal protection of the laws under the Fourteenth Amendment. In each of the cases other than the Delaware case, a three-judge federal district court denied relief to the plaintiffs on the so-called "separate but equal" doctrine announced by this Court in *Plessy v. Ferguson*, 163 U.S. 537. Under that doctrine, equality of treatment is accorded when the races are provided substantially equal facilities, even though these facilities be separate. . . .

The plaintiffs contend that segregated public schools are not "equal" and cannot be made "equal," and that hence they are deprived of the equal protection of the laws. Because of the obvious importance of the question presented, the Court took jurisdiction. Argument was heard in the 1952 Term, and reargument was heard this Term on certain questions propounded by the Court.

Reargument was largely devoted to the circumstances surrounding the adoption of the Fourteenth Amendment in 1868. It covered exhaustively consideration of the Amendment in Congress, ratification by the states, then existing practices in racial segregation, and the views of proponents and opponents of the Amendment. This discussion and our own investigation convince us that, although these sources cast some light, it is not enough to resolve the problem with which we are faced.

At best, they are inconclusive. The most avid proponents of the post-War Amendments undoubtedly intended them to remove all legal distinctions among "all persons born or naturalized in the United States." Their opponents, just as certainly, were antagonistic to both the letter and the spirit of the Amendments and wished them to have the most limited effect. What others in Congress and the state legislatures had in mind cannot be determined with any degree of certainty.

An additional reason for the inconclusive nature of the Amendment's history, with respect to segregated schools, is the status of public education at that time. In the South, the movement toward free common schools, supported by general taxation, had not yet taken hold. Education of white children was largely in the hands of private groups. Education of Negroes was almost nonexistent, and practically all of the race were illiterate. In fact, any education of Negroes was forbidden by law in some states. Today, in contrast, many Negroes have achieved outstanding success in the arts and sciences as well as in the business and professional world. It is true that public school education at the time of the Amendment had advanced further in the North, but the effect of the Amendment on Northern States was generally ignored in the congressional debates. Even in the North, the conditions of public education did not approximate those existing today. The curriculum was usually rudimentary; ungraded schools were common in rural areas; the school term was but three months a year in many states; and compulsory school attendance was virtually unknown. As a consequence, it is not surprising that there should be so little in the history of the Fourteenth Amendment relating to its intended effect on public education.

In the first cases in this Court construing the Fourteenth Amendment, decided shortly after its adoption, the Court interpreted it as proscribing all state-imposed discriminations against the Negro race. The doctrine of "separate but equal" did not make its appearance in this court until 1896 in the case of *Plessy v. Ferguson*, supra, involving not education but transportation. American courts have since labored with the doctrine for over half a century. In this Court, there have been six cases involving the 'separate but equal' doctrine in the field of public education. . . . In more recent cases, all on the graduate school level, inequality was found in that specific benefits enjoyed by white students were denied to Negro students of the same educational qualifications. In none of these cases was it necessary to re-examine the doctrine to grant relief to the Negro plaintiff. And in *Sweatt v. Painter* [339 U.S. 629 (1950)], the Court expressly reserved decision on the question whether *Plessy v. Ferguson* should be held inapplicable to public education.

In the instant cases, that question is directly presented. Here, unlike *Sweatt v. Painter*, there are findings below that the Negro and white schools involved have been equalized, or are being equalized, with respect to buildings, curricula, qualifications and salaries of teachers, and other "tangible" factors. Our decision, therefore, cannot turn on merely a comparison of these tangible factors in the Negro and white schools involved in each of the cases. We must look instead to the effect of segregation itself on public education.

In approaching this problem, we cannot turn the clock back to 1868 when the Amendment was adopted, or even to 1896 when *Plessy v. Ferguson* was written. We must consider public education in the light of its full development and its present place in American life throughout the Nation. Only in this way can it be determined if segregation in public schools deprives these plaintiffs of the equal protection of the laws.

Today, education is perhaps the most important function of state and local governments. Compulsory school attendance laws and the great expenditures for education both demonstrate our recognition of the importance of education to our democratic society. . . . In these days, it is doubtful that any child may reasonably be expected to succeed in life if he is denied the opportunity of an education. Such an opportunity, where the state has undertaken to provide it, is a right which must be made available to all on equal terms.

We come then to the question presented: Does segregation of children in public schools solely on the basis of race, even though the physical facilities and other "tangible" factors may be equal, deprive the children of the minority group of equal educational opportunities? We believe that it does.

In *Sweatt v. Painter*, in finding that a segregated law school for Negroes could not provide them equal educational opportunities, this Court relied in large part on "those qualities which are incapable of objective measurement but which make for greatness in a law school." In *McLaurin v. Oklahoma State Regents*, 339 U.S. 637 . . . (1950), the Court, in requiring that a Negro admitted to a white graduate school be treated like all other students, again resorted to intangible considerations: " . . . his ability to study, to engage in discussions and exchange views with other students, and, in general, to learn his profession." Such considerations apply with added force to children in grade and high schools. To separate them from others of similar age and qualifications solely because of their race generates a feeling of inferiority as to their status in the community that may affect their hearts and minds in a way unlikely ever to be undone. The effect of this separation on their educational opportunities was well stated by a finding in the Kansas case by a court which nevertheless felt compelled to rule against the Negro plaintiffs:

Segregation of white and colored children in public schools has a detrimental effect upon the colored children. The impact is greater when it has the sanction of the law; for the policy of separating the races is usually interpreted as denoting the inferiority of the negro group. A sense of inferiority affects the motivation of a child to learn. Segregation with the sanction of law, therefore, has a tendency to [retard] the educational and mental development of Negro children and to deprive them of some of the benefits they would receive in a racial[ly] integrated school system.

Whatever may have been the extent of psychological knowledge at the time of *Plessy v. Ferguson*, this finding is amply supported by modern authority. Any language in *Plessy v. Ferguson* contrary to this finding is rejected.

We conclude that in the field of public education the doctrine of 'separate but equal' has no place. Separate educational facilities are inherently unequal. Therefore, we hold that the plaintiffs and others similarly situated for whom the actions have been brought are, by reason of the segregation complained of, deprived of the equal protection of the laws guaranteed by the Fourteenth Amendment. . . .

Loving v. Virginia
388 U.S. 1 (1967)

•

Mr. Chief Justice WARREN delivered the opinion of the Court.

This case presents a constitutional question never addressed by this Court: whether a statutory scheme adopted by the State of Virginia to prevent marriages between persons solely on the basis of racial classifications violates the Equal Protection and Due Process Clauses of the Fourteenth Amendment. For reasons which seem to us to reflect the central meaning of those constitutional commands, we conclude that these statutes cannot stand consistently with the Fourteenth Amendment.

In June 1958, two residents of Virginia, Mildred Jeter, a Negro woman, and Richard Loving, a white man, were married in the District of Columbia pursuant to its laws. Shortly after their marriage, the Lovings returned to Virginia and established their marital abode in Caroline County. . . . [T]he Circuit Court of Caroline County, a grand jury issued an indictment charging the Lovings with violating Virginia's ban on interracial marriages. . . . [T]he Lovings pleaded guilty to the charge and were sentenced to one year in jail; however, the trial judge suspended the sentence for a period of 25 years on the condition that the Lovings leave the State and not return to Virginia together for 25 years. . . .

The State argues that the meaning of the Equal Protection Clause, as illuminated by the statements of the Framers, is only that state penal laws containing an interracial element as part of the definition of the offense must apply equally to whites and Negroes in the sense that members of each race are punished to the same degree. The State contends that, because its miscegenation statutes punish equally both the white and the Negro participants in an interracial marriage, these statutes, despite their reliance on racial classifications do not constitute an invidious discrimination based upon race. The second argument advanced by the State assumes the validity of its equal application theory. The argument is that, if the Equal Protection Clause does not outlaw miscegenation statutes because of their reliance on racial classifications, the question of constitutionality would thus become whether there was any rational basis for a State to treat interracial marriages differently from other marriages. On this question, the State argues, the scientific evidence is substantially in doubt and, consequently, this Court should defer to the wisdom of the state legislature in adopting its policy of discouraging interracial marriages.

Because we reject the notion that the mere "equal application" of a statute containing racial classifications is enough to remove the classifications from the Fourteenth Amendment's proscription of all invidious racial discriminations, we do not accept the State's contention that these statutes should be upheld if there is any possible basis for concluding that they serve a rational purpose. . . .

[T]he Equal Protection Clause requires the consideration of whether the classifications drawn by any statute constitute an arbitrary and invidious discrimination. The clear and central purpose of the Fourteenth Amendment was to eliminate all official state sources of invidious racial discrimination in the States. . . .

There can be no question but that Virginia's miscegenation statutes rest solely upon distinctions drawn according to race. The statutes proscribe generally accepted conduct if engaged in by members of different races. . . . At the very least, the Equal Protection Clause demands that racial classifications, especially suspect in criminal statutes, be subjected to the "most rigid scrutiny," *Korematsu v. United States*, 323 U.S. 214, 216 (1944), and, if they are ever to be upheld, they must be shown to be necessary to the accomplishment of some permissible state objective, independent of the racial discrimination which it was the object of the Fourteenth Amendment to eliminate.

There is patently no legitimate overriding purpose independent of invidious racial discrimination which justifies this classification. The fact that Virginia prohibits only interracial marriages involving white persons demonstrates that the racial classifications must stand on their own justification, as measures designed to maintain White Supremacy. We have consistently denied the constitutionality of measures which restrict the rights of citizens on account of race. There can be no doubt that restricting the freedom to marry solely because of racial classifications violates the central meaning of the Equal Protection Clause.

These statutes also deprive the Lovings of liberty without due process of law in violation of the Due Process Clause of the Fourteenth Amendment. The freedom to marry has long been recognized as one of the vital personal rights essential to the orderly pursuit of happiness by free men. . . . To deny this fundamental freedom on so unsupportable a basis as the racial classifications embodied in these statutes, classifications so directly subversive of the principle of equality at the heart of the Fourteenth Amendment, is surely to deprive all the State's citizens of liberty without due process of law. . . .

Grutter v. Bollinger
539 U.S. 306 (2003)

•

The Supreme Court's first major decision on the issue of "affirmative action"—minority-race government preferences in education, contracting, or employment—came in *Regents of University of California v. Bakke* (1978) and involved a minority quota for students admitted to a public university's medical school. The Court was deeply divided: a 5–4 majority rejected racial quotas and set-asides, but a different 5–4 majority allowed consideration of race as a "factor." Justice Powell, who cast the deciding vote, concluded that quotas were forbidden by statute and by the Constitution, but that race could be considered as a "plus factor" in admissions decisions that relied on other criteria. Eight justices rejected the distinction between quotas and "plus-factors" for race, but Justice Lewis Powell's opinion—joined by no other justice—became the holding of the case.

In *Grutter v. Bollinger* (2003), a 5–4 majority of the Court endorsed Justice Powell's approach and upheld the University of Michigan Law School's affirmative-action admissions system. In *Gratz v. Bollinger*, a companion case decided the same day, a 6–3 majority struck down Michigan's somewhat different undergraduate program, which gave a twenty-point bonus (out of one hundred) for racial-minority status in its admissions algorithm. Only Justice O'Connor and Justice Breyer joined both results.

✪

JUSTICE O'CONNOR DELIVERED THE OPINION OF THE COURT.

This case requires us to decide whether the use of race as a factor in student admissions by the University of Michigan Law School (Law School) is unlawful. . . .

We last addressed the use of race in public higher education over 25 years ago. In the landmark [*Regents of University of California v.*] *Bakke* case, we reviewed a racial set-aside program that reserved 16 out of 100 seats in a medical school class for members of certain minority groups.

The decision produced six separate opinions, none of which commanded a majority of the Court. Four Justices would have upheld the program against all attack on the ground that the government can use race to "remedy disadvantages cast on minorities by past racial prejudice." Four other Justices avoided the constitutional question altogether and struck down the program on statutory grounds. Justice Powell provided a fifth vote not only for invalidating the set-aside program, but also for reversing the state court's injunction against any use of race whatsoever. . . .

Justice Powell began by stating that "[t]he guarantee of equal protection cannot mean one thing when applied to one individual and something else when applied to a person of another color. If both are not accorded the same protection, then it is not equal." In Justice Powell's view, when governmental decisions "touch upon an individual's race or ethnic background, he is entitled to a judicial determination that the burden he is asked to bear on that basis is precisely tailored to serve a compelling governmental interest." Under this exacting standard, only one of the interests asserted by the university survived Justice Powell's scrutiny.

First, Justice Powell rejected an interest in "'reducing the historic deficit of traditionally disfavored minorities in medical schools and in the medical profession'" as an unlawful interest in racial balancing. Second, Justice Powell rejected an interest in remedying societal discrimination because such measures would risk placing unnecessary burdens on innocent third parties "who bear no responsibility for whatever harm the beneficiaries of the special admissions program are thought to have suffered." Third, Justice Powell rejected an interest in "increasing the number of physicians who will practice in communities currently underserved," concluding that even if such an interest could be compelling in some circumstances the program under review was not "geared to promote that goal." Justice Powell approved the university's use of race to further only one interest: "the attainment of a diverse student body." . . . Justice Powell was, however, careful to emphasize that in his view race "is only one element in a range of factors a university properly may consider in attaining the goal of a heterogeneous student body."

In the wake of our fractured decision in *Bakke*, courts have struggled to discern whether Justice Powell's diversity rationale, set forth in part of the opinion joined by no other Justice, is nonetheless binding precedent. . . . [F]or the reasons set out below, today we endorse Justice

Powell's view that student body diversity is a compelling state interest that can justify the use of race in university admissions. . . .

Because the Fourteenth Amendment "protect[s] *persons*, not *groups*," all "governmental action based on race—a *group* classification long recognized as in most circumstances irrelevant and therefore prohibited-should be subjected to detailed judicial inquiry to ensure that the *personal* right to equal protection of the laws has not been infringed." *Adarand Constructors, Inc. v. Peña* (1995). It follows from that principle that "government may treat people differently because of their race only for the most compelling reasons." . . . It is true that some language in [earlier] opinions might be read to suggest that remedying past discrimination is the only permissible justification for race-based governmental action. But we have never held that the only governmental use of race that can survive strict scrutiny is remedying past discrimination. . . . Today, we hold that the Law School has a compelling interest in attaining a diverse student body.

The Law School's educational judgment that such diversity is essential to its educational mission is one to which we defer. . . . The Law School has determined, based on its experience and expertise, that a "critical mass" of underrepresented minorities is necessary to further its compelling interest in securing the educational benefits of a diverse student body. . . .

[A] university may consider race or ethnicity only as a "'plus' in a particular applicant's file," without "insulat[ing] the individual from comparison with all other candidates for the available seats." *Bakke* (Opinion of Powell, J.) . . . [T]he Law School engages in a highly individualized, holistic review of each applicant's file, giving serious consideration to all the ways an applicant might contribute to a diverse educational environment. . . . There is no policy, either *de jure* or *de facto*, of automatic acceptance or rejection based on any single "soft" variable. Unlike the program at issue in *Gratz v. Bollinger*, ante, the Law School awards no mechanical, predetermined diversity "bonuses" based on race or ethnicity. . . .

[In] the context of its individualized inquiry into the possible diversity contributions of all applicants, the Law School's race-conscious admissions program does not unduly harm nonminority applicants. We are mindful, however, that "[a] core purpose of the Fourteenth Amendment was to do away with all governmentally imposed discrimination based on race." *Palmore v. Sidoti*, (1984). Accordingly, race-conscious admissions policies must be limited in time. This requirement reflects that racial classifications, however compelling their goals, are potentially so dangerous that they may be employed no more broadly than the interest demands. Enshrining a permanent justification for racial preferences would offend this fundamental equal protection principle. We see no reason to exempt race-conscious admissions programs from the requirement that all governmental use of race must have a logical end point. . . . In the context of higher education, the durational requirement can be met by sunset provisions in race-conscious admissions policies and periodic reviews to determine whether racial preferences are still necessary to achieve student body diversity. . . . It has been 25 years since Justice Powell first approved the use of race to further an interest in student body diversity in the context of public higher education. . . . We expect that 25 years from now, the use of racial preferences will no longer be necessary to further the interest approved today.

JUSTICE THOMAS . . . CONCURRING IN PART AND DISSENTING IN PART.

Frederick Douglass, speaking to a group of abolitionists almost 140 years ago, delivered a message lost on today's majority:

> "[I]n regard to the colored people, there is always more that is benevolent, I perceive, than just, manifested towards us. What I ask for the negro is not benevolence, not pity, not sympathy, but simply *justice.* The American people have always been anxious to know what they shall do with us. . . . I have had but one answer from the beginning. Do nothing with us! Your doing with us has already played the mischief with us. Do nothing with us! If the apples will not remain on the tree of their own strength, if they are worm-eaten at the core, if they are early ripe and disposed to fall, let them fall! . . . And if the negro cannot stand on his own legs, let him fall also. All I ask is, give him a chance to stand on his own legs! Let him alone! . . . [Y]our interference is doing him positive injury."

What the Black Man Wants: An Address Delivered in Boston, Massachusetts, on 26 January 1865, reprinted in 4 The Frederick Douglass Papers 59, 68 (J. Blassingame & J. McKivigan eds. 1991) (emphasis in original).
Like Douglass, I believe blacks can achieve in every avenue of

American life without the meddling of university administrators. Because I wish to see all students succeed whatever their color, I share, in some respect, the sympathies of those who sponsor the type of discrimination advanced by the University of Michigan Law School. The Constitution does not, however, tolerate institutional devotion to the status quo in admissions policies when such devotion ripens into racial discrimination. Nor does the Constitution countenance the unprecedented deference the Court gives to the Law School, an approach inconsistent with the very concept of "strict scrutiny."

No one would argue that a university could set up a lower general admissions standard and then impose heightened requirements only on black applicants. Similarly, a university may not maintain a high admissions standard and grant exemptions to favored races. The Law School, of its own choosing, and for its own purposes, maintains an exclusionary admissions system that it knows produces racially disproportionate results. Racial discrimination is not a permissible solution to the self-inflicted wounds of this elitist admissions policy.

The majority upholds the Law School's racial discrimination not by interpreting the people's Constitution, but by responding to a faddish slogan of the cognoscenti. Nevertheless, I concur in part in the Court's opinion. First, I agree with the Court insofar as its decision, which approves of only one racial classification, confirms that further use of race in admissions remains unlawful. Second, I agree with the Court's holding that racial discrimination in higher education admissions will be illegal in 25 years. . . . I respectfully dissent from the remainder of the Court's opinion and the judgment, however, because I believe that the Law School's current use of race violates the Equal Protection Clause and that the Constitution means the same thing today as it will in 300 months. . . .

The Law School maintains that it wishes to obtain "educational benefits that flow from student body diversity." This statement must be evaluated carefully, because it implies that both "diversity" and "educational benefits" are components of the Law School's compelling state interest. Additionally, the Law School's refusal to entertain certain changes in its admissions process and status indicates that the compelling state interest it seeks to validate is actually broader than might appear at first glance.

Undoubtedly there are other ways to "better" the education of law students aside from ensuring that the student body contains a "critical mass" of underrepresented minority students. Attaining "diversity," whatever it means, is the mechanism by which the Law School obtains educational benefits, not an end of itself. The Law School, however, apparently believes that only a racially mixed student body can lead to the educational benefits it seeks. How, then, is the Law School's interest in these allegedly unique educational "benefits" *not* simply the forbidden interest in "racial balancing," that the majority expressly rejects? A distinction between these two ideas . . . is purely sophistic—so much so that the majority uses them interchangeably. . . .

The Law School adamantly disclaims any race-neutral alternative that would reduce "academic selectivity," which would in turn "require the Law School to become a very different institution, and to sacrifice a core part of its educational mission." . . . In other words, the Law School seeks to improve marginally the education it offers without sacrificing too much of its exclusivity and elite status. . . . Under the proper standard, there is no pressing public necessity in maintaining a public law school at all and, it follows, certainly not an elite law school. Likewise, marginal improvements in legal education do not qualify as a compelling state interest. While legal education at a public university may be good policy or otherwise laudable, it is obviously not a pressing public necessity[.] . . . Michigan has no compelling interest in having a law school at all, much less an *elite* one. . . .

An infinite variety of admissions methods are available to the Law School. Considering all of the radical thinking that has historically occurred at this country's universities, the Law School's intractable approach toward admissions is striking. The Court will not even deign to make the Law School try other methods, however, preferring instead to grant a 25-year license to violate the Constitution. And the same Court that had the courage to order the desegregation of all public schools in the South now fears, on the basis of platitudes rather than principle, to force the Law School to abandon a decidedly imperfect admissions regime that provides the basis for racial discrimination. . . .

Beyond the harm the Law School's racial discrimination visits upon its test subjects, no social science has disproved the notion that this discrimination "engender[s] attitudes of superiority or, alternatively, provoke[s] resentment among those who believe that they have been wronged by the government's use of race." *Adarand* (Thomas, J., concurring). "These programs stamp minorities with a badge of inferiority and may cause them to develop dependencies or to adopt an attitude that they are 'entitled' to preferences."

It is uncontested that each year, the Law School admits a handful of blacks who would be admitted in the absence of racial discrimination. . . . Who can differentiate between those who belong and those who do not? The majority of blacks are admitted to the Law School because of discrimination, and because of this policy all are tarred as undeserving. This problem of stigma does not depend on determinacy as to whether those stigmatized are actually the "beneficiaries" of racial discrimination. When blacks take positions in the highest places of government, industry, or academia, it is an open question today whether their skin color played a part in their advancement. The question itself is the stigma—because either racial discrimination did play a role, in which case the person may be deemed "otherwise unqualified," or it did not, in which case asking the question itself unfairly marks those blacks who would succeed without discrimination. . . .

"Our Constitution is color-blind, and neither knows nor tolerates classes among citizens." *Plessy v. Ferguson* (1896) (Harlan, J., dissenting). It has been nearly 140 years since Frederick Douglass asked the intellectual ancestors of the Law School to "[d]o nothing with us!" and the Nation adopted the Fourteenth Amendment. Now we must wait another 25 years to see this principle of equality vindicated. I therefore respectfully dissent from the remainder of the Court's opinion and the judgment.

Craig v. Boren
429 U.S. 190 (1976)

•

Craig v. Boren (1976) is the unlikely modern landmark on sex discrimination. The Court struck down, by a vote of 7–2, an Oklahoma law setting a higher minimum beer-drinking age for men than for women, as a violation of the Equal Protection Clause. The Court adopted an "intermediate" standard for reviewing sex-based classifications, which is less stringent than the "strict scrutiny" applied to racial discrimination but more stringent than the relaxed, "rational basis" standard applied to economic legislation.

MR. JUSTICE BRENNAN DELIVERED THE OPINION OF THE COURT.

The interaction of two sections of an Oklahoma statute . . . prohibits the sale of "nonintoxicating" 3.2% beer to males under the age of 21 and to females under the age of 18. The question to be decided is whether such a gender-based differential constitutes a denial to males 18–20 years of age of the equal protection of the laws in violation of the Fourteenth Amendment. . . .

To withstand constitutional challenge, previous cases establish that classifications by gender must serve important governmental objectives and must be substantially related to achievement of those objectives. Thus, in *Reed* [*v. Reed* (1971)], the objectives of "reducing the workload on probate courts," and "avoiding intrafamily controversy," were deemed of insufficient importance to sustain use of an overt gender criterion in the appointment of administrators of intestate decedents' estates. Decisions following *Reed* similarly have rejected administrative ease and convenience as sufficiently important objectives to justify gender-based classifications. . . .

Reed v. Reed has also provided the underpinning for decisions that have invalidated statutes employing gender as an inaccurate proxy for other, more germane bases of classification. Hence, "archaic and overbroad" generalizations concerning the financial position of servicewomen and working women could not justify use of a gender line in determining eligibility for certain governmental entitlements. Similarly, increasingly outdated misconceptions concerning the role of females in the home rather than in the "marketplace and world of ideas" were rejected as loose-fitting characterizations incapable of supporting state statutory schemes that were premised upon their accuracy. In light of the weak congruence between gender and the characteristic or trait that gender purported to represent, it was necessary that the legislatures choose either to realign their substantive laws in a gender-neutral fashion, or to adopt procedures for identifying those instances where the sex-centered generalization actually comported with fact. . . .

We turn then to the question whether, under *Reed*, the difference between males and females with respect to the purchase of 3.2% beer warrants the differential in age drawn by the Oklahoma statute. We conclude that it does not. . . .

We accept for purposes of discussion the District Court's identification of the objective underlying [sections] 241 and 245 as the enhancement of traffic safety. Clearly, the protection of public health and safety represents an important function of state and local governments. However, appellees' statistics in our view cannot support the conclusion that the gender-based distinction closely serves to achieve that objective and therefore the distinction cannot under *Reed* withstand equal protection challenge.

The appellees introduced a variety of statistical surveys. First, an analysis of arrest statistics for 1973 demonstrated that 18–20-year-old male arrests for "driving under the influence" and "drunkenness" substantially exceeded female arrests for that same age period. Similarly, youths aged 17–21 were found to be overrepresented among those killed or injured in traffic accidents, with males again numerically exceeding females in this regard. Third, a random roadside survey in Oklahoma City revealed that young males were more inclined to drive and drink beer than were their female counterparts. . . .

Even were this statistical evidence accepted as accurate, it nevertheless offers only a weak answer to the equal protection question presented here. The most focused and relevant of the statistical surveys, arrests of 18–20-year-olds for alcohol-related driving offenses, exemplifies the ultimate unpersuasiveness of this evidentiary record. Viewed in terms of the correlation between sex and the actual activity that Oklahoma seeks to regulate driving while under the influence of alcohol the statistics broadly establish that .18% of females and 2% of males in that age group were arrested for that offense. While such a disparity is not trivial in a statistical sense, it hardly can form the basis for employment of a gender line as a classifying device. Certainly if maleness is to serve as a proxy for drinking and driving, a correlation of 2% must be considered an unduly tenuous "fit." Indeed, prior cases have consistently rejected the use of sex as a decision-making factor even though the statutes in question certainly rested on far more predictive empirical relationships than this.

. . . It is unrealistic to expect either members of the judiciary or state officials to be well versed in the rigors of experimental or statistical technique. But this merely illustrates that proving broad sociological propositions by statistics is a dubious business, and one that inevitably is in tension with the normative philosophy that underlies the Equal Protection Clause. Suffice to say that the showing offered by the appellees does not satisfy us that sex represents a legitimate, accurate proxy for the regulation of drinking and driving. . . .

MR. JUSTICE REHNQUIST, DISSENTING.

The Court's disposition of this case is objectionable on two grounds. First is its conclusion that men challenging a gender-based statute which treats them less favorably than women may invoke a more stringent standard of judicial review than pertains to most other types of classifications. Second is the Court's enunciation of this standard, without citation to any source, as being that "classifications by gender must serve important governmental objectives and must be substantially related to achievement of those objectives." . . .

The Court's conclusion that a law which treats males less favorably than females "must serve important governmental objectives and must be substantially related to achievement of those objectives" apparently comes out of thin air. The Equal Protection Clause contains no such language, and none of our previous cases adopt that standard. . . . How is this Court to divine what objectives are important? How is it to determine whether a particular law is "substantially" related to the achievement of such objective, rather than related in some other way to its achievement? Both of the phrases used are so diaphanous and elastic as to invite subjective judicial preferences or prejudices relating to particular types of legislation, masquerading as judgments whether such legislation is directed at "important" objectives or, whether the relationship to those objectives is "substantial" enough. . . .

The Court's criticism of the statistics relied on by the District Court conveys the impression that a legislature in enacting a new law is to be subjected to the judicial equivalent of a doctoral examination in statistics. Legislatures are not held to any rules of evidence such as those which may govern courts or other administrative bodies, and are entitled to draw factual conclusions on the basis of the determination of probable cause which an arrest by a police officer normally represents. In this situation, they could reasonably infer that the incidence of drunk driving is a good deal higher than the incidence of arrest. . . .

Nor is it unreasonable to conclude from the expressed preference for beer by four-fifths of the age-group males that that beverage was a predominant source of their intoxication-related arrests. Taking that as the predicate, the State could reasonably bar those males from any purchases of alcoholic beer, including that of the 3.2% variety. This Court lacks the expertise or the data to evaluate the intoxicating properties of that beverage, and in that posture our only appropriate course is to defer to the reasonable inference supporting the statute that taken in sufficient quantity this beer has the same effect as any alcoholic beverage.

Quite apart from these alleged methodological deficiencies in the statistical evidence, the Court appears to hold that that evidence, on its face, fails to support the distinction drawn in the statute. The Court notes that only 2% of males (as against .18% of females) in the age group were arrested for drunk driving, and that this very low figure establishes "an unduly tenuous 'fit'" between maleness and drunk driving in the 18–20-year-old group. On this point the Court misconceives the nature of the equal protection inquiry.

The rationality of a statutory classification for equal protection purposes does not depend upon the statistical "fit" between the class and the trait sought to be singled out. It turns on whether there may be a sufficiently higher incidence of the trait within the included class than in the excluded class to justify different treatment. Therefore the present equal protection challenge to this gender-based discrimination poses only the question whether the incidence of drunk driving among young men is sufficiently greater than among young women to justify differential treatment. Notwithstanding the Court's critique of the statistical evidence, that evidence suggests clear differences between the drinking and driving habits of young men and women. Those differences are grounds enough for the State reasonably to conclude that young males pose by far the greater drunk-driving hazard, both in terms of sheer numbers and in terms of hazard on a per-driver basis. The gender-based difference in treatment in this case is therefore not irrational.

EQUAL PROTECTION AND
VOTING RIGHTS

⚜

*I*n a series of controversial and consequential decisions beginning in the 1960s, the Supreme Court held that the Equal
Protection Clause of the Fourteenth Amendment includes a
"one person, one vote" requirement that bars unequal treatment of the
right to vote within a state. *Baker v. Carr* (1962) decided by a vote of 7–2
that federal courts could appropriately review state election processes
under the Equal Protection Clause. *Reynolds v. Sims* (1964) held, by a
vote of 8–1, that the Equal Protection Clause requires that state election
districts be drawn so as to give substantially equal weight to each vote.
Harper v. Virginia Board of Elections (1966) struck down state poll taxes
by a vote of 6–3.

Bush v. Gore (2000) applied *Baker* and *Reynolds* to reverse an election
recount treating disputed ballots differently in different parts of the
state, ending a contested election for President of the United States. The
vote was 7–2 that the recount procedures violated the Equal Protection
Clause, but 5–4 as to the appropriate remedy.

✪

Baker v. Carr
369 U.S. 186 (1962)

•

MR. JUSTICE BRENNAN DELIVERED THE OPINION OF THE
COURT:

. . . The complaint alleg[ed] that by means of a 1901 statute of Tennessee apportioning the members of the General Assembly among the
State's 95 counties, "these plaintiffs and others similarly situated, are
denied the equal protection of the laws accorded them by the Fourteenth Amendment to the Constitution of the United States by virtue
of the debasement of their votes." . . . We understand the District Court
to have read [our prior] cases as compelling the conclusion that since
the appellants sought to have a legislative apportionment held unconstitutional, their suit presented a 'political question' and was therefore
nonjusticiable. . . . [I]t is argued that apportionment cases, whatever the
actual wording of the complaint, can involve no federal constitutional
right except one resting on the guaranty of a republican form of government, and that complaints based on that clause have been held to present political questions which are nonjusticiable. We hold that the claim
pleaded here neither rests upon nor implicates the Guaranty Clause and
that its justiciability is therefore not foreclosed by our decisions of cases
involving that clause. . . .

Prominent on the surface of any case held to involve a political question is found a textually demonstrable constitutional commitment of
the issue to a coordinate political department; or a lack of judicially dis-
coverable and manageable standards for resolving it; or the impossibility
of deciding without an initial policy determination of a kind clearly
for nonjudicial discretion; or the impossibility of a court's undertaking
independent resolution without expressing lack of the respect due coordinate branches of government; or an unusual need for unquestioning
adherence to a political decision already made; or the potentiality of
embarrassment from multifarious pronouncements by various departments on one question. Unless one of these formulations is inextricable
from the case at bar, there should be no dismissal for non-justiciability
on the ground of a political question's presence. . . .

But it is argued that this case shares the characteristics of decisions that constitute a category not yet considered, cases concerning the Constitution's guaranty, in Art. IV, § 4, of a republican form of government. . . . Guaranty Clause claims involve those elements which define a 'political question,' and for that reason and no other, they are nonjusticiable. . . . The question here is the consistency of state action with the Federal Constitution. We have no question decided, or to be decided, by a political branch of government coequal with this Court. Nor do we risk embarrassment of our government abroad, or grave disturbance at home if we take issue with Tennessee as to the constitutionality of her action here challenged. Nor need the appellants, in order to succeed in this action, ask the Court to enter upon policy determinations for which judicially manageable standards are lacking. . . .

We conclude that the complaint's allegations of a denial of equal protection present a justiciable constitutional cause of action upon which appellants are entitled to a trial and a decision. The right asserted is within the reach of judicial protection under the Fourteenth Amendment. . . .

MR. JUSTICE FRANKFURTER, WHOM MR. JUSTICE HARLAN JOINS, DISSENTING.

The Court today reverses a uniform course of decision established by a dozen cases, including one by which the very claim now sustained was unanimously rejected only five years ago. The impressive body of rulings thus cast aside reflected the equally uniform course of our political history regarding the relationship between population and legislative representation—a wholly different matter from denial of the franchise to individuals because of race, color, religion or sex. Such a massive repudiation of the experience of our whole past in asserting destructively novel judicial power demands a detailed analysis of the role of this Court in our constitutional scheme. Disregard of inherent limits in the effective exercise of the Court's 'judicial Power' not only presages the futility of judicial intervention in the essentially political conflict of forces by which the relation between population and representation has time out of mind been and now is determined. . . . The Court's authority—possessed of neither the purse nor the sword—ultimately rests on sustained public confidence in its moral sanction. Such feeling must be nourished by the Court's complete detachment, in fact and in appearance, from political entanglements and by abstention from injecting itself into the clash of political forces in political settlements. . . .

The present case involves all of the elements that have made the Guarantee Clause cases non-justiciable. It is, in effect, a Guarantee Clause claim masquerading under a different label. But it cannot make the case more fit for judicial action that appellants invoke the Fourteenth Amendment rather than Art. IV, § 4, where, in fact, the gist of their complaint is the same—unless it can be found that the Fourteenth Amendment speaks with greater particularity to their situation. . . .

To find such a political conception legally enforceable in the broad and unspecific guarantee of equal protection is to rewrite the Constitution. Certainly, 'equal protection' is no more secure a foundation for judicial judgment of the permissibility of varying forms of representative government than is 'Republican Form.' . . . The notion that representation proportioned to the geographic spread of population is so universally accepted as a necessary element of equality between man and man that it must be taken to be the standard of a political equality preserved by the Fourteenth Amendment . . . is, to put it bluntly, not true. However desirable and however desired by some among the great political thinkers and framers of our government, it has never been generally practiced, today or in the past. It was not the English system, it was not the colonial system, it was not the system chosen for the national government by the Constitution, it was not the system exclusively or even predominantly practiced by the States at the time of adoption of the Fourteenth Amendment, it is not predominantly practiced by the States today.

. . . Apportionment, by its character, is a subject of extraordinary complexity, involving—even after the fundamental theoretical issues concerning what is to be represented in a representative legislature have been fought out or compromised—considerations of geography, demography, electoral convenience . . . and a host of others. . . . Apportionment battles are overwhelmingly party or intra-party contests. It will add a virulent source of friction and tension in federal-state relations to embroil the federal judiciary in them.

Reynolds v. Sims
377 U.S. 533 (1964)

•

CHIEF JUSTICE WARREN DELIVERED THE OPINION OF THE COURT:

Legislators represent people, not trees or acres. Legislators are elected by voters, not farms or cities or economic interests. As long as ours is a representative form of government, and our legislatures are those instruments of government elected directly by and directly representative of the people, the right to elect legislators in a free and unimpaired fashion is a bedrock of our political system. It could hardly be gainsaid that a constitutional claim had been asserted by an allegation that certain otherwise qualified voters had been entirely prohibited from voting for members of their state legislature. And, if a State should provide that the votes of citizens in one part of the State should be given two times, or five times, or 10 times the weight of votes of citizens in another part of the State, it could hardly be contended that the right to vote of those residing in the disfavored areas had not been effectively diluted. . . . Weighting the votes of citizens differently, by any method or means, merely because of where they happen to reside, hardly seems justifiable. . . .

[T]he concept of equal protection has been traditionally viewed as requiring the uniform treatment of persons standing in the same relation to the governmental action questioned or challenged. With respect to the allocation of legislative representation, all voters, as citizens of a State, stand in the same relation regardless of where they live. Any suggested criteria for the differentiation of citizens are insufficient to justify any discrimination, as to the weight of their votes, unless relevant to the permissible purposes of legislative apportionment. Since the achieving of fair and effective representation for all citizens is concededly the basic aim of legislative apportionment, we conclude that the Equal Protection Clause guarantees the opportunity for equal participation by all voters in the election of state legislators. Diluting the weight of votes because of place of residence impairs basic constitutional rights under the Fourteenth Amendment just as much as invidious discriminations based upon factors such as race, or economic status. . . .

We are told that the matter of apportioning representation in a state legislature is a complex and many-faceted one. We are advised that States can rationally consider factors other than population in apportioning legislative representation. We are admonished not to restrict the power of the States to impose differing views as to political philosophy on their citizens. We are cautioned about the dangers of entering into political thickets and mathematical quagmires. Our answer is this: a denial of constitutionally protected rights demands judicial protection; our oath and our office require no less of us. . . .

We hold that, as a basic constitutional standard, the Equal Protection Clause requires that the seats in both houses of a bicameral state legislature must be apportioned on a population basis. Simply stated, an individual's right to vote for state legislators is unconstitutionally impaired when its weight is in a substantial fashion diluted when compared with votes of citizens living on other parts of the State. . . .

Much has been written since our decision in *Baker v. Carr* about the applicability of the so-called federal analogy to state legislative apportionment arrangements. . . . [T]he court below concluded that no conceivable analogy could be drawn between the federal scheme and the apportionment of seats in the Alabama Legislature under the proposed constitutional amendment. We agree with the District Court, and find the federal analogy inapposite and irrelevant to state legislative districting schemes. Attempted reliance on the federal analogy appears often to be little more than an after-the-fact rationalization offered in defense of maladjusted state apportionment arrangements. The original constitutions of 36 of our States provided that representation in both houses of the state legislatures would be based completely, or predominantly, on population. And the Founding Fathers clearly had no intention of establishing a pattern or model for the apportionment of seats in state legislatures when the system of representation in the Federal Congress was adopted. Demonstrative of this is the fact that the Northwest Ordinance, adopted in the same year, 1787, as the Federal Constitution, provided for the apportionment of seats in territorial legislatures solely on the basis of population.

The system of representation in the two Houses of the Federal Congress is one ingrained in our Constitution, as part of the law of the land. It is one conceived out of compromise and concession indispensable to the establishment of our federal republic. Arising from unique historical circumstances, it is based on the consideration that in establishing our type of federalism a group of formerly independent States bound themselves together under one national government. . . .

Political subdivisions of States—counties, cities, or whatever—never were and never have been considered as sovereign entities. Rather, they have been traditionally regarded as subordinate governmental instrumentalities created by the State to assist in the carrying out of state governmental functions. . . . The relationship of the States to the Federal Government could hardly be less analogous. . . .

Harper v. Virginia Board of Elections
383 U.S. 663 (1966)

•

JUSTICE DOUGLAS DELIVERED THE OPINION OF THE COURT:

. . . We conclude that a State violates the Equal Protection Clause of the Fourteenth Amendment whenever it makes the affluence of the voter or payment of any fee an electoral standard. Voter qualifications have no relation to wealth nor to paying or not paying this or any other tax. Our cases demonstrate that the Equal Protection Clause of the Fourteenth Amendment restrains the States from fixing voter qualifications which invidiously discriminate. . . .

Recently in *Reynolds v. Sims*, 377 U.S. 533, 561–562, we said, 'Undoubtedly, the right of suffrage is a fundamental matter in a free and democratic society. Especially since the right to exercise the franchise in a free and unimpaired manner is preservative of other basic civil and political rights, any alleged infringement of the right of citizens to vote must be carefully and meticulously scrutinized.' . . . We say the same whether the citizen, otherwise qualified to vote, has $1.50 in his pocket or nothing at all, pays the fee or fails to pay it. The principle that denies the State the right to dilute a citizen's vote on account of his economic status or other such factors by analogy bars a system which excludes those unable to pay a fee to vote or who fail to pay.

It is argued that a State may exact fees from citizens for many different kinds of licenses; that if it can demand from all an equal fee for a driver's license, it can demand from all an equal poll tax for voting. But we must remember that the interest of the State, when it comes to voting, is limited to the power to fix qualifications. Wealth, like race, creed, or color, is not germane to one's ability to participate intelligently in the electoral process. . . . To introduce wealth or payment of a fee as a measure of a voter's qualifications is to introduce a capricious or irrelevant factor. The degree of the discrimination is irrelevant. In this context—that is, as a condition of obtaining a ballot—the requirement of fee paying causes an 'invidious' discrimination that runs afoul of the Equal Protection Clause. . . .

[T]he Equal Protection Clause is not shackled to the political theory of a particular era. In determining what lines are unconstitutionally discriminatory, we have never been confined to historic notions of equality, any more than we have restricted due process to a fixed catalogue of what was at a given time deemed to be the limits of fundamental rights. Notions of what constitutes equal treatment for purposes of the Equal Protection Clause do change. . . .

In a recent searching re-examination of the Equal Protection Clause, we held, as already noted, that 'the opportunity for equal participation by all voters in the election of state legislators' is required. *Reynolds v. Sims.* We decline to qualify that principle by sustaining this poll tax. . . . [W]ealth or fee paying has, in our view, no relation to voting qualifications; the right to vote is too precious, too fundamental to be so burdened or conditioned.

MR. JUSTICE BLACK, DISSENTING.

. . . The mere fact that a law results in treating some groups differently from others does not, of course, automatically amount to a violation of the Equal Protection Clause.

. . . A study of our cases shows that this Court has refused to use the general language of the Equal Protection Clause as though it provided a handy instrument to strike down state laws which the Court feels are based on bad governmental policy. . . . Although I join the Court in disliking the policy of the poll tax, this is not in my judgment a justifiable reason for holding this poll tax law unconstitutional. Such a holding on my part would, in my judgment, be an exercise of power which the Constitution does not confer upon me. . . .

The Court's justification for consulting its own notions rather than following the original meaning of the Constitution, as I would, apparently is based on the belief of the majority of the Court that for this Court to be bound by the original meaning of the Constitution is an intolerable and debilitating evil; that our Constitution should not be 'shackled to the political theory of a particular era,' and that to save the country from the original Constitution the Court must have constant power to renew it and keep it abreast of this Court's more enlightening theories of what is best for our society. It seems to me that this is an attack not only on the great value of our Constitution itself but also on the concept of a written constitution which is to survive through the years as originally written unless changed through the amendment process which the Framers wisely provided. Moreover, when a 'political theory' embodied in our Constitution becomes outdated, it seems to me that a majority of the nine members of this Court are not only without constitutional power but are far less qualified to choose a new constitutional political theory than the people of this country proceeding in the manner provided by Article V. . . .

Bush v. Gore
531 U.S. 98 (2000)

•

THE COURT DELIVERED A PER CURIAM OPINION.

On December 8, 2000, the Supreme Court of Florida ordered that the Circuit Court of Leon County tabulate by hand 9,000 ballots in Miami-Dade County. It also ordered the inclusion in the certified vote totals of 215 votes identified in Palm Beach County and 168 votes identified in Miami-Dade County for Vice President Albert Gore, Jr., and Senator Joseph Lieberman, Democratic candidates for President and Vice President. The State Supreme Court . . . held that relief would require manual recounts in all Florida counties where so-called "undervotes" had not been subject to manual tabulation. The court ordered all manual recounts to begin at once. Governor Bush and Richard

Cheney, Republican candidates for President and Vice President, filed an emergency application for a stay of this mandate. On December 9, we granted the application[.] . . .

The petition presents the following questions: whether the Florida Supreme Court established new standards for resolving Presidential election contests, thereby violating Art. II, § 1, cl. 2, of the United States Constitution and failing to comply with 3 U.S.C. § 5, and whether the use of standardless manual recounts violates the Equal Protection and Due Process Clauses. With respect to the equal protection question, we find a violation of the Equal Protection Clause.

. . . When the state legislature vests the right to vote for President in its people, the right to vote as the legislature has prescribed is fundamental; and one source of its fundamental nature lies in the equal weight accorded to each vote and the equal dignity owed to each voter. . . . The right to vote is protected in more than the initial allocation of the franchise. Equal protection applies as well to the manner of its exercise. Having once granted the right to vote on equal terms, the State may not, by later arbitrary and disparate treatment, value one person's vote over that of another. See, e.g., *Harper v. Virginia Bd. of Elections* (1966) ("[O]nce the franchise is granted to the electorate, lines may not be drawn which are inconsistent with the Equal Protection Clause of the Fourteenth Amendment"). It must be remembered that "the right of suffrage can be denied by a debasement or dilution of the weight of a citizen's vote just as effectively as by wholly prohibiting the free exercise of the franchise." *Reynolds v. Sims* (1964).

There is no difference between the two sides of the present controversy on these basic propositions. Respondents say that the very purpose of vindicating the right to vote justifies the recount procedures now at issue. The question before us, however, is whether the recount procedures the Florida Supreme Court has adopted are consistent with its obligation to avoid arbitrary and disparate treatment of the members of its electorate.

. . . As seems to have been acknowledged at oral argument, the standards for accepting or rejecting contested ballots might vary not only from county to county but indeed within a single county from one recount team to another.

The record provides some examples. A monitor in Miami-Dade County testified at trial that he observed that three members of the county canvassing board applied different standards in defining a legal vote. And testimony at trial also revealed that at least one county changed its evaluative standards during the counting process. . . . This is not a process with sufficient guarantees of equal treatment.

An early case in our one person, one vote jurisprudence arose when a State accorded arbitrary and disparate treatment to voters in its different counties. *Gray v. Sanders* (1963). The Court found a constitutional violation. We relied on these principles in the context of the Presidential selection process in *Moore v. Ogilvie* (1969), where we invalidated a county-based procedure that diluted the influence of citizens in larger counties in the nominating process. There we observed that "[t]he idea that one group can be granted greater voting strength than another is hostile to the one man, one vote basis of our representative government."

The State Supreme Court ratified this uneven treatment. It mandated that the recount totals from two counties, Miami-Dade and Palm Beach, be included in the certified total. The court also appeared to hold *sub silentio* that the recount totals from Broward County, which were not completed until after the original November 14 certification by the Secretary, were to be considered part of the new certified vote totals even though the county certification was not contested by Vice President Gore. Yet each of the counties used varying standards to determine what was a legal vote. Broward County used a more forgiving standard than Palm Beach County, and uncovered almost three times as many new votes, a result markedly disproportionate to the difference in population between the counties. . . .

The recount process, in its features here described, is inconsistent with the minimum procedures necessary to protect the fundamental right of each voter in the special instance of a statewide recount under the authority of a single state judicial officer. Our consideration is limited to the present circumstances, for the problem of equal protection in election processes generally presents many complexities. . . .

Upon due consideration of the difficulties identified to this point, it is obvious that the recount cannot be conducted in compliance with the requirements of equal protection and due process without substantial additional work. It would require not only the adoption (after opportunity for argument) of adequate statewide standards for determining what is a legal vote, and practicable procedures to implement them, but also orderly judicial review of any disputed matters that might arise. . . .

The Supreme Court of Florida has said that the legislature intended the State's electors to "participat[e] fully in the federal electoral process," as provided in 3 U.S.C. § 5. That statute, in turn, requires that any controversy or contest that is designed to lead to a conclusive selection of electors be completed by December 12. That date is upon us, and there is no recount procedure in place under the State Supreme Court's order that comports with minimal constitutional standards. Because it is evident that any recount seeking to meet the December 12 date will be unconstitutional for the reasons we have discussed, we reverse the judgment of the Supreme Court of Florida ordering a recount to proceed.

Seven Justices of the Court agree that there are constitutional problems with the recount ordered by the Florida Supreme Court that demand a remedy. . . . The only disagreement is as to the remedy. Because the Florida Supreme Court has said that the Florida Legislature intended to obtain the safe-harbor benefits of 3 U.S.C. § 5, Justice BREYER's proposed remedy—remanding to the Florida Supreme Court for its ordering of a constitutionally proper contest until December 18—contemplates action in violation of the Florida Election Code . . . The judgment of the Supreme Court of Florida is reversed. . . .

JUSTICE STEVENS, WITH WHOM JUSTICE GINSBURG AND JUSTICE BREYER JOIN, DISSENTING.

The Constitution assigns to the States the primary responsibility for determining the manner of selecting the Presidential electors. See Art. II, § 1, cl. 2. When questions arise about the meaning of state laws, including election laws, it is our settled practice to accept the opinions of the highest courts of the States as providing the final answers. On rare occasions, however, either federal statutes or the Federal Constitution may require federal judicial intervention in state elections. This is not such an occasion.

The federal questions that ultimately emerged in this case are not substantial. Article II provides that "[e]ach *State* shall appoint, in such Manner as the Legislature *thereof* may direct, a Number of Electors." It does not create state legislatures out of whole cloth, but rather takes them as they come—as creatures born of, and constrained by, their state constitutions. . . . The legislative power in Florida is subject to judicial review pursuant to Article V of the Florida Constitution, and nothing in Article II of the Federal Constitution frees the state legislature from the constraints in the State Constitution that created it. Moreover, the Florida Legislature's own decision to employ a unitary code for all elections indicates that it intended the Florida Supreme Court to play the same role in Presidential elections that it has historically played in resolving electoral disputes. The Florida Supreme Court's exercise of appellate jurisdiction therefore was wholly consistent with, and indeed contemplated by, the grant of authority in Article II.

JUSTICE BREYER, DISSENTING.

The Court was wrong to take this case. It was wrong to grant a stay. It should now vacate that stay and permit the Florida Supreme Court to decide whether the recount should resume. The political implications of this case for the country are momentous. But the federal legal questions presented, with one exception, are insubstantial.

. . . The majority concludes that the Equal Protection Clause requires that a manual recount be governed not only by the uniform general standard of the "clear intent of the voter," but also by uniform subsidiary standards (for example, a uniform determination whether indented, but not perforated, "undervotes" should count). . . . [S]ince the use of different standards could favor one or the other of the candidates, since time was, and is, too short to permit the lower courts to iron out significant differences through ordinary judicial review, and since the relevant distinction was embodied in the order of the State's highest court, I agree that, in these very special circumstances, basic principles of fairness may well have counseled the adoption of a uniform standard to address the problem. . . .

Nonetheless, there is no justification for the majority's remedy, which is simply to reverse the lower court and halt the recount entirely. An appropriate remedy would be, instead, to remand this case with instructions that, even at this late date, would permit the Florida Supreme Court to require recounting *all* undercounted votes in Florida . . . in accordance with a single uniform standard. . . .

THE FIRST AMENDMENT

*T*he period from 1960 to 1990 marked some particularly important developments and refinements in the Court's interpretation of the First Amendment freedoms of speech, the press, and religion, and set forth principles that have endured to the present. The Court ruled that government generally may not restrict speech because of its content, no matter how offensive or vulgar (*Cohen v. California*, 1971, 5–3), not even if it advocates unlawful conduct (*Brandenburg v. Ohio*, 1969, unanimous). Conduct, such as the burning of a draft card or the American flag, may be restricted by neutral laws, but not because of any symbolic message it sends (*United States v. O'Brien*, 1968, 8–1; *Texas v. Johnson*, 1989, 5–4). Government, generally, may neither keep the press from publishing what it sees fit (*The Pentagon Papers Case*, 1971, 6–3) nor punish the libel of public figures in most cases, unless intentional (*New York Times Co. v. Sullivan*, 1964, unanimous).

With respect to religious freedom, the Court held that official, government-sanctioned prayer in public school was an impermissible "establishment" of religion (*Engel v. Vitale*, 1962, 8–1), but that religious speech on public property did not otherwise violate the Establishment Clause. On the contrary, the First Amendment required equal treatment of religious speech and forbade discrimination against religion (*Widmar v. Vincent*, 1981, 8--1). Finally, the Court wrestled with how broadly to protect the "free exercise" of religion, returning in 1990 to a narrower reading in *Employment Division v. Smith* (5–4).

✪

Cohen v. California
403 U.S. 15 (1971)

•

MR. JUSTICE HARLAN DELIVERED THE OPINION OF THE COURT.

This case may seem at first blush too inconsequential to find its way into our books, but the issue it presents is of no small constitutional significance.

Appellant Paul Robert Cohen was convicted in the Los Angeles Municipal Court of violating that part of California Penal Code § 415 which prohibits "maliciously and willfully disturbing the peace or quiet of any neighborhood or person . . . by . . . offensive conduct . . . ." He was given 30 days' imprisonment. . . .

On April 26, 1968, the defendant was observed in the Los Angeles County Courthouse in the corridor outside of division 20 of the municipal court wearing a jacket bearing the words "Fuck the Draft" which were plainly visible. There were women and children present in the corridor. The defendant was arrested. The defendant testified that he wore the jacket knowing that the words were on the jacket as a means of informing the public of the depth of his feelings against the Vietnam War and the draft.

I

. . . The conviction quite clearly rests upon the asserted offensiveness of the words Cohen used to convey his message to the public. The only "conduct" which the State sought to punish is the fact of communication. Thus, we deal here with a conviction resting solely upon "speech," not upon any separately identifiable conduct which allegedly was intended by Cohen to be perceived by others as expressive of particular views but which, on its face, does not necessarily convey any message and hence arguably could be regulated without effectively repressing Cohen's ability to express himself. Further, the State certainly lacks power to punish Cohen for the underlying content of the message the inscription conveyed. At least so long as there is no showing of an intent to incite disobedience to or disruption of the draft, Cohen could not, consistently with the First and Fourteenth Amendments, be punished for asserting the evident position on the inutility or immorality of the draft his jacket reflected.

Appellant's conviction, then, rests squarely upon his exercise of the "freedom of speech" protected from arbitrary governmental interference by the Constitution and can be justified, if at all, only as a valid regulation of the manner in which he exercised that freedom, not as a permissible prohibition on the substantive message it conveys. This does not end the inquiry, of course, for the First and Fourteenth Amendments have never been thought to give absolute protection to every individual to speak whenever or wherever he pleases or to use any form of address in any circumstances that he chooses. In this vein, too, however, we think it important to note that several issues typically associated with such problems are not presented here. . . .

[T]his case cannot be said to fall within those relatively few categories of instances where prior decisions have established the power of government to deal more comprehensively with certain forms of individual expression simply upon a showing that such a form was employed. This is not, for example, an obscenity case. Whatever else may be necessary to give rise to the States' broader power to prohibit obscene expression, such expression must be, in some significant way, erotic. *Roth v. United States*, 354 U.S. 476 (1957). It cannot plausibly be maintained that this vulgar allusion to the Selective Service System would conjure up such psychic stimulation in anyone likely to be confronted with Cohen's crudely defaced jacket.

This Court has also held that the States are free to ban the simple use, without a demonstration of additional justifying circumstances, of so-called "fighting words," those personally abusive epithets which, when addressed to the ordinary citizen, are, as a matter of common knowledge, inherently likely to provoke violent reaction. *Chaplinsky v.*

New Hampshire, 315 U.S. 568 (1942). . . . No individual actually or likely to be present could reasonably have regarded the words on appellant's jacket as a direct personal insult. Nor do we have here an instance of the exercise of the State's police power to prevent a speaker from intentionally provoking a given group to hostile reaction. . . .

Finally, in arguments before this Court much has been made of the claim that Cohen's distasteful mode of expression was thrust upon unwilling or unsuspecting viewers, and that the State might therefore legitimately act as it did in order to protect the sensitive from otherwise unavoidable exposure to appellant's crude form of protest. Of course, the mere presumed presence of unwitting listeners or viewers does not serve automatically to justify curtailing all speech capable of giving offense. . . . The ability of government, consonant with the Constitution, to shut off discourse solely to protect others from hearing it is, in other words, dependent upon a showing that substantial privacy interests are being invaded in an essentially intolerable manner. Any broader view of this authority would effectively empower a majority to silence dissidents simply as a matter of personal predilections.

In this regard, persons confronted with Cohen's jacket were in a quite different posture than, say, those subjected to the raucous emissions of sound trucks blaring outside their residences. Those in the Los Angeles courthouse could effectively avoid further bombardment of their sensibilities simply by averting their eyes. . . . [I]f Cohen's "speech" was otherwise entitled to constitutional protection, we do not think the fact that some unwilling "listeners" in a public building may have been briefly exposed to it can serve to justify this breach of the peace conviction where, as here, there was no evidence that persons powerless to avoid appellant's conduct did in fact object to it . . . .

II

Against this background, the issue flushed by this case stands out in bold relief. It is whether California can excise, as "offensive conduct," one particular scurrilous epithet from the public discourse, either upon the theory of the court below that its use is inherently likely to cause violent reaction or upon a more general assertion that the States, acting as guardians of public morality, may properly remove this offensive word from the public vocabulary.

The rationale of the California court is plainly untenable. . . . We have been shown no evidence that substantial numbers of citizens are standing ready to strike out physically at whoever may assault their sensibilities with execrations like that uttered by Cohen. There may be some persons about with such lawless and violent proclivities, but that is an insufficient base upon which to erect, consistently with constitutional values, a governmental power to force persons who wish to ventilate their dissident views into avoiding particular forms of expression. The argument amounts to little more than the self-defeating proposition that to avoid physical censorship of one who has not sought to provoke such a response by a hypothetical coterie of the violent and lawless, the States may more appropriately effectuate that censorship themselves. . . .

Admittedly, it is not so obvious that the First and Fourteenth Amendments must be taken to disable the States from punishing public utterance of this unseemly expletive in order to maintain what they regard as a suitable level of discourse within the body politic. We think, however, that examination and reflection will reveal the shortcomings of a contrary viewpoint.

At the outset, we cannot overemphasize that, in our judgment, most situations where the State has a justifiable interest in regulating speech will fall within one or more of the various established exceptions, discussed above but not applicable here, to the usual rule that governmental bodies may not prescribe the form or content of individual expression. Equally important to our conclusion is the constitutional backdrop against which our decision must be made. The constitutional right of free expression is powerful medicine in a society as diverse and populous as ours. It is designed and intended to remove governmental restraints from the arena of public discussion, putting the decision as to what views shall be voiced largely into the hands of each of us, in the hope that use of such freedom will ultimately produce a more capable citizenry and more perfect polity and in the belief that no other approach would comport with the premise of individual dignity and choice upon which our political system rests.

To many, the immediate consequence of this freedom may often appear to be only verbal tumult, discord, and even offensive utterance. These are, however, within established limits, in truth necessary side effects of the broader enduring values which the process of open debate permits us to achieve. That the air may at times seem filled with verbal cacophony is, in this sense not a sign of weakness but of strength. . . .

[T]he principle contended for by the State seems inherently boundless. How is one to distinguish this from any other offensive word? Surely the State has no right to cleanse public debate to the point where it is grammatically palatable to the most squeamish among us. Yet no readily ascertainable general principle exists for stopping short of that result were we to affirm the judgment below. For, while the particular four-letter word being litigated here is perhaps more distasteful than most others of its genre, it is nevertheless often true that one man's vulgarity is another's lyric. Indeed, we think it is largely because governmental officials cannot make principled distinctions in this area that the Constitution leaves matters of taste and style so largely to the individual.

Additionally, we cannot overlook the fact, because it is well illustrated by the episode involved here, that much linguistic expression serves a dual communicative function: it conveys not only ideas capable of relatively precise, detached explication, but otherwise inexpressible emotions as well. In fact, words are often chosen as much for their emotive as their cognitive force. We cannot sanction the view that the Constitution, while solicitous of the cognitive content of individual speech has little or no regard for that emotive function which practically speaking, may often be the more important element of the overall message sought to be communicated. . . .

Finally, and in the same vein, we cannot indulge the facile assumption that one can forbid particular words without also running a substantial risk of suppressing ideas in the process. Indeed, governments might soon seize upon the censorship of particular words as a convenient guise for banning the expression of unpopular views. We have been able, as noted above, to discern little social benefit that might result from running the risk of opening the door to such grave results.

It is, in sum, our judgment that, absent a more particularized and compelling reason for its actions, the State may not, consistently with the First and Fourteenth Amendments, make the simple public display here involved of this single four-letter expletive a criminal offense. Because that is the only arguably sustainable rationale for the conviction here at issue, the judgment below must be reversed.

Brandenburg v. Ohio
395 U.S. 444 (1969)

•

PER CURIAM

The appellant, a leader of a Ku Klux Klan group, was convicted under the Ohio Criminal Syndicalism statute for 'advocat[ing] . . . the duty, necessity, or propriety of crime, sabotage, violence, or unlawful methods of terrorism as a means of accomplishing industrial or political reform' and for 'voluntarily assembl[ing] with any society, group, or assemblage of persons formed to teach or advocate the doctrines of criminal syndicalism.' He was fined $1,000 and sentenced to one to 10 years' imprisonment. . . .

The record shows that a man, identified at trial as the appellant, telephoned an announcer-reporter on the staff of a Cincinnati television station and invited him to come to a Ku Klux Klan 'rally' to be held at a farm in Hamilton County. With the cooperation of the organizers, the reporter and a cameraman attended the meeting and filmed the events. Portions of the films were later broadcast on the local station and on a national network. . . . One film showed 12 hooded figures, some of whom carried firearms. They were gathered around a large wooden cross, which they burned. No one was present other than the participants and the newsmen who made the film. Most of the words uttered during the scene were incomprehensible when the film was projected, but scattered phrases could be understood that were derogatory of Negroes and, in one instance, of Jews. Another scene on the same film showed the appellant, in Klan regalia, making a speech. The speech, in full, was as follows:

This is an organizers' meeting. We have had quite a few members here today which are—we have hundreds, hundreds of members throughout the State of Ohio. I can quote from a newspaper clipping from the Columbus, Ohio Dispatch, five weeks ago Sunday morning. The Klan has more members in the State of Ohio than does any other organization. We're not a revengent [sic] organization, but if our President, our Congress, our Supreme Court, continues to suppress the white, Caucasian race, it's possible that there might have to be some revengeance taken.

We are marching on Congress July the Fourth, four hundred

thousand strong. From there we are dividing into two groups, one group to march on St. Augustine, Florida, the other group to march into Mississippi. Thank you.

. . . In 1927, this Court sustained the constitutionality of California's Criminal Syndicalism Act, the text of which is quite similar to that of the laws of Ohio. *Whitney v. California*, 274 U.S. 357 (1927). The Court upheld the statute on the ground that, without more, 'advocating' violent means to effect political and economic change involves such danger to the security of the State that the State may outlaw it. . . . But *Whitney* has been thoroughly discredited by later decisions. See *Dennis v. United States*, 341 U.S. 494, at 507 (1951). These later decisions have fashioned the principle that the constitutional guarantees of free speech and free press do not permit a State to forbid or proscribe advocacy of the use of force or of law violation except where such advocacy is directed to inciting or producing imminent lawless action and is likely to incite or produce such action. . . .

Measured by this test, Ohio's Criminal Syndicalism Act cannot be sustained. The Act punishes persons who 'advocate or teach the duty, necessity, or propriety' of violence 'as a means of accomplishing industrial or political reform'; or who publish or circulate or display any book or paper containing such advocacy; or who 'justify' the commission of violent acts 'with intent to exemplify, spread or advocate the propriety of the doctrines of criminal syndicalism'; or who 'voluntarily assemble' with a group formed 'to teach or advocate the doctrines of criminal syndicalism.' . . .

[W]e are here confronted with a statute which, by its own words and as applied, purports to punish mere advocacy and to forbid, on pain of criminal punishment, assembly with others merely to advocate the described type of action. Such a statute falls within the condemnation of the First and Fourteenth Amendments. The contrary teaching of *Whitney v. California*, supra, cannot be supported, and that decision is therefore overruled.

United States v. O'Brien
391 U.S. 367 (1968)

•

MR. CHIEF JUSTICE WARREN DELIVERED THE OPINION OF THE COURT.

On the morning of March 31, 1966, David Paul O'Brien and three companions burned their Selective Service registration certificates on the steps of the South Boston Courthouse. A sizable crowd, including several agents of the Federal Bureau of Investigation, witnessed the event. Immediately after the burning, members of the crowd began attacking O'Brien and his companions. An FBI agent ushered O'Brien to safety inside the courthouse. After he was advised of his right to counsel and to silence, O'Brien stated to FBI agents that he had burned his registration certificate because of his beliefs, knowing that he was violating federal law. He produced the charred remains of the certificate, which, with his consent, were photographed. . . .

[T]he Universal Military Training and Service Act of 1948 . . . was amended by Congress in 1965 . . . so that, at the time O'Brien burned his certificate, an offense was committed by any person, "who forges, alters, knowingly destroys, knowingly mutilates, or in any manner changes any such certificate. . . ."

. . . [T]he Court of Appeals . . . held the 1965 Amendment unconstitutional as a law abridging freedom of speech. . . . We hold that the 1965 Amendment is constitutional both as enacted and as applied.

I

. . . We note at the outset that the 1965 Amendment plainly does not abridge free speech on its face, and we do not understand O'Brien to argue otherwise. Amended § 12(b)(3) on its face deals with conduct having no connection with speech. It prohibits the knowing destruction of certificates issued by the Selective Service System, and there is nothing necessarily expressive about such conduct. The Amendment does not distinguish between public and private destruction, and it does not punish only destruction engaged in for the purpose of expressing views. A law prohibiting destruction of Selective Service certificates no more abridges free speech on its face than a motor vehicle law prohibiting the destruction of drivers' licenses, or a tax law prohibiting the destruction of books and records.

O'Brien nonetheless argues that the 1965 Amendment is unconstitutional in its application to him, and is unconstitutional as enacted because what he calls the "purpose" of Congress was "to suppress freedom of speech." We consider these arguments separately.

II

O'Brien first argues that the 1965 Amendment is unconstitutional as applied to him because his act of burning his registration certificate was protected "symbolic speech" within the First Amendment. His argument is that the freedom of expression which the First Amendment guarantees includes all modes of "communication of ideas by conduct," and that his conduct is within this definition because he did it in "demonstration against the war and against the draft."

We cannot accept the view that an apparently limitless variety of conduct can be labeled "speech" whenever the person engaging in the conduct intends thereby to express an idea. However, even on the assumption that the alleged communicative element in O'Brien's conduct is sufficient to bring into play the First Amendment, it does not necessarily follow that the destruction of a registration certificate is constitutionally protected activity. This Court has held that when "speech" and "nonspeech" elements are combined in the same course of conduct, a sufficiently important governmental interest in regulating the nonspeech element can justify incidental limitations on First Amendment freedoms. . . . [A] government regulation is sufficiently justified if it is within the constitutional power of the Government; if it furthers an important or substantial governmental interest; if the governmental interest is unrelated to the suppression of free expression; and if the incidental restriction on alleged First Amendment freedoms is no greater than is essential to the furtherance of that interest. We find that the 1965 Amendment to § 12(b)(3) of the Universal Military Training and Service Act meets all of these requirements, and consequently that O'Brien can be constitutionally convicted for violating it. . . .

The many functions performed by Selective Service certificates establish beyond doubt that Congress has a legitimate and substantial interest in preventing their wanton and unrestrained destruction and assuring their continuing availability by punishing people who knowingly and willfully destroy or mutilate them. . . .

We think it apparent that the continuing availability to each registrant of his Selective Service certificates substantially furthers the smooth and proper functioning of the system that Congress has established to raise armies. We think it also apparent that the Nation has a vital interest in having a system for raising armies that functions with maximum efficiency and is capable of easily and quickly responding to continually changing circumstances. For these reasons, the Government has a substantial interest in assuring the continuing availability of issued Selective Service certificates.

It is equally clear that the 1965 Amendment specifically protects this substantial governmental interest. . . . The 1965 Amendment prohibits such conduct and does nothing more. In other words, both the governmental interest and the operation of the 1965 Amendment are limited to the noncommunicative aspect of O'Brien's conduct. The governmental interest and the scope of the 1965 Amendment are limited to preventing harm to the smooth and efficient functioning of the Selective Service System. When O'Brien deliberately rendered unavailable his registration certificate, he wilfully frustrated this governmental interest. For this noncommunicative impact of his conduct, and for nothing else, he was convicted. . . .

III

O'Brien finally argues that the 1965 Amendment is unconstitutional as enacted because what he calls the "purpose" of Congress was "to suppress freedom of speech." We reject this argument because under settled principles the purpose of Congress, as O'Brien uses that term, is not a basis for declaring this legislation unconstitutional.

It is a familiar principle of constitutional law that this Court will not strike down an otherwise constitutional statute on the basis of an alleged illicit legislative motive. . . . Inquiries into congressional motives or purposes are a hazardous matter. When the issue is simply the interpretation of legislation, the Court will look to statements by legislators for guidance as to the purpose of the legislature, because the benefit to sound decision-making in this circumstance is thought sufficient to risk the possibility of misreading Congress' purpose. It is entirely a different matter when we are asked to void a statute that is, under well-settled criteria, constitutional on its face, on the basis of what fewer than a handful of Congressmen said about it. What motivates one legislator to make a speech about a statute is not necessarily what motivates scores of others to enact it, and the stakes are sufficiently high for us to eschew guesswork. We decline to void essentially on the ground that it is unwise legislation which Congress had the undoubted power to enact and which could be reenacted in its exact form if the same or another legislator made a "wiser" speech about it. . . .

Texas v. Johnson
491 U.S. 397 (1989)

•

JUSTICE BRENNAN DELIVERED THE OPINION OF THE COURT.

After publicly burning an American flag as a means of political protest, Gregory Lee Johnson was convicted of desecrating a flag in violation of Texas law. This case presents the question whether his conviction is consistent with the First Amendment. We hold that it is not. . . .

The First Amendment literally forbids the abridgment only of "speech," but we have long recognized that its protection does not end at the spoken or written word. While we have rejected "the view that an apparently limitless variety of conduct can be labeled 'speech' whenever the person engaging in the conduct intends thereby to express an idea [*United States v. O'Brien*]," we have acknowledged that conduct may be "sufficiently imbued with elements of communication to fall within the scope of the First and Fourteenth Amendments." [*Spence v. Washington*, 418 U.S. 405 (1974)].

In deciding whether particular conduct possesses sufficient communicative elements to bring the First Amendment into play, we have asked whether "[a]n intent to convey a particularized message was present, and [whether] the likelihood was great that the message would be understood by those who viewed it" [*Spence*]. . . . The State of Texas conceded for purposes of its oral argument in this case that Johnson's conduct was expressive conduct[.] . . . Johnson burned an American flag as part—indeed, as the culmination—of a political demonstration that coincided with the convening of the Republican Party and its re-nomination of Ronald Reagan for President. The expressive, overtly po-litical nature of this conduct was both intentional and overwhelmingly apparent. . . .

The government generally has a freer hand in restricting expressive conduct than it has in restricting the written or spoken word. It may not, however, proscribe particular conduct *because* it has expressive ele-ments. . . . It is, in short, not simply the verbal or nonverbal nature of the expression, but the governmental interest at stake, that helps to de-termine whether a restriction on that expression is valid. Thus, although we have recognized that where "'speech' and 'nonspeech' elements are combined in the same course of conduct, a sufficiently important gov-ernmental interest in regulating the nonspeech element can justify in-cidental limitations on First Amendment freedoms," we have limited the applicability of *O'Brien*'s relatively lenient standard to those cases in which "the governmental interest is unrelated to the suppression of free expression." *O'Brien*. . . . The State offers two separate interests to justify this conviction: preventing breaches of the peace and preserving the flag as a symbol of nationhood and national unity. We hold that the first interest is not implicated on this record and that the second is related to the suppression of expression. . . .

The only evidence offered by the State at trial to show the reaction to Johnson's actions was the testimony of several persons who had been seriously offended by the flag burning. The State's position, therefore, amounts to a claim that an audience that takes serious offense at par-ticular expression is necessarily likely to disturb the peace and that the expression may be prohibited on this basis. Our precedents do not countenance such a presumption. On the contrary, they recognize that a principal "function of free speech under our system of government is to invite dispute. It may indeed best serve its high purpose when it induces a condition of unrest, creates dissatisfaction with conditions as they are, or even stirs people to anger." *Terminiello v. Chicago*, 337 U.S. 1, 4 (1949). . . .

The State also asserts an interest in preserving the flag as a symbol of nationhood and national unity. In *Spence*, we acknowledged that the government's interest in preserving the flag's special symbolic value "is directly related to expression in the context of activity" such as affixing a peace symbol to a flag. We are equally persuaded that this interest is related to expression in the case of Johnson's burning of the flag. The State, apparently, is concerned that such conduct will lead people to believe either that the flag does not stand for nationhood and national unity, but instead reflects other, less positive concepts, or that the concepts reflected in the flag do not in fact exist, that is, that we do not enjoy unity as a Nation. These concerns blossom only when a person's treatment of the flag communicates some message, and thus are related "to the suppression of free expression" within the meaning of *O'Brien*.

It remains to consider whether the State's interest in preserving the flag as a symbol of nationhood and national unity justifies Johnson's conviction. As in *Spence*, "[w]e are confronted with a case of prosecution for the expression of an idea through activity." . . . Johnson was not, we add, prosecuted for the expression of just any idea; he was prosecuted for his expression of dissatisfaction with the policies of this country, expression situated at the core of our First Amendment values. Moreover, Johnson was prosecuted because he knew that his politically charged expression would cause "serious offense." If he had burned the flag as a means of disposing of it because it was dirty or torn, he would not have been convicted of flag desecration under this Texas law: federal law designates burning as the preferred means of disposing of a flag "when it is in such condition that it is no longer a fitting emblem for display" and Texas has no quarrel with this means of disposal. The Texas law is thus not aimed at protecting the physical integrity of the flag in all circumstances, but is designed instead to protect it only against impairments that would cause serious offense to others. . . .

[T]he State's claim is that it has an interest in preserving the flag as a symbol of *nationhood* and *national unity*, a symbol with a determinate range of meanings. According to Texas, if one physically treats the flag in a way that would tend to cast doubt on either the idea that nationhood and national unity are the flag's referents or that national unity actually exists, the message conveyed thereby is a harmful one and therefore may be prohibited.

If there is a bedrock principle underlying the First Amendment, it is that the government may not prohibit the expression of an idea simply because society finds the idea itself offensive or disagreeable. . . . Texas' focus on the precise nature of Johnson's expression, moreover, misses the point of our prior decisions: their enduring lesson, that the government may not prohibit expression simply because it disagrees with its message, is not dependent on the particular mode in which one chooses to express an idea. . . . We never before have held that the Government may ensure that a symbol be used to express only one view of that symbol or its referents. . . . To conclude that the government may permit designated symbols to be used to communicate only a limited set of messages would be to enter territory having no discernible or defensible boundaries. Could the government, on this theory, prohibit the burning of state flags? Of copies of the Presidential seal? Of the Constitution? In evaluating these choices under the First Amendment, how would we decide which symbols were sufficiently special to warrant this unique status? To do so, we would be forced to consult our own political preferences, and impose them on the citizenry, in the very way that the First Amendment forbids us to do. . . .

The way to preserve the flag's special role is not to punish those who feel differently about these matters. It is to persuade them that they are wrong. . . . We can imagine no more appropriate response to burning a flag than waving one's own, no better way to counter a flag burner's message than by saluting the flag that burns, no surer means of preserving the dignity even of the flag that burned than by—as one witness here did—according its remains a respectful burial. We do not consecrate the flag by punishing its desecration, for in doing so we dilute the freedom that this cherished emblem represents. . . .

CHIEF JUSTICE REHNQUIST, WITH WHOM JUSTICE WHITE AND JUSTICE O'CONNOR JOIN, DISSENTING.

The American flag . . . throughout more than 200 years of our history, has come to be the visible symbol embodying our Nation. . . . [T]he public burning of the American flag by Johnson was no essential part of any exposition of ideas, and at the same time it had a tendency to incite a breach of the peace. . . . As with "fighting words," so with flag burning, for purposes of the First Amendment: It is "no essential part of any exposition of ideas, and [is] of such slight social value as a step to truth that any benefit that may be derived from [it] is clearly outweighed" by the public interest in avoiding a probable breach of the peace. . . .

The Texas statute deprived Johnson of only one rather inarticulate symbolic form of protest—a form of protest that was profoundly offensive to many—and left him with a full panoply of other symbols and every conceivable form of verbal expression to express his deep disapproval of national policy. Thus, in no way can it be said that Texas is punishing him because his hearers—or any other group of people—were profoundly opposed to the message that he sought to convey. Such opposition is no proper basis for restricting speech or expression under the First Amendment. It was Johnson's use of this particular symbol, and not the idea that he sought to convey by it or by his many other expressions, for which he was punished. . . .

The Pentagon Papers Case: *New York Times Co. v. United States*, 403 U.S. 713 (1971)

•

PER CURIAM.

We granted certiorari in these cases in which the United States seeks to enjoin the New York Times and the Washington Post from publishing the contents of a classified study entitled "History of U.S. Decision-Making Process on Viet Nam Policy."

"Any system of prior restraints of expression comes to this Court bearing a heavy presumption against its constitutional validity." *Bantam Books, Inc. v. Sullivan* (1963). The Government "thus carries a heavy burden of showing justification for the imposition of such a restraint." *Organization for a Better Austin v. Keefe* (1971). [The lower courts] held that the Government had not met that burden. We agree. . . .

MR. JUSTICE BLACK, WITH WHOM MR. JUSTICE DOUGLAS JOINS, CONCURRING.

I adhere to the view that the Government's case against the Washington Post should have been dismissed and that the injunction against the New York Times should have been vacated without oral argument when the cases were first presented to this Court. I believe that every moment's continuance of the injunctions against these newspapers amounts to a flagrant, indefensible, and continuing violation of the First Amendment. . . .

Our Government was launched in 1789 with the adoption of the Constitution. The Bill of Rights, including the First Amendment, followed in 1791. Now, for the first time in the 182 years since the founding of the Republic, the federal courts are asked to hold that the First Amendment does not mean what it says, but rather means that the Government can halt the publication of current news of vital importance to the people of this country.

In seeking injunctions against these newspapers and in its presentation to the Court, the Executive Branch seems to have forgotten the essential purpose and history of the First Amendment. . . . In the First Amendment the Founding Fathers gave the free press the protection it must have to fulfill its essential role in our democracy. The press was to serve the governed, not the governors. The Government's power to censor the press was abolished so that the press would remain forever free to censure the Government. The press was protected so that it could bare the secrets of government and inform the people. Only a free and unrestrained press can effectively expose deception in government. . . . The Government's case here is based on premises entirely different from those that guided the Framers of the First Amendment. . . . To find that the President has "inherent power" to halt the publication of news by resort to the courts would wipe out the First Amendment and destroy the fundamental liberty and security of the very people the Government hopes to make 'secure.' No one can read the history of the adoption of the First Amendment without being convinced beyond any doubt that it was injunctions like those sought here that Madison and his collaborators intended to outlaw in this Nation for all time. . . .

MR. JUSTICE BRENNAN, CONCURRING.

. . . [T]he First Amendment tolerates absolutely no prior judicial restraints of the press predicated upon surmise or conjecture that untoward consequences may result. Our cases, it is true, have indicated that there is a single, extremely narrow class of cases in which the First Amendment's ban on prior judicial restraint may be overridden. Our cases have thus far indicated that such cases may arise only when the Nation "is at war," *Schenck v. United States* (1919), during which times "(n)o one would question but that a government might prevent actual obstruction to its recruiting service or the publication of the sailing dates of transports or the number and location of troops." *Near v. Minnesota ex rel. Olson* (1931). Even if the present world situation were assumed to be tantamount to a time of war, or if the power of presently available armaments would justify even in peacetime the suppression of information that would set in motion a nuclear holocaust, in neither of these actions has the Government presented or even alleged that publication of items from or based upon the material at issue would cause the happening of an event of that nature. "(T)he chief purpose of (the First Amendment's) guaranty (is) to prevent previous restraints upon publication." *Near v. Minnesota*. Thus, only governmental allegation and proof that publication must inevitably, directly, and immediately cause the occurrence of an event kindred to imperiling the safety of a transport already at sea can support even the issuance of an interim restraining order. . . . Unless and until the Government has clearly made out its case, the First Amendment commands that no injunction may issue.

MR. JUSTICE STEWART, WITH WHOM MR. JUSTICE WHITE JOINS, CONCURRING.

In the governmental structure created by our Constitution, the Executive is endowed with enormous power in the two related areas of national defense and international relations. This power, largely unchecked by the Legislative and Judicial branches, has been pressed to the very hilt since the advent of the nuclear missile age. . . .

The responsibility must be where the power is. If the Constitution gives the Executive a large degree of unshared power in the conduct of foreign affairs and the maintenance of our national defense, then under the Constitution the Executive must have the largely unshared duty to determine and preserve the degree of internal security necessary to exercise that power successfully. . . .

Undoubtedly Congress has the power to enact specific and appropriate criminal laws to protect government property and preserve government secrets. Congress has passed such laws, and several of them are of very colorable relevance to the apparent circumstances of these cases. And if a criminal prosecution is instituted, it will be the responsibility of the courts to decide the applicability of the criminal law under which the charge is brought. . . .

But in the cases before us we are asked neither to construe specific regulations nor to apply specific laws. We are asked, instead, to perform a function that the Constitution gave to the Executive, not the Judiciary. We are asked, quite simply, to prevent the publication by two newspapers of material that the Executive Branch insists should not, in the national interest, be published. I am convinced that the Executive is correct with respect to some of the documents involved. But I cannot say that disclosure of any of them will surely result in direct, immediate, and irreparable damage to our Nation or its people. That being so, there can under the First Amendment be but one judicial resolution of the issues before us. I join the judgments of the Court.

MR. JUSTICE MARSHALL, CONCURRING.

. . . The problem here is whether in these particular cases the Executive Branch has authority to invoke the equity jurisdiction of the courts to protect what it believes to be the national interest. . . . The Government argues that in addition to the inherent power of any government to protect itself, the President's power to conduct foreign affairs and his position as Commander in Chief give him authority to impose censorship on the press to protect his ability to deal effectively with foreign nations and to conduct the military affairs of the country. Of course, it is beyond cavil that the President has broad powers by virtue of his primary responsibility for the conduct of our foreign affairs and his position as Commander in Chief. . . .

It would, however, be utterly inconsistent with the concept of separation of powers for this Court to use its power of contempt to prevent behavior that Congress has specifically declined to prohibit. There would be a similar damage to the basic concept of these co-equal branches of Government if when the Executive Branch has adequate authority granted by Congress to protect "national security" it can choose instead to invoke the contempt power of a court to enjoin the threatened conduct. . . .

[W]e are not faced with a situation where Congress has failed to provide the Executive with broad power to protect the Nation from disclosure of damaging state secrets. Congress has on several occasions given extensive consideration to the problem of protecting the military and strategic secrets of the United States. This consideration has resulted in the enactment of statutes making it a crime to receive, disclose, communicate, withhold, and publish certain documents, photographs, instruments, appliances, and information. . . . At least one of the many statutes in this area seems relevant to these cases. . . . Either the Government has the power under statutory grant to use traditional criminal law to protect the country or, if there is no basis for arguing that Congress has made the activity a crime, it is plain that Congress has specifically refused to grant the authority the Government seeks from this Court. In either case this Court does not have authority to grant the requested relief. It is not for this Court to fling itself into every breach perceived by some Government official nor is it for this Court to take on itself the burden of enacting law, especially a law that Congress has refused to pass.

MR. JUSTICE HARLAN, WITH WHOM THE CHIEF JUSTICE AND MR. JUSTICE BLACKMUN JOIN, DISSENTING.

These cases forcefully call to mind the wise admonition of Mr. Justice Holmes, dissenting in *Northern Securities Co. v. United States*, 193 U.S. 197, 400–401 (1904): "Great cases, like hard cases, make bad law. For great cases are called great, not by reason of their real importance in shaping the law of the future, but because of some accident of immediate overwhelming interest which appeals to the feelings and distorts the judgment. These immediate interests exercise a kind of hydraulic pressure which makes what previously was clear seem doubtful, and before which even well settled principles of law will bend."

With all respect, I consider that the Court has been almost irresponsibly feverish in dealing with these cases. . . .

It is plain to me that the scope of the judicial function in passing upon the activities of the Executive Branch of the Government in the field of foreign affairs is very narrowly restricted. This view is, I think, dictated by the concept of separation of powers upon which our constitutional system rests.

In a speech on the floor of the House of Representatives, Chief Justice John Marshall, then a member of that body, stated: "The President is the sole organ of the nation in its external relations, and its sole representative with foreign nations." From that time, shortly after the founding of the Nation, to this, there has been no substantial challenge to this description of the scope of executive power. . . .

I agree that, in performance of its duty to protect the values of the First Amendment against political pressures, the judiciary must review the initial Executive determination to the point of satisfying itself that the subject matter of the dispute does lie within the proper compass of the President's foreign relations power. . . . But in my judgment the judiciary may not properly . . . redetermine for itself the probable impact of disclosure on the national security. . . .

New York Times Co. v. Sullivan
376 U.S. 254 (1964)

•

MR. JUSTICE BRENNAN DELIVERED THE OPINION OF THE COURT.

We are required in this case to determine for the first time the extent to which the constitutional protections for speech and press limit a State's power to award damages in a libel action brought by a public official against critics of his official conduct.

Respondent L. B. Sullivan is one of the three elected Commissioners of the City of Montgomery, Alabama. . . . He brought this civil libel action against the four individual petitioners, who are Negroes and Alabama clergymen, and against petitioner the New York Times Company, a New York corporation which publishes the New York Times, a daily newspaper. A jury in the Circuit Court of Montgomery County awarded him damages of $500,000, the full amount claimed, against all the petitioners, and the Supreme Court of Alabama affirmed.

Respondent's complaint alleged that he had been libeled by statements in a full-page advertisement that was carried in the New York Times on March 29, 1960. Entitled "Heed Their Rising Voices," the advertisement began by stating that "As the whole world knows by now, thousands of Southern Negro students are engaged in widespread non-violent demonstrations in positive affirmation of the right to live in human dignity as guaranteed by the U.S. Constitution and the Bill of Rights." It went on to charge that "in their efforts to uphold these guarantees, they are being met by an unprecedented wave of terror by those who would deny and negate that document which the whole world looks upon as setting the pattern for modern freedom. . . . " Succeeding paragraphs purported to illustrate the "wave of terror" by describing certain alleged events. The text concluded with an appeal for funds for three purposes: support of the student movement, "the struggle for the right to vote," and the legal defense of Dr. Martin Luther King, Jr., leader of the movement, against a perjury indictment then pending in Montgomery. . . .

We hold that the rule of law applied by the Alabama courts is constitutionally deficient for failure to provide the safeguards for freedom of speech and of the press that are required by the First and Fourteenth Amendments in a libel action brought by a public official against critics of his official conduct. . . .

The general proposition that freedom of expression upon public questions is secured by the First Amendment has long been settled by our decisions. . . .

Authoritative interpretations of the First Amendment guarantees have consistently refused to recognize an exception for any test of truth—whether administered by judges, juries, or administrative officials—and especially one that puts the burden of proving truth on the speaker. . . . [E]rroneous statement is inevitable in free debate, and . . . must be protected if the freedoms of expression are to have the "breathing space" that they "need . . . to survive. . . .

A rule compelling the critic of official conduct to guarantee the truth of all his factual assertions—and to do so on pain of libel judgments virtually unlimited in amount—leads to . . . "self-censorship." Allowance of the defense of truth, with the burden of proving it on the defendant, does not mean that only false speech will be deterred. . . . Under such a rule, would-be critics of official conduct may be deterred from voicing their criticism, even though it is believed to be true and even though it is in fact true, because of doubt whether it can be proved in court or fear of the expense of having to do so. . . . The rule thus dampens the vigor and limits the variety of public debate. It is inconsistent with the First and Fourteenth Amendments.

The constitutional guarantees require, we think, a federal rule that prohibits a public official from recovering damages for a defamatory falsehood relating to his official conduct unless he proves that the statement was made with "actual malice"—that is, with knowledge that it was false or with reckless disregard of whether it was false or not. . . . We think the evidence against the Times supports at most a finding of negligence in failing to discover the misstatements, and is constitutionally insufficient to show the recklessness that is required for a finding of actual malice. . . .

Engel v. Vitale
370 U.S. 421 (1962)

•

MR. JUSTICE BLACK DELIVERED THE OPINION OF THE COURT.

The respondent Board of Education of Union Free School District No. 9, New Hyde Park, New York, acting in its official capacity under state law, directed the School District's principal to cause the following prayer to be said aloud by each class in the presence of a teacher at the beginning of each school day:

'Almighty God, we acknowledge our dependence upon Thee, and we beg Thy blessings upon us, our parents, our teachers and our Country.'

This daily procedure was adopted on the recommendation of the State Board of Regents, a governmental agency created by the State Constitution to which the New York Legislature has granted broad supervisory, executive, and legislative powers over the State's public school system. These state officials composed the prayer which they recommended and published as a part of their 'Statement on Moral and Spiritual Training in the Schools.' . . .

We think that by using its public school system to encourage recitation of the Regents' prayer, the State of New York has adopted a practice wholly inconsistent with the Establishment Clause. . . . [T]he constitutional prohibition against laws respecting an establishment of religion must at least mean that in this country it is no part of the business of government to compose official prayers for any group of the American people to recite as a part of a religious program carried on by government.

It is a matter of history that this very practice of establishing governmentally composed prayers for religious services was one of the reasons which caused many of our early colonists to leave England and seek religious freedom in America. . . . By the time of the adoption of the Constitution, our history shows that there was a widespread awareness among many Americans of the dangers of a union of Church and State. These people knew, some of them from bitter personal experience, that one of the greatest dangers to the freedom of the individual to worship in his own way lay in the Government's placing its official stamp of approval upon one particular kind of prayer or one particular form of religious services. . . . Under that Amendment's prohibition against governmental establishment of religion . . . government in this country, be it state or federal, is without power to prescribe by law any particular form of prayer which is to be used as an official prayer in carrying on any program of governmentally sponsored religious activity. . . .

Neither the fact that the prayer may be denominationally neutral nor the fact that its observance on the part of the students is voluntary can serve to free it from the limitations of the Establishment Clause, as it might from the Free Exercise Clause. . . . Although these two clauses may in certain instances overlap, they forbid two quite different kinds of governmental encroachment upon religious freedom. The Establishment Clause, unlike the Free Exercise Clause, does not depend upon any showing of direct governmental compulsion and is violated by the enactment of laws which establish an official religion whether those laws operate directly to coerce nonobserving individuals or not. This is not to say, of course, that laws officially prescribing a particular form of religious worship do not involve coercion of such individuals. When the power, prestige and financial support of government is placed behind a particular religious belief, the indirect coercive pressure upon religious minorities to conform to the prevailing officially approved religion is plain. But the purposes underlying the Establishment Clause go much further than that. Its first and most immediate purpose rested on the belief that a union of government and religion tends to destroy government and to degrade religion. . . .

"It has been argued that to apply the Constitution in such a way as to prohibit state laws respecting an establishment of religious services in public schools is to indicate a hostility toward religion or toward prayer. Nothing, of course, could be more wrong. . . . [The First Amendment]

was written to quiet well-justified fears . . . arising out of an awareness that governments of the past had shackled men's tongues to make
them speak only the religious thoughts that government wanted them
to speak and to pray only to the God that government wanted them
to pray to. It is neither sacrilegious nor antireligious to say that each
separate government in this country should stay out of the business of
writing or sanctioning official prayers and leave that purely religious
function to the people themselves and to those the people choose to look
to for religious guidance." . . .

MR. JUSTICE STEWART, DISSENTING.

A local school board in New York has provided that those pupils
who wish to do so may join in a brief prayer at the beginning of each
school day, acknowledging their dependence upon God and asking His
blessing upon them and upon their parents, their teachers, and their
country. . . . With all respect, I think the Court has misapplied a great
constitutional principle. I cannot see how an 'official religion' is established by letting those who want to say a prayer say it. On the contrary,
I think that to deny the wish of these school children to join in reciting
this prayer is to deny them the opportunity of sharing in the spiritual
heritage of our Nation. . . .

At the opening of each day's Session of this Court we stand, while
one of our officials invokes the protection of God. Since the days of
John Marshall our Crier has said, 'God save the United States and this
Honorable Court.' Each of our Presidents, from George Washington to
John F. Kennedy, has upon assuming his Office asked the protection
and help of God. . . . Countless similar examples could be listed, but
there is no need to belabor the obvious. . . . I do not believe that this
Court, or the Congress, or the President has by the actions and practices
I have mentioned established an 'official religion' in violation of the
Constitution. And I do not believe the State of New York has done so
in this case. What each has done has been to recognize and to follow
the deeply entrenched and highly cherished spiritual traditions of our
Nation—traditions which come down to us from those who almost
two hundred years ago avowed their 'firm Reliance on the Protection of
Divine Providence' when they proclaimed the freedom and independence of this brave new world. I dissent.

Widmar v. Vincent
454 U.S. 263 (1981)

•

JUSTICE POWELL DELIVERED THE OPINION OF THE COURT.

This case presents the question whether a state university, which makes its facilities generally available for the activities of registered student groups, may close its facilities to a registered student group desiring to use the facilities for religious worship and religious discussion.

I

It is the stated policy of the University of Missouri at Kansas City to encourage the activities of student organizations. The University officially recognizes over 100 student groups. It routinely provides University facilities for the meetings of registered organizations. . . . From 1973 until 1977, a registered religious group named Cornerstone regularly sought and received permission to conduct its meetings in University facilities. In 1977, however, the University informed the group that it could no longer meet in University buildings. The exclusion was based on a regulation, adopted by the Board of Curators in 1972, that prohibits the use of University buildings or grounds "for purposes of religious worship or religious teaching." Eleven University students, all members of Cornerstone, brought suit to challenge the regulation[.] . . . They alleged that the University's discrimination against religious activity and discussion violated their rights to free exercise of religion, equal protection, and freedom of speech under the First and Fourteenth Amendments to the Constitution of the United States. . . .

II

Through its policy of accommodating their meetings, the University has created a forum generally open for use by student groups. Having done so, the University has assumed an obligation to justify its discriminations and exclusions under applicable constitutional norms. The Constitution forbids a State to enforce certain exclusions from a forum generally open to the public, even if it was not required to create the forum in the first place. . . . Here, UMKC has discriminated against student groups and speakers based on their desire to use a generally open forum to engage in religious worship and discussion. These are forms of speech and association protected by the First Amendment. . . . In order to justify discriminatory exclusion from a public forum based on the religious content of a group's intended speech, the University must . . . show that its regulation is necessary to serve a compelling state interest, and that it is narrowly drawn to achieve that end.

III

In this case, the University claims a compelling interest in maintaining strict separation of church and State. . . . We agree that the interest of the University in complying with its constitutional obligations may be characterized as compelling. It does not follow, however, that an "equal access" policy would be incompatible with this Court's Establishment Clause cases. . . .

The University's argument misconceives the nature of this case. The question is not whether the creation of a religious forum would violate the Establishment Clause. The University has opened its facilities for use by student groups, and the question is whether it can now exclude groups because of the content of their speech. In this context, we are unpersuaded that the primary effect of the public forum, open to all forms of discourse, would be to advance religion.

We are not oblivious to the range of an open forum's likely effects. It is possible—perhaps even foreseeable—that religious groups will ben-efit from access to University facilities. But this Court has explained that a religious organization's enjoyment of merely "incidental" benefits does not violate the prohibition against the "primary advancement" of religion.

We are satisfied that any religious benefits of an open forum at UMKC would be "incidental" within the meaning of our cases. Two factors are especially relevant.

First, an open forum in a public university does not confer any im-primatur of state approval on religious sects or practices. As the Court of Appeals quite aptly stated, such a policy "would no more commit the University . . . to religious goals" than it is "now committed to the goals of the Students for a Democratic Society, the Young Socialist Alliance," or any other group eligible to use its facilities.

Second, the forum is available to a broad class of nonreligious, as well as religious, speakers; there are over 100 recognized student groups at UMKC. The provision of benefits to so broad a spectrum of groups is an important index of secular effect. If the Establishment Clause barred the extension of general benefits to religious groups, "a church could not be protected by the police and fire departments, or have its public sidewalk kept in repair." [1976] *Roemer v. Maryland Public Works Bd.* . . .

IV

Our holding in this case in no way undermines the capacity of the University to establish reasonable time, place, and manner regulations. Nor do we question the right of the University to make academic judgments as to how best to allocate scarce resources . . . [or] to exclude even First Amendment activities that violate reasonable campus rules or substantially interfere with the opportunity of other students to obtain an education. . . . Having created a forum generally open to student groups, the University seeks to enforce a content-based exclusion of religious speech. Its exclusionary policy violates the fundamental principle that a state regulation of speech should be content-neutral. . . .

Employment Division v. Smith
494 U.S. 872 (1990)

•

JUSTICE SCALIA DELIVERED THE OPINION OF THE COURT.

This case requires us to decide whether the Free Exercise Clause of the First Amendment permits the State of Oregon to include religiously inspired peyote use within the reach of its general criminal prohibition on use of that drug, and thus permits the State to deny unemployment benefits to persons dismissed from their jobs because of such religiously inspired use.

Oregon law prohibits the knowing or intentional possession of . . . the drug peyote, a hallucinogen derived from the plant *Lophophora williamsii Lemaire*.

Respondents Alfred Smith and Galen Black (hereinafter respondents) were fired from their jobs with a private drug rehabilitation organization because they ingested peyote for sacramental purposes at a ceremony of the Native American Church, of which both are members. When respondents applied to petitioner Employment Division . . . for unemployment compensation, they were determined to be ineligible for benefits. . . . Respondents' claim for relief rests on our decisions in *Sherbert v. Verner* . . . in which we held that a State could not condition the availability of unemployment insurance on an individual's willingness to forgo conduct required by his religion. . . .

The Free Exercise Clause of the First Amendment, which has been made applicable to the States by incorporation into the Fourteenth Amendment, provides that "Congress shall make no law respecting an establishment of religion, or *prohibiting the free exercise thereof.*" The free exercise of religion means, first and foremost, the right to believe and profess whatever religious doctrine one desires. Thus, the First Amendment obviously excludes all "governmental regulation of religious *beliefs* as such." *Sherbert v. Verner.* The government may not compel affirmation of religious belief . . . punish the expression of religious doctrines it believes to be false, impose special disabilities on the basis of religious views or religious status . . . or lend its power to one or the other side in controversies over religious authority or dogma.

But the "exercise of religion" often involves not only belief and profession but the performance of (or abstention from) physical acts: assembling with others for a worship service, participating in sacramental use of bread and wine, proselytizing, abstaining from certain foods or certain modes of transportation. It would be true, we think . . . that a State would be "prohibiting the free exercise [of religion]" if it sought to ban such acts or abstentions only when they are engaged in for religious reasons, or only because of the religious belief that they display. It would doubtless be unconstitutional, for example, to ban the casting of "statues that are to be used for worship purposes," or to prohibit bowing down before a golden calf.

Respondents in the present case, however, seek to carry the meaning of "prohibiting the free exercise [of religion]" one large step further. They contend that their religious motivation for using peyote places them beyond the reach of a criminal law that is not specifically directed at their religious practice, and that is concededly constitutional as applied to those who use the drug for other reasons. They assert, in other words, that "prohibiting the free exercise [of religion]" includes requiring any individual to observe a generally applicable law that requires (or forbids) the performance of an act that his religious belief forbids (or requires). As a textual matter, we do not think the words must be given that meaning. It is no more necessary to regard the collection of a general tax, for example, as "prohibiting the free exercise [of religion]" by those citizens who believe support of organized government to be sinful, than it is to regard the same tax as "abridging the freedom . . . of the press" of those publishing companies that must pay the tax as a condition of staying in business. It is a permissible reading of the text, in the one case as in the other, to say that if prohibiting the exercise of religion (or burdening the activity of printing) is not the object of the tax but merely the incidental effect of a generally applicable and otherwise valid provision, the First Amendment has not been offended. . . .

Our decisions reveal that the latter reading is the correct one. We have never held that an individual's religious beliefs excuse him from compliance with an otherwise valid law prohibiting conduct that the State is free to regulate. We first had occasion to assert that principle in *Reynolds v. United States*, 98 U.S. 145 (1878), where we rejected the claim that criminal laws against polygamy could not be constitutionally applied to those whose religion commanded the practice. "Laws," we said, "are made for the government of actions, and while they cannot interfere with mere religious belief and opinions, they may with practices. . . . Can a man excuse his practices to the contrary because of his religious belief? To permit this would be to make the professed doctrines of religious belief superior to the law of the land, and in effect to permit every citizen to become a law unto himself."

The only decisions in which we have held that the First Amendment bars application of a neutral, generally applicable law to religiously motivated action have involved not the Free Exercise Clause alone, but the Free Exercise Clause in conjunction with other constitutional protections, such as freedom of speech and of the press; or the right of parents . . . to direct the education of their children, see *Wisconsin v. Yoder*, 406 U.S. 205 (1972) (invalidating compulsory school-attendance laws as applied to Amish parents who refused on religious grounds to send their children to school). Some of our cases prohibiting compelled expression, decided exclusively upon free speech grounds, have also involved freedom of religion. . . .

The present case does not present such a hybrid situation, but a free exercise claim unconnected with any communicative activity or parental right. Respondents urge us to hold, quite simply, that when otherwise prohibitable conduct is accompanied by religious convictions, not only the convictions but the conduct itself must be free from governmental regulation. We have never held that, and decline to do so now. . . .

Respondents argue that even though exemption from generally applicable criminal laws need not automatically be extended to religiously motivated actors, at least the claim for a religious exemption must be evaluated under the balancing test set forth in *Sherbert v. Verner*, 374 U.S. 398 (1963). Under the *Sherbert* test, governmental actions that substantially burden a religious practice must be justified by a compelling governmental interest. . . . We have never invalidated any governmental action on the basis of the *Sherbert* test except the denial of unemployment compensation.

Even if we were inclined to breathe into *Sherbert* some life beyond the unemployment compensation field, we would not apply it to require exemptions from a generally applicable criminal law. . . . We conclude today that the sounder approach, and the approach in accord with the vast majority of our precedents, is to hold the test inapplicable to such challenges. The government's ability to enforce generally applicable prohibitions of socially harmful conduct, like its ability to carry out other aspects of public policy, "cannot depend on measuring the effects of a governmental action on a religious objector's spiritual development." [*Lyng v. Northwest Indian Cemetery* (1988)]. To make an individual's obligation to obey such a law contingent upon the law's coincidence with his religious beliefs, except where the State's interest is "compelling"— permitting him, by virtue of his beliefs, "to become a law unto himself," *Reynolds v. United States*—contradicts both constitutional tradition and common sense.

The "compelling government interest" requirement seems benign, because it is familiar from other fields. But using it as the standard that must be met before the government may accord different treatment on the basis of race . . . or before the government may regulate the content of speech . . . is not remotely comparable to using it for the purpose asserted here. What it produces in those other fields—equality of treatment and an unrestricted flow of contending speech—are constitutional norms; what it would produce here—a private right to ignore generally applicable laws—is a constitutional anomaly. . . .

Any society adopting such a system would be courting anarchy, but that danger increases in direct proportion to the society's diversity of religious beliefs, and its determination to coerce or suppress none of them. Precisely because . . . we value and protect that religious divergence, we cannot afford the luxury of deeming *presumptively invalid*, as applied to the religious objector, every regulation of conduct that does not protect an interest of the highest order. . . . The First Amendment's protection of religious liberty does not require this. . . .

JUSTICE O'CONNOR, WITH WHOM JUSTICE BRENNAN, JUSTICE MARSHALL, AND JUSTICE BLACKMUN JOIN AS TO PARTS I AND II, CONCURRING IN THE JUDGMENT.

Although I agree with the result the Court reaches in this case, I cannot join its opinion. In my view, today's holding dramatically departs from well-settled First Amendment jurisprudence, appears unnecessary to resolve the question presented, and is incompatible with our Nation's fundamental commitment to individual religious liberty. . . .

The Court today . . . interprets the [Free Exercise] Clause to permit the government to prohibit, without justification, conduct mandated by an individual's religious beliefs, so long as that prohibition is generally applicable. But a law that prohibits certain conduct—conduct that happens to be an act of worship for someone—manifestly does prohibit that person's free exercise of his religion. A person who is barred from engaging in religiously motivated conduct is barred from freely exercising his religion. Moreover, that person is barred from freely exercising his religion regardless of whether the law prohibits the conduct only when engaged in for religious reasons, only by members of that religion, or by all persons. . . .

The Court responds that generally applicable laws are "one large step" removed from laws aimed at specific religious practices. The First Amendment, however, does not distinguish between laws that are generally applicable and laws that target particular religious practices.

Indeed, few States would be so naive as to enact a law directly prohibiting or burdening a religious practice as such. Our free exercise cases
have all concerned generally applicable laws that had the effect of significantly burdening a religious practice. If the First Amendment is to
have any vitality, it ought not be construed to cover only the extreme
and hypothetical situation in which a State directly targets a religious
practice. . . .

To say that a person's right to free exercise has been burdened, of
course, does not mean that he has an absolute right to engage in the
conduct. Under our established First Amendment jurisprudence, we
have recognized that the freedom to act, unlike the freedom to believe, cannot be absolute. . . . Instead, we have respected both the First
Amendment's express textual mandate and the governmental interest in
regulation of conduct by requiring the government to justify any substantial burden on religiously motivated conduct by a compelling state
interest and by means narrowly tailored to achieve that interest. . . .

THE SECOND AMENDMENT

☙

*T*he Supreme Court gave its first extended analysis of the Second Amendment right to keep and bear arms in two modern cases. In *District of Columbia v. Heller* (2008), the Court held by a vote of 5–4 that the right was an individual right, not merely a right of state militias. In *McDonald v. City of Chicago* (2010), the Court held by a vote of 5–4 that the individual right to gun ownership limited the powers of state governments. The Court held that the Fourteenth Amendment incorporated the Second Amendment as a limitation on the states. Justice Alito's opinion for four justices rested this conclusion on the Due Process Clause of the amendment, reflecting traditional judicial precedent. Justice Thomas's concurrence argued that the Privileges or Immunities Clause of the amendment provided a sounder textual basis for the same conclusion.

The opinions in *McDonald* distill the analysis in *Heller* on the meaning of the Second Amendment and contain a significant discussion of how the Fourteenth Amendment is best understood as embracing the specific individual liberties of the Bill of Rights.

✪

McDonald v. City of Chicago
130 S. Ct. 3020 (2010)

•

JUSTICE ALITO ANNOUNCED THE JUDGMENT OF THE
COURT . . .

Two years ago, in *District of Columbia v. Heller*, we held that the Second
Amendment protects the right to keep and bear arms for the purpose
of self-defense, and we struck down a District of Columbia law that
banned the possession of handguns in the home. The city of Chicago
(City) and the village of Oak Park, a Chicago suburb, have laws that are
similar to the District of Columbia's, but Chicago and Oak Park argue
that their laws are constitutional because the Second Amendment has
no application to the States. We have previously held that most of the
provisions of the Bill of Rights apply with full force to both the Federal
Government and the States. Applying the standard that is well established in our case law, we hold that the Second Amendment right is
fully applicable to the States. . . .

Petitioners argue that the Chicago and Oak Park laws violate the
right to keep and bear arms for two reasons. Petitioners' primary submission is that this right is among the "privileges or immunities of
citizens of the United States" and that the narrow interpretation of the
Privileges or Immunities Clause adopted in the *Slaughter-House Cases*
should now be rejected. As a secondary argument, petitioners contend
that the Fourteenth Amendment's Due Process Clause "incorporates"
the Second Amendment . . .

The Bill of Rights, including the Second Amendment, originally
applied only to the Federal Government. In [*Barron v. Baltimore* (see
p. 71)], the Court, in an opinion by Chief Justice Marshall, explained
that this question was "of great importance" but "not of much difficulty." In less than four pages, the Court firmly rejected the proposition
that the first eight Amendments operate as limitations on the States,
holding that they apply only to the Federal Government. . . .

The constitutional Amendments adopted in the aftermath of the
Civil War fundamentally altered our country's federal system. The provision at issue in this case, § 1 of the Fourteenth Amendment, provides,

among other things, that a State may not abridge "the privileges or immunities of citizens of the United States" or deprive "any person of life, liberty, or property, without due process of law."

Four years after the adoption of the Fourteenth Amendment, this Court was asked to interpret the Amendment's reference to "the privileges or immunities of citizens of the United States." *The Slaughter-House Cases* involved challenges to a Louisiana law permitting the creation of a state-sanctioned monopoly on the butchering of animals within the city of New Orleans. Justice Samuel Miller's opinion for the Court concluded that the Privileges or Immunities Clause protects only those rights "which owe their existence to the Federal government, its National character, its Constitution, or its laws." The Court held that other fundamental rights—rights that predated the creation of the Federal Government and that "the State governments were created to establish and secure"—were not protected by the Clause. . . .

Today, many legal scholars dispute the correctness of the narrow Slaughter-House interpretation. . . .We see no need to reconsider that interpretation here. For many decades, the question of the rights protected by the Fourteenth Amendment against state infringement has been analyzed under the Due Process Clause of that Amendment and not under the Privileges or Immunities Clause. We therefore decline to disturb the Slaughter-House holding. . . .

In the late 19th century, the Court began to consider whether the Due Process Clause prohibits the States from infringing rights set out in the Bill of Rights. . . . An alternative theory regarding the relationship between the Bill of Rights and § 1 of the Fourteenth Amendment was championed by Justice Black. This theory held that § 1 of the Fourteenth Amendment totally incorporated all of the provisions of the Bill of Rights. As Justice Black noted, the chief congressional proponents of the Fourteenth Amendment espoused the view that the Amendment made the Bill of Rights applicable to the States and, in so doing, overruled this Court's decision in *Barron*. . . . Nonetheless, the Court never has embraced Justice Black's "total incorporation" theory. . . . While Justice Black's theory was never adopted, the Court eventually moved in that direction by initiating what has been called a process of "selective incorporation," i.e., the Court began to hold that the Due Process Clause fully incorporates particular rights contained in the first eight Amendments. . . .

The decisions during this time . . . inquired whether a particular Bill of Rights guarantee is fundamental to our scheme of ordered liberty and system of justice. . . . The Court eventually incorporated almost all of the provisions of the Bill of Rights. . . .

With this framework in mind, we now turn directly to the question whether the Second Amendment right to keep and bear arms is incorporated in the concept of due process. In answering that question, as just explained, we must decide whether the right to keep and bear arms is fundamental to our scheme of ordered liberty, or as we have said in a related context, whether this right is "deeply rooted in this Nation's history and tradition[.]"

Our decision in *Heller* points unmistakably to the answer. Self-defense is a basic right, recognized by many legal systems from ancient times to the present day, and in *Heller*, we held that individual self-defense is "the central component" of the Second Amendment right. Heller makes it clear that this right is "deeply rooted in this Nation's history and tradition." . . .

The right to keep and bear arms was considered no less fundamental by those who drafted and ratified the Bill of Rights. . . . Antifederalists and Federalists alike agreed that the right to bear arms was fundamental to the newly formed system of government. . . . By the 1850's, the perceived threat that had prompted the inclusion of the Second Amendment in the Bill of Rights—the fear that the National Government would disarm the universal militia—had largely faded as a popular concern, but the right to keep and bear arms was highly valued for purposes of self-defense. . . .

After the Civil War, many of the over 180,000 African Americans who served in the Union Army returned to the States of the old Confederacy, where systematic efforts were made to disarm them and other blacks. . . . The laws of some States formally prohibited African Americans from possessing firearms. . . . Throughout the South, armed parties, often consisting of ex-Confederate soldiers serving in the state militias, forcibly took firearms from newly freed slaves. . . .

Union Army commanders took steps to secure the right of all citizens to keep and bear arms, but the 39th Congress concluded that legislative action was necessary. Its efforts to safeguard the right to keep and bear arms demonstrate that the right was still recognized to be fundamental.

The most explicit evidence of Congress' aim appears in § 14 of the

Freedmen's Bureau Act of 1866, which provided that "the right . . . to have full and equal benefit of all laws and proceedings concerning personal liberty, personal security, and the acquisition, enjoyment, and disposition of estate, real and personal, including the constitutional right to bear arms, shall be secured to and enjoyed by all the citizens . . . without respect to race or color, or previous condition of slavery." . . . The Civil Rights Act of 1866, which was considered at the same time as the Freedmen's Bureau Act, similarly sought to protect the right of all citizens to keep and bear arms. . . .

Congress, however, ultimately deemed these legislative remedies insufficient. Southern resistance, Presidential vetoes, and this Court's pre–Civil War precedent persuaded Congress that a constitutional amendment was necessary to provide full protection for the rights of blacks. Today, it is generally accepted that the Fourteenth Amendment was understood to provide a constitutional basis for protecting the rights set out in the Civil Rights Act of 1866. . . .

In debating the Fourteenth Amendment, the 39th Congress referred to the right to keep and bear arms as a fundamental right deserving of protection. . . . Even those who thought the Fourteenth Amendment unnecessary believed that blacks, as citizens, "have equal right to protection, and to keep and bear arms for self-defense." . . .

In sum, it is clear that the Framers and ratifiers of the Fourteenth Amendment counted the right to keep and bear arms among those fundamental rights necessary to our system of ordered liberty. . . .

Municipal respondents argue, finally, that the right to keep and bear arms is unique among the rights set out in the first eight Amendments "because the reason for codifying the Second Amendment (to protect the militia) differs from the purpose (primarily, to use firearms to engage in self-defense) that is claimed to make the right implicit in the concept of ordered liberty." Municipal respondents suggest that the Second Amendment right differs from the rights heretofore incorporated because the latter were "valued for [their] own sake." But we have never previously suggested that incorporation of a right turns on whether it has intrinsic as opposed to instrumental value, and quite a few of the rights previously held to be incorporated—for example the right to counsel and the right to confront and subpoena witnesses—are clearly instrumental by any measure. Moreover, this contention repackages one of the chief arguments that we rejected in *Heller*, i.e., that the scope of the Second Amendment right is defined by the immediate threat that led to the inclusion of that right in the Bill of Rights. In *Heller*, we recognized that the codification of this right was prompted by fear that the Federal Government would disarm and thus disable the militias, but we rejected the suggestion that the right was valued only as a means of preserving the militias. On the contrary, we stressed that the right was also valued because the possession of firearms was thought to be essential for self-defense. As we put it, self-defense was "the central component of the right itself." . . .

In *Heller*, we held that the Second Amendment protects the right to possess a handgun in the home for the purpose of self-defense. Unless considerations of stare decisis counsel otherwise, a provision of the Bill of Rights that protects a right that is fundamental from an American perspective applies equally to the Federal Government and the States. . . . We therefore hold that the Due Process Clause of the Fourteenth Amendment incorporates the Second Amendment right recognized in Heller. . . .

JUSTICE THOMAS, CONCURRING IN PART AND CONCURRING IN THE JUDGMENT.

I agree with the Court that the Fourteenth Amendment makes the right to keep and bear arms set forth in the Second Amendment "fully applicable to the States." I write separately because I believe there is a more straightforward path to this conclusion, one that is more faithful to the Fourteenth Amendment's text and history.

Applying what is now a well-settled test, the plurality opinion concludes that the right to keep and bear arms applies to the States through the Fourteenth Amendment's Due Process Clause because it is "fundamental" to the American "scheme of ordered liberty," and " 'deeply rooted in this Nation's history and tradition'. . . . I agree with that description of the right. But I cannot agree that it is enforceable against the States through a clause that speaks only to "process." Instead, the right to keep and bear arms is a privilege of American citizenship that applies to the States through the Fourteenth Amendment's Privileges or Immunities Clause. . . .

The notion that a constitutional provision that guarantees only "process" before a person is deprived of life, liberty, or property could define the substance of those rights strains credulity for even the most casual user of words. Moreover, this fiction is a particularly dangerous one. The one theme that links the Court's substantive due process precedents together is their lack of a guiding principle to distinguish "fundamental" rights that warrant protection from nonfundamental rights that do not. . . . [A]ny serious argument over the scope of the Due Process Clause must acknowledge that neither its text nor its history suggests that it protects the many substantive rights this Court's cases now claim it does.

I cannot accept a theory of constitutional interpretation that rests on such tenuous footing. . . . I believe the original meaning of the Fourteenth Amendment offers a superior alternative, and that a return to that meaning would allow this Court to enforce the rights the Fourteenth Amendment is designed to protect with greater clarity and predictability than the substantive due process framework has so far managed.

I acknowledge the volume of precedents that have been built upon the substantive due process framework, and I further acknowledge the importance of stare decisis to the stability of our Nation's legal system. But stare decisis is only an "adjunct" of our duty as judges to decide by our best lights what the Constitution means. . . .

The Privileges or Immunities Clause of the Fourteenth Amendment declares that "[n]o State . . . shall abridge the privileges or immunities of citizens of the United States." . . . At the time of Reconstruction, the terms "privileges" and "immunities" had an established meaning as synonyms for "rights." The two words, standing alone or paired together, were used interchangeably with the words "rights," "liberties," and "freedoms," and had been since the time of Blackstone. . . . The group of rights-bearers to whom the Privileges or Immunities Clause applies is, of course, "citizens." By the time of Reconstruction, it had long been established that both the States and the Federal Government existed to preserve their citizens' inalienable rights, and that these rights were considered "privileges" or "immunities" of citizenship. . . .

Even though the Bill of Rights did not apply to the States, other provisions of the Constitution did limit state interference with individual rights. Article IV, § 2, cl. 1 provides that "[t]he Citizens of each State shall be entitled to all Privileges and Immunities of Citizens in the several States." The text of this provision resembles the Privileges or Immunities Clause, and it can be assumed that the public's understanding of the latter was informed by its understanding of the former.

Article IV, § 2 was derived from a similar clause in the Articles of Confederation, and reflects the dual citizenship the Constitution provided to all Americans after replacing that "league" of separate sovereign States. By virtue of a person's citizenship in a particular State, he was guaranteed whatever rights and liberties that State's constitution and laws made available. Article IV, § 2 vested citizens of each State with an additional right: the assurance that they would be afforded the "privileges and immunities" of citizenship in any of the several States in the Union to which they might travel. . . .

The text . . . demonstrates three points about the meaning of the Privileges or Immunities Clause in § 1. First, "privileges" and "immunities" were synonyms for "rights." Second, both the States and the Federal Government had long recognized the inalienable rights of their citizens. Third, Article IV, § 2 of the Constitution protected traveling citizens against state discrimination with respect to the fundamental rights of state citizenship.

Two questions still remain . . . The first involves the nature of the rights at stake: Are the privileges or immunities of "citizens of the United States" recognized by § 1 the same as the privileges and immunities of "citizens in the several States" to which Article IV, § 2 refers? The second involves the restriction imposed on the States: Does § 1, like Article IV, § 2, prohibit only discrimination with respect to certain rights if the State chooses to recognize them, or does it require States to recognize those rights? . . . [As to the first question,] Section 1 protects the rights of citizens "of the United States" specifically. The evidence overwhelmingly demonstrates that the privileges and immunities of such citizens included individual rights enumerated in the Constitution, including the right to keep and bear arms. . . .

[As to the second question], I begin, again, with the text. The Privileges or Immunities Clause opens with the command that " No State shall " abridge the privileges or immunities of citizens of the United States." The very same phrase opens Article I, § 10 of the Constitution, which prohibits the States from "pass[ing] any Bill of Attainder" or "ex post facto Law," among other things. Article I, § 10 is one of the few constitutional provisions that limits state authority. In *Barron*, when Chief Justice Marshall interpreted the Bill of Rights as lacking "plain and intelligible language" restricting state power to infringe upon individual liberties, he pointed to Article I, § 10 as an example of text that would have accomplished that task. . . . Thus, the fact that the Privileges or Immunities Clause uses the command "[n]o State shall"— which Article IV, § 2 does not—strongly suggests that the former imposes a greater restriction on state power than the latter.

This interpretation is strengthened when one considers that the Privileges or Immunities Clause uses the verb "abridge," rather than "discriminate," to describe the limit it imposes on state authority. The Webster's dictionary in use at the time of Reconstruction defines the word "abridge" to mean "[t]o deprive; to cut off; . . . as, to abridge one of his rights." . . . The Clause is thus best understood to impose a limitation on state power to infringe upon pre-existing substantive rights. It raises no indication that the Framers of the Clause used the word "abridge" to prohibit only discrimination. . . .

As the Court makes crystal clear, if the Fourteenth Amendment "had outlawed only those laws that discriminate on the basis of race or previous condition of servitude, African Americans in the South would likely have remained vulnerable to attack by many of their worst abusers: the state militia and state peace officers." . . .

This history confirms what the text of the Privileges or Immunities Clause most naturally suggests: Consistent with its command that "[n]o State shall . . . abridge" the rights of United States citizens, the Clause establishes a minimum baseline of federal rights, and the constitutional right to keep and bear arms plainly was among them. . . .

JUSTICE STEVENS, DISSENTING.

. . . I agree with the plurality's refusal to accept petitioners' primary submission. Their briefs marshal an impressive amount of historical evidence for their argument that the Court interpreted the Privileges or Immunities Clause too narrowly in the Slaughter-House Cases. But the original meaning of the Clause is not as clear as they suggest—and not nearly as clear as it would need to be to dislodge 137 years of precedent. The burden is severe for those who seek radical change in such an established body of constitutional doctrine. . . .

CRIMINAL LAW

✿

*I*n the 1960s, the Supreme Court dramatically expanded the procedural protections accorded to criminal defendants. *Miranda v. Arizona* (1966) is perhaps the best known such case and is illustrative of the Court's approach. A 5–4 majority famously declared that arrested criminal suspects must be given "warnings" of their rights to remain silent and to a lawyer. Even though the Fifth Amendment did not itself require such warnings, the majority believed them important as safeguards of Fifth Amendment rights and as checks on police interrogation practices.

✪

Miranda v. Arizona
384 U.S. 436 (1966)

•

MR. CHIEF JUSTICE WARREN DELIVERED THE OPINION OF
THE COURT.

The cases before us raise questions which go to the roots of our concepts of American criminal jurisprudence: the restraints society must
observe consistent with the Federal Constitution in prosecuting individuals for crime. More specifically, we deal with the admissibility of
statements obtained from an individual who is subjected to custodial
police interrogation and the necessity for procedures which assure that
the individual is accorded his privilege under the Fifth Amendment to
the Constitution not to be compelled to incriminate himself. . . .

Our holding will be spelled out with some specificity in the pages
which follow but briefly stated it is this: the prosecution may not use
statements, whether exculpatory or inculpatory, stemming from custodial interrogation of the defendant unless it demonstrates the use of
procedural safeguards effective to secure the privilege against self-
incrimination. Prior to any questioning, the person must be warned
that he has a right to remain silent, that any statement he does make
may be used as evidence against him, and that he has a right to the
presence of an attorney, either retained or appointed. The defendant
may waive effectuation of these rights, provided the waiver is made
voluntarily, knowingly and intelligently. If, however, he indicates in any
manner and at any stage of the process that he wishes to consult with an
attorney before speaking there can be no questioning. Likewise, if the
individual is alone and indicates in any manner that he does not wish to
be interrogated, the police may not question him. The mere fact that he
may have answered some questions or volunteered some statements on
his own does not deprive him of the right to refrain from answering any
further inquiries until he has consulted with an attorney and thereafter
consents to be questioned.

. . . An understanding of the nature and setting of this in-custody
interrogation is essential to our decisions today. . . . [T]he modern practice of in-custody interrogation is psychologically rather than physically

oriented. . . . The officers are told by the manuals that the "principal psychological factor contributing to a successful interrogation is privacy—
being alone with the person under interrogation." . . . To highlight the
isolation and unfamiliar surroundings, the manuals instruct the police
to display an air of confidence in the suspect's guilt and from outward
appearance to maintain only an interest in confirming certain details.
The guilt of the subject is to be posited as a fact. The interrogator
should direct his comments toward the reasons why the subject committed the act, rather than court failure by asking the subject whether
he did it. Like other men, perhaps the subject has had a bad family life,
had an unhappy childhood, had too much to drink, had an unrequited
desire for women. The officers are instructed to minimize the moral
seriousness of the offense, to cast blame on the victim or on society.
These tactics are designed to put the subject in a psychological state
where his story is but an elaboration of what the police purport to know
already—that he is guilty. Explanations to the contrary are dismissed
and discouraged. . . .

The interrogators sometimes are instructed to induce a confession out
of trickery. The technique here is quite effective in crimes which require
identification or which run in series. In the identification situation, the
interrogator may take a break in his questioning to place the subject
among a group of men in a line-up. "The witness or complainant (previously coached, if necessary) studies the line-up and confidently points
out the subject as the guilty party." Then the questioning resumes "as
though there were now no doubt about the guilt of the subject." . . .

The manuals also contain instructions for police on how to handle the
individual who refuses to discuss the matter entirely, or who asks for an
attorney or relatives. The examiner is to concede him the right to remain
silent. "This usually has a very undermining effect. First of all, he is
disappointed in his expectation of an unfavorable reaction on the part of
the interrogator. Secondly, a concession of this right to remain silent im-
presses the subject with the apparent fairness of his interrogator." After
this psychological conditioning, however, the officer is told to point out
the incriminating significance of the suspect's refusal to talk:

> "Joe, you have a right to remain silent. That's your privilege and
> I'm the last person in the world who'll try to take it away from you.
> If that's the way you want to leave this, O.K. But let me ask you this.

Suppose you were in my shoes and I were in yours and you called me in to ask me about this and I told you, 'I don't want to answer any of your questions.' You'd think I had something to hide, and you'd probably be right in thinking that. That's exactly what I'll have to think about you, and so will everybody else. So let's sit here and talk this whole thing over."

Few will persist in their initial refusal to talk, it is said, if this monologue is employed correctly. . . .

[W]e concern ourselves primarily with this interrogation atmosphere and the evils it can bring. . . . In these cases, we might not find the defendants' statements to have been involuntary in traditional terms. Our concern for adequate safeguards to protect precious Fifth Amendment rights is, of course, not lessened in the slightest. In each of the cases, the defendant was thrust into an unfamiliar atmosphere and run through menacing police interrogation procedures. The potentiality for compulsion is forcefully apparent, for example, in Miranda, where the indigent Mexican defendant was a seriously disturbed individual with pronounced sexual fantasies[.] . . .

We are satisfied that all the principles embodied in the privilege apply to informal compulsion exerted by law-enforcement officers during in-custody questioning. . . . In order to combat these pressures and to permit a full opportunity to exercise the privilege against self-incrimination, the accused must be adequately and effectively apprised of his rights and the exercise of those rights must be fully honored. . . .

[W]e cannot say that the Constitution necessarily requires adherence to any particular solution for the inherent compulsions of the interrogation process as it is presently conducted. Our decision in no way creates a constitutional straitjacket which will handicap sound efforts at reform, nor is it intended to have this effect. We encourage Congress and the States to continue their laudable search for increasingly effective ways of protecting the rights of the individual while promoting efficient enforcement of our criminal laws. However, unless we are shown other procedures which are at least as effective in apprising accused persons of their right of silence and in assuring a continuous opportunity to exercise it, [these] safeguards must be observed. . . .

If the individual indicates in any manner, at any time prior to or during questioning, that he wishes to remain silent, the interrogation must cease. . . . If the interrogation continues without the presence of an attorney and a statement is taken, a heavy burden rests on the government to demonstrate that the defendant knowingly and intelligently waived his privilege against self-incrimination and his right to retained or appointed counsel. . . . The requirement of warnings and waiver of rights is a fundamental with respect to the Fifth Amendment privilege and not simply a preliminary ritual to existing methods of interrogation.

Mr. Justice HARLAN, whom Mr. Justice STEWART and Mr. Justice WHITE join, dissenting.

I believe the decision of the Court represents poor constitutional law and entails harmful consequences for the country at large. . . . The new rules are not designed to guard against police brutality or other unmistakably banned forms of coercion. Those who use third-degree tactics and deny them in court are equally able and destined to lie as skillfully about warnings and waivers. Rather, the thrust of the new rules is to negate all pressures, to reinforce the nervous or ignorant suspect, and ultimately to discourage any confession at all. The aim in short is toward "voluntariness" in a utopian sense, or to view it from a different angle, voluntariness with a vengeance. . . .

The Court's opinion in my view reveals no adequate basis for extending the Fifth Amendment's privilege against self-incrimination to the police station. Far more important, it fails to show that the Court's new rules are well supported, let alone compelled, by Fifth Amendment precedents. . . . Historically, the privilege against self-incrimination did not bear at all on the use of extra-legal confessions[.] . . .

The more important premise is that pressure on the suspect must be eliminated though it be only the subtle influence of the atmosphere and surroundings. The Fifth Amendment, however, has never been thought to forbid all pressure to incriminate one's self in the situations covered by it. . . . Interrogation is no doubt often inconvenient and unpleasant for the suspect. However, it is no less so for a man to be arrested and jailed, to have his house searched, or to stand trial in court, yet all this may properly happen to the most innocent given probable cause, a warrant, or an indictment. . . .

[I]t may make the analysis more graphic to consider the actual facts of one of the four cases reversed by the Court. *Miranda v. Arizona* serves best, being neither the hardest nor easiest of the four under the Court's standards.

On March 3, 1963, an 18-year-old girl was kidnapped and forcibly raped near Phoenix, Arizona. Ten days later, on the morning of March 13, petitioner Miranda was arrested and taken to the police station. At this time Miranda was 23 years old, indigent, and educated to the extent of completing half the ninth grade. He had "an emotional illness" of the schizophrenic type, according to the doctor who eventually examined him; the doctor's report also stated that Miranda was "alert and oriented as to time, place, and person," intelligent within normal limits, competent to stand trial, and sane within the legal definition. At the police station, the victim picked Miranda out of a lineup, and two officers then took him into a separate room to interrogate him, starting about 11:30 a.m. Though at first denying his guilt, within a short time Miranda gave a detailed oral confession and then wrote out in his own hand and signed a brief statement admitting and describing the crime. All this was accomplished in two hours or less without any force, threats or promises and—I will assume this though the record is uncertain— without any effective warnings at all.

Miranda's oral and written confessions are now held inadmissible under the Court's new rules. One is entitled to feel astonished that the Constitution can be read to produce this result. These confessions were obtained during brief, daytime questioning conducted by two officers and unmarked by any of the traditional indicia of coercion. They assured a conviction for a brutal and unsettling crime, for which the police had and quite possibly could obtain little evidence other than the victim's identifications, evidence which is frequently unreliable. There was, in sum, a legitimate purpose, no perceptible unfairness, and certainly little risk of injustice in the interrogation. Yet the resulting confessions, and the responsible course of police practice they represent, are to be sacrificed to the Court's own finespun conception of fairness which I seriously doubt is shared by many thinking citizens in this country. . . .

Nothing in the letter or the spirit of the Constitution or in the precedents squares with the heavy-handed and one-sided action that is so precipitously taken by the Court in the name of fulfilling its constitutional responsibilities.

MODERN CIVIL RIGHTS
LEGISLATION

 ౿

*O*ver the years, Congress has invoked various legislative powers to enact legislation forbidding many types of discrimination and to further civil and constitutional rights. In 1883, The *Civil Rights Cases* (see pp. 176) struck down the provisions of the Civil Rights Act of 1875 that prohibited racial discrimination, by private businesses providing services to the general public, as exceeding Congress's power to enforce the Thirteenth and Fourteenth Amendments. In *Heart of Atlanta Motel v. United States* (1964), however, the Supreme Court unanimously upheld the Civil Rights Act of 1964's prohibitions of racial discrimination in public accommodations—including in hotels, restaurants, theaters, and sports arenas—as a valid exercise of Congress's power to regulate *commerce*.

Then, in *Jones v. Alfred H. Mayer Co.* (1968), the Court adopted a broader view of Congress's power to enforce the Thirteenth Amendment than it had in the 1883 *Civil Rights Cases*, finding that Congress had the power to pass all laws "necessary and proper" for the elimination of racial barriers to the acquisition of real and personal property, and upholding a broad interpretation of the Civil Rights Act of 1866 on this ground. Two justices dissented on statutory interpretation grounds, without reaching the constitutional issue.

In *City of Boerne v. Flores* (1997), the Court again considered the scope of Congress's powers in enforcing the Fourteenth Amendment's provisions protecting individual liberties against state government interference. By a vote of 6–3, the Court held that Congress is limited to enforcing the Supreme Court's understanding of the Fourteenth Amendment and cannot use its power under section five to enact legislation embodying a more expansive view of such rights.

✪

Heart of Atlanta Motel v. United States
379 U.S. 241 (1964)

•

Mr. Justice CLARK delivered the opinion of the Court.

This is a declaratory judgment action attacking the constitutionality of Title II of the Civil Rights Act of 1964. . . . The case comes here on admissions and stipulated facts. Appellant owns and operates the Heart of Atlanta Motel which has 216 rooms available to transient guests. . . . Prior to passage of the Act the motel had followed a practice of refusing to rent rooms to Negroes, and it alleged that it intended to continue to do so. In an effort to perpetuate that policy this suit was filed.

The appellant contends that Congress in passing this Act exceeded its power to regulate commerce under Art. I, § 8, cl. 3, of the Constitution of the United States; that the Act violates the Fifth Amendment because appellant is deprived of the right to choose its customers and operate its business as it wishes, resulting in a taking of its liberty and property without due process of law and a taking of its property without just compensation; and, finally, that by requiring appellant to rent available rooms to Negroes against its will, Congress is subjecting it to involuntary servitude in contravention of the Thirteenth Amendment.

The appellees counter that the unavailability to Negroes of adequate accommodations interferes significantly with interstate travel, and that Congress, under the Commerce Clause, has power to remove such obstructions and restraints; that the Fifth Amendment does not forbid reasonable regulation and that consequential damage does not constitute a 'taking' within the meaning of that amendment; that the Thirteenth Amendment claim fails because it is entirely frivolous to say that an amendment directed to the abolition of human bondage and the removal of widespread disabilities associated with slavery places discrimination in public accommodations, beyond the reach of both federal and state law.

. . . The Senate Commerce Committee made it quite clear that the fundamental object of Title II was to vindicate 'the deprivation of personal dignity that surely accompanies denials of equal access to public establishments.' At the same time, however, it noted that such an objective has been and could be readily achieved 'by congressional action based on the commerce power of the Constitution.' Our study of the legislative record, made in the light of prior cases, has brought us to the conclusion that Congress possessed ample power in this regard, and we have therefore not considered the other grounds relied upon. This is not to say that the remaining authority upon which it acted was not adequate, a question upon which we do not pass, but merely that since the commerce power is sufficient for our decision here we have considered it alone. . . .

In light of our ground for decision, it might be well at the outset to discuss the Civil Rights Cases, supra, which declared provisions of the Civil Rights Act of 1875 unconstitutional. We think that decision inapposite, and without precedential value in determining the constitutionality of the present Act. Unlike Title II of the present legislation, the 1875 Act broadly proscribed discrimination in 'inns, public conveyances on land or water, theaters, and other places of public amusement,' without limiting the categories of affected businesses to those impinging upon interstate commerce. In contrast, the applicability of Title II is carefully limited to enterprises having a direct and substantial relation to the interstate flow of goods and people, except where state action is involved. Further, the fact that certain kinds of businesses may not in 1875 have been sufficiently involved in interstate commerce to warrant bringing them within the ambit of the commerce power is not necessarily dispositive of the same question today. Our populace had not reached its present mobility, nor were facilities, goods and services circulating as readily in interstate commerce as they are today. . . . Finally, there is language in the Civil Rights Cases which indicates that the Court did not fully consider whether the 1875 Act could be sustained as an exercise of the commerce power. Though the Court observed that 'no one will contend that the power to pass it was contained in the constitution before the adoption of the last three amendments (Thirteenth, Fourteenth, and Fifteenth),' the Court went on specifically to note that the Act was not 'conceived' in terms of the commerce power and expressly pointed out:

'Of course, these remarks (as to lack of congressional power) do not apply to those cases in which congress is clothed with direct and plenary powers of legislation over the whole subject, accompanied with an express or implied denial of such power to the states, as in the regulation of commerce with foreign nations, among the several states, and with the Indian tribes[.] . . . In these cases congress has power to pass laws for regulating the subjects specified, in every detail, and the conduct and transactions of individuals in respect thereof.' . . .

In framing Title II of this Act Congress was also dealing with what it considered a moral problem. But that fact does not detract from the overwhelming evidence of the disruptive effect that racial discrimination has had on commercial intercourse. It was this burden which empowered Congress to enact appropriate legislation, and, given this basis for the exercise of its power, Congress was not restricted by the fact that the particular obstruction to interstate commerce with which it was dealing was also deemed a moral and social wrong. . . .

Nor does the Act deprive appellant of liberty or property under the Fifth Amendment. The commerce power invoked here by the Congress is a specific and plenary one authorized by the Constitution itself. The only questions are: (1) whether Congress had a rational basis for finding that racial discrimination by motels affected commerce, and (2) if it had such a basis, whether the means it selected to eliminate that evil are reasonable and appropriate. If they are, appellant has no 'right' to select its guests as it sees fit, free from governmental regulation. . . . Neither do we find any merit in the claim that the Act is a taking of property without just compensation. . . .

We find no merit in the remainder of appellant's contentions, including that of 'involuntary servitude.' As we have seen, 32 States prohibit racial discrimination in public accommodations. These laws but codify the common-law innkeeper rule which long predated the Thirteenth Amendment. It is difficult to believe that the Amendment was intended to abrogate this principle. . . .

Jones v. Alfred H. Mayer Co.
392 U.S. 409 (1968)

•

MR. JUSTICE STEWART DELIVERED THE OPINION OF THE COURT.

In this case, we are called upon to determine the scope and the constitutionality of an Act of Congress, 42 U.S.C. § 1982, which provides that:

"All citizens of the United States shall have the same right, in every State and Territory, as is enjoyed by white citizens thereof to inherit, purchase lease, sell, hold, and convey real and personal property."

On September 2, 1965, the petitioners filed a complaint in the District Court for the Eastern District of Missouri, alleging that the respondents had refused to sell them a home in the Paddock Woods community of St. Louis County for the sole reason that petitioner Joseph Lee Jones is a Negro. . . .

[The] question is whether Congress has power under the Constitution to do what § 1982 purports to do: to prohibit all racial discrimination, private and public, in the sale and rental of property. Our starting point is the Thirteenth Amendment, for it was pursuant to that constitutional provision that Congress originally enacted what is now § 1982. The Amendment consists of two parts. Section 1 states: "Neither slavery nor involuntary servitude, except as a punishment for crime whereof the party shall have been duly convicted, shall exist within the United States, or any place subject to their jurisdiction." Section 2 provides: "Congress shall have power to enforce this article by appropriate legislation."

As its text reveals, the Thirteenth Amendment "is not a mere prohibition of State laws establishing or upholding slavery, but an absolute declaration that slavery or involuntary servitude shall not exist in any part of the United States" [*Civil Rights Cases*]. It has never been doubted, therefore, "that the power vested in Congress to enforce the article by appropriate legislation," includes the power to enact laws "direct and primary, operating upon the acts of individuals, whether sanctioned by State legislation or not."

Thus, the fact that § 1982 operates upon the unofficial acts of private individuals, whether or not sanctioned by state law, presents no constitutional problem. If Congress has power under the Thirteenth Amendment to eradicate conditions that prevent Negroes from buying and renting property because of their race or color, then no federal statute calculated to achieve that objective can be thought to exceed the constitutional power of Congress simply because it reaches beyond state action to regulate the conduct of private individuals. The constitutional question in this case, therefore, comes to this: does the authority of Congress to enforce the Thirteenth Amendment "by appropriate legislation" include the power to eliminate all racial barriers to the acquisition of real and personal property? We think the answer to that question is plainly yes.

"By its own unaided force and effect," the Thirteenth Amendment "abolished slavery, and established universal freedom" [*Civil Rights Cases*]. Whether or not the Amendment itself did any more than that—a question not involved in this case—it is at least clear that the Enabling Clause of that Amendment empowered Congress to do much more. For that clause clothed "Congress with power to pass *all laws necessary and proper for abolishing all badges and incidents of slavery in the United States.*"

Those who opposed passage of the Civil Rights Act of 1866 argued, in effect that the Thirteenth Amendment merely authorized Congress to dissolve the legal bond by which the Negro slave was held to his master. Yet many had earlier opposed the Thirteenth Amendment on the very ground that it would give Congress virtually unlimited power to enact laws for the protection of Negroes in every State. And the majority leaders in Congress—who were, after all, the authors of the Thirteenth Amendment—had no doubt that its Enabling Clause contemplated the sort of positive legislation that was embodied in the 1866 Civil Rights Act. Their chief spokesman, Senator Trumbull of Illinois, the Chairman of the Judiciary Committee, had brought the Thirteenth Amendment to the floor of the Senate in 1864. In defending the constitutionality of the 1866 Act, he argued that, if the narrower construction of the Enabling Clause were correct, then

"the trumpet of freedom that we have been blowing throughout the land has given an 'uncertain sound,' and the promised freedom is a delusion. Such was not the intention of Congress, which proposed the constitutional amendment, nor is such the fair meaning of the amendment itself. . . . I have no doubt that, under this provision . . . , we may destroy all these discriminations in civil rights against the black man, and if we cannot, our constitutional amendment amounts to nothing. It was for that purpose that the second clause of that amendment was adopted, which says that Congress shall have authority, by appropriate legislation, to carry into effect the article prohibiting slavery. Who is to decide what that appropriate legislation is to be? The Congress of the United States, and it is for Congress to adopt such appropriate legislation as it may think proper, so that it be a means to accomplish the end."

Surely Senator Trumbull was right. Surely Congress has the power under the Thirteenth Amendment rationally to determine what are the badges and the incidents of slavery, and the authority to translate that determination into effective legislation. Nor can we say that the determination Congress has made is an irrational one. For this Court recognized long ago that, whatever else they may have encompassed, the badges and incidents of slavery—its "burdens and disabilities"—included restraints upon "those fundamental rights which are the essence of civil freedom, namely, the same right . . . to inherit, purchase, lease, sell and convey property, as is enjoyed by white citizens" [*Civil Rights Cases*]. Just as the Black Codes, enacted after the Civil War to restrict the free exercise of those rights, were substitutes for the slave system, so the exclusion of Negroes from white communities became a substitute for the Black Codes. And when racial discrimination herds men into ghettos and makes their ability to buy property turn on the color of their skin, then it too is a relic of slavery.

Negro citizens, North and South, who saw in the Thirteenth Amendment a promise of freedom—freedom to "go and come at pleasure" and to "buy and sell when they please"—would be left with "a mere paper guarantee" if Congress were powerless to assure that a dollar in the hands of a Negro will purchase the same thing as a dollar in the hands of a white man. At the very least, the freedom that Congress is empowered to secure under the Thirteenth Amendment includes the freedom to buy whatever a white man can buy, the right to live wherever a white man can live. . . .

City of Boerne v. Flores
521 U.S. 507 (1997)

•

JUSTICE KENNEDY DELIVERED THE OPINION OF THE COURT.

A decision by local zoning authorities to deny a church a building permit was challenged under the Religious Freedom Restoration Act of 1993 (RFRA or Act). The case calls into question the authority of Congress to enact RFRA. We conclude the statute exceeds Congress' power. . . .

Congress enacted RFRA in direct response to the Court's decision in *Employment Div., Dept. of Human Resources of Oregon v. Smith* (1990). There we considered a Free Exercise Clause claim brought by members of the Native American Church who were denied unemployment benefits when they lost their jobs because they had used peyote. Their practice was to ingest peyote for sacramental purposes, and they challenged an Oregon statute of general applicability which made use of the drug criminal. In evaluating the claim, we declined to apply the balancing test set forth in *Sherbert v. Verner*, 374 U.S. 398 (1963), under which we would have asked whether Oregon's prohibition substantially burdened a religious practice and, if it did, whether the burden was justified by a compelling government interest. . . .

The application of the *Sherbert* test, the *Smith* decision explained, would have produced an anomaly in the law, a constitutional right to ignore neutral laws of general applicability. . . . Four Members of the Court disagreed. They argued the law placed a substantial burden on the Native American Church members so that it could be upheld only if the law served a compelling state interest and was narrowly tailored to achieve that end. . . .

These points of constitutional interpretation were debated by Members of Congress in hearings and floor debates. Many criticized the Court's reasoning, and this disagreement resulted in the passage of RFRA. Congress announced:

(1) [T]he framers of the Constitution, recognizing free exercise of religion as an unalienable right, secured its protection in the First Amendment to the Constitution;

(2) laws 'neutral' toward religion may burden religious exercise as surely as laws intended to interfere with religious exercise;

(3) governments should not substantially burden religious exercise without compelling justification;

(4) in *Employment Division v. Smith*, 494 U.S. 872 (1990), the Supreme Court virtually eliminated the requirement that the government justify burdens on religious exercise imposed by laws neutral toward religion; and

(5) the compelling interest test as set forth in prior Federal court rulings is a workable test for striking sensible balances between religious liberty and competing prior governmental interests." . . .

RFRA prohibits "[g]overnment" from "substantially burden[ing]" a person's exercise of religion even if the burden results from a rule of general applicability unless the government can demonstrate the burden "(1) is in furtherance of a compelling governmental interest; and (2) is the least restrictive means of furthering that compelling governmental interest." The Act's mandate applies to any "branch, department, agency, instrumentality, and official . . . of the United States," as well as to any "State, or . . . subdivision of a State." . . .

Congress relied on its Fourteenth Amendment enforcement power in enacting the most far reaching and substantial of RFRA's provisions, those which impose its requirements on the States. . . .The Fourteenth Amendment provides, in relevant part: . . . "Section 5. The Congress shall have power to enforce, by appropriate legislation, the provisions of this article." . . . Congress, it is said, is only protecting by legislation one of the liberties guaranteed by the Fourteenth Amendment's Due Process Clause, the free exercise of religion, beyond what is necessary under *Smith*. . . . In *Ex parte Virginia* (1879), we explained the scope of Congress' § 5 power in the following broad terms:

Whatever legislation is appropriate, that is, adapted to carry out the objects the amendments have in view, whatever tends to enforce submission to the prohibitions they contain, and to secure to all persons the enjoyment of perfect equality of civil rights and the equal protection of the laws against State denial or invasion, if not prohibited, is brought within the domain of congressional power.

Legislation which deters or remedies constitutional violations can fall within the sweep of Congress' enforcement power even if in the process it prohibits conduct which is not itself unconstitutional[.] . . .

For example, the Court upheld a suspension of literacy tests and similar voting requirements under Congress' parallel power to enforce the provisions of the Fifteenth Amendment as a measure to combat racial discrimination in voting. We have also concluded that other measures protecting voting rights are within Congress' power to enforce the Fourteenth and Fifteenth Amendments, despite the burdens those measures placed on the States. . . .

In assessing the breadth of § 5's enforcement power, we begin with its text. Congress has been given the power "to enforce" the "provisions of this article." We agree with respondent, of course, that Congress can enact legislation under § 5 enforcing the constitutional right to the free exercise of religion. . . .

Congress' power under § 5, however, extends only to "enforc[ing]" the provisions of the Fourteenth Amendment. . . . The design of the Amendment and the text of § 5 are inconsistent with the suggestion that Congress has the power to decree the substance of the Fourteenth Amendment's restrictions on the States. Legislation which alters the meaning of the Free Exercise Clause cannot be said to be enforcing the Clause. Congress does not enforce a constitutional right by changing what the right is. It has been given the power "to enforce," not the power to determine what constitutes a constitutional violation.

While the line between measures that remedy or prevent unconstitutional actions and measures that make a substantive change in the governing law is not easy to discern, and Congress must have wide latitude in determining where it lies, the distinction exists and must be observed. There must be a congruence and proportionality between the injury to be prevented or remedied and the means adopted to that end. Lacking such a connection, legislation may become substantive in operation and effect. . . .

The Fourteenth Amendment's history confirms the remedial, rather than substantive, nature of the Enforcement Clause. The Joint Committee on Reconstruction of the 39th Congress began drafting what would become the Fourteenth Amendment in January 1866. The objections to the Committee's first draft of the Amendment, and the rejection of the draft, have a direct bearing on the central issue of defining Congress' enforcement power. In February, Republican Representative John Bingham of Ohio reported the following draft Amendment to the House of Representatives on behalf of the Joint Committee:

The Congress shall have power to make all laws which shall be necessary and proper to secure to the citizens of each State all privileges and immunities of citizens in the several States, and to all persons in the several States equal protection in the rights of life, liberty, and property.

Cong. Globe, 39th Cong., 1st Sess., 1034 (1866).

The proposal encountered immediate opposition[.] . . . Members of Congress from across the political spectrum criticized the Amendment, and the criticisms had a common theme: The proposed Amendment gave Congress too much legislative power at the expense of the existing constitutional structure. . . . The Amendment in its early form was not again considered. Instead, the Joint Committee began drafting a new article of Amendment, which it reported to Congress on April 30, 1866.

Section 1 of the new draft Amendment imposed self-executing limits on the States. Section 5 prescribed that "[t]he Congress shall have power to enforce, by appropriate legislation, the provisions of this article." Under the revised Amendment, Congress' power was no longer plenary but remedial. Congress was granted the power to make the substantive constitutional prohibitions against the States effective. . . .

As enacted, the Fourteenth Amendment confers substantive rights against the States which, like the provisions of the Bill of Rights, are self-executing. . . . The power to interpret the Constitution in a case or controversy remains in the Judiciary. . . .

If Congress could define its own powers by altering the Fourteenth Amendment's meaning, no longer would the Constitution be "superior paramount law, unchangeable by ordinary means." It would be "on a level with ordinary legislative acts, and, like other acts, . . . alterable when the legislature shall please to alter it." *Marbury v. Madison*, 1 Cranch, at 177. Under this approach, it is difficult to conceive of a principle that would limit congressional power. . . .

RFRA cannot be considered remedial, preventive legislation, if those terms are to have any meaning. RFRA is so out of proportion to a supposed remedial or preventive object that it cannot be understood as responsive to, or designed to prevent, unconstitutional behavior. It appears, instead, to attempt a substantive change in constitutional protections. . . .

Our national experience teaches that the Constitution is preserved best when each part of the Government respects both the Constitution and the proper actions and determinations of the other branches. When the Court has interpreted the Constitution, it has acted within the province of the Judicial Branch, which embraces the duty to say what the law is. *Marbury v. Madison.* When the political branches of the Government act against the background of a judicial interpretation of the Constitution already issued, it must be understood that in later cases and controversies the Court will treat its precedents with the respect due them under settled principles, including *stare decisis,* and contrary expectations must be disappointed. RFRA was designed to control cases and controversies, such as the one before us; but as the provisions of the federal statute here invoked are beyond congressional authority, it is this Court's precedent, not RFRA, which must control.

JUSTICE O'CONNOR, . . . DISSENTING.

I dissent from the Court's disposition of this case. I agree with the Court that the issue before us is whether the Religious Freedom Restoration Act of 1993 (RFRA) is a proper exercise of Congress' power to enforce § 5 of the Fourteenth Amendment. But as a yardstick for measuring the constitutionality of RFRA, the Court uses its holding in *Employment Div., Dept. of Human Resources of Oregon v. Smith,* the decision that prompted Congress to enact RFRA as a means of more rigorously enforcing the Free Exercise Clause. I remain of the view that Smith was wrongly decided, and I would use this case to reexamine the Court's holding there. . . . If the Court were to correct the misinterpretation of the Free Exercise Clause set forth in *Smith,* it would simultaneously put our First Amendment jurisprudence back on course and allay the legitimate concerns of a majority in Congress who believed that Smith improperly restricted religious liberty. We would then be in a position to review RFRA in light of a proper interpretation of the Free Exercise Clause. . . . [I]f I agreed with the Court's standard in *Smith,* I would join the opinion.

SUBSTANTIVE DUE PROCESS
AND PRIVACY RIGHTS

*I*n *Griswold v. Connecticut* (1965), the Supreme Court held 7–2 that married couples have a constitutional right to use contraception. The Court did not identify which provision of the Constitution provides that right, relying instead on the "penumbras" and "emanations" of several constitutional rights, without resting on any one specifically. The case was a significant innovation and an important transitional case leading to the Court's declaration of a constitutional right to abortion in *Roe v. Wade*.

Roe v. Wade (1973) has been the most controversial Supreme Court decision of the modern era. By a vote of 7–2, the Court held that "substantive due process"—the same legal principle used in *Dred Scott* and *Lochner*—conferred a constitutional right to abortion throughout pregnancy. Under *Roe*, women may have abortions for any reason during the first six months of pregnancy and for health reasons during the last three months. *Roe*'s companion case, *Doe v. Bolton*, defined health reasons as including psychological, emotional, family, and social reasons for abortion.

In *Planned Parenthood v. Casey* (1992), the Court surprised observers with an equally if not more important abortion decision. Though the justices declined to embrace *Roe* as rightly decided, a 5–4 majority reaffirmed *Roe*'s central holding on the basis of the doctrine of *"stare decisis,"* the judicial policy of adhering to prior decisions.

In *Lawrence v. Texas* (2003), the Court revisited the question of whether the Constitution contains a substantive due process right to engage in homosexual sexual activity. An earlier decision, *Bowers v. Hardwick* (1986), had rejected such a claim. In *Lawrence*, the Court overruled *Bowers* by a vote of 6–3, based on what it regarded as changed public attitudes toward homosexuality. The Court held that the doctrine of *stare decisis* did not require adherence to *Bowers*, which the Court had come to view as wrongly decided.

✪

Griswold v. Connecticut
381 U.S. 479 (1965)

•

MR. JUSTICE DOUGLAS DELIVERED THE OPINION OF THE COURT.

The statutes whose constitutionality is involved in this appeal . . . [provide]:

'Any person who uses any drug, medicinal article or instrument for the purpose of preventing conception shall be fined not less than fifty dollars or imprisoned not less than sixty days nor more than one year or be both fined and imprisoned.' . . .

'Any person who assists, abets, counsels, causes, hires or commands another to commit any offense may be prosecuted and punished as if he were the principal offender.' . . .

[W]e are met with a wide range of questions that implicate the Due Process Clause of the Fourteenth Amendment. Overtones of some arguments suggest that *Lochner v. State of New York*, 198 U.S. 45 should be our guide. But we decline that invitation . . . We do not sit as a super-legislature to determine the wisdom, need, and propriety of laws that touch economic problems, business affairs, or social conditions. This law, however, operates directly on an intimate relation of husband and wife and their physician's role in one aspect of that relation.

The association of people is not mentioned in the Constitution nor in the Bill of Rights. The right to educate a child in a school of the parents' choice—whether public or private or parochial—is also not mentioned. Nor is the right to study any particular subject or any foreign language. Yet the First Amendment has been construed to include certain of those rights. . . . In *NAACP v. State of Alabama*, 357 U.S. 449, 462 we protected the 'freedom to associate and privacy in one's associations,' noting that freedom of association was a peripheral First Amendment right. Disclosure of membership lists of a constitutionally valid association, we held, was invalid 'as entailing the likelihood of a substantial restraint upon the exercise by petitioner's members of their right to freedom of association.' In other words, the First Amendment has a penumbra where privacy is protected from governmental intrusion. . . .

The foregoing cases suggest that specific guarantees in the Bill of Rights have penumbras, formed by emanations from those guarantees that help give them life and substance. . . . Various guarantees create zones of privacy. The right of association contained in the penumbra of the First Amendment is one, as we have seen. The Third Amendment in its prohibition against the quartering of soldiers 'in any house' in time of peace without the consent of the owner is another facet of that privacy. The Fourth Amendment explicitly affirms the 'right of the people to be secure in their persons, houses, papers, and effects, against unreasonable searches and seizures.' The Fifth Amendment in its Self-Incrimination Clause enables the citizen to create a zone of privacy which government may not force him to surrender to his detriment. The Ninth Amendment provides: 'The enumeration in the Constitution, of certain rights, shall not be construed to deny or disparage others retained by the people.' . . .

The present case, then, concerns a relationship lying within the zone of privacy created by several fundamental constitutional guarantees. And it concerns a law which, in forbidding the use of contraceptives rather than regulating their manufacture or sale, seeks to achieve its goals by means having a maximum destructive impact upon that relationship. . . . Would we allow the police to search the sacred precincts of marital bedrooms for telltale signs of the use of contraceptives? The very idea is repulsive to the notions of privacy surrounding the marriage relationship.

MR. JUSTICE GOLDBERG, WHOM THE CHIEF JUSTICE AND
MR. JUSTICE BRENNAN JOIN, CONCURRING.

. . . This Court, in a series of decisions, has held that the Fourteenth
Amendment absorbs and applies to the States those specifics of the first
eight amendments which express fundamental personal rights. The language and history of the Ninth Amendment reveal that the Framers of
the Constitution believed that there are additional fundamental rights,
protected from governmental infringement, which exist alongside those
fundamental rights specifically mentioned in the first eight constitutional amendments.

The Ninth Amendment reads, 'The enumeration in the Constitution, of certain rights, shall not be construed to deny or disparage others
retained by the people.' The Amendment is almost entirely the work of
James Madison. It was introduced in Congress by him and passed the
House and Senate with little or no debate and virtually no change in
language. It was proffered to quiet expressed fears that a bill of specifically enumerated rights could not be sufficiently broad to cover all essential rights and that the specific mention of certain rights would be
interpreted as a denial that others were protected.

In presenting the proposed Amendment, Madison said:

'It has been objected also against a bill of rights, that, by enumer-
ating particular exceptions to the grant of power, it would disparage
those rights which were not placed in that enumeration; and it might
follow by implication, that those rights which were not singled out,
were intended to be assigned into the hands of the General Government, and were consequently insecure. This is one of the most plausible
arguments I have ever heard urged against the admission of a bill of
rights into this system; but, I conceive, that it may be guarded against.
I have attempted it, as gentlemen may see by turning to the last clause
of the fourth resolution (the Ninth Amendment).' I Annals of Congress
439 (Gales and Seaton ed. 1834). . . .

To hold that a right so basic and fundamental and so deep-rooted in
our society as the right of privacy in marriage may be infringed because
that right is not guaranteed in so many words by the first eight amendments to the Constitution is to ignore the Ninth Amendment and to
give it no effect whatsoever. Moreover, a judicial construction that this
fundamental right is not protected by the Constitution because it is

not mentioned in explicit terms by one of the first eight amendments or elsewhere in the Constitution would violate the Ninth Amendment, which specifically states that '(t)he enumeration in the Constitution, of certain rights shall not be construed to deny or disparage others retained by the people.' . . . I do not mean to imply that the Ninth Amendment is applied against the States by the Fourteenth. Nor do I mean to state that the Ninth Amendment constitutes an independent source of rights protected from infringement by either the States or the Federal Government. . . . The Ninth Amendment simply shows the intent of the Constitution's authors that other fundamental personal rights should not be denied such protection or disparaged in any other way simply because they are not specifically listed in the first eight constitutional amendments. . . .

Although the Constitution does not speak in so many words of the right of privacy in marriage, I cannot believe that it offers these fundamental rights no protection. The fact that no particular provision of the Constitution explicitly forbids the State from disrupting the traditional relation of the family—a relation as old and as fundamental as our entire civilization—surely does not show that the Government was meant to have the power to do so. Rather, as the Ninth Amendment expressly recognizes, there are fundamental personal rights such as this one, which are protected from abridgment by the Government though not specifically mentioned in the Constitution. . . .

The logic of the dissents would sanction federal or state legislation that seems to me even more plainly unconstitutional than the statute before us. Surely the Government, absent a showing of a compelling subordinating state interest, could not decree that all husbands and wives must be sterilized after two children have been born to them. Yet by their reasoning such an invasion of marital privacy would not be subject to constitutional challenge because, while it might be 'silly,' no provision of the Constitution specifically prevents the Government from curtailing the marital right to bear children and raise a family. While it may shock some of my Brethren that the Court today holds that the Constitution protects the right of marital privacy, in my view it is far more shocking to believe that the personal liberty guaranteed by the Constitution does not include protection against such totalitarian limitation of family size, which is at complete variance with our constitutional concepts. . . .

Finally, it should be said of the Court's holding today that it in no way interferes with a State's proper regulation of sexual promiscuity or misconduct. As my Brother Harlan so well stated in his dissenting opinion in *Poe v. Ullman*, 367 U.S. at 553: 'Adultery, homosexuality and the like are sexual intimacies which the State forbids . . . but the intimacy of husband and wife is necessarily an essential and accepted feature of the institution of marriage, an institution which the State not only must allow, but which always and in every age it has fostered and protected.' . . .

Mr. Justice BLACK, with whom Mr. Justice STEWART joins, dissenting.

. . . The Court talks about a constitutional 'right of privacy' as though there is some constitutional provision or provisions forbidding any law ever to be passed which might abridge the 'privacy' of individuals. But there is not. There are, of course, guarantees in certain specific constitutional provisions which are designed in part to protect privacy at certain times and places with respect to certain activities. . . .

One of the most effective ways of diluting or expanding a constitutionally guaranteed right is to substitute for the crucial word or words of a constitutional guarantee another word or words, more or less flexible and more or less restricted in meaning. This fact is well illustrated by the use of the term 'right of privacy' as a comprehensive substitute for the Fourth Amendment's guarantee against 'unreasonable searches and seizures.' 'Privacy' is a broad, abstract and ambiguous concept which can easily be shrunken in meaning but which can also, on the other hand, easily be interpreted as a constitutional ban against many things other than searches and seizures. . . . I like my privacy as well as the next one, but I am nevertheless compelled to admit that government has a right to invade it unless prohibited by some specific constitutional provision. . . .

The due process argument . . . is based . . . on the premise that this Court is vested with power to invalidate all state laws that it consider to be arbitrary, capricious, unreasonable, or oppressive, or this Court's belief that a particular state law under scrutiny has no 'rational or justifying' purpose, or is offensive to a 'sense of fairness and justice.' If these formulas based on 'natural justice,' or others which mean the same thing, are to prevail, they require judges to determine what is or is not constitutional on the basis of their own appraisal of what laws are unwise or unnecessary. The power to make such decisions is of course that of a legislative body. Surely it has to be admitted that no provision of the Constitution specifically gives such blanket power to courts to exercise such a supervisory veto over the wisdom and value of legislative policies and to hold unconstitutional those laws which they believe unwise or dangerous. . . .

My Brother GOLDBERG has adopted the recent discovery that the Ninth Amendment as well as the Due Process Clause can be used by this Court as authority to strike down all state legislation which this Court thinks violates 'fundamental principles of liberty and justice,' or is contrary to the 'traditions and (collective) conscience of our people.' . . . If any broad, unlimited power to hold laws unconstitutional because they offend what this Court conceives to be the '(collective) conscience of our people' is vested in this Court by the Ninth Amendment, the Fourteenth Amendment, or any other provision of the Constitution, it was not given by the Framers, but rather has been bestowed on the Court by the Court. This fact is perhaps responsible for the peculiar phenomenon that for a period of a century and a half no serious suggestion was ever made that the Ninth Amendment, enacted to protect state powers against federal invasion, could be used as a weapon of federal power to prevent state legislatures from passing laws they consider appropriate to govern local affairs. . . .

I realize that many good and able men have eloquently spoken and written, sometimes in rhapsodical strains, about the duty of this Court to keep the Constitution in tune with the times. The idea is that the Constitution must be changed from time to time and that this Court is charged with a duty to make those changes. For myself, I must with all deference reject that philosophy. The Constitution makers knew the need for change and provided for it. Amendments suggested by the people's elected representatives can be submitted to the people or their selected agents for ratification. That method of change was good for our Fathers, and being somewhat old fashioned I must add it is good enough for me. And so, I cannot rely on the Due Process Clause or the Ninth Amendment or any mysterious and uncertain natural law concept as a reason for striking down this state law. The Due Process Clause . . . was liberally used by this Court to strike down economic legislation in the early decades of this century, threatening, many people thought, the tranquility and stability of the Nation [citing *Lochner*]. That formula, based on subjective considerations of 'natural justice,' is no less dangerous when used to enforce this Court's views about personal rights than those about economic rights. I had thought that we had laid that formula, as a means for striking down state legislation, to rest once and for all in cases like *West Coast Hotel Co. v. Parrish*. . . .

MR. JUSTICE STEWART, WHOM MR. JUSTICE BLACK JOINS, DISSENTING.

Since 1879 Connecticut has had on its books a law which forbids the use of contraceptives by anyone. I think this is an uncommonly silly law. As a practical matter, the law is obviously unenforceable, except in the oblique context of the present case. As a philosophical matter, I believe the use of contraceptives in the relationship of marriage should be left to personal and private choice, based upon each individual's moral, ethical, and religious beliefs. As a matter of social policy, I think professional counsel about methods of birth control should be available to all, so that each individual's choice can be meaningfully made. But we are not asked in this case to say whether we think this law is unwise, or even asinine. We are asked to hold that it violates the United States Constitution. And that I cannot do.

In the course of its opinion the Court refers to no less than six Amendments to the Constitution: the First, the Third, the Fourth, the Fifth, the Ninth, and the Fourteenth. But the Court does not say which of these Amendments, if any, it thinks is infringed by this Connecticut law.

We are told that the Due Process Clause of the Fourteenth Amendment is not, as such, the 'guide' in this case. With that much I agree[.] . . . As to the First, Third, Fourth, and Fifth Amendments, I can find nothing in any of them to invalidate this Connecticut law. . . . [U]nless the solemn process of constitutional adjudication is to descend to the level of a play on words, there is not involved here any abridgment of 'the freedom of speech, or of the press; or the right of the people peaceably to assemble, and to petition the Government for a redress of grievances.' No soldier has been quartered in any house. There has been no search, and no seizure. Nobody has been compelled to be a witness against himself.

The Court also quotes the Ninth Amendment, and my Brother GOLDBERG's concurring opinion relies heavily upon it. But to say that the Ninth Amendment has anything to do with this case is to turn somersaults with history. The Ninth Amendment, like its companion the Tenth . . . was framed by James Madison and adopted by the States simply to make clear that the adoption of the Bill of Rights did not alter the plan that the Federal Government was to be a government of express and limited powers, and that all rights and powers not delegated to it were retained by the people and the individual States. Until today no member of this Court has ever suggested that the Ninth Amendment meant anything else, and the idea that a federal court could ever use the Ninth Amendment to annul a law passed by the elected representatives of the people of the State of Connecticut would have caused James Madison no little wonder.

What provision of the Constitution, then, does make this state law invalid? The Court says it is the right of privacy 'created by several fundamental constitutional guarantees.' With all deference, I can find no such general right of privacy in the Bill of Rights, in any other part of the Constitution, or in any case ever before decided by this Court.

The Court does not say how far the new constitutional right of privacy announced today extends. . . . At the oral argument in this case we were told that the Connecticut law does not 'conform to current community standards.' But it is not the function of this Court to decide cases on the basis of community standards. We are here to decide cases 'agreeably to the Constitution and laws of the United States.' It is the essence of judicial duty to subordinate our own personal views, our own ideas of what legislation is wise and what is not. If, as I should surely hope, the law before us does not reflect the standards of the people of Connecticut, the people of Connecticut can freely exercise their true Ninth and Tenth Amendment rights to persuade their elected representatives to repeal it. That is the constitutional way to take this law off the books.

Roe v. Wade
410 U.S. 113 (1973)

•

MR. JUSTICE BLACKMUN DELIVERED THE OPINION OF THE COURT.

This Texas federal appeal and its Georgia companion, *Doe v. Bolton*, 410 U.S. 179, present constitutional challenges to state criminal abortion legislation. . . .

We forthwith acknowledge our awareness of the sensitive and emotional nature of the abortion controversy, of the vigorous opposing views, even among physicians, and of the deep and seemingly absolute convictions that the subject inspires. One's philosophy, one's experiences, one's exposure to the raw edges of human existence, one's religious training, one's attitudes toward life and family and their values, and the moral standards one establishes and seeks to observe, are all likely to influence and to color one's thinking and conclusions about abortion. . . .

The principal thrust of appellant's attack on the Texas statutes is that they improperly invade a right, said to be possessed by the pregnant woman, to choose to terminate her pregnancy. Appellant would discover this right in the concept of personal "liberty" embodied in the Fourteenth Amendment's Due Process Clause; or in personal marital, familial, and sexual privacy said to be protected by the Bill of Rights or its penumbras, see *Griswold v. Connecticut*, 381 U.S. 479 (1965); or among those rights reserved to the people by the Ninth Amendment, *Griswold v. Connecticut*, 381 U.S., at 486. . . .

The Constitution does not explicitly mention any right of privacy. In a line of decisions, however . . . the Court has recognized that a right of personal privacy, or a guarantee of certain areas or zones of privacy, does exist under the Constitution. In varying contexts, the Court or individual Justices have, indeed, found at least the roots of that right in the First Amendment . . . in the Fourth and Fifth Amendments . . . in the penumbras of the Bill of Rights, *Griswold v. Connecticut*; in the Ninth Amendment, *id*; or in the concept of liberty guaranteed by the first section of the Fourteenth Amendment. These decisions make it clear that only personal rights that can be deemed "fundamental" or "implicit in the concept of ordered liberty," are included in this guarantee of personal privacy. They also make it clear that the right has some extension to activities relating to marriage, *Loving v. Virginia* (1967); procreation; contraception; family relationships; . . . and child rearing and education.

This right of privacy, whether it be founded in the Fourteenth Amendment's concept of personal liberty and restrictions upon state action, as we feel it is, or, as the District Court determined, in the Ninth Amendment's reservation of rights to the people, is broad enough to encompass a woman's decision whether or not to terminate her pregnancy. The detriment that the State would impose upon the pregnant woman by denying this choice altogether is apparent. Specific and direct harm medically diagnosable even in early pregnancy may be involved. Maternity, or additional offspring, may force upon the woman a distressful life and future. Psychological harm may be imminent. Mental and physical health may be taxed by child care. There is also the distress, for all concerned, associated with the unwanted child, and there is the problem of bringing a child into a family already unable, psychologically and otherwise, to care for it. In other cases, as in this one, the additional difficulties and continuing stigma of unwed motherhood may be involved. All these are factors the woman and her responsible physician necessarily will consider in consultation.

. . . The Court's decisions recognizing a right of privacy also acknowledge that some state regulation in areas protected by that right is appropriate. As noted above, a State may properly assert important interests in safeguarding health, in maintaining medical standards, and in protecting potential life. At some point in pregnancy, these respective interests become sufficiently compelling to sustain regulation of the factors that govern the abortion decision. The privacy right involved, therefore, cannot be said to be absolute. . . . We, therefore, conclude that the right of personal privacy includes the abortion decision, but that this right is not unqualified and must be considered against important state interests in regulation. . . .

The appellee and certain *amici* argue that the fetus is a "person" within the language and meaning of the Fourteenth Amendment. In support of this, they outline at length and in detail the well-known facts of fetal development. If this suggestion of personhood is established, the appellant's case, of course, collapses, for the fetus' right to life would then be guaranteed specifically by the Amendment. . . . The Constitution does not define "person" in so many words. . . . But in nearly all . . . instances [where it appears], the use of the word is such that it has application only postnatally. None indicates, with any assurance, that it has any possible prenatal application. All this, together with our observation, that throughout the major portion of the 19th century prevailing legal abortion practices were far freer than they are today, persuades us that the word "person," as used in the Fourteenth Amendment, does not include the unborn. . . .

Texas urges that, apart from the Fourteenth Amendment, life begins at conception and is present throughout pregnancy, and that, therefore, the State has a compelling interest in protecting that life from and after conception. We need not resolve the difficult question of when life begins. When those trained in the respective disciplines of medicine, philosophy, and theology are unable to arrive at any consensus, the judiciary, at this point in the development of man's knowledge, is not in a position to speculate as to the answer. . . . In areas other than criminal abortion, the law has been reluctant to endorse any theory that life, as we recognize it, begins before live birth or to accord legal rights to the unborn except in narrowly defined situations. . . . In short, the unborn have never been recognized in the law as persons in the whole sense.

In view of all this, we do not agree that, by adopting one theory of life, Texas may override the rights of the pregnant woman that are at stake. We repeat, however, that the State does have an important and legitimate interest in preserving and protecting the health of the pregnant woman, whether she be a resident of the State or a non-resident who seeks medical consultation and treatment there, and that it has still another important and legitimate interest in protecting the potentiality of human life. These interests are separate and distinct. Each grows in substantiality as the woman approaches term and, at a point during pregnancy, each becomes "compelling."

With respect to the State's important and legitimate interest in the health of the mother, the "compelling" point, in the light of present medical knowledge, is at approximately the end of the first trimester. This is so because of the now-established medical fact that until the end of the first trimester mortality in abortion may be less than mortality in normal childbirth. It follows that, from and after this point, a State may regulate the abortion procedure to the extent that the regulation reasonably relates to the preservation and protection of maternal health.

Examples of permissible state regulation in this area are requirements as to the qualifications of the person who is to perform the abortion; as to the licensure of that person; as to the facility in which the procedure is to be performed, that is, whether it must be a hospital or may be a clinic or some other place of less-than-hospital status; as to the licensing of the facility; and the like. . . .

With respect to the State's important and legitimate interest in potential life, the "compelling" point is at viability. This is so because the fetus then presumably has the capability of meaningful life outside the mother's womb. State regulation protective of fetal life after viability thus has both logical and biological justifications. If the State is interested in protecting fetal life after viability, it may go so far as to proscribe abortion during that period, except when it is necessary to preserve the life or health of the mother.

Measured against these standards, [the Texas statute], in restricting legal abortions to those "procured or attempted by medical advice for the purpose of saving the life of the mother," sweeps too broadly. The statute makes no distinction between abortions performed early in pregnancy and those performed later, and it limits to a single reason, "saving" the mother's life, the legal justification for the procedure. The statute, therefore, cannot survive the constitutional attack made upon it here. . . .

MR. JUSTICE REHNQUIST, DISSENTING.

. . . I have difficulty in concluding, as the Court does, that the right of "privacy" is involved in this case. Texas, by the statute here challenged, bars the performance of a medical abortion by a licensed physician on a plaintiff such as Roe. A transaction resulting in an operation such as this is not "private" in the ordinary usage of that word. Nor is the "privacy" that the Court finds here even a distant relative of the freedom from searches and seizures protected by the Fourth Amendment to the Constitution, which the Court has referred to as embodying a right to privacy. . . .

While the Court's opinion quotes from the dissent of Mr. Justice Holmes in *Lochner v. New York* (1905), the result it reaches is more closely attuned to the majority opinion of Mr. Justice Peckham in that case. As in *Lochner* and similar cases applying substantive due process standards to economic and social welfare legislation, the adoption of the compelling state interest standard will inevitably require this Court to examine the legislative policies and pass on the wisdom of these policies in the very process of deciding whether a particular state interest put forward may or may not be "compelling." The decision here to break pregnancy into three distinct terms and to outline the permissible restrictions the State may impose in each one, for example, partakes more of judicial legislation than it does of a determination of the intent of the drafters of the Fourteenth Amendment. . . .

To reach its result, the Court necessarily has had to find within the Scope of the Fourteenth Amendment a right that was apparently completely unknown to the drafters of the Amendment. . . . By the time of the adoption of the Fourteenth Amendment in 1868, there were at least 36 laws enacted by state or territorial legislatures limiting abortion. . . . There apparently was no question concerning the validity of this provision or of any of the other state statutes when the Fourteenth Amendment was adopted. The only conclusion possible from this history is that the drafters did not intend to have the Fourteenth Amendment withdraw from the States the power to legislate with respect to this matter. . . .

MR. JUSTICE WHITE, WITH WHOM MR. JUSTICE
REHNQUIST JOINS, DISSENTING.

At the heart of the controversy in these cases are those recurring pregnancies that pose no danger whatsoever to the life or health of the mother but are, nevertheless, unwanted for any one or more of a variety of reasons—convenience, family planning, economics, dislike of children, the embarrassment of illegitimacy, etc.. The common claim before us is that for any one of such reasons, or for no reason at all, and without asserting or claiming any threat to life or health, any woman is entitled to an abortion at her request if she is able to find a medical advisor willing to undertake the procedure.

. . . With all due respect, I dissent. I find nothing in the language or history of the Constitution to support the Court's judgments. The Court simply fashions and announces a new constitutional right for pregnant women and, with scarcely any reason or authority for its action, invests that right with sufficient substance to override most existing state abortion statutes. The upshot is that the people and the legislatures of the

50 States are constitutionally disentitled to weigh the relative importance of the continued existence and development of the fetus, on the
one hand, against a spectrum of possible impacts on the mother, on the
other hand. As an exercise of raw judicial power, the Court perhaps has
authority to do what it does today; but in my view its judgment is an
improvident and extravagant exercise of the power of judicial review
that the Constitution extends to this Court.

The Court apparently values the convenience of the pregnant woman
more than the continued existence and development of the life or potential life that she carries. Whether or not I might agree with that mar-
shaling of values, I can in no event join the Court's judgment because I
find no constitutional warrant for imposing such an order of priorities on
the people and legislatures of the States. . . . I cannot accept the Court's
exercise of its clear power of choice by interposing a constitutional barrier to state efforts to protect human life and by investing women and
doctors with the constitutionally protected right to exterminate it. This
issue, for the most part, should be left with the people and to the political processes the people have devised to govern their affairs. . . .

Planned Parenthood v. Casey
505 U.S. 833 (1992)

•

JUSTICE O'CONNOR, JUSTICE KENNEDY, AND JUSTICE
SOUTER ANNOUNCED THE JUDGMENT OF THE COURT AND
DELIVERED THE OPINION OF THE COURT[.] . . .

I

Liberty finds no refuge in a jurisprudence of doubt. Yet 19 years after
our holding that the Constitution protects a woman's right to terminate her pregnancy in its early stages, *Roe v. Wade*, 410 U.S. 113 (1973),
that definition of liberty is still questioned. Joining the respondents
as amicus curiae, the United States, as it has done in five other cases
in the last decade, again asks us to overrule *Roe*. . . . After considering

the fundamental constitutional questions resolved by *Roe*, principles of institutional integrity, and the rule of *stare decisis*, we are led to conclude this: the essential holding of *Roe v. Wade* should be retained and once again reaffirmed. . . .

II

Constitutional protection of the woman's decision to terminate her pregnancy derives from the Due Process Clause of the Fourteenth Amendment. It declares that no State shall "deprive any person of life, liberty, or property, without due process of law." The controlling word in the cases before us is "liberty." Although a literal reading of the Clause might suggest that it governs only the procedures by which a State may deprive persons of liberty, for at least 105 years, the Clause has been understood to contain a substantive component as well[.] . . . Neither the Bill of Rights nor the specific practices of States at the time of the adoption of the Fourteenth Amendment marks the outer limits of the substantive sphere of liberty which the Fourteenth Amendment protects. . . . The inescapable fact is that adjudication of substantive due process claims may call upon the Court in interpreting the Constitution to exercise that same capacity which by tradition courts always have exercised: reasoned judgment. . . .

Our law affords constitutional protection to personal decisions relating to marriage, procreation, contraception, family relationships, child rearing, and education. . . . These matters, involving the most intimate and personal choices a person may make in a lifetime, choices central to personal dignity and autonomy, are central to the liberty protected by the Fourteenth Amendment. At the heart of liberty is the right to define one's own concept of existence, of meaning, of the universe, and of the mystery of human life. Beliefs about these matters could not define the attributes of personhood were they formed under compulsion of the State.

These considerations begin our analysis of the woman's interest in terminating her pregnancy but cannot end it, for this reason: though the abortion decision may originate within the zone of conscience and belief, it is more than a philosophic exercise. Abortion is a unique act. It is an act fraught with consequences for others: for the woman who must live with the implications of her decision; for the persons who perform and assist in the procedure; for the spouse, family, and society which must confront the knowledge that these procedures exist, procedures some deem nothing short of an act of violence against innocent human life; and, depending on one's beliefs, for the life or potential life that is aborted. Though abortion is conduct, it does not follow that the State is entitled to proscribe it in all instances. That is because the liberty of the woman is at stake in a sense unique to the human condition and so unique to the law. The mother who carries a child to full term is subject to anxieties, to physical constraints, to pain that only she must bear. That these sacrifices have from the beginning of the human race been endured by woman with a pride that ennobles her in the eyes of others and gives to the infant a bond of love cannot alone be grounds for the State to insist she make the sacrifice. Her suffering is too intimate and personal for the State to insist, without more, upon its own vision of the woman's role, however dominant that vision has been in the course of our history and our culture. The destiny of the woman must be shaped to a large extent on her own conception of her spiritual imperatives and her place in society.

It should be recognized, moreover, that in some critical respects the abortion decision is of the same character as the decision to use contraception, to which *Griswold v. Connecticut, Eisenstadt v. Baird*, and *Carey v. Population Services International* afford constitutional protection. We have no doubt as to the correctness of those decisions. They support the reasoning in *Roe* relating to the woman's liberty because they involve personal decisions concerning not only the meaning of procreation but also human responsibility and respect for it. . . .

While we appreciate the weight of the arguments made on behalf of the State in the cases before us, arguments which in their ultimate formulation conclude that *Roe* should be overruled, the reservations any of us may have in reaffirming the central holding of *Roe* are outweighed by the explication of individual liberty we have given combined with the force of *stare decisis*. . . .

III

A

The obligation to follow precedent begins with necessity, and a contrary necessity marks its outer limit. . . . [N]o judicial system could do society's work if it eyed each issue afresh in every case that raised it. Indeed, the very concept of the rule of law underlying our own Constitution requires such continuity over time that a respect for precedent is, by definition, indispensable. At the other extreme, a different necessity would make itself felt if a prior judicial ruling should come to be seen so clearly as error that its enforcement was for that very reason doomed.

Even when the decision to overrule a prior case is not, as in the rare, latter instance, virtually foreordained, it is common wisdom that the rule of stare decisis is not an "inexorable command," and certainly it is not such in every constitutional case. Rather, when this Court reexamines a prior holding, its judgment is customarily informed by a series of prudential and pragmatic considerations designed to test the consistency of overruling a prior decision with the ideal of the rule of law, and to gauge the respective costs of reaffirming and overruling a prior case. Thus, for example, we may ask whether the rule has proven to be intolerable simply in defying practical workability; whether the rule is subject to a kind of reliance that would lend a special hardship to the consequences of overruling and add inequity to the cost of repudiation; whether related principles of law have so far developed as to have left the old rule no more than a remnant of abandoned doctrine; or whether facts have so changed, or come to be seen so differently, as to have robbed the old rule of significant application or justification.

. . .

The sum of the precedential enquiry . . . shows *Roe*'s underpinnings unweakened in any way affecting its central holding. While it has engendered disapproval, it has not been unworkable. An entire generation has come of age free to assume *Roe*'s concept of liberty in defining the capacity of women to act in society, and to make reproductive decisions; no erosion of principle going to liberty or personal autonomy has left *Roe*'s central holding a doctrinal remnant; *Roe* portends no developments at odds with other precedent for the analysis of personal liberty; and no changes of fact have rendered viability more or less appropriate as the point at which the balance of interests tips. Within the bounds of normal stare decisis analysis, then, and subject to the considerations on which it customarily turns, the stronger argument is for affirming *Roe*'s central holding, with whatever degree of personal reluctance any of us may have, not for overruling it.

B

. . . Because neither the factual underpinnings of *Roe*'s central holding nor our understanding of it has changed (and because no other indication of weakened precedent has been shown), the Court could not pretend to be reexamining the prior law with any justification beyond a present doctrinal disposition to come out differently from the Court of 1973. To overrule prior law for no other reason than that would run counter to the view repeated in our cases, that a decision to overrule should rest on some special reason over and above the belief that a prior case was wrongly decided. . . .

C

. . .

Where, in the performance of its judicial duties, the Court decides a case in such a way as to resolve the sort of intensely divisive controversy reflected in *Roe* and those rare, comparable cases, its decision has a dimension that the resolution of the normal case does not carry. It is the dimension present whenever the Court's interpretation of the Constitution calls the contending sides of a national controversy to end their national division by accepting a common mandate rooted in the Constitution.

The Court is not asked to do this very often, having thus addressed the Nation only twice in our lifetime, in the decisions of *Brown* and *Roe*. But when the Court does act in this way, its decision requires an equally rare precedential force to counter the inevitable efforts to overturn it and to thwart its implementation. Some of those efforts may be mere unprincipled emotional reactions; others may proceed from principles worthy of profound respect. But whatever the premises of opposition may be, only the most convincing justification under accepted standards of precedent could suffice to demonstrate that a later decision overruling the first was anything but a surrender to political pressure, and an unjustified repudiation of the principle on which the Court staked its authority in the first instance. So to overrule under fire in the absence of the most compelling reason to reexamine a watershed decision would subvert the Court's legitimacy beyond any serious question. . . . A decision to overrule *Roe*'s essential holding under the existing circumstances would address error, if error there was, at the cost of both profound and unnecessary damage to the Court's legitimacy, and to the Nation's commitment to the rule of law. It is therefore imperative to adhere to the essence of *Roe*'s original decision, and we do so today.

IV

. . . We reject the trimester framework, which we do not consider to be part of the essential holding of *Roe*. Measures aimed at ensuring that a woman's choice contemplates the consequences for the fetus do not necessarily interfere with the right recognized in *Roe*, although those measures have been found to be inconsistent with the rigid trimester framework announced in that case. A logical reading of the central holding in *Roe* itself, and a necessary reconciliation of the liberty of the woman and the interest of the State in promoting prenatal life, require, in our view, that we abandon the trimester framework as a rigid prohibition on all previability regulation aimed at the protection of fetal life. . . .

In our view, the undue burden standard is the appropriate means of reconciling the State's interest with the woman's constitutionally protected liberty. . . . A finding of an undue burden is a shorthand for the conclusion that a state regulation has the purpose or effect of placing a substantial obstacle in the path of a woman seeking an abortion of a nonviable fetus. A statute with this purpose is invalid because the means chosen by the State to further the interest in potential life must be calculated to inform the woman's free choice, not hinder it. . . . [A] State may not prohibit any woman from making the ultimate decision to terminate her pregnancy before viability.

We also reaffirm *Roe*'s holding that "subsequent to viability, the State in promoting its interest in the potentiality of human life may, if it chooses, regulate, and even proscribe, abortion except where it is necessary, in appropriate medical judgment, for the preservation of the life or health of the mother." . . .

V

. . . Our Constitution is a covenant running from the first generation of Americans to us and then to future generations. It is a coherent succession. Each generation must learn anew that the Constitution's written terms embody ideas and aspirations that must survive more ages than one. We accept our responsibility not to retreat from interpreting the full meaning of the covenant in light of all of our precedents. We invoke it once again to define the freedom guaranteed by the Constitution's own promise, the promise of liberty. . . .

JUSTICE BLACKMUN, CONCURRING IN PART, CONCURRING IN THE JUDGMENT IN PART, AND DISSENTING IN PART.

. . . Three years ago, in *Webster v. Reproductive Health Services*, 492 U.S. 490 (1989), four Members of this Court appeared poised to "cas[t] into darkness the hopes and visions of every woman in this country" who had come to believe that the Constitution guaranteed her the right to reproductive choice. All that remained between the promise of *Roe* and the darkness of the plurality was a single, flickering flame. Decisions since *Webster* gave little reason to hope that this flame would cast much light. But now, just when so many expected the darkness to fall, the flame has grown bright.

. . . Make no mistake, the joint opinion of Justices O'CONNOR, KENNEDY, and SOUTER is an act of personal courage and constitutional principle. . . . In the 19 years since *Roe* was decided, that case has shaped more than reproductive planning—"[a]n entire generation has come of age free to assume *Roe*'s concept of liberty in defining the capacity of women to act in society, and to make reproductive decisions." The Court understands that, having "call[ed] the contending sides . . . to end their national division by accepting a common mandate rooted in the Constitution," a decision to overrule *Roe* "would seriously weaken the Court's capacity to exercise the judicial power and to function as the Supreme Court of a Nation dedicated to the rule of law." What has happened today should serve as a model for future Justices and a warning to all who have tried to turn this Court into yet another political branch. . . .

In one sense, the Court's approach is worlds apart from that of THE CHIEF JUSTICE and Justice SCALIA. And yet, in another sense, the distance between the two approaches is short—the distance is but a single vote. I am 83 years old. I cannot remain on this Court forever, and when I do step down, the confirmation process for my successor well may focus on the issue before us today. That, I regret, may be exactly where the choice between the two worlds will be made.

CHIEF JUSTICE REHNQUIST, WITH WHOM JUSTICE WHITE, JUSTICE SCALIA, AND JUSTICE THOMAS JOIN, CONCURRING IN THE JUDGMENT IN PART AND DISSENTING IN PART.

. . . We believe that *Roe* was wrongly decided, and that it can and should be overruled consistently with our traditional approach to *stare decisis* in constitutional cases. . . .

The joint opinion of Justices O'CONNOR, KENNEDY, and SOUTER cannot bring itself to say that *Roe* was correct as an original matter, but the authors are of the view that "the immediate question is not the soundness of *Roe's* resolution of the issue, but the precedential force that must be accorded to its holding." Instead of claiming that *Roe* was correct as a matter of original constitutional interpretation, the opinion therefore contains an elaborate discussion of *stare decisis*. . . . *Roe* analyzed abortion regulation under a rigid trimester framework, a framework which has guided this Court's decisionmaking for 19 years. The joint opinion rejects that framework.

Stare decisis is defined in Black's Law Dictionary as meaning "to abide by, or adhere to, decided cases." Whatever the "central holding" of *Roe* that is left after the joint opinion finishes dissecting it is surely not the result of that principle. While purporting to adhere to precedent, the joint opinion instead revises it. . . . [Two precedents] are frankly overruled . . . under the "undue burden" standard expounded in the joint opinion.

In our view, authentic principles of *stare decisis* do not require that any portion of the reasoning in *Roe* be kept intact. "*Stare decisis* is not . . . a universal, inexorable command," especially in cases involving the interpretation of the Federal Constitution. Erroneous decisions in such constitutional cases are uniquely durable, because correction through legislative action, save for constitutional amendment, is impossible. It is therefore our duty to reconsider constitutional interpretations that "depar[t] from a proper understanding" of the Constitution. Our constitutional watch does not cease merely because we have spoken before on an issue; when it becomes clear that a prior constitutional interpretation is unsound we are obliged to reexamine the question. See, e.g., *West Virginia Bd. of Ed. v. Barnette* (1943); *Erie R. Co. v. Tompkins* (1938).

The joint opinion discusses several *stare decisis* factors which, it asserts, point toward retaining a portion of *Roe*. Two of these factors are that the main "factual underpinning" of *Roe* has remained the same, and that its doctrinal foundation is no weaker now than it was in 1973. Of course, what might be called the basic facts which gave rise to *Roe* have remained the same—women become pregnant, there is a point somewhere, depending on medical technology, where a fetus becomes viable, and women give birth to children. But this is only to say that the same facts which gave rise to *Roe* will continue to give rise to similar cases. It is not a reason, in and of itself, why those cases must be decided in the same incorrect manner as was the first case to deal with the question. And surely there is no requirement, in considering whether to depart from *stare decisis* in a constitutional case, that a decision be more wrong now than it was at the time it was rendered. If that were true, the most outlandish constitutional decision could survive forever, based simply on the fact that it was no more outlandish later than it was when originally rendered. . . .

The joint opinion also points to the reliance interests involved in this context in its effort to explain why precedent must be followed for precedent's sake. . . . But, as the joint opinion apparently agrees, any traditional notion of reliance is not applicable here. . . . In the end, having failed to put forth any evidence to prove any true reliance, the joint opinion's argument is based solely on generalized assertions about the national psyche, on a belief that the people of this country have grown accustomed to the *Roe* decision over the last 19 years and have "ordered their thinking and living around" it. . . . [But] at various points in the past, the same could have been said about this Court's erroneous decisions that the Constitution allowed "separate but equal" treatment of minorities, see *Plessy v. Ferguson*, or that "liberty" under the Due Process Clause protected "freedom of contract," . . . *Lochner v. New York* (1905). The "separate but equal" doctrine lasted 58 years after *Plessy*, and *Lochner's* protection of contractual freedom lasted 32 years. However, the simple fact that a generation or more had grown used to these major decisions did not prevent the Court from correcting its errors in those cases, nor should it prevent us from correctly interpreting the Constitution here.

Apparently realizing that conventional *stare decisis* principles do not support its position, the joint opinion advances a belief that retaining a portion of *Roe* is necessary to protect the "legitimacy" of this Court. . . . But the joint opinion goes on to state that when the Court "resolve[s] the sort of intensely divisive controversy reflected in *Roe* and those rare, comparable cases," its decision is exempt from reconsideration under established principles of *stare decisis* in constitutional cases. This is so, the joint opinion contends, because in those "intensely divisive" cases the Court has "call[ed] the contending sides of a national controversy to end their national division by accepting a common mandate rooted in the Constitution," and must therefore take special care not to be perceived as "surrender[ing] to political pressure" and continued opposition. . . . Under this principle, when the Court has ruled on a divisive issue, it is apparently prevented from overruling that decision for the sole reason that it was incorrect, unless opposition to the original decision has died away.

. . . The question of whether a particular issue is "intensely divisive" enough to qualify for special protection is entirely subjective and dependent on the individual assumptions of the Members of this Court. In addition, because the Court's duty is to ignore public opinion and criticism on issues that come before it, its Members are in perhaps the worst position to judge whether a decision divides the Nation deeply enough to justify such uncommon protection. Although many of the Court's decisions divide the populace to a large degree, we have not previously on that account shied away from applying normal rules of *stare decisis* when urged to reconsider earlier decisions. Over the past 21 years, for example, the Court has overruled in whole or in part 34 of its previous constitutional decisions. . . .

In assuming that the Court is perceived as "surrender[ing] to political pressure" when it overrules a controversial decision, the joint opinion forgets that there are two sides to any controversy. The joint opinion asserts that, in order to protect its legitimacy, the Court must refrain from overruling a controversial decision lest it be viewed as favoring those who oppose the decision. But a decision to adhere to prior precedent is subject to the same criticism, for in such a case one can easily argue that the Court is responding to those who have demonstrated in favor of the original decision. . . . But this perceived dilemma arises only if one assumes, as the joint opinion does, that the Court should make its decisions with a view toward speculative public perceptions. If one assumes instead, as the Court surely did in both *Brown* and *West Coast Hotel*, that the Court's legitimacy is enhanced by faithful interpretation of the Constitution irrespective of public opposition, such self-engendered difficulties may be put to one side. . . .

JUSTICE SCALIA, WITH WHOM THE CHIEF JUSTICE, JUS-
TICE WHITE, AND JUSTICE THOMAS JOIN, CONCURRING IN
THE JUDGMENT IN PART AND DISSENTING IN PART.

. . . The Court's reliance upon *stare decisis* can best be described as
contrived. . . . It seems to me that *stare decisis* ought to be applied even
to the doctrine of *stare decisis*, and I confess never to have heard of this
new, keep-what-you-want-and-throw-away-the-rest version. . . . It is
particularly difficult, in the circumstances of the present decision, to
sit still for the Court's lengthy lecture upon the virtues of 'constancy,'
of 'remain[ing] steadfast,' and adhering to 'principle'. Among the five
justices who purportedly adhere to *Roe*, at most three agree upon the
principle that constitutes adherence . . . and that principle is inconsistent
with *Roe*. . . . To make matters worse, two of the three, in order thus to
remain steadfast, had to abandon previously stated positions. . . .

There is a poignant aspect to today's opinion. Its length, and what
might be called its epic tone, suggest that its authors believe they are
bringing to an end a troublesome era in the history of our Nation and
of our Court. "It is the dimension" of authority, they say, to "cal[l] the
contending sides of national controversy to end their national division
by accepting a common mandate rooted in the Constitution." There
comes vividly to mind a portrait by Emanuel Leutze that hangs in
the Harvard Law School: Roger Brooke Taney, painted in 1859, the
82d year of his life, the 24th of his Chief Justiceship, the second after
his opinion in *Dred Scott*. He is all in black, sitting in a shadowed red
armchair, left hand resting upon a pad of paper in his lap, right hand
hanging limply, almost lifelessly, beside the inner arm of the chair. He
sits facing the viewer and staring straight out. There seems to be on
his face, and in his deep-set eyes, an expression of profound sadness
and disillusionment. Perhaps he always looked that way, even when
dwelling upon the happiest of thoughts. But those of us who know how
the lustre of his great Chief Justiceship came to be eclipsed by *Dred
Scott* cannot help believing that he had that case—its already apparent
consequences for the Court and its soon-to-be-played-out consequences
for the Nation—burning on his mind. I expect that two years earlier
he, too, had thought himself "call[ing] the contending sides of national
controversy to end their national division by accepting a common mandate rooted in the Constitution."

It is no more realistic for us in this litigation, than it was for him in that, to think that an issue of the sort they both involved—an issue involving life and death, freedom and subjugation—can be "speedily and finally settled" by the Supreme Court, as President James Buchanan in his inaugural address said the issue of slavery in the territories would be. Quite to the contrary, by foreclosing all democratic outlet for the deep passions this issue arouses, by banishing the issue from the political forum . . . the Court merely prolongs and intensifies the anguish. . . .

Lawrence v. Texas
539 U.S. 558 (2003)

•

JUSTICE KENNEDY DELIVERED THE OPINION OF THE COURT.

Liberty protects the person from unwarranted government intrusions into a dwelling or other private places. In our tradition the State is not omnipresent in the home. And there are other spheres of our lives and existence, outside the home, where the State should not be a dominant presence. Freedom extends beyond spatial bounds. Liberty presumes an autonomy of self that includes freedom of thought, belief, expression, and certain intimate conduct. The instant case involves liberty of the person both in its spatial and in its more transcendent dimensions.

The question before the Court is the validity of a Texas statute making it a crime for two persons of the same sex to engage in certain intimate sexual conduct. . . . The complaints described [petitioners'] crime as "deviate sexual intercourse, namely anal sex, with a member of the same sex (man)." . . . The petitioners were adults at the time of the alleged offense. Their conduct was in private and consensual.

We conclude the case should be resolved by determining whether the petitioners were free as adults to engage in the private conduct in the exercise of their liberty under the Due Process Clause of the Fourteenth Amendment to the Constitution. For this inquiry we deem it necessary to reconsider the Court's holding in Bowers [v. Hardwick (1986)]. . . . The laws involved in Bowers and here are, to be sure, statutes that purport to do no more than prohibit a particular sexual act. Their penalties and purposes, though, have more far-reaching consequences, touching upon the most private human conduct, sexual behavior, and in the most private of places, the home. The statutes do seek to control a personal relationship that, whether or not entitled to formal recognition in the law, is within the liberty of persons to choose without being punished as criminals. . . . When sexuality finds overt expression in intimate conduct with another person, the conduct can be but one element in a personal bond that is more enduring. The liberty protected by the Constitution allows homosexual persons the right to make this choice. . . .

[W]e think that our laws and traditions in the past half century are of most relevance here. These references show an emerging awareness that liberty gives substantial protection to adult persons in deciding how to conduct their private lives in matters pertaining to sex. . . . [A]lmost five years before *Bowers* was decided the European Court of Human Rights considered a case with parallels to *Bowers* and to today's case. An adult male resident in Northern Ireland alleged he was a practicing homosexual who desired to engage in consensual homosexual conduct. The laws of Northern Ireland forbade him that right. . . . The court held that the laws proscribing the conduct were invalid under the European Convention on Human Rights. . . . Other nations, too, have taken action consistent with an affirmation of the protected right of homosexual adults to engage in intimate, consensual conduct. The right the petitioners seek in this case has been accepted as an integral part of human freedom in many other countries. . . .

The doctrine of stare decisis is essential to the respect accorded to the judgments of the Court and to the stability of the law. It is not, however, an inexorable command. . . . In [*Planned Parenthood v.*] *Casey* we noted that when a court is asked to overrule a precedent recognizing a constitutional liberty interest, individual or societal reliance on the existence of that liberty cautions with particular strength against reversing course. . . . The holding in *Bowers*, however, has not induced detrimental reliance comparable to some instances where recognized individual rights are involved. . . . *Bowers* was not correct when it was decided, and it is not correct today. It ought not to remain binding precedent. *Bowers v. Hardwick* should be and now is overruled.

The present case does not involve minors. It does not involve persons who might be injured or coerced or who are situated in relationships where consent might not easily be refused. It does not involve public conduct or prostitution. It does not involve whether the government must give formal recognition to any relationship that homosexual persons seek to enter. The case does involve two adults who, with full and mutual consent from each other, engaged in sexual practices common to a homosexual lifestyle. . . . Had those who drew and ratified the Due Process Clauses of the Fifth Amendment or the Fourteenth Amendment known the components of liberty in its manifold possibilities, they might have been more specific. . . . As the Constitution endures, persons in every generation can invoke its principles in their own search for greater freedom. . . .

JUSTICE O'CONNOR, CONCURRING IN THE JUDGMENT.

. . . I agree with the Court that Texas' statute banning same-sex sodomy is unconstitutional. Rather than relying on the substantive component of the Fourteenth Amendment's Due Process Clause, as the Court does, I base my conclusion on the Fourteenth Amendment's Equal Protection Clause. . . .

The statute at issue here makes sodomy a crime only if a person "engages in deviate sexual intercourse with another individual of the same sex." Sodomy between opposite-sex partners, however, is not a crime in Texas. That is, Texas treats the same conduct differently based solely on the participants. . . .

This case raises a different issue than *Bowers*: whether, under the Equal Protection Clause, moral disapproval is a legitimate state interest to justify by itself a statute that bans homosexual sodomy, but not heterosexual sodomy. It is not. . . .

That this law as applied to private, consensual conduct is unconstitutional under the Equal Protection Clause does not mean that other laws distinguishing between heterosexuals and homosexuals would similarly fail under rational basis review. Texas cannot assert any legitimate state interest here, such as national security or preserving the traditional institution of marriage. Unlike the moral disapproval of same-sex relations—the asserted state interest in this case—other reasons exist to promote the institution of marriage beyond mere moral disapproval of an excluded group. . . .

JUSTICE SCALIA, WITH WHOM THE CHIEF JUSTICE AND
JUSTICE THOMAS JOIN, DISSENTING.

. . . I begin with the Court's surprising readiness to reconsider a
decision rendered a mere 17 years ago in *Bowers v. Hardwick*. I do not
myself believe in rigid adherence to *stare decisis* in constitutional cases;
but I do believe that we should be consistent rather than manipula-
tive in invoking the doctrine. Today's opinions in support of reversal
do not bother to distinguish—or indeed, even bother to mention—the
paean to *stare decisis* coauthored by three Members of today's majority in
Planned Parenthood v. Casey. There, when *stare decisis* meant preservation
of judicially invented abortion rights, the widespread criticism of *Roe*
was strong reason to reaffirm it[.] . . . Today, however, the widespread
opposition to *Bowers*, a decision resolving an issue as "intensely divisive"
as the issue in *Roe*, is offered as a reason in favor of overruling it. . . .

[I]t does not surprise me, and should surprise no one, that the Court
has chosen today to revise the standards of *stare decisis* set forth in *Casey*.
It has thereby exposed *Casey*'s extraordinary deference to precedent for
the result-oriented expedient that it is.

Having decided that it need not adhere to stare decisis, the Court
still must establish that *Bowers* was wrongly decided and that the Texas
statute, as applied to petitioners, is unconstitutional. [The Texas law]
undoubtedly imposes constraints on liberty. So do laws prohibiting
prostitution, recreational use of heroin, and, for that matter, working
more than 60 hours per week in a bakery. But there is no right to "liberty" under the Due Process Clause, though today's opinion repeatedly
makes that claim. The Fourteenth Amendment *expressly allows* States
to deprive their citizens of "liberty," *so long as "due process of law" is provided*. . . . The Court today . . . embraces . . . Justice Stevens' declaration
in his *Bowers* dissent, that "the fact that a governing majority in a State
has traditionally viewed a particular practice as immoral is not a sufficient reason for upholding a law prohibiting the practice." . . . This effectively decrees the end of all morals legislation. If, as the Court asserts,
the promotion of majoritarian sexual morality is not even a *legitimate*
state interest, none of the above-mentioned laws can survive[.] . . .

Finally, I turn to petitioners' equal-protection challenge, which no
Member of the Court save Justice O'CONNOR embraces: On its face
[the law] applies equally to all persons. Men and women, heterosexuals

and homosexuals, are all subject to its prohibition of deviate sexual intercourse with someone of the same sex. To be sure, [the law] does distinguish between the sexes insofar as concerns the partner with whom the sexual acts are performed: men can violate the law only with other men, and women only with other women. But this cannot itself be a denial of equal protection, since it is precisely the same distinction regarding partner that is drawn in state laws prohibiting marriage with someone of the same sex while permitting marriage with someone of the opposite sex.

The objection is made, however, that the antimiscegenation laws invalidated in *Loving v. Virginia*, 388 U.S. 1, 8 (1967), similarly were applicable to whites and blacks alike, and only distinguished between the races insofar as the partner was concerned. In *Loving*, however . . . the Virginia statute was "designed to maintain White Supremacy." . . . No purpose to discriminate against men or women as a class can be gleaned from the Texas law. . . . Justice O'CONNOR argues that the discrimination in this law which must be justified is not its discrimination with regard to the sex of the partner but its discrimination with regard to the sexual proclivity of the principal actor. . . . This reasoning leaves on pretty shaky grounds state laws limiting marriage to opposite-sex couples. Justice O'CONNOR seeks to preserve them by the conclusory statement that "preserving the traditional institution of marriage" is a legitimate state interest. But "preserving the traditional institution of marriage" is just a kinder way of describing the State's moral disapproval of same-sex couples. . . .

Social perceptions of sexual and other morality change over time, and every group has the right to persuade its fellow citizens that its view of such matters is the best. . . . But persuading one's fellow citizens is one thing, and imposing one's views in absence of democratic majority will is something else. I would no more require a State to criminalize homosexual acts—or, for that matter, display any moral disapprobation of them—than I would forbid it to do so. What Texas has chosen to do is well within the range of traditional democratic action, and its hand should not be stayed through the invention of a brand-new "constitutional right" by a Court that is impatient of democratic change. . . .

PRESIDENTIAL AUTONOMY
AND AUTHORITY

꯭ᐤ꯭

*U*nited States v. Nixon, the "Nixon Tapes Case," is famous for rejecting President Richard Nixon's claim of "executive privilege" to withhold tape recordings of presidential conversations in the White House from a special prosecutor appointed by the attorney general. The Supreme Court held that the prosecutor, a subordinate executive officer, could issue a subpoena to the president, the chief executive, and that the courts could command compliance with such a subpoena, overruling claims of presidential autonomy and confidentiality. The decision was unanimous and Nixon turned over the tapes, quickly leading to his resignation—the only time a U.S. president has resigned from office.

Morrison v. Olson upheld the constitutionality of a statute that built on the special prosecutor arrangement in *Nixon* by providing for the judicial appointment of an "independent counsel" to investigate and prosecute alleged misconduct by executive branch officials. Justice Scalia was the only dissenter, but his opinion received considerable attention after an independent counsel investigation led to the impeachment of President Clinton several years later. The independent counsel statute was renewed several times after its initial enactment, but Congress allowed it to expire after the Clinton impeachment. The Court's rulings

in *Nixon* and *Morrison,* and the independent counsel arrangement generally, had a significant impact on the Constitution's separation of powers
and the nation's politics for more than a quarter century.

✪

United States v. Nixon
418 U.S. 683 (1974)

•

MR. CHIEF JUSTICE BURGER DELIVERED THE OPINION OF
THE COURT.

This litigation presents for review the denial of a motion, filed in
the District Court on behalf of the President of the United States . . .
to quash a third-party *subpoena duces tecum* issued by the United States
District Court for the District of Columbia . . . direct[ing] the President to produce certain tape recordings and documents relating to his
conversations with aides and advisers. . . . On March 1, 1974, a grand
jury of the United States District Court for the District of Columbia
returned an indictment charging seven named individuals . . . with
various offenses, including conspiracy to defraud the United States and
to obstruct justice. Although he was not designated as such in the indictment, the grand jury named the President, among others, as an
unindicted coconspirator. . . . On April 18, 1974, upon motion of the
Special Prosecutor, a subpoena *duces tecum* was issued . . . to the President . . . requir[ing] the production, in advance of the September 9 trial
date, of certain tapes, memoranda, papers, transcripts, or other writings
relating to certain precisely identified meetings between the President
and others. . . .

In the District Court, the President's counsel argued that the court
lacked jurisdiction to issue the subpoena because the matter was an
intra-branch dispute between a subordinate and superior officer of
the Executive Branch and hence not subject to judicial resolution. . . .
[I]t is contended that a President's decision is final in determining what
evidence is to be used in a given criminal case. Although his counsel

concedes that the President has delegated certain specific powers to the Special Prosecutor, he has not "waived nor delegated to the Special Prosecutor the President's duty to claim privilege as to all materials . . . which fall within the President's inherent authority to refuse to disclose to any executive officer." Brief for the President 42. . . .

Our starting point is the nature of the proceeding for which the evidence is sought—here a pending criminal prosecution. It is a judicial proceeding in a federal court alleging violation of federal laws and is brought in the name of the United States as sovereign. . . . [T]he Attorney General has delegated the authority to represent the United States in these particular matters to a Special Prosecutor with unique authority and tenure. The regulation gives the Special Prosecutor explicit power to contest the invocation of executive privilege in the process of seeking evidence deemed relevant to the performance of these specially delegated duties. . . . So long as this regulation remains in force the Executive Branch is bound by it, and indeed the United States as the sovereign composed of the three branches is bound to respect and to enforce it. . . .

[W]e turn to the claim that the subpoena should be quashed because it demands "confidential conversations between a President and his close advisors that it would be inconsistent with the public interest to produce." The first contention is a broad claim that the separation of powers doctrine precludes judicial review of a President's claim of privilege. The second contention is that if he does not prevail on the claim of absolute privilege, the court should hold as a matter of constitutional law that the privilege prevails over the subpoena *duces tecum*.

In the performance of assigned constitutional duties each branch of the Government must initially interpret the Constitution, and the interpretation of its powers by any branch is due great respect from the others. The President's counsel, as we have noted, reads the Constitution as providing an absolute privilege of confidentiality for all Presidential communications. Many decisions of this Court, however, have unequivocally reaffirmed the holding of *Marbury v. Madison*, 1 Cranch 137 (1803), that "[it] is emphatically the province and duty of the judicial department to say what the law is." . . . Our system of government "requires that federal courts on occasion interpret the Constitution in a manner at variance with the construction given the document by another branch." *Powell v. McCormack* (1969). . . .

Notwithstanding the deference each branch must accord the others, the "judicial Power of the United States" vested in the federal courts by Art. III, § 1, of the Constitution can no more be shared with the Executive Branch than the Chief Executive, for example, can share with the Judiciary the veto power, or the Congress share with the Judiciary the power to override a Presidential veto. Any other conclusion would be contrary to the basic concept of separation of powers and the checks and balances that flow from the scheme of a tripartite government. . . .

In support of his claim of absolute privilege, the President's counsel urges two grounds, one of which is common to all governments and one of which is peculiar to our system of separation of powers. The first ground is the valid need for protection of communications between high Government officials and those who advise and assist them in the performance of their manifold duties; the importance of this confidentiality is too plain to require further discussion. Human experience teaches that those who expect public dissemination of their remarks may well temper candor with a concern for appearances and for their own interests to the detriment of the decisionmaking process. Whatever the nature of the privilege of confidentiality of Presidential communications in the exercise of Art. II powers, the privilege can be said to derive from the supremacy of each branch within its own assigned area of constitutional duties. Certain powers and privileges flow from the nature of enumerated powers; the protection of the confidentiality of Presidential communications has similar constitutional underpinnings.

The second ground asserted by the President's counsel in support of the claim of absolute privilege rests on the doctrine of separation of powers. Here it is argued that the independence of the Executive Branch within its own sphere . . . insulates a President from a judicial subpoena in an ongoing criminal prosecution, and thereby protects confidential Presidential communications.

However, neither the doctrine of separation of powers, nor the need for confidentiality of high-level communications, without more, can sustain an absolute, unqualified Presidential privilege of immunity from judicial process under all circumstances. The President's need for complete candor and objectivity from advisers calls for great deference from the courts. However, when the privilege depends solely on the broad, undifferentiated claim of public interest in the confidentiality of such conversations, a confrontation with other values arises. Absent a claim of need to protect military, diplomatic, or sensitive national security secrets, we find it difficult to accept the argument that even the very important interest in confidentiality of Presidential communications is significantly diminished by production of such material for *in camera* inspection with all the protection that a district court will be obliged to provide.

The impediment that an absolute, unqualified privilege would place in the way of the primary constitutional duty of the Judicial Branch to do justice in criminal prosecutions would plainly conflict with the function of the courts under Art. III. . . . To read the Art. II powers of the President as providing an absolute privilege as against a subpoena essential to enforcement of criminal statutes on no more than a generalized claim of the public interest in confidentiality of nonmilitary and nondiplomatic discussions would upset the constitutional balance of "a workable government" and gravely impair the role of the courts under Art. III. . . .

Since we conclude that the legitimate needs of the judicial process may outweigh Presidential privilege, it is necessary to resolve those competing interests in a manner that preserves the essential functions of each branch. . . . In this case we must weigh the importance of the general privilege of confidentiality of Presidential communications in performance of the President's responsibilities against the inroads of such a privilege on the fair administration of criminal justice. The interest in preserving confidentiality is weighty indeed and entitled to great respect. However, we cannot conclude that advisers will be moved to temper the candor of their remarks by the infrequent occasions of disclosure because of the possibility that such conversations will be called for in the context of a criminal prosecution. . . .

On the other hand, the allowance of the privilege to withhold evidence that is demonstrably relevant in a criminal trial would cut deeply into the guarantee of due process of law and gravely impair the basic function of the courts. A President's acknowledged need for confidentiality in the communications of his office is general in nature, whereas the constitutional need for production of relevant evidence in a criminal proceeding is specific and central to the fair adjudication of a particular criminal case in the administration of justice. Without access to specific facts a criminal prosecution may be totally frustrated. The President's broad interest in confidentiality of communications will not be vitiated by disclosure of a limited number of conversations preliminarily shown to have some bearing on the pending criminal cases.

We conclude that when the ground for asserting privilege as to subpoenaed materials sought for use in a criminal trial is based only on the generalized interest in confidentiality, it cannot prevail over the fundamental demands of due process of law in the fair administration of criminal justice. The generalized assertion of privilege must yield to the demonstrated, specific need for evidence in a pending criminal trial. . . .

Morrison v. Olson
487 U.S. 654 (1988)

•

CHIEF JUSTICE REHNQUIST DELIVERED THE OPINION OF THE COURT.

This case presents us with a challenge to the independent counsel provisions of the Ethics in Government Act of 1978[.] . . . We hold today that these provisions of the Act do not . . . impermissibly interfere with the President's authority under Article II in violation of the constitutional principle of separation of powers.

Briefly stated, Title VI of the Ethics in Government Act . . . allows for the appointment of an "independent counsel" to investigate and, if appropriate, prosecute certain high ranking Government officials for violations of federal criminal laws. . . . With respect to all matters within the independent counsel's jurisdiction, the Act grants the counsel "full power and independent authority to exercise all investigative and prosecutorial functions and powers of the Department of Justice[.]" . . .

We now turn to consider whether the Act is invalid under the constitutional principle of separation of powers. Two related issues must be addressed: The first is whether the provision of the Act restricting the Attorney General's power to remove the independent counsel to only those instances in which he can show "good cause," taken by itself, impermissibly interferes with the President's exercise of his constitutionally appointed functions. The second is whether, taken as a whole, the Act violates the separation of powers by reducing the President's ability to control the prosecutorial powers wielded by the independent counsel. . . .

[T]he real question is whether the removal restrictions are of such a nature that they impede the President's ability to perform his constitutional duty, and the functions of the officials in question must be analyzed in that light. Considering for the moment the "good cause" removal provision in isolation from the other parts of the Act at issue in this case, we cannot say that the imposition of a "good cause" standard for removal by itself unduly trammels on executive authority. . . . Although the counsel exercises no small amount of discretion and judgment in deciding how to carry out his or her duties under the Act, we simply do not see how the President's need to control the exercise of that discretion is so central to the functioning of the Executive Branch as to require as a matter of constitutional law that the counsel be terminable at will by the President.

Nor do we think that the "good cause" removal provision at issue here impermissibly burdens the President's power to control or supervise the independent counsel, as an executive official, in the execution of his or her duties under the Act. . . . Here, as with the provision of the Act conferring the appointment authority of the independent counsel on the special court, the congressional determination to limit the removal power of the Attorney General was essential, in the view of Congress, to establish the necessary independence of the office. . . .

The final question to be addressed is whether the Act, taken as a whole, violates the principle of separation of powers by unduly interfering with the role of the Executive Branch. . . . [W]e do not think that the Act "impermissibly undermine[s]" the powers of the Executive Branch, or "disrupts the proper balance between the coordinate branches [by] prevent[ing] the Executive Branch from accomplishing its constitutionally assigned functions[.]" It is undeniable that the Act reduces the amount of control or supervision that the Attorney General and, through him, the President exercises over the investigation and prosecution of a certain class of alleged criminal activity. . . . [T]he Attorney General retains the power to remove the counsel for "good cause," a power that we have already concluded provides the Executive with substantial ability to ensure that the laws are "faithfully executed" by an independent counsel. No independent counsel may be appointed without a specific request by the Attorney General, and the Attorney

General's decision not to request appointment if he finds "no reasonable grounds to believe that further investigation is warranted" is committed to his unreviewable discretion. The Act thus gives the Executive a degree of control over the power to initiate an investigation by the independent counsel. . . . [I]n our view these features of the Act give the Executive Branch sufficient control over the independent counsel to ensure that the President is able to perform his constitutionally assigned duties. . . .

JUSTICE SCALIA, DISSENTING.

It is the proud boast of our democracy that we have "a government of laws and not of men." Many Americans are familiar with that phrase; not many know its derivation. It comes from Part the First, Article XXX, of the Massachusetts Constitution of 1780, which reads in full as follows:

> In the government of this Commonwealth, the legislative department shall never exercise the executive and judicial powers, or either of them: The executive shall never exercise the legislative and judicial powers, or either of them: The judicial shall never exercise the legislative and executive powers, or either of them: to the end it may be a government of laws and not of men.

The Framers of the Federal Constitution similarly viewed the principle of separation of powers as the absolutely central guarantee of a just Government. In No. 47 of The Federalist, Madison wrote that "[n]o political truth is certainly of greater intrinsic value, or is stamped with the authority of more enlightened patrons of liberty." The Federalist No. 47. Without a secure structure of separated powers, our Bill of Rights would be worthless, as are the bills of rights of many nations of the world that have adopted, or even improved upon, the mere words of ours.

But just as the mere words of a Bill of Rights are not self-effectuating, the Framers recognized "[t]he insufficiency of a mere parchment delineation of the boundaries" to achieve the separation of powers. Federalist No. 73 (A. Hamilton). "[T]he great security," wrote Madison, "against a gradual concentration of the several powers in the same department consists in giving to those who administer each department the necessary constitutional means and personal motives to resist encroachments of the others. The provision for defense must in this, as in all other cases, be made commensurate to the danger of attack." Federalist No. 51. Madison continued:

> But it is not possible to give to each department an equal power of self-defense. In republican government, the legislative authority necessarily predominates. The remedy for this inconveniency is to divide the legislature into different branches; and to render them, by different modes of election and different principles of action, as little connected with each other as the nature of their common functions and their common dependence on the society will admit. . . . As the weight of the legislative authority requires that it should be thus divided, the weakness of the executive may require, on the other hand, that it should be fortified.

The major "fortification" provided, of course, was the veto power. But in addition to providing fortification, the Founders conspicuously and very consciously declined to sap the Executive's strength in the same way they had weakened the Legislature: by dividing the executive power. Proposals to have multiple executives, or a council of advisers with separate authority were rejected. Thus, while "[a]ll legislative Powers herein granted shall be vested in a Congress of the United States, which shall consist of a Senate *and* House of Representatives," U.S. Const., Art. I, § 1 [emphasis added], "[t]he executive Power shall be vested in *a President of the United States*," Art. II, § 1, cl. 1 (emphasis added).

That is what this suit is about. Power. The allocation of power among Congress, the President, and the courts in such fashion as to preserve the equilibrium the Constitution sought to establish—so that "a gradual concentration of the several powers in the same department," Federalist No. 51 (J. Madison), can effectively be resisted. Frequently an issue of this sort will come before the Court clad, so to speak, in sheep's clothing: the potential of the asserted principle to effect important change in the equilibrium of power is not immediately evident, and must be discerned by a careful and perceptive analysis. But this wolf comes as a wolf.

The present case began when the Legislative and Executive Branches became "embroiled in a dispute concerning the scope of the congressional investigatory power," . . . which—as is often the case with such interbranch conflicts—became quite acrimonious. . . .

Certain Members of the House remained angered by the confrontation, particularly by the role played by the Department of Justice. . . . Accordingly, staff counsel of the House Judiciary Committee were commissioned . . . to investigate the Justice Department's role in the controversy. That investigation lasted 2 1/2 years, and produced a 3,000-page report issued by the Committee over the vigorous dissent of all but one of its minority-party members. That report, which among other charges questioned the truthfulness of certain statements made by Assistant Attorney General Olson during testimony in front of the Committee during the early stages of its investigation, was sent to the Attorney General along with a formal request that he appoint an independent counsel to investigate Mr. Olson and others. . . .

Thus, by the application of this statute in the present case, Congress has effectively compelled a criminal investigation of a high-level appointee of the President in connection with his actions arising out of a bitter power dispute between the President and the Legislative Branch. Mr. Olson may or may not be guilty of a crime; we do not know. But we do know that the investigation of him has been commenced, not necessarily because the President or his authorized subordinates believe it is in the interest of the United States . . . but only because the Attorney General cannot affirm, as Congress demands, that there are *no reasonable grounds to believe* that further investigation is warranted. The decisions regarding the scope of that further investigation, its duration, and, finally, whether or not prosecution should ensue, are likewise beyond the control of the President and his subordinates. . . .

If to describe this case is not to decide it, the concept of a government of separate and coordinate powers no longer has meaning. . . .

To repeat, Article II, § 1, cl. 1, of the Constitution provides:

"The executive Power shall be vested in a President of the United States."

As I described at the outset of this opinion, this does not mean *some of* the executive power, but *all of* the executive power. It seems to me, therefore, that the decision of the Court of Appeals invalidating the present statute must be upheld on fundamental separation-of-powers principles if the following two questions are answered affirmatively: (1) Is the conduct of a criminal prosecution (and of an investigation to decide whether to prosecute) the exercise of purely executive power? (2) Does the statute deprive the President of the United States of exclusive control over the exercise of that power? Surprising to say, the Court appears to concede an affirmative answer to both questions, but seeks to avoid the inevitable conclusion that since the statute vests some purely executive power in a person who is not the President of the United States it is void.

The Court concedes that "[t]here is no real dispute that the functions performed by the independent counsel are 'executive'"[.] . . . There is no possible doubt that the independent counsel's functions fit this description. She is vested with the "full power and independent authority to exercise all *investigative and prosecutorial* functions and powers of the Department of Justice [and] the Attorney General." Governmental investigation and prosecution of crimes is a quintessentially executive function.

As for the second question, whether the statute before us deprives the President of exclusive control over that quintessentially executive activity: The Court does not, and could not possibly, assert that it does not. That is indeed the whole object of the statute. Instead, the Court points out that the President, through his Attorney General, has at least *some* control. That concession is alone enough to invalidate the statute, but I cannot refrain from pointing out that the Court greatly exaggerates the extent of that "some" Presidential control. "Most importan[t]" among these controls, the Court asserts, is the Attorney General's "power to remove the counsel for 'good cause.'" This is somewhat like referring to shackles as an effective means of locomotion. . . .

. . . [I]t is ultimately irrelevant *how much* the statute reduces Presidential control. The case is over when the Court acknowledges, as it must, that "[i]t is undeniable that the Act reduces the amount of control or supervision that the Attorney General and, through him, the President exercises over the investigation and prosecution of a certain class of alleged criminal activity." It effects a revolution in our constitutional jurisprudence for the Court, once it has determined that (1) purely executive functions are at issue here, and (2) those functions have been given to a person whose actions are not fully within the supervision and control of the President, nonetheless to proceed further to sit in judgment of whether "the President's need to control the exercise of [the independent counsel's] discretion is *so central* to the functioning of the Executive Branch" as to require complete control[.] . . . It is not for us to determine, and we have never presumed to determine, how much of the purely executive powers of government must be within the full control of the President. The Constitution prescribes that they *all* are.

. . .

Is it unthinkable that the President should have such exclusive power, even when alleged crimes by him or his close associates are at issue? No more so than that Congress should have the exclusive power of legislation, even when what is at issue is its own exemption from the burdens of certain laws. . . . A system of separate and coordinate powers necessarily involves an acceptance of exclusive power that can theoretically be abused. . . . The checks against any branch's abuse of its exclusive powers are twofold: First, retaliation by one of the other branch's use of *its* exclusive powers: Congress, for example, can impeach the executive who willfully fails to enforce the laws; the executive can decline to prosecute under unconstitutional statutes; and the courts can dismiss malicious prosecutions. Second, and ultimately, there is the political check that the people will replace those in the political branches . . . who are guilty of abuse. Political pressures produced special prosecutors—for Teapot Dome and for Watergate, for example—long before this statute created the independent counsel. . . .

In sum, this statute does deprive the President of substantial control over the prosecutory functions performed by the independent counsel, and it does substantially affect the balance of powers. That the Court could possibly conclude otherwise demonstrates both the wisdom of our former constitutional system, in which the degree of reduced control and political impairment were irrelevant, since *all* purely executive power had to be in the President; and the folly of the new system of standardless judicial allocation of powers we adopt today. . . .

A government of laws means a government of rules. Today's decision on the basic issue of fragmentation of executive power is ungoverned by rule, and hence ungoverned by law. It extends into the very heart of our most significant constitutional function the "totality of the circumstances" mode of analysis that this Court has in recent years become fond of. Taking all things into account, we conclude that the power taken away from the President here is not really *too* much. The next time executive power is assigned to someone other than the President we may conclude, taking all things into account, that it *is* too much. That opinion, like this one, will not be confined by any rule. We will describe, as we have today (though I hope more accurately) the effects of the provision in question, and will authoritatively announce: "The President's need to control the exercise of the [subject officer's] discretion *is* so central to the functioning of the Executive Branch as to require complete control." This is not analysis; it is *ad hoc* judgment. And it fails to explain why it is not true that—as the text of the Constitution seems to require, as the Founders seemed to expect, and as our past cases have uniformly assumed—all purely executive power must be under the control of the President.

The ad hoc approach to constitutional adjudication has real attraction, even apart from its work-saving potential. It is guaranteed to produce a result, in every case, that will make a majority of the Court happy with the law. The law is, by definition, precisely what the majority thinks, taking all things into account, it *ought* to be. I prefer to rely upon the judgment of the wise men who constructed our system, and of the people who approved it, and of two centuries of history that have shown it to be sound. Like it or not, that judgment says, quite plainly, that "[t]he executive Power shall be vested in a President of the United States."

WAR POWERS

꧂

S ome of the most important modern interpretations of the Constitution's allocation of war powers have come in the form of enactments by Congress rather than decisions of the Supreme Court. The War Powers Resolution of 1973 sought to regulate the president's use of armed force in situations arguably short of "war". President Richard Nixon vetoed the resolution, arguing that it was unconstitutional. However, Congress overrode the veto by two-thirds majorities of the House and Senate. Since 1973, Congress and the president have often been at odds regarding the resolution's constitutionality.

Following the attacks of September 11, 2001, Congress enacted a sweeping Authorization for Use of Military Force (AUMF) against persons, groups, and nations connected with the attacks or attackers. The Supreme Court subsequently decided several cases interpreting both the AUMF and presidential war powers with respect to the capture, detention, and military punishment of enemy combatants.

In *Hamdi v. Rumsfeld* (2004), a divided Court held that the president's military power as commander in chief permitted him, in time of constitutionally authorized war, to hold and detain enemy combatants for the duration of hostilities, including American citizens alleged to have been fighting for the enemy, but that the Due Process Clause required that

American citizens be granted a hearing to challenge the propriety of their detention. Justice O'Connor's opinion for a plurality of four justices stated the narrowest reasoning in support of the two holdings.

In *Hamdan v. Rumsfeld* (2006), the Court invalidated, by a 5–3 vote, the use of a military tribunal to try an alleged enemy war criminal captured in Afghanistan and held at Guantánamo Bay, Cuba. The Court held that such tribunals were not authorized, either by Congress or by the president's own constitutional powers. Congress responded by enacting the Military Commissions Act of 2006 (MCA), specifically granting the president the authority that the Court in *Hamdan* had said he did not possess.

In *Boumediene v. Bush* (2008), the Court struck down, 5–4, a provision of the Military Commissions Act withdrawing habeas corpus jurisdiction for non-citizens in military custody. The Court held that non-citizen enemy combatants have a U.S. constitutional right to the writ of habeas corpus in order to challenge their military detention abroad and that judicial review of military determinations was an inadequate substitute.

The opinions in these cases are extraordinarily lengthy. *Hamdi* and *Boumediene* are excerpted here to present their most significant holdings and the dissenting positions.

✪

The War Powers Resolution of 1973

•

Resolved by the Senate and House of Representatives of the United States of America in Congress assembled . . .

Section 2. <u>Purpose and Policy</u>.

(a) It is the purpose of this joint resolution to fulfill the intent of the framers of the Constitution of the United States and insure that the collective judgment of both the Congress and the President will apply to the introduction of United States Armed Forces into hostilities, or into situations where imminent involvement in hostilities is clearly indicated by the circumstances, and to the continued use of such forces[.] . . .

(c) The constitutional powers of the President as Commander-in-Chief to introduce United States Armed Forces into hostilities, or into situations where imminent involvement in hostilities is clearly indicated by the circumstances, are exercised only pursuant to (1) a declaration of war, (2) specific statutory authorization, or (3) a national emergency created by attack upon the United States, its territories or possessions, or its armed forces. . . .

Section 5. Congressional Action. . . .

(b) Within sixty calendar days after a report is submitted . . . the President shall terminate any use of United States Armed Forces with respect to which such report was submitted . . . unless the Congress (1) has declared war or enacted a specific authorization for such use of the United States Armed Forces, (2) has extended by law such sixty-day period, or (3) is physically unable to meet as a result of an armed attack upon the United States. . . .

(c) Notwithstanding subsection (b), at any time that United States Armed Forces are engaged in hostilities outside the territory of the United States, its possessions and territories without a declaration of war or specific statutory authorization, such forces shall be removed by the President if the Congress so directs by concurrent resolution. . . .

Section 8. Interpretation of Joint Resolution

(a) Authority to introduce United States Armed Forces into hostilities or into situations wherein involvement in hostilities is clearly indicated by the circumstances shall not be inferred—

(1) from any provision of law . . . including any provision contained in an appropriation Act, unless such provision specifically authorizes the introduction of United States Armed Forces into hostilities or into such situations and states that it is intended to constitute specific statutory authorization within the meaning of this joint resolution; or

(2) from any treaty heretofore or hereafter ratified unless such treaty is implemented by legislation specifically authorizing the introduction of United States Armed Forces into hostilities or into such situations and stating that it is intended to constitute specific statutory authorization within the meaning of this joint resolution. . . .

(c) Nothing in this joint resolution—

(1) is intended to alter the constitutional authority of the Congress or of the President, or the provisions of existing treaties; or

(2) shall be construed as granting any authority to the President with respect to the introduction of United States Armed Forces . . .

which authority he would not have had in the absence of this joint
resolution . . .

Statement Vetoing the War Powers Resolution (1973)
RICHARD NIXON

•

To the House of Representatives:

I hereby return without my approval House Joint Resolution 542—
the War Powers Resolution. While I am in accord with the desire of the
Congress to assert its proper role in the conduct of our foreign affairs,
the restrictions which this resolution would impose upon the authority
of the President are both unconstitutional and dangerous to the best
interests of our Nation.

The proper roles of the Congress and the Executive in the conduct of foreign affairs have been debated since the founding of our
country. Only recently, however, has there been a serious challenge to
the wisdom of the Founding Fathers in choosing not to draw a precise
and detailed line of demarcation between the foreign policy powers of
the two branches.

The Founding Fathers understood the impossibility of foreseeing
every contingency that might arise in this complex area. They acknowledged the need for flexibility in responding to changing circumstances.
They recognized that foreign policy decisions must be made through
close cooperation between the two branches and not through rigidly
codified procedures.

These principles remain as valid today as they were when our Constitution was written. Yet House Joint Resolution 542 would violate
those principles by defining the President's powers in ways which would
strictly limit his constitutional authority.

House Joint Resolution 542 would attempt to take away, by a mere
legislative act, authorities which the President has properly exercised
under the Constitution for almost 200 years. One of its provisions would
automatically cut off certain authorities after sixty days unless the Congress extended them. Another would allow the Congress to eliminate
certain authorities merely by the passage of a concurrent resolution—an

action which does not normally have the force of law, since it denies the President his constitutional role in approving legislation.

I believe that both these provisions are unconstitutional. The only way in which the constitutional powers of a branch of the Government can be altered is by amending the Constitution—and any attempt to make such alterations by legislation alone is clearly without force. . . .

Authorization for Use of Military Force (September 18, 2001)

•

Joint Resolution: To authorize the use of United States Armed Forces against those responsible for the recent attacks launched against the United States

Whereas, on September 11, 2001, acts of treacherous violence were committed against the United States and its citizens; and

Whereas, such acts render it both necessary and appropriate that the United States exercise its rights to self-defense and to protect United States citizens both at home and abroad; and

Whereas, in light of the threat to the national security and foreign policy of the United States posed by these grave acts of violence; and

Whereas, such acts continue to pose an unusual and extraordinary threat to the national security and foreign policy of the United States; and

Whereas, the President has authority under the Constitution to take action to deter and prevent acts of international terrorism against the United States: Now, therefore, be it

Resolved by the Senate and House of Representatives of the United States of America in Congress assembled,

. . .

Section 2. Authorization for Use of United States Armed Forces.

(a) In General—That the President is authorized to use all necessary and appropriate force against those nations, organizations, or persons he determines planned, authorized, committed or aided the terrorist attacks that occurred on September 11, 2001, or harbored such organizations or persons, in order to prevent any future acts of international terrorism against the United States by such nations, organizations, or persons.

(b) War Powers Resolution Requirements—

(1) Specific Statutory Authorization.—Consistent with section 8(a) (1) of the War Powers Resolution, the Congress declares that this section is intended to constitute specific statutory authorization within the meaning of section 5(b) of the War Powers Resolution.

(2) Applicability of Other Requirements.—Nothing in this resolution supersedes any requirement of the War Powers Resolution.

Hamdi v. Rumsfeld
542 U.S. 507 (2004)

•

JUSTICE O'CONNOR ANNOUNCED THE JUDGMENT OF THE COURT AND DELIVERED AN OPINION, IN WHICH THE CHIEF JUSTICE, JUSTICE KENNEDY, AND JUSTICE BREYER JOIN.

At this difficult time in our Nation's history, we are called upon to consider the legality of the Government's detention of a United States citizen on United States soil as an "enemy combatant" and to address the process that is constitutionally owed to one who seeks to challenge his classification as such. . . . We hold that although Congress authorized the detention of combatants in the narrow circumstances alleged here, due process demands that a citizen held in the United States as an enemy combatant be given a meaningful opportunity to contest the factual basis for that detention before a neutral decisionmaker.

I

On September 11, 2001, the al Qaeda terrorist network used hijacked commercial airliners to attack prominent targets in the United States. Approximately 3,000 people were killed in those attacks. One week later, in response to these "acts of treacherous violence," Congress passed a resolution [the Authorization for Use of Military Force (AUMF)] authorizing the President to "use all necessary and appropriate force against those nations, organizations, or persons he determines planned, authorized, committed, or aided the terrorist attacks" or "harbored such organizations or persons, in order to prevent any future acts of international terrorism against the United States by such nations, organizations or persons." . . .

This case arises out of the detention of a man whom the Government alleges took up arms with the Taliban during this conflict. . . . Born in Louisiana in 1980, Hamdi moved with his family to Saudi Arabia as a child. By 2001, the parties agree, he resided in Afghanistan. At some point that year, he was seized by members of the Northern Alliance, a coalition of military groups opposed to the Taliban government, and eventually was turned over to the United States military. . . . The Government contends that Hamdi is an "enemy combatant," and that this status justifies holding him in the United States indefinitely—without formal charges or proceedings—unless and until it makes the determination that access to counsel or further process is warranted. . . .

II

The threshold question before us is whether the Executive has the authority to detain citizens who qualify as "enemy combatants." . . . [W]e agree with the Government's position, that Congress has in fact authorized Hamdi's detention, through the AUMF. . . .

There can be no doubt that individuals who fought against the United States in Afghanistan as part of the Taliban, an organization known to have supported the al Qaeda terrorist network responsible for those attacks, are individuals Congress sought to target in passing the AUMF. We conclude that detention of individuals falling into the limited category we are considering, for the duration of the particular conflict in which they were captured, is so fundamental and accepted an incident to war as to be an exercise of the "necessary and appropriate force" Congress has authorized the President to use.

The capture and detention of lawful combatants and the capture, detention, and trial of unlawful combatants, by "universal agreement and practice," are "important incident[s] of war." *Ex parte Quirin*. The purpose of detention is to prevent captured individuals from returning to the field of battle and taking up arms once again. . . .

There is no bar to this Nation's holding one of its own citizens as an enemy combatant. In *Quirin*, one of the detainees, Haupt, alleged that he was a naturalized United States citizen. We held that "[c]itizens who associate themselves with the military arm of the enemy government, and with its aid, guidance and direction enter this country bent on hostile acts, are enemy belligerents within the meaning of . . . the law of war." While Haupt was tried for violations of the law of war, nothing in *Quirin* suggests that his citizenship would have precluded his mere detention for the duration of the relevant hostilities. . . .

It is a clearly established principle of the law of war that detention may last no longer than active hostilities. . . . The United States may detain, for the duration of these hostilities, individuals legitimately determined to be Taliban combatants who "engaged in an armed conflict against the United States." If the record establishes that United States troops are still involved in active combat in Afghanistan, those detentions are part of the exercise of "necessary and appropriate force," and therefore are authorized by the AUMF.

. . . [O]ur opinion only finds legislative authority to detain under the AUMF once it is sufficiently clear that the individual is, in fact, an enemy combatant; whether that is established by concession or by some other process that verifies this fact with sufficient certainty seems beside the point.

III

Even in cases in which the detention of enemy combatants is legally authorized, there remains the question of what process is constitutionally due to a citizen who disputes his enemy-combatant status. . . .

It is beyond question that substantial interests lie on both sides of the scale in this case. . . . [A]s critical as the Government's interest may be in detaining those who actually pose an immediate threat to the national security of the United States during ongoing international conflict, history and common sense teach us that an unchecked system of detention carries the potential to become a means for oppression and abuse of others who do not present that sort of threat. . . . We reaffirm today the fundamental nature of a citizen's right to be free from involuntary confinement by his own government without due process of law, and we weigh the opposing governmental interests against the curtailment of liberty that such confinement entails. . . .

[We] hold that a citizen-detainee seeking to challenge his classification as an enemy combatant must receive notice of the factual basis for his classification, and a fair opportunity to rebut the Government's factual assertions before a neutral decisionmaker. . . . At the same time, the exigencies of the circumstances may demand that, aside from these core elements, enemy-combatant proceedings may be tailored to alleviate their uncommon potential to burden the Executive at a time of ongoing military conflict. Hearsay, for example, may need to be accepted as the most reliable available evidence from the Government in such a proceeding. Likewise, the Constitution would not be offended by a presumption in favor of the Government's evidence, so long as that presumption remained a rebuttable one and fair opportunity for rebuttal were provided.

. . . We think it unlikely that this basic process will have the dire impact on the central functions of warmaking that the Government forecasts. The parties agree that initial captures on the battlefield need not receive the process we have discussed here; that process is due only when the determination is made to *continue* to hold those who have been seized. . . . While we accord the greatest respect and consideration to the judgments of military authorities in matters relating to the actual prosecution of a war, and recognize that the scope of that discretion necessarily is wide, it does not infringe on the core role of the military for the courts to exercise their own time-honored and constitutionally mandated roles of reviewing and resolving claims like those presented here. . . .

In sum, while the full protections that accompany challenges to detentions in other settings may prove unworkable and inappropriate in the enemy-combatant setting, the threats to military operations posed by a basic system of independent review are not so weighty as to trump a citizen's core rights to challenge meaningfully the Government's case and to be heard by an impartial adjudicator. . . .

In so holding, we necessarily reject the Government's assertion that separation of powers principles mandate a heavily circumscribed role for the courts in such circumstances. Indeed, the position that the courts must forgo any examination of the individual case and focus exclusively on the legality of the broader detention scheme cannot be mandated by any reasonable view of separation of powers, as this approach serves only to *condense* power into a single branch of government. We have long since made clear that a state of war is not a blank check for the President when it comes to the rights of the Nation's citizens. *Youngstown Sheet & Tube*. Whatever power the United States Constitution envisions for the Executive in its exchanges with other nations or with enemy organizations in times of conflict, it most assuredly envisions a role for all three branches when individual liberties are at stake. . . .

There remains the possibility that the standards we have articulated could be met by an appropriately authorized and properly constituted military tribunal. Indeed, it is notable that military regulations already provide for such process in related instances, dictating that tribunals be made available to determine the status of enemy detainees who assert prisoner-of-war status under the Geneva Convention. In the absence of such process, however, a court that receives a petition for a writ of habeas corpus from an alleged enemy combatant must itself ensure that the minimum requirements of due process are achieved. . . .

JUSTICE SCALIA, WITH WHOM JUSTICE STEVENS JOINS, DISSENTING.

Petitioner Yaser Hamdi, a presumed American citizen, has been imprisoned without charge or hearing in the Norfolk and Charleston Naval Brigs for more than two years, on the allegation that he is an enemy combatant who bore arms against his country for the Taliban. His father claims to the contrary, that he is an inexperienced aid worker caught in the wrong place at the wrong time. . . .

Where the Government accuses a citizen of waging war against it, our constitutional tradition has been to prosecute him in federal court for treason or some other crime. Where the exigencies of war prevent that, the Constitution's Suspension Clause, Art. I, § 9, cl. 2, allows Congress to relax the usual protections temporarily. Absent suspension, however, the Executive's assertion of military exigency has not been thought sufficient to permit detention without charge. No one contends that the congressional Authorization for Use of Military Force, on which the Government relies to justify its actions here, is an implementation of the Suspension Clause. Accordingly, I would reverse the judgment below.

. . . The gist of the Due Process Clause, as understood at the founding and since, was to force the Government to follow those common-law procedures traditionally deemed necessary before depriving a person of life, liberty, or property. When a citizen was deprived of liberty because of alleged criminal conduct, those procedures typically required committal by a magistrate followed by indictment and trial. . . .

The allegations here, of course, are no ordinary accusations of criminal activity. Yaser Esam Hamdi has been imprisoned because the Government believes he participated in the waging of war against the United States. The relevant question, then, is whether there is a different, special procedure for imprisonment of a citizen accused of wrongdoing *by aiding the enemy in wartime*. . . .

[I]n *Ex parte Milligan* (1866) . . . the Court issued the writ to an American citizen who had been tried by military commission for offenses that included conspiring to overthrow the Government, seize munitions, and liberate prisoners of war. The Court rejected in no uncertain terms the Government's assertion that military jurisdiction was proper "under the 'laws and usages of war.'" . . .

[T]he reasoning and conclusion of *Milligan* logically cover the present case. The Government justifies imprisonment of Hamdi on principles of the law of war and admits that, absent the war, it would have no such authority. But if the law of war cannot be applied to citizens where courts are open, then Hamdi's imprisonment without criminal trial is no less unlawful than Milligan's trial by military tribunal. . . .

The Government argues that our more recent jurisprudence ratifies its indefinite imprisonment of a citizen within the territorial jurisdiction of federal courts. It places primary reliance upon *Ex parte Quirin* (1942), a World War II case upholding the trial by military commission of eight German saboteurs, one of whom, Herbert Haupt, was a U.S. citizen. The case was not this Court's finest hour. . . . In my view [*Quirin*] seeks to revise *Milligan* rather than describe it. . . .

It follows from what I have said that Hamdi is entitled to a habeas decree requiring his release unless (1) criminal proceedings are promptly brought, or (2) Congress has suspended the writ of habeas corpus. A suspension of the writ could, of course, lay down conditions for continued detention, similar to those that today's opinion prescribes under the Due Process Clause. . . .

Having found a congressional authorization for detention of citizens where none clearly exists; and having discarded the categorical procedural protection of the Suspension Clause; the plurality then proceeds, under the guise of the Due Process Clause, to prescribe what procedural protections *it* thinks appropriate. It "weigh[s] the private interest . . . against the Government's asserted interest" . . . and—just as though writing a new Constitution—comes up with an unheard-of system in which the citizen rather than the Government bears the burden of proof, testimony is by hearsay rather than live witnesses, and the presiding officer may well be a "neutral" military officer rather than judge and jury. . . .

Many think it not only inevitable but entirely proper that liberty give way to security in times of national crisis—that, at the extremes of military exigency, *inter arma silent leges*. Whatever the general merits of the view that war silences law or modulates its voice, that view has no place in the interpretation and application of a Constitution designed precisely to confront war and, in a manner that accords with democratic principles, to accommodate it. Because the Court has proceeded to meet the current emergency in a manner the Constitution does not envision, I respectfully dissent.

JUSTICE THOMAS, DISSENTING.

The Executive Branch, acting pursuant to the powers vested in the President by the Constitution and with explicit congressional approval, has determined that Yaser Hamdi is an enemy combatant and should be detained. This detention falls squarely within the Federal Government's war powers, and we lack the expertise and capacity to second-guess that decision. As such, petitioners' habeas challenge should fail, and there is no reason to remand the case. . . .

The Founders intended that the President have primary responsibility—along with the necessary power—to protect the national security and to conduct the Nation's foreign relations. They did so principally because the structural advantages of a unitary Executive are essential in these domains. "Energy in the executive is a leading character in the definition of good government. It is essential to the protection of the community against foreign attacks." [*The Federalist*], No. 70 (A. Hamilton). The principle "ingredien[t]" for "energy in the executive" is "unity." This is because "[d]ecision, activity, secrecy, and dispatch will generally characterise the proceedings of one man, in a much more eminent degree, than the proceedings of any greater number."

These structural advantages are most important in the national-security and foreign-affairs contexts. "Of all the cares or concerns of

government, the direction of war most peculiarly demands those qualities which distinguish the exercise of power by a single hand." *Id.*, No.
74 (A. Hamilton). . . . This Court has long recognized these features
and has accordingly held that the President has *constitutional* authority
to protect the national security and that this authority carries with it
broad discretion. . . .

I agree with the plurality that the Federal Government has power to
detain those that the Executive Branch determines to be enemy combatants. . . . But I do not think that the plurality has adequately explained
the breadth of the President's authority to detain enemy combatants, an
authority that includes making virtually conclusive factual findings. . . .

In this context, due process requires nothing more than a good-faith
executive determination. To be clear: The Court has held that an Executive, acting pursuant to statutory and constitutional authority, may,
consistent with the Due Process Clause, unilaterally decide to detain an
individual if the Executive deems this necessary for the public safety
even if he is mistaken. . . . The Government's asserted authority to detain
an individual that the President has determined to be an enemy combatant, at least while hostilities continue, comports with the Due Process
Clause. . . . I therefore cannot agree with Justice SCALIA's conclusion
that the Government must choose between using standard criminal
processes and suspending the writ. . . .

By detaining Hamdi, the President, in the prosecution of a war and
authorized by Congress, has acted well within his authority. Hamdi
thereby received all the process to which he was due under the circumstances. I therefore believe that this is no occasion to balance the competing interests, as the plurality unconvincingly attempts to do.

Boumediene v. Bush
553 U.S. 723 (2008)

•

JUSTICE KENNEDY DELIVERED THE OPINION OF THE COURT.

Petitioners are aliens designated as enemy combatants and detained
at the United States Naval Station at Guantanamo Bay, Cuba. . . .

Petitioners present a question not resolved by our earlier cases relating to the detention of aliens at Guantanamo: whether they have the constitutional privilege of *habeas corpus*, a privilege not to be withdrawn except in conformance with the Suspension Clause, Art. I, § 9, cl. 2. We hold these petitioners do have the habeas corpus privilege. . . . [Section] 7 of the Military Commissions Act of 2006, operates as an unconstitutional suspension of the writ. . . .

Under the Authorization for Use of Military Force (AUMF) . . . the President is authorized "to use all necessary and appropriate force against those nations, organizations, or persons he determines planned, authorized, committed, or aided the terrorist attacks that occurred on September 11, 2001, or harbored such organizations or persons, in order to prevent any future acts of international terrorism against the United States by such nations, organizations or persons."

Interpreting the AUMF, the Department of Defense ordered the detention of these petitioners, and they were transferred to Guantanamo. Some of these individuals were apprehended on the battlefield in Afghanistan, others in places as far away from there as Bosnia and Gambia. All are foreign nationals . . . Each denies he is a member of the al Qaeda terrorist network that carried out the September 11 attacks or of the Taliban regime that provided sanctuary for al Qaeda. Each . . . has sought a writ of habeas corpus[.] . . . [The Military Commissions Act, §7, provides that] "(1) No court, justice, or judge shall have jurisdiction to hear or consider an application for a writ of habeas corpus filed by or on behalf of an alien detained by the United States who has been determined by the United States to have been properly detained as an enemy combatant or is awaiting such determination." . . .

In deciding the constitutional questions now presented we must determine whether petitioners are barred from seeking the writ or invoking the protections of the Suspension Clause either because of their status, i.e., petitioners' designation by the Executive Branch as enemy combatants, or their physical location, i.e., their presence at Guantanamo Bay. The Government contends that noncitizens designated as enemy combatants and detained in territory located outside our Nation's borders have no constitutional rights and no privilege of habeas corpus. Petitioners contend they do have cognizable constitutional rights and that Congress, in seeking to eliminate recourse to habeas corpus as a means to assert those rights, acted in violation of the Suspension Clause. . . .

The Framers viewed freedom from unlawful restraint as a fundamental precept of liberty, and they understood the writ of habeas corpus as a vital instrument to secure that freedom. . . . That the Framers considered the writ a vital instrument for the protection of individual liberty is evident from the care taken to specify the limited grounds for its suspension: "The Privilege of the Writ of Habeas Corpus shall not be suspended, unless when in Cases of Rebellion or Invasion the public Safety may require it." Art. I, § 9, cl. 2[.] . . .

As [Alexander Hamilton] explained in *The Federalist* No. 84:

"[T]he practice of arbitrary imprisonments, have been, in all ages, the favorite and most formidable instruments of tyranny. The observations of the judicious Blackstone . . . are well worthy of recital: 'To bereave a man of life . . . or by violence to confiscate his estate, without accusation or trial, would be so gross and notorious an act of despotism as must at once convey the alarm of tyranny throughout the whole nation; but confinement of the person, by secretly hurrying him to jail, where his sufferings are unknown or forgotten, is a less public, a less striking, and therefore a *more dangerous engine* of arbitrary government.' And as a remedy for this fatal evil he is everywhere peculiarly emphatical in his encomiums on the *habeas corpus* act, which in one place he calls 'the BULWARK of the British Constitution.' " . . .

[T]he parties in these cases have examined historical sources to construct a view of the common-law writ as it existed in 1789[.] . . . Diligent search by all parties reveals no certain conclusions. . . . We know that at common law a petitioner's status as an alien was not a categorical bar to habeas corpus relief. See, e.g., *Sommersett's Case*, (1772) (ordering an African slave freed upon finding the custodian's return insufficient) [.] . . . We know as well that common-law courts entertained habeas petitions brought by enemy aliens detained in England—"entertained" at least in the sense that the courts held hearings to determine the threshold question of entitlement to the writ. . . .

Guantanamo Bay is not formally part of the United States. . . . We therefore do not question the Government's position that Cuba, not the United States, maintains sovereignty, in the legal and technical sense of the term, over Guantanamo Bay. But this does not end the analysis. . . . [I]t is not altogether uncommon for a territory to be under the *de jure* sovereignty of one nation, while under the plenary control, or practical sovereignty, of another. . . .

[I]n *Johnson v. Eisentrager* (1950) . . . the Court addressed whether habeas corpus jurisdiction extended to enemy aliens who had been convicted of violating the laws of war. The prisoners were detained at Landsberg Prison in Germany during the Allied Powers' postwar occupation. . . . [T]he Court in *Eisentrager* denied access to the writ, and it noted the prisoners "at no relevant time were within any territory over which the United States is sovereign, and [that] the scenes of their offense, their capture, their trial and their punishment were all beyond the territorial jurisdiction of any court of the United States." . . .

[W]e do not accept the idea that the above-quoted passage from *Eisentrager* is the only authoritative language in the opinion[.] . . . [B]ecause the United States lacked both *de jure* sovereignty and plenary control over Landsberg Prison . . . it is far from clear that the *Eisentrager* Court used the term sovereignty only in the narrow technical sense and not to connote the degree of control the military asserted over the facility. . . . Nothing in *Eisentrager* says that *de jure* sovereignty is or has ever been the only relevant consideration in determining the geographic reach of the Constitution or of habeas corpus. . . .

The Government's formal sovereignty-based test raises troubling separation-of-powers concerns as well. The political history of Guantanamo illustrates the deficiencies of this approach. The United States has maintained complete and uninterrupted control of the bay for over 100 years. . . . Yet the Government's view is that the Constitution had no effect there, at least as to noncitizens, because the United States disclaimed sovereignty in the formal sense of the term. The necessary implication of the argument is that by surrendering formal sovereignty over any unincorporated territory to a third party, while at the same time entering into a lease that grants total control over the territory back to the United States, it would be possible for the political branches to govern without legal constraint.

Our basic charter cannot be contracted away like this. The Constitution grants Congress and the President the power to acquire, dispose of, and govern territory, not the power to decide when and where its terms apply. . . .

[T]he *Eisentrager* Court found relevant that each petitioner:

"(a) is an enemy alien; (b) has never been or resided in the United States; (c) was captured outside of our territory and there held in military custody as a prisoner of war; (d) was tried and convicted by a

Military Commission sitting outside the United States; (e) for offenses against laws of war committed outside the United States; (f) and is at all times imprisoned outside the United States." . . .

[T]he petitioners, like those in *Eisentrager*, are not American citizens. But the petitioners in *Eisentrager* did not contest, it seems, the Court's assertion that they were "enemy alien[s]." . . . [U]nlike in *Eisentrager*, there has been no trial by military commission for violations of the laws of war. . . . [T]he detainees here are similarly situated to the *Eisentrager* petitioners in that the sites of their apprehension and detention are technically outside the sovereign territory of the United States. . . . But there are critical differences between Landsberg Prison, circa 1950, and the United States Naval Station at Guantanamo Bay in 2008. Unlike its present control over the naval station, the United States' control over the prison in Germany was neither absolute nor indefinite. . . . The United States was . . . answerable to its Allies for all activities occurring there. . . .

It is true that before today the Court has never held that noncitizens detained by our Government in territory over which another country maintains *de jure* sovereignty have any rights under our Constitution. But the cases before us lack any precise historical parallel. They involve individuals detained by executive order for the duration of a conflict that, if measured from September 11, 2001, to the present, is already among the longest wars in American history. . . . The detainees, moreover, are held in a territory that, while technically not part of the United States, is under the complete and total control of our Government. Under these circumstances the lack of a precedent on point is no barrier to our holding.

We hold that Art. I, § 9, cl. 2, of the Constitution has full effect at Guantanamo Bay. If the privilege of habeas corpus is to be denied to the detainees now before us, Congress must act in accordance with the requirements of the Suspension Clause. . . . The MCA does not purport to be a formal suspension of the writ; and the Government, in its submissions to us, has not argued that it is. Petitioners, therefore, are entitled to the privilege of habeas corpus to challenge the legality of their detention. . . .

JUSTICE SCALIA, WITH WHOM THE CHIEF JUSTICE, JUSTICE THOMAS, AND JUSTICE ALITO JOIN, DISSENTING.

Today, for the first time in our Nation's history, the Court confers a constitutional right to habeas corpus on alien enemies detained abroad by our military forces in the course of an ongoing war. The Chief Justice's dissent, which I join, shows that the procedures prescribed by Congress in the Detainee Treatment Act provide the essential protections that habeas corpus guarantees; there has thus been no suspension of the writ, and no basis exists for judicial intervention beyond what the Act allows. My problem with today's opinion is more fundamental still: The writ of habeas corpus does not, and never has, run in favor of aliens abroad[.] . . .

America is at war with radical Islamists. . . . On September 11, 2001, the enemy brought the battle to American soil, killing 2,749 at the Twin Towers in New York City, 184 at the Pentagon in Washington, D. C., and 40 in Pennsylvania. . . . It has threatened further attacks against our homeland; one need only walk about buttressed and barricaded Washington, or board a plane anywhere in the country, to know that the threat is a serious one. Our Armed Forces are now in the field against the enemy, in Afghanistan and Iraq. Last week, 13 of our countrymen in arms were killed.

The game of bait-and-switch that today's opinion plays upon the Nation's Commander in Chief will make the war harder on us. It will almost certainly cause more Americans to be killed. That consequence would be tolerable if necessary to preserve a time-honored legal principle vital to our constitutional Republic. But it is this Court's blatant abandonment of such a principle that produces the decision today. The President relied on our settled precedent in *Johnson v. Eisentrager* (1950), when he established the prison at Guantanamo Bay for enemy aliens. Citing that case, the President's Office of Legal Counsel advised him "that the great weight of legal authority indicates that a federal district court could not properly exercise habeas jurisdiction over an alien detained at [Guantánamo Bay]." . . . Had the law been otherwise, the military surely would not have transported prisoners there, but would have kept them in Afghanistan, transferred them to another of our foreign military bases, or turned them over to allies for detention. Those other facilities might well have been worse for the detainees themselves. . . .

The Court admits that it cannot determine whether the writ historically extended to aliens held abroad, and it concedes (necessarily) that Guantanamo Bay lies outside the sovereign territory of the United States. . . . Together, these two concessions establish that . . . the Court has no basis to strike down the Military Commissions Act, and must leave undisturbed the considered judgment of the coequal branches. . . .

The Court purports to derive from our precedents a "functional" test for the extraterritorial reach of the writ, which shows that the Military Commissions Act unconstitutionally restricts the scope of habeas. That is remarkable because the most pertinent of those precedents, *Johnson v. Eisentrager*, conclusively establishes the opposite. There we were confronted with the claims of 21 Germans held at Landsberg Prison, an American military facility located in the American Zone of occupation in postwar Germany. . . . Like the petitioners here, the Germans claimed that their detentions violated the Constitution and international law, and sought a writ of habeas corpus. Writing for the Court, Justice Jackson held that American courts lacked habeas jurisdiction:

"We are cited to [*sic*] no instance where a court, in this or any other country where the writ is known, has issued it on behalf of an alien enemy who, at no relevant time and in no stage of his captivity, has been within its territorial jurisdiction. Nothing in the text of the Constitution extends such a right, nor does anything in our statutes." . . .

Eisentrager thus held—*held* beyond any doubt—that the Constitution does not ensure habeas for aliens held by the United States in areas over which our Government is not sovereign. . . . *Eisentrager* nowhere mentions a "functional" test, and the notion that it is based upon such a principle is patently false. . . . There is simply no support for the Court's assertion that constitutional rights extend to aliens held outside U.S. sovereign territory . . . and *Eisentrager* could not be clearer that the privilege of habeas corpus does not extend to aliens abroad. . . .

Putting aside the conclusive precedent of *Eisentrager*, it is clear that the original understanding of the Suspension Clause was that habeas corpus was not available to aliens abroad[.] . . . It is entirely clear that, at English common law, the writ of habeas corpus did not extend beyond the sovereign territory of the Crown. . . . What history teaches is confirmed by the nature of the limitations that the Constitution places upon suspension of the common-law writ. It can be suspended only "in Cases of Rebellion or Invasion." Art. I, § 9, cl. 2. The latter case (invasion) is plainly limited to the territory of the United States; and while it is conceivable that a rebellion could be mounted by American citizens abroad, surely the overwhelming majority of its occurrences would be domestic. If the extraterritorial scope of habeas turned on flexible, "functional" considerations, as the Court holds, why would the Constitution limit its suspension almost entirely to instances of domestic crisis? . . .

Today the Court warps our Constitution in a way that goes beyond the narrow issue of the reach of the Suspension Clause, invoking judicially brainstormed separation-of-powers principles to establish a manipulable "functional" test for the extraterritorial reach of habeas corpus[.] . . . It blatantly misdescribes important precedents, most conspicuously Justice Jackson's opinion for the Court in *Johnson v. Eisentrager.* It breaks a chain of precedent as old as the common law that prohibits judicial inquiry into detentions of aliens abroad absent statutory authorization. And, most tragically, it sets our military commanders the impossible task of proving to a civilian court, under whatever standards this Court devises in the future, that evidence supports the confinement of each and every enemy prisoner.

The Nation will live to regret what the Court has done today. I dissent.

FEDERALISM AND
ENUMERATED POWERS

*O*ne of the enduring areas of constitutional controversy in the nation's history has been the scope of the national government's enumerated powers. Several important recent cases have revisited this perennial issue. In *United States v. Lopez* (1995), the Court, for the first time since 1937, struck down, by vote of 5–4, a federal statute, the Gun-Free School Zones Act, as exceeding Congress's power to regulate interstate commerce. The majority opinion in *Lopez* collected and distilled prior decisions defining and limiting the scope of that power.

In an important decision concerning the scope of national legislative power, a divided Court, in *National Federation of Independent Business v. Sebelius* (2012), upheld the "individual mandate" provision of the Patient Protection and Affordable Care Act of 2010 as an exercise of Congress's taxing power but not as an exercise of Congress's power to regulate commerce. A 5–4 majority held that the law's requirement that all individuals purchase health insurance exceeded Congress's powers under the Commerce and Necessary and Proper Clauses. A different 5–4 majority, however, held that the mandate could be sustained under Congress's power to impose taxes. Chief Justice Roberts was the only justice in both majorities. His opinion was not, in all respects, joined by a majority, but it stated the controlling rationale on all points. The Court also held, 7–2, that the law's provisions conditioning all federal Medicaid funding to states on state enactment of certain laws exceeded Congress's spending power.

✪

United States v. Lopez
514 U.S. 549 (1995)

•

CHIEF JUSTICE REHNQUIST DELIVERED THE OPINION OF THE COURT.

In the Gun-Free School Zones Act of 1990, Congress made it a federal offense "for any individual knowingly to possess a firearm at a place that the individual knows, or has reasonable cause to believe, is a school zone." . . . The Act neither regulates a commercial activity nor contains a requirement that the possession be connected in any way to interstate commerce. We hold that the Act exceeds the authority of Congress "[t]o regulate Commerce . . . among the several States. . . ." U.S. Const., Art. I, § 8, cl. 3.

. . . We start with first principles. The Constitution creates a Federal Government of enumerated powers. As James Madison wrote: "The powers delegated by the proposed Constitution to the federal government are few and defined. Those which are to remain in the State governments are numerous and indefinite." The Federalist No. 45. . . . The Constitution delegates to Congress the power "[t]o regulate Commerce with foreign Nations, and among the several States, and with the Indian Tribes." Art. I, § 8, cl. 3. The Court, through Chief Justice Marshall, first defined the nature of Congress' commerce power in *Gibbons v. Ogden* (1824):

"Commerce, undoubtedly, is traffic, but it is something more: it is intercourse. It describes the commercial intercourse between nations, and parts of nations, in all its branches, and is regulated by prescribing rules for carrying on that intercourse."

The commerce power "is the power to regulate; that is, to prescribe the rule by which commerce is to be governed. This power, like all others vested in congress, is complete in itself, may be exercised to its utmost extent, and acknowledges no limitations, other than are prescribed in the constitution." The *Gibbons* Court, however, acknowledged that limitations on the commerce power are inherent in the very language of the Commerce Clause.

> It is not intended to say that these words comprehend that commerce, which is completely internal, which is carried on between man and man in a State, or between different parts of the same State, and which does not extend to or affect other States. Such a power would be inconvenient, and is certainly unnecessary.
>
> Comprehensive as the word 'among' is, it may very properly be restricted to that commerce which concerns more States than one. . . . The enumeration presupposes something not enumerated; and that something, if we regard the language, or the subject of the sentence, must be the exclusively internal commerce of a State.

. . . [W]e have identified three broad categories of activity that Congress may regulate under its commerce power. . . . First, Congress may regulate the use of the channels of interstate commerce. . . . Second, Congress is empowered to regulate and protect the instrumentalities of interstate commerce, or persons or things in interstate commerce, even though the threat may come only from intrastate activities. . . . Finally, Congress' commerce authority includes the power to regulate those activities having a substantial relation to interstate commerce, i.e., those activities that substantially affect interstate commerce. . . .

We now turn to consider the power of Congress, in the light of this framework, to enact § 922(q). The first two categories of authority may be quickly disposed of: § 922(q) is not a regulation of the use of the channels of interstate commerce, nor is it an attempt to prohibit the interstate transportation of a commodity through the channels of commerce; nor can § 922(q) be justified as a regulation by which Congress has sought to protect an instrumentality of interstate commerce or a thing in interstate commerce. Thus, if § 922(q) is to be sustained, it must be under the third category as a regulation of an activity that substantially affects interstate commerce.

. . . [W]e have upheld a wide variety of congressional Acts regulating intrastate economic activity where we have concluded that the activity substantially affected interstate commerce. Examples include the regulation of intrastate coal mining, intrastate extortionate credit transactions, restaurants utilizing substantial interstate supplies, inns and hotels catering to interstate guests, and production and consumption of homegrown wheat [citing *Wickard v. Filburn*, p. 219]. These examples are by no means exhaustive, but the pattern is clear. Where economic activity substantially affects interstate commerce, legislation regulating that activity will be sustained. Even *Wickard*, which is perhaps the most far-reaching example of Commerce Clause authority over intrastate activity, involved economic activity in a way that the possession of a gun in a school zone does not. . . .

Section 922(q) is a criminal statute that by its terms has nothing to do with "commerce" or any sort of economic enterprise, however broadly one might define those terms. Section 922(q) is not an essential part of a larger regulation of economic activity, in which the regulatory scheme could be undercut unless the intrastate activity were regulated. It cannot, therefore, be sustained under our cases upholding regulations of activities that arise out of or are connected with a commercial transaction, which viewed in the aggregate, substantially affects interstate commerce. . . .

The Government's essential contention, *in fine*, is that we may determine here that § 922(q) is valid because possession of a firearm in a local school zone does indeed substantially affect interstate commerce. The Government argues that possession of a firearm in a school zone may result in violent crime and that violent crime can be expected to affect the functioning of the national economy in two ways. First, the costs of violent crime are substantial, and, through the mechanism of insurance, those costs are spread throughout the population. Second, violent crime reduces the willingness of individuals to travel to areas within the country that are perceived to be unsafe. The Government also argues that the presence of guns in schools poses a substantial threat to the educational process by threatening the learning environment. A handicapped educational process, in turn, will result in a less productive citizenry. That, in turn, would have an adverse effect on the Nation's economic well-being. As a result, the Government argues that Congress could rationally have concluded that § 922(q) substantially affects interstate commerce.

We pause to consider the implications of the Government's arguments. The Government admits, under its "costs of crime" reasoning, that Congress could regulate not only all violent crime, but all activities that might lead to violent crime, regardless of how tenuously they relate to interstate commerce. Similarly, under the Government's "national productivity" reasoning, Congress could regulate any activity that it found was related to the economic productivity of individual citizens: family law (including marriage, divorce, and child custody), for example. Under the theories that the Government presents in support of § 922(q), it is difficult to perceive any limitation on federal power, even in areas such as criminal law enforcement or education where States historically have been sovereign. Thus, if we were to accept the Government's arguments, we are hard pressed to posit any activity by an individual that Congress is without power to regulate.

. . . The possession of a gun in a local school zone is in no sense an economic activity that might, through repetition elsewhere, substantially affect any sort of interstate commerce. Respondent was a local student at a local school; there is no indication that he had recently moved in interstate commerce, and there is no requirement that his possession of the firearm have any concrete tie to interstate commerce.

To uphold the Government's contentions here, we would have to pile inference upon inference in a manner that would bid fair to convert congressional authority under the Commerce Clause to a general police power of the sort retained by the States. Admittedly, some of our prior cases have taken long steps down that road, giving great deference to congressional action. The broad language in these opinions has suggested the possibility of additional expansion, but we decline here to proceed any further. To do so would require us to conclude that the Constitution's enumeration of powers does not presuppose something not enumerated, cf. *Gibbons v. Ogden*, and that there never will be a distinction between what is truly national and what is truly local, cf. *Jones & Laughlin Steel*. This we are unwilling to do. . . .

JUSTICE KENNEDY, WITH WHOM JUSTICE O'CONNOR JOINS, CONCURRING.

The history of the judicial struggle to interpret the Commerce Clause during the transition from the economic system the Founders knew to the single, national market still emergent in our own era counsels great restraint before the Court determines that the Clause is insufficient to support an exercise of the national power. That history gives me some pause about today's decision, but I join the Court's opinion with these observations on what I conceive to be its necessary though limited holding.

Chief Justice Marshall announced that the national authority reaches "that commerce which concerns more States than one" and that the commerce power "is complete in itself, may be exercised to its utmost extent, and acknowledges no limitations, other than are prescribed in the constitution." *Gibbons v. Ogden.* His statements can be understood now as an early and authoritative recognition that the Commerce Clause grants Congress extensive power and ample discretion to determine its appropriate exercise. The progression of our Commerce Clause cases from *Gibbons* to the present was not marked, however, by a coherent or consistent course of interpretation. . . . Furthermore, for almost a century after the adoption of the Constitution, the Court's Commerce Clause decisions did not concern the authority of Congress to legislate. Rather, the Court faced the related but quite distinct question of the authority of the States to regulate matters that would be within the commerce power had Congress chosen to act. The simple fact was that in the early years of the Republic, Congress seldom perceived the necessity to exercise its power in circumstances where its authority would be called into question. The Court's initial task, therefore, was to elaborate the theories that would permit the States to act where Congress had not done so. Not the least part of the problem was the unresolved question whether the congressional power was exclusive, a question reserved by Chief Justice Marshall in *Gibbons v. Ogden*[.] . . .

The case that seems to mark the Court's definitive commitment to the practical conception of the commerce power is *NLRB v. Jones & Laughlin Steel Corp.* (1937), where the Court sustained labor laws that applied to manufacturing facilities[.] . . .

The history of our Commerce Clause decisions contains at least two lessons of relevance to this case. The first, as stated at the outset, is the imprecision of content-based boundaries used without more to define the limits of the Commerce Clause. The second, related to the first but of even greater consequence, is that the Court as an institution and the legal system as a whole have an immense stake in the stability of our Commerce Clause jurisprudence as it has evolved to this point. *Stare decisis* operates with great force in counseling us not to call in question the essential principles now in place respecting the congressional power to regulate transactions of a commercial nature. That fundamental restraint on our power forecloses us from reverting to an understanding of commerce that would serve only an 18th-century economy, dependent then upon production and trading practices that had changed but little over the preceding centuries; it also mandates against returning to the time when congressional authority to regulate undoubted commercial activities was limited by a judicial determination that those matters had an insufficient connection to an interstate system. Congress can regulate in the commercial sphere on the assumption that we have a single market and a unified purpose to build a stable national economy. . . .

JUSTICE THOMAS, CONCURRING.

The Court today properly concludes that the Commerce Clause does not grant Congress the authority to prohibit gun possession within 1,000 feet of a school, as it attempted to do in the Gun-Free School Zones Act of 1990. Although I join the majority, I write separately to observe that our case law has drifted far from the original understanding of the Commerce Clause. In a future case, we ought to temper our Commerce Clause jurisprudence in a manner that both makes sense of our more recent case law and is more faithful to the original understanding of that Clause.

We have said that Congress may regulate not only "Commerce . . . among the several States," U.S. Const., Art. I, § 8, cl. 3, but also anything that has a "substantial effect" on such commerce. This test, if taken to its logical extreme, would give Congress a "police power" over all aspects of American life. Unfortunately, we have never come to grips with this implication of our substantial effects formula. Although we have supposedly applied the substantial effects test for the past 60 years, we *always* have rejected readings of the Commerce Clause and the scope of federal power that would permit Congress to exercise a police power; our cases are quite clear that there are real limits to federal power. . . . In an appropriate case, I believe that we must further reconsider our "substantial effects" test with an eye toward constructing a standard that reflects the text and history of the Commerce Clause without totally rejecting our more recent Commerce Clause jurisprudence. . . .

JUSTICE BREYER, WITH WHOM JUSTICE STEVENS, JUSTICE SOUTER, AND JUSTICE GINSBURG JOIN, DISSENTING.

The issue in this case is whether the Commerce Clause authorizes Congress to enact a statute that makes it a crime to possess a gun in, or near, a school. In my view, the statute falls well within the scope of the commerce power as this Court has understood that power over the last half century.

In reaching this conclusion, I apply three basic principles of Commerce Clause interpretation. First, the power to "regulate Commerce . . . among the several States," U.S. Const., Art. I, § 8, cl. 3, encompasses the power to regulate local activities insofar as they significantly affect interstate commerce. . . . Second, in determining whether a local activity will likely have a significant effect upon interstate commerce, a court must consider, not the effect of an individual act (a single instance of gun possession), but rather the cumulative effect of all similar instances (i.e., the effect of all guns possessed in or near schools). . . . Third, the Constitution requires us to judge the connection between a regulated activity and interstate commerce, not directly, but at one remove. Courts must give Congress a degree of leeway in determining the existence of a significant factual connection between the regulated activity and interstate commerce—both because the Constitution delegates the commerce power directly to Congress and because the determination requires an empirical judgment of a kind that a legislature is more likely than a court to make with accuracy. The traditional words "rational basis" capture this leeway. . . .

Applying these principles to the case at hand, we must ask whether Congress could have had a *rational basis* for finding a significant (or substantial) connection between gun-related school violence and interstate commerce. . . . Numerous reports and studies—generated both inside and outside government—make clear that Congress could reasonably have found the empirical connection that its law, implicitly or explicitly, asserts. . . . Congress could therefore have found a substantial educational problem—teachers unable to teach, students unable to learn— and concluded that guns near schools contribute substantially to the size and scope of that problem.

Having found that guns in schools significantly undermine the quality of education in our Nation's classrooms, Congress could also have found, given the effect of education upon interstate and foreign commerce, that gun-related violence in and around schools is a commercial, as well as a human, problem. Education, although far more than a matter of economics, has long been inextricably intertwined with the Nation's economy. . . .

National Federation of Independent Business v. Sebelius
457 U.S. ___ (2012)

•

CHIEF JUSTICE ROBERTS ANNOUNCED THE JUDGMENT OF THE COURT . . .

Today we resolve constitutional challenges to two provisions of the Patient Protection and Affordable Care Act of 2010: the individual mandate, which requires individuals to purchase a health insurance policy providing a minimum level of coverage; and the Medicaid expansion, which gives funds to the States on the condition that they provide specified health care to all citizens whose income falls below a certain threshold. . . .

In our federal system, the National Government possesses only limited powers; the States and the people retain the remainder. Nearly two centuries ago, Chief Justice Marshall observed that "the question respecting the extent of the powers actually granted" to the Federal Government "is perpetually arising, and will probably continue to arise, as long as our system shall exist." *McCulloch v. Maryland* (1819). . . . The Federal Government "is acknowledged by all to be one of enumerated powers." *Ibid.* The enumeration of powers is also a limitation of powers, because "[t]he enumeration presupposes something not enumerated." *Gibbons v. Ogden* (1824). The Constitution's express conferral of some powers makes clear that it does not grant others. . . .

Today, the restrictions on government power foremost in many Americans' minds are likely to be affirmative prohibitions, such as contained in the Bill of Rights. These affirmative prohibitions come into play, however, only where the Government possesses authority to act in the first place. If no enumerated power authorizes Congress to pass a certain law, that law may not be enacted, even if it would not violate any of the express prohibitions in the Bill of Rights or elsewhere in the Constitution.

Indeed, the Constitution did not initially include a Bill of Rights at least partly because the Framers felt the enumeration of powers sufficed to restrain the Government. As Alexander Hamilton put it, "the Constitution is itself, in every rational sense, and to every useful purpose, A BILL OF RIGHTS." The Federalist No. 84. And when the Bill of Rights was ratified, it made express what the enumeration of powers necessarily implied: "The powers not delegated to the United States by the Constitution . . . are reserved to the States respectively, or to the people." U. S. Const., Amdt. 10. The Federal Government has expanded dramatically over the past two centuries, but it still must show that a constitutional grant of power authorizes each of its actions.

The same does not apply to the States, because the Constitution is not the source of their power. The Constitution may restrict state governments—as it does, for example, by forbidding them to deny any person the equal protection of the laws. But where such prohibitions do not apply, state governments do not need constitutional authorization to act. The States thus can and do perform many of the vital functions of modern government—punishing street crime, running public schools, and zoning property for development, to name but a few—even though the Constitution's text does not authorize any government to do so. Our cases refer to this general power of governing, possessed by the States but not by the Federal Government, as the "police power." . . .

This case concerns two powers that the Constitution does grant the Federal Government, but which must be read carefully to avoid creating a general federal authority akin to the police power. The Constitution authorizes Congress to "regulate Commerce with foreign Nations, and among the several States, and with the Indian Tribes." Art. I, §8, cl. 3. Our precedents read that to mean that Congress may regulate "the channels of interstate commerce," "persons or things in interstate commerce," and "those activities that substantially affect interstate commerce." *United States v. Morrison* (2000). The power over activities that substantially affect interstate commerce can be expansive. That power has been held to authorize federal regulation of such seemingly local matters as a farmer's decision to grow wheat for himself and his livestock, and a loan shark's extortionate collections from a neighborhood butcher shop. See *Wickard v. Filburn* (1942); *Perez v. United States* (1971).

Congress may also "lay and collect Taxes, Duties, Imposts and Excises, to pay the Debts and provide for the common Defence and general Welfare of the United States." U.S. Const., Art. I, §8, cl. 1. Put simply, Congress may tax and spend. This grant gives the Federal Government considerable influence even in areas where it cannot directly regulate. The Federal Government may enact a tax on an activity that it cannot authorize, forbid, or otherwise control. See, e.g., *License Tax Cases* (1867). And in exercising its spending power, Congress may offer funds to the States, and may condition those offers on compliance with specified conditions. These offers may well induce the States to adopt policies that the Federal Government itself could not impose. See, e.g., *South Dakota v. Dole* (1987) (conditioning federal highway funds on States raising their drinking age to 21).

The reach of the Federal Government's enumerated powers is broader still because the Constitution authorizes Congress to "make all Laws which shall be necessary and proper for carrying into Execution the foregoing Powers." Art. I, §8, cl. 18. We have long read this provision to give Congress great latitude in exercising its powers: "Let the end be legitimate, let it be within the scope of the constitution, and all means which are appropriate, which are plainly adapted to that end, which are not prohibited, but consist with the letter and spirit of the constitution, are constitutional." *McCulloch.*

Our permissive reading of these powers is explained in part by a general reticence to invalidate the acts of the Nation's elected leaders. . . . Members of this Court are vested with the authority to interpret the law; we possess neither the expertise nor the prerogative to make policy judgments. Those decisions are entrusted to our Nation's elected leaders, who can be thrown out of office if the people disagree with them. It is not our job to protect the people from the consequences of their political choices.

Our deference in matters of policy cannot, however, become abdication in matters of law. "The powers of the legislature are defined and limited; and that those limits may not be mistaken, or forgotten, the constitution is written." *Marbury v. Madison* (1803). Our respect for Congress's policy judgments thus can never extend so far as to disavow restraints on federal power that the Constitution carefully constructed.

. . . And there can be no question that it is the responsibility of this Court to enforce the limits on federal power by striking down acts of Congress that transgress those limits. *Marbury v. Madison.* . . .

The individual mandate requires most Americans to maintain "minimum essential" health insurance coverage. . . . Beginning in 2014, those who do not comply with the mandate must make a "[s]hared responsibility payment" to the Federal Government. That payment, which the Act describes as a "penalty," is calculated as a percentage of household income, subject to a floor based on a specified dollar amount and a ceiling based on the average annual premium the individual would have to pay for qualifying private health insurance. §5000A(c). The Act provides that the penalty will be paid to the Internal Revenue Service with an individual's taxes, and "shall be assessed and collected in the same manner" as tax penalties, such as the penalty for claiming too large an income tax refund. . . .

The Government advances two theories for the proposition that Congress had constitutional authority to enact the individual mandate. First, the Government argues that Congress had the power to enact the mandate under the Commerce Clause. Under that theory, Congress may order individuals to buy health insurance because the failure to do so affects interstate commerce, and could undercut the Affordable Care Act's other reforms. Second, the Government argues that if the commerce power does not support the mandate, we should nonetheless uphold it as an exercise of Congress's power to tax. According to the Government, even if Congress lacks the power to direct individuals to buy insurance, the only effect of the individual mandate is to raise taxes on those who do not do so, and thus the law may be upheld as a tax.

The Government's first argument is that the individual mandate is a valid exercise of Congress's power under the Commerce Clause and the Necessary and Proper Clause. According to the Government, the health care market is characterized by a significant cost-shifting problem. Everyone will eventually need health care at a time and to an extent they cannot predict, but if they do not have insurance, they often will not be able to pay for it. Because state and federal laws nonetheless require hospitals to provide a certain degree of care to individuals without regard to their ability to pay, hospitals end up receiving compensation for only a portion of the services they provide. To recoup the losses, hospitals pass on the cost to insurers through higher rates, and insurers, in turn, pass on the cost to policy holders in the form of higher premiums. . . .

The individual mandate was Congress's solution to these problems. By requiring that individuals purchase health insurance, the mandate prevents cost-shifting by those who would otherwise go without it. In addition, the mandate forces into the insurance risk pool more healthy individuals, whose premiums on average will be higher than their health care expenses. This allows insurers to subsidize the costs of covering the unhealthy individuals the reforms require them to accept. The Government claims that Congress has power under the Commerce and Necessary and Proper Clauses to enact this solution.

. . . The path of our Commerce Clause decisions has not always run smooth, but it is now well established that Congress has broad authority under the Clause. We have recognized, for example, that "[t]he power of Congress over interstate commerce is not confined to the regulation of commerce among the states," but extends to activities that "have a substantial effect on interstate commerce." *United States v. Darby* (1941). Congress's power, moreover, is not limited to regulation of an activity that by itself substantially affects interstate commerce, but also extends to activities that do so only when aggregated with similar activities of others. See *Wickard*.

Given its expansive scope, it is no surprise that Congress has employed the commerce power in a wide variety of ways to address the pressing needs of the time. But Congress has never attempted to rely on that power to compel individuals not engaged in commerce to purchase an unwanted product. . . .

The Constitution grants Congress the power to "*regulate* Commerce." . . . The power to *regulate* commerce presupposes the existence of commercial activity to be regulated. If the power to "regulate" something included the power to create it, many of the provisions in the Constitution would be superfluous. For example, the Constitution gives Congress the power to "coin Money," in addition to the power to "regulate the Value thereof." . . . Our precedent also reflects this understanding. As expansive as our cases construing the scope of the commerce power have been, they all have one thing in common: They uniformly describe the power as reaching "activity." . . .

The individual mandate, however, does not regulate existing commercial activity. It instead compels individuals to *become* active in commerce by purchasing a product, on the ground that their failure to do so affects interstate commerce. Construing the Commerce Clause to permit Congress to regulate individuals precisely *because* they are doing nothing would open a new and potentially vast domain to congressional authority. Every day individuals do not do an infinite number of things. In some cases they decide not to do something; in others they simply fail to do it. Allowing Congress to justify federal regulation by pointing to the effect of inaction on commerce would bring countless decisions an individual could *potentially* make within the scope of federal regulation, and—under the Government's theory—empower Congress to make those decisions for him. . . .

Indeed, the Government's logic would justify a mandatory purchase to solve almost any problem. . . . To consider a different example in the health care market, many Americans do not eat a balanced diet. That group makes up a larger percentage of the total population than those without health insurance. The failure of that group to have a healthy diet increases health care costs, to a greater extent than the failure of the uninsured to purchase insurance. Those increased costs are borne in part by other Americans who must pay more, just as the uninsured shift costs to the insured. . . . Under the Government's theory, Congress could address the diet problem by ordering everyone to buy vegetables.

People, for reasons of their own, often fail to do things that would be good for them or good for society. Those failures—joined with the similar failures of others—can readily have a substantial effect on interstate commerce. Under the Government's logic, that authorizes Congress to use its commerce power to compel citizens to act as the Government would have them act.

That is not the country the Framers of our Constitution envisioned. . . . Congress already enjoys vast power to regulate much of what we do. Accepting the Government's theory would give Congress the same license to regulate what we do not do, fundamentally changing the relation between the citizen and the Federal Government.

To an economist, perhaps, there is no difference between activity and inactivity; both have measurable economic effects on commerce. But the distinction between doing something and doing nothing would not have been lost on the Framers, who were "practical statesmen," not metaphysical philosophers. . . . The Framers gave Congress the power to *regulate* commerce, not to *compel* it, and for over 200 years both our decisions and Congress's actions have reflected this understanding. There is no reason to depart from that understanding now. . . .

The Government regards it as sufficient to trigger Congress's authority that almost all those who are uninsured will, at some unknown point in the future, engage in a health care transaction. . . . The proposition that Congress may dictate the conduct of an individual today because of prophesied future activity finds no support in our precedent. We have said that Congress can anticipate the *effects* on commerce of an economic activity. But we have never permitted Congress to anticipate that activity itself in order to regulate individuals not currently engaged in commerce. . . .

Everyone will likely participate in the markets for food, clothing, transportation, shelter, or energy; that does not authorize Congress to direct them to purchase particular products in those or other markets today. The Commerce Clause is not a general license to regulate an individual from cradle to grave, simply because he will predictably engage in particular transactions. Any police power to regulate individuals as such, as opposed to their activities, remains vested in the States.

The Government next contends that Congress has the power under the Necessary and Proper Clause to enact the individual mandate because the mandate is an "integral part of a comprehensive scheme of economic regulation . . .

Under this argument, it is not necessary to consider the effect that an individual's inactivity may have on interstate commerce; it is enough that Congress regulate commercial activity in a way that requires regulation of inactivity to be effective.

The power to "make all Laws which shall be necessary and proper for carrying into Execution" the powers enumerated in the Constitution, Art. I, §8, cl. 18, vests Congress with authority to enact provisions "incidental to the [enumerated] power, and conducive to its beneficial exercise," *McCulloch*. Although the Clause gives Congress authority to "legislate on that vast mass of incidental powers which must be involved in the constitution," it does not license the exercise of any "great substantive and independent power[s]" beyond those specifically enumerated. Instead, the Clause is "'merely a declaration, for the removal of all uncertainty, that the means of carrying into execution those [powers] otherwise granted are included in the grant.'" *Kinsella v. United States ex rel. Singleton* (1960) (quoting . . . James Madison . . .).

As our jurisprudence under the Necessary and Proper Clause has developed, we have been very deferential to Congress's determination that a regulation is "necessary." . . . But we have also carried out our responsibility to declare unconstitutional those laws that undermine the structure of government established by the Constitution. . . .

[T]he individual mandate cannot be sustained under the Necessary and Proper Clause as an essential component of the insurance reforms. Each of our prior cases upholding laws under that Clause involved exercises of authority derivative of, and in service to, a granted power. The individual mandate, by contrast, vests Congress with the extraordinary ability to create the necessary predicate to the exercise of an enumerated power. . . . [S]uch a conception of the Necessary and Proper Clause would work a substantial expansion of federal authority. No longer would Congress be limited to regulating under the Commerce Clause those who by some preexisting activity bring themselves within the sphere of federal regulation. Instead, Congress could reach beyond the natural limit of its authority and draw within its regulatory scope those who otherwise would be outside of it. Even if the individual mandate is "necessary" to the Act's insurance reforms, such an expansion of federal power is not a "proper" means for making those reforms effective.

. . .

That is not the end of the matter. Because the Commerce Clause does not support the individual mandate, it is necessary to turn to the Government's second argument: that the mandate may be upheld as within Congress's enumerated power to "lay and collect Taxes." Art. I, §8, cl. 1.

. . . The most straightforward reading of the mandate is that it commands individuals to purchase insurance. After all, it states that individuals "shall" maintain health insurance. Congress thought it could enact such a command under the Commerce Clause, and the Government primarily defended the law on that basis. But, for the reasons explained above, the Commerce Clause does not give Congress that power. Under our precedent, it is therefore necessary to ask whether the Government's alternative reading of the statute—that it only imposes a tax on those without insurance—is a reasonable one. . . .

It is of course true that the Act describes the payment as a "penalty," not a "tax." But . . . that label . . . does not determine whether the payment may be viewed as an exercise of Congress's taxing power. . . . We have . . . held that exactions not labeled taxes nonetheless were authorized by Congress's power to tax. In the *License Tax Cases* [1867], for example, we held that federal licenses to sell liquor and lottery tickets—for which the licensee had to pay a fee—could be sustained as exercises of the taxing power. And in *New York v. United States* [1992] we upheld as a tax a "surcharge" on out-of-state nuclear waste shipments, a portion of which was paid to the Federal Treasury. We thus ask whether the shared responsibility payment falls within Congress's taxing power, "[d]isregarding the designation of the exaction, and viewing its substance and application." *United States v. Constantine* (1935); cf. *Quill Corp. v. North Dakota* (1992) ("[M]agic words or labels" should not "disable an otherwise constitutional levy"). . . .

[T]he shared responsibility payment may for constitutional purposes be considered a tax, not a penalty: First, for most Americans the amount due will be far less than the price of insurance, and, by statute, it can never be more. It may often be a reasonable financial decision to make the payment rather than purchase insurance, unlike the "prohibitory" financial punishment in [*Bailey v. Drexel Furniture* (1922)]. Second, the individual mandate contains no scienter requirement. Third, the payment is collected solely by the IRS through the normal means of taxation—except that the Service is *not* allowed to use those means most suggestive of a punitive sanction, such as criminal prosecution. The reasons the Court in *Drexel Furniture* held that what was called a "tax" there was a penalty support the conclusion that what is called a "penalty" here may be viewed as a tax.

None of this is to say that the payment is not intended to affect individual conduct. Although the payment will raise considerable revenue, it is plainly designed to expand health insurance coverage. But taxes that seek to influence conduct are nothing new. Some of our earliest federal taxes sought to deter the purchase of imported manufactured goods in order to foster the growth of domestic industry. Today, federal and state taxes can compose more than half the retail price of cigarettes, not just to raise more money, but to encourage people to quit smoking. And we have upheld such obviously regulatory measures as taxes on selling marijuana and sawed-off shotguns. . . . That §5000A seeks to shape decisions about whether to buy health insurance does not mean that it cannot be a valid exercise of the taxing power. . . .

There may, however, be a more fundamental objection to a tax on those who lack health insurance. Even if only a tax, the payment under

§5000A(b) remains a burden that the Federal Government imposes for an omission, not an act. If it is troubling to interpret the Commerce Clause as authorizing Congress to regulate those who abstain from commerce, perhaps it should be similarly troubling to permit Congress to impose a tax for not doing something.

Three considerations allay this concern. First, and most importantly, it is abundantly clear the Constitution does not guarantee that individuals may avoid taxation through inactivity. A capitation, after all, is a tax that everyone must pay simply for existing, and capitations are expressly contemplated by the Constitution. The Court today holds that our Constitution protects us from federal regulation under the Commerce Clause so long as we abstain from the regulated activity. But from its creation, the Constitution has made no such promise with respect to taxes. See Letter from Benjamin Franklin to M. Le Roy (Nov. 13, 1789) ("Our new Constitution is now established . . . but in this world nothing can be said to be certain, except death and taxes"). . . .

Second, Congress's ability to use its taxing power to influence conduct is not without limits. . . . Because the tax at hand is within even those strict limits, we need not here decide the precise point at which an exaction becomes so punitive that the taxing power does not authorize it. . . .

Third, although the breadth of Congress's power to tax is greater than its power to regulate commerce, the taxing power does not give Congress the same degree of control over individual behavior. . . . Congress's authority under the taxing power is limited to requiring an individual to pay money into the Federal Treasury, no more.

The States also contend that the Medicaid expansion exceeds Congress's authority under the Spending Clause. They claim that Congress is coercing the States to adopt the changes it wants by threatening to withhold all of a State's Medicaid grants, unless the State accepts the new expanded funding and complies with the conditions that come with it. This, they argue, violates the basic principle that the "Federal Government may not compel the States to enact or administer a federal regulatory program" [*New York v. United States* (1992)]. . . .

The Spending Clause grants Congress the power "to pay the Debts and provide for the . . . general Welfare of the United States." U. S. Const., Art. I, §8, cl. 1. We have long recognized that Congress may use this power to grant federal funds to the States, and may condition such a grant upon the States' "taking certain actions that Congress could not require them to take." . . . The conditions imposed by Congress ensure that the funds are used by the States to "provide for the . . . general Welfare" in the manner Congress intended.

At the same time, our cases have recognized limits on Congress's power under the Spending Clause to secure state compliance with federal objectives. . . . "[T]he Constitution has never been understood to confer upon Congress the ability to require the States to govern according to Congress' instructions." *New York*. . . . That insight . . . has led us to scrutinize Spending Clause legislation to ensure that Congress is not using financial inducements to exert a "power akin to undue influence." *Steward Machine Co. v. Davis* (1937). Congress may use its spending power to create incentives for States to act in accordance with federal policies. But when "pressure turns into compulsion," *ibid.*, the legislation runs contrary to our system of federalism. "[T]he Constitution simply does not give Congress the authority to require the States to regulate." *New York*. That is true whether Congress directly commands a State to regulate or indirectly coerces a State to adopt a federal regulatory system as its own. . . .

The States . . . argue that . . . Congress has "crossed the line distinguishing encouragement from coercion," *New York*, in the way it has structured the funding: Instead of simply refusing to grant the new funds to States that will not accept the new conditions, Congress has also threatened to withhold those States' existing Medicaid funds. The States claim that this threat serves no purpose other than to force unwilling States to sign up for the dramatic expansion in health care coverage effected by the Act.

Given the nature of the threat and the programs at issue here, we must agree. We have upheld Congress's authority to condition the receipt of funds on the States' complying with restrictions on the use of those funds, because that is the means by which Congress ensures that the funds are spent according to its view of the "general Welfare." Conditions that do not here govern the use of the funds, however, cannot be justified on that basis. When, for example, such conditions take the form of threats to terminate other significant independent grants, the conditions are properly viewed as a means of pressuring the States to accept policy changes. . . .

In this case, the financial "inducement" Congress has chosen is much more than "relatively mild encouragement"—it is a gun to the head. . . . A State that opts out of the Affordable Care Act's expansion in health care coverage . . . stands to lose not merely "a relatively small percentage" of its existing Medicaid funding, but *all* of it. Medicaid spending accounts for over 20 percent of the average State's total budget, with federal funds covering 50 to 83 percent of those costs. . . . The threatened loss of over 10 percent of a State's overall budget . . . is economic dragooning that leaves the States with no real option but to acquiesce in the Medicaid expansion. . . .

The question remains whether today's holding affects other provisions of the Affordable Care Act. In considering that question, "[w]e seek to determine what Congress would have intended in light of the Court's constitutional holding." *United States v. Booker* (2005). . . . We are confident that Congress would have wanted to preserve the rest of the Act. . . .

JUSTICE GINSBURG, CONCURRING IN THE JUDGMENT IN PART, AND DISSENTING IN PART.

I agree . . . that the minimum coverage provision is a proper exercise of Congress' taxing power. . . . Unlike THE CHIEF JUSTICE, however, I would hold, alternatively, that the Commerce Clause authorizes Congress to enact the minimum coverage provision. . . .

Rather than evaluating the constitutionality of the minimum coverage provision in the manner established by our precedents, THE CHIEF JUSTICE relies on a newly minted constitutional doctrine. The commerce power does not, THE CHIEF JUSTICE announces, permit Congress to "compe[l] individuals to become active in commerce by purchasing a product."

THE CHIEF JUSTICE's novel constraint on Congress' commerce power gains no force from our precedent and for that reason alone warrants disapprobation. But even assuming, for the moment, that Congress lacks authority under the Commerce Clause to "compel individuals not engaged in commerce to purchase an unwanted product," such a limitation would be inapplicable here. Everyone will, at some point, consume health-care products and services. Thus, if THE CHIEF JUSTICE is correct that an insurance purchase requirement can be applied only to those who "actively" consume health care, the minimum coverage provision fits the bill. . . .

If unwanted today, medical service secured by insurance may be desperately needed tomorrow. Virtually everyone, I reiterate, consumes health care at some point in his or her life. Health insurance is a means of paying for this care, nothing more. In requiring individuals to obtain insurance, Congress is therefore not mandating the purchase of a discrete, unwanted product. Rather, Congress is merely defining the terms on which individuals pay for an interstate good they consume: Persons subject to the mandate must now pay for medical care in advance (instead of at the point of service) and through insurance (instead of out of pocket). Establishing payment terms for goods in or affecting interstate commerce is quintessential economic regulation well within Congress' domain. . . .

For the reasons explained above, the minimum coverage provision is valid Commerce Clause legislation. When viewed as a component of the entire ACA, the provision's constitutionality becomes even plainer.

The Necessary and Proper Clause "empowers Congress to enact laws in effectuation of its [commerce] powe[r] that are not within its authority to enact in isolation." [*Gonzales v.*] *Raich* (SCALIA, J., concurring in judgment). . . . Recall that one of Congress' goals in enacting the Affordable Care Act was to eliminate the insurance industry's practice of charging higher prices or denying coverage to individuals with preexisting medical conditions. The commerce power allows Congress to ban this practice, a point no one disputes.

Congress knew, however, that simply barring insurance companies from relying on an applicant's medical history would not work in practice. Without the individual mandate, Congress learned, guaranteed-issue and community-rating requirements would trigger an adverse-selection death-spiral in the health-insurance market: Insurance premiums would skyrocket, the number of uninsured would increase, and insurance companies would exit the market. When complemented by an insurance mandate, on the other hand, guaranteed issue and community rating would work as intended, increasing access to insurance and reducing uncompensated care. The minimum coverage provision is thus an "essential par[t] of a larger regulation of economic activity"; without the provision, "the regulatory scheme [w]ould be undercut." *Raich*, 545 U. S., at 24–25 (internal quotation marks omitted). Put differently, the minimum coverage provision, together with the guaranteed-issue and community-rating requirements, is "'reasonably adapted' to the attainment of a legitimate end under the commerce power": the elimination of pricing and sales practices that take an applicant's medical history into account. . . .

JUSTICE SCALIA, JUSTICE KENNEDY, JUSTICE THOMAS, AND JUSTICE ALITO, DISSENTING.

. . . What is absolutely clear, affirmed by the text of the 1789 Constitution, by the Tenth Amendment ratified in 1791, and by innumerable cases of ours in the 220 years since, is that there are structural limits upon federal power—upon what it can prescribe with respect to private conduct, and upon what it can impose upon the sovereign States. Whatever may be the conceptual limits upon the Commerce Clause and upon the power to tax and spend, they cannot be such as will enable the Federal Government to regulate all private conduct and to compel the States to function as administrators of federal programs. . . . The Act before us here exceeds federal power both in mandating the purchase of health insurance and in denying nonconsenting States all Medicaid funding. These parts of the Act are central to its design and operation, and all the Act's other provisions would not have been enacted without them. In our view it must follow that the entire statute is inoperative.

A few respectful responses to JUSTICE GINSBURG's dissent on the issue of the Mandate are in order. That dissent duly recites the test of Commerce Clause power that our opinions have applied, but disregards the premise the test contains. It is true enough that Congress needs only a "'rational basis' for concluding that the *regulated activity* substantially affects interstate commerce." But it must be *activity* affecting commerce that is regulated, and not merely the failure to engage in commerce. And one is not now purchasing the health care covered by the insurance mandate simply because one is likely to be purchasing it in the future. . . . If all inactivity affecting commerce is commerce, commerce is everything. Ultimately the dissent is driven to saying that there is really no difference between action and inaction, a proposition that has never recommended itself, neither to the law nor to common sense. To say, for example, that the inaction here consists of activity in "the self-insurance market," *ibid.*, seems to us wordplay. By parity of reasoning the failure to buy a car can be called participation in the non-private-car-transportation market. Commerce becomes everything.

. . . The dissent treats the Constitution as though it is an enumeration of those problems that the Federal Government can address . . . The Constitution is not that. It enumerates not federally soluble *problems*, but federally available *powers*. The Federal Government can address whatever problems it wants but can bring to their solution only those powers that the Constitution confers, among which is the power to regulate commerce. . . . Article I contains no whatever-it-takes-to-solve-a-national-problem power. . . .

As far as §5000A is concerned, we would stop there. Congress has attempted to regulate beyond the scope of its Commerce Clause authority, and §5000A is therefore invalid. . . . The issue is not whether Congress had the *power* to frame the minimum-coverage provision as a tax, but whether it *did* so. . . . In this case, there is simply no way . . . to escape what Congress enacted: a mandate that individuals maintain minimum essential coverage, enforced by a penalty. . . .

[T]o say that the Individual Mandate merely imposes a tax is not to interpret the statute but to rewrite it. . . . We have no doubt that Congress knew precisely what it was doing when it rejected an earlier version of this legislation that imposed a tax instead of a requirement-with-penalty. Imposing a tax through judicial legislation inverts the constitutional scheme, and places the power to tax in the branch of government least accountable to the citizenry.

Seven Members of the Court agree that the Medicaid Expansion, as enacted by Congress, is unconstitutional. . . . Because the Medicaid Expansion is unconstitutional, the question of remedy arises. The most natural remedy would be to invalidate the Medicaid Expansion. . . . The Court today opts for permitting the cut-off of only incremental Medicaid funding. . . . The Court severs nothing, but simply revises [the statute] to read as the Court would desire. . . .

The Court today decides to save a statute Congress did not write. It rules that what the statute declares to be a requirement with a penalty is instead an option subject to a tax. And it changes the intentionally coercive sanction of a total cut-off of Medicaid funds to a supposedly noncoercive cut-off of only the incremental funds that the Act makes available. The Court regards its strained statutory interpretation as judicial modesty. It is not. It amounts instead to a vast judicial overreaching. . . .

The 101 Most Significant
Supreme Court
Interpretations of the Constitution†

1. ***Marbury v. Madison***, 5 U.S. (1 Cranch) 137 (1803): Famous Supreme Court decision first explicitly defending the propriety of "judicial review" of the constitutionality of legislative acts in cases presenting constitutional questions.
2. *Martin v. Hunter's Lessee*, 14 U.S. (1 Wheat.) 304 (1816): Important early case upholding jurisdiction of U.S. Supreme Court to review state supreme court decisions on matters of federal law.
3. ***McCulloch v. Maryland***, 17 U.S. 316 (1819): Foundational case adopting a broad view of enumerated national legislative powers, including Necessary and Proper Clause, and striking down a state law interfering with the operation of a federal statute.
4. *Cohens v. Virginia*, 19 U.S. (6 Wheat.) 264 (1821): Upheld authority of Supreme Court in cases involving federal law, even where a state was a party. Rejected Virginia's argument that state sovereignty barred federal judicial authority over such cases.

---

† Cases in bold are excerpted in the book.

5. *Gibbons v. Ogden*, 22 U.S. (9 Wheat.) 1 (1824): Important early case interpreting scope of Congress's power under the Commerce Clause and invalidating a state law that conflicted with federal regulation of commerce.

6. *Cherokee Nation v. Georgia*, 30 U.S. 1 (1831): Foundational case classifying Native American Indian tribes as "domestic dependent nations" rather than "foreign states" in their relationship to the nation and to state governments.

7. **Barron v. Baltimore**, 32 U.S. 243 (1833): Leading case holding that the provisions of the Bill of Rights limited the powers of the national government only, not those of the states. Superseded by adoption of the Fourteenth Amendment in 1868.

8. *Prigg v. Pennsylvania*, 41 U.S. 539 (1842): Landmark decision upholding the constitutionality of the federal Fugitive Slave Act of 1793. Held that national power barred state legislation on the subject of fugitive slaves and struck down Pennsylvania's prosecution of a slave-catcher for kidnapping.

9. *Luther v. Borden*, 48 U.S. 1 (1849): Held that some constitutional issues are "political questions" to be decided by Congress and the president, not the courts. At issue was the question of which group constituted the lawful government of Rhode Island, for purposes of applying Article IV's mandate that the national government guarantee each state a "Republican Form of Government."

10. **Dred Scott v. Sandford**, 60 U.S. 393 (1857): Enormously important case holding that blacks, whether slave or free, had no legal rights and could never be considered citizens. Struck down the Missouri Compromise ban on slavery in Northern federal territories as a denial of a substantive "Due Process" right to own black slaves. Overturned by the Civil War and the Thirteenth and Fourteenth Amendments.

11. The **Prize Cases**, 67 U.S. 635 (1863): Landmark Civil War decision concerning the allocation of war powers between Congress and the president. Upheld President Lincoln's blockade of Southern ports as within the president's military power as commander in chief.

12. **Ex parte Milligan**, 71 U.S. 2 (1866): Held that military commissions may not be used to try U.S citizens not affiliated with

enemy forces for treason, in Union states where civilian courts remained open.

13. *Mississippi v. Johnson*, 71 U.S. 475 (1867); *Georgia v. Stanton*, 73 U.S. 50 (1868): Historically important decisions holding that courts lacked the authority to enjoin executive branch enforcement of Reconstruction Acts.

14. *Ex parte McCardle*, 74 U.S. 506 (1868): Upheld Congress's power, under the Exceptions Clause of Article III, to remove cases from the Supreme Court's appellate jurisdiction. This decision prevented Supreme Court review of a case challenging the constitutionality of Reconstruction policies.

15. ***Slaughterhouse Cases***, 83 U.S. 36 (1873): Watershed case first interpreting the Thirteenth Amendment and the Fourteenth Amendment's Privileges or Immunities, Due Process, and Equal Protection clauses. Upheld a Louisiana law granting an exclusive franchise to operate a meat slaughterhouse business in New Orleans.

16. ***Bradwell v. Illinois***, 83 U.S. 130 (1873): Held that, under *Slaughterhouse*, an Illinois law forbidding women to be licensed attorneys did not violate Fourteenth Amendment.

17. ***Minor v. Happersett***, 88 U.S. 162 (1874): Held that the Fourteenth Amendment did not give women the right to vote. The Nineteenth Amendment granted this right in 1920.

18. ***Reynolds v. United States***, 98 U.S. 145 (1879): Leading case narrowly reading Free Exercise of Religion Clause as not permitting the exercise of such religious convictions in conflict with religion-neutral general laws. Upheld Congress's power to prohibit practice of polygamy in the territories, where engaged in as a matter of religious belief.

19. ***Strauder v. West Virginia***, 100 U.S. 303 (1880): Held that exclusion of blacks from serving on juries violates the Equal Protection Clause of Fourteenth Amendment.

20. The ***Civil Rights Cases*** (1883): Watershed decision holding that Congress's power to enforce the Fourteenth Amendment's provisions does not include authority to pass civil rights laws forbidding discrimination by private businesses in transportation, inns, and public amusement.

21. *Elk v. Wilkins*, 112 U.S. 94 (1884): Held that Native American

citizens who are members of Indian Tribes are not birthright U.S. citizens under the Fourteenth Amendment and are not entitled to the right to vote under the Fifteenth Amendment. Superseded by federal statute granting citizenship to Native Americans in 1924.

22. The Chinese Exclusion Case: *Chae Chan Ping v. United States*, 130 U.S. 581 (1889): Adopted a broad view of Congress's power over immigration, naturalization, and exclusion of aliens and affirmed that a federal statute may supersede the provisions of a treaty.

23. *Plessy v. Ferguson*, 163 U.S. 537 (1896): Held that enforced legal segregation by race does not violate the Equal Protection Clause of Fourteenth Amendment, adopting a doctrine permitting "separate but equal" facilities for different races of citizens.

24. The *Insular Cases*, 182 U.S. 1 (1901): Historically important set of cases holding that not all of the Constitution's provisions necessarily apply in all U.S. territories. Specifically, held that certain individual rights and limitations on government did not apply in territories acquired following the Spanish-American War not contemplated for admission to statehood.

25. *Giles v. Harris*, 189 U.S. 475 (1903): Held that judicial relief was unavailable to remedy alleged conspiracy to deprive blacks in Alabama of their constitutional right to vote under the Fifteenth Amendment.

26. *Lochner v. New York*, 198 U.S. 45 (1905): Employed the doctrine of substantive due process to find that the Fourteenth Amendment prohibited laws unduly interfering with liberty of contract by economic and labor regulations.

27. *Schenck v. United States*, 249 U.S. 47 (1919); **Debs v. United States**, 249 U.S. 211 (1919): *Schenck* upheld a Sedition Act conviction for the circulation of a leaflet arguing that the draft was unconstitutional and urging readers to oppose the draft. The Court held that the pamphlet's words created a "clear and present danger" of a harm Congress could lawfully prohibit. *Debs* upheld the conviction of Socialist former presidential candidate Eugene Debs for making a speech urging draft resistance, on the basis of the holding in *Schenck*.

28. *Missouri v. Holland*, 252 U.S. 416 (1920): Held that Congress possesses the legislative power to enact laws necessary and proper for executing treaties with other nations.

29. *Myers v. United States*, 272 U.S. 52 (1926): Leading case holding that the president's constitutional power to direct and control the execution of federal law entails the authority to remove subordinate executive branch officers as he thinks appropriate.

30. *Pierce v. Society of Sisters*, 268 U.S. 510 (1925): Struck down Oregon law requiring parents to send their children to public schools—rather than to private and religious schools—as a violation of rights of religious liberty and free expression embraced by the Fourteenth Amendment.

31. *Buck v. Bell*, 274 U.S. 200 (1927): Upheld the involuntary state sterilization of a young mother because of her mental impairment. Rejected Equal Protection Clause objection to adverse treatment because of disability, embracing a pro-eugenics position.

32. *Home Building & Loan Association v. Blaisdell*, 290 U.S. 398 (1934): Upheld a Depression-era state law abrogating foreclosure provisions of private mortgage contracts, rejecting a challenge, brought under the Contracts Clause, that the law impaired "the obligation of Contracts."

33. *United States v. Butler*, 297 U.S. 1 (1936): Held that the Constitution confers on Congress power to spend money for purposes beyond those authorized by its specifically enumerated powers.

34. *United States v. Curtiss-Wright Export Corp.*, 299 U.S. 304 (1936): Articulated a broad view of the president's power over foreign affairs as the sole constitutional representative of the nation.

35. **West Coast Hotel v. Parrish**, 300 U.S. 379 (1937): Landmark decision upholding a state minimum wage law for women and rejecting the substantive due process reasoning of *Lochner v. New York* (1905).

36. **National Labor Relations Board v. Jones & Laughlin Steel Corp.**, 301 U.S. 1 (1937): Landmark case upholding the National Labor Relations Act as within Congress's power under the Commerce Clause and the Necessary and Proper Clause.

37. *Erie Railroad Co. v. Tompkins*, 304 U.S. 64 (1938): Held that federal courts lacked the power to create substantive "common

law" rules of decision in cases within their diversity-of-citizen-ship jurisdiction but were bound instead by applicable state law. Overruled the longstanding contrary decision in *Swift v. Tyson*, 41 U.S. 1 (1842).

38. ***United States v. Carolene Products Co.***, 304 U.S. 144 (1938): Upheld a law prohibiting interstate shipment of certain milk products against a substantive due process challenge, rejecting *Lochner*'s approach and substituting deferential review of eco-nomic regulations. Includes a famous footnote embracing a generally broader judicial power to examine laws violating indi-vidual constitutional rights or discriminating against minorities.

39. ***Minersville School District v. Gobitis***, 310 U.S. 586 (1940): Rejected Free Exercise of Religion claim of Jehovah's Witnesses schoolchildren to be free from being forced to recite the Pledge of Allegiance and salute the flag against religious conscience.

40. ***United States v. Darby***, 312 U.S. 100 (1941): Upheld the Fair Labor Standards Act of 1938 as an exercise of Congress's power under the Commerce Clause and the Necessary and Proper Clause. Overruled a prior decision holding that Congress may not forbid the interstate shipment of goods produced in facto-ries employing child labor.

41. ***Ex parte Quirin***, 317 U.S. 1 (1942): Landmark decision up-holding presidential use of military commissions to try alleged Nazi saboteurs for violations of the law of war.

42. ***Wickard v. Filburn***, 317 U.S. 111 (1942): Upheld a federal law limiting agricultural production, as applied to home-grown wheat, as within Congress's power under the Commerce Clause and the Necessary and Proper Clause.

43. ***West Virginia State Board of Education v. Barnette***, 319 U.S. 642 (1943): Landmark decision embracing the First Amend-ment Free Speech Clause right of schoolchildren to be free from being forced to recite the Pledge of Allegiance and salute the flag. Overruled *Minersville School District v. Gobitis*, 310 U.S. 586 (1940).

44. ***Korematsu v. United States***, 323 U.S. 214 (1944); *Hirabayashi v. United States*, 320 U.S. 81 (1943): *Hirabayashi* upheld a military curfew order during World War II that applied only to persons of Japanese ancestry. *Korematsu* upheld the constitutionality of

a military-exclusion order removing such persons from their homes and ultimately interning them in relocation camps.

45. ***Youngstown Sheet & Tube Co. v. Sawyer***, 343 U.S. 579 (1952): Famous separation-of-powers case holding unconstitutional President Truman's seizure of the nation's steel industry to avert a labor strike during Korean War.

46. ***Brown v. Board of Education***, 347 U.S. 483 (1954) ("Brown I") and 349 U.S. 294 (1955) ("Brown II"): Landmark case holding state racial segregation in education unconstitutional under the Equal Protection Clause and repudiating "separate but equal" doctrine of *Plessy v. Ferguson* (1896). "Brown II" ordered district courts to fashion remedies to achieve desegregation "with all deliberate speed."

47. *Cooper v. Aaron*, 358 U.S. 1 (1958): Unanimously affirmed school desegregation order in the face of state resistance and asserted the supremacy of the Supreme Court's interpretations of the Constitution.

48. *Mapp v. Ohio*, 367 U.S. 643 (1961): Held that the Fourth Amendment forbids the use in court of evidence resulting from an unconstitutional search or seizure.

49. ***Baker v. Carr***, 369 U.S. 186 (1962); ***Reynolds v. Sims***, 377 U.S. 533 (1964): *Baker* embraced judicial authority to hear and decide Equal Protection Clause challenges to unequal state legislative representation. *Reynolds* held that Equal Protection Clause required states to balance legislative districts under a "one person, one vote" principle.

50. ***Engel v. Vitale***, 370 U.S. 421 (1962): Struck down the practice of daily classroom recitation of state-written prayer as part of an official public school program, under the Establishment of Religion Clause of the First Amendment.

51. *Gideon v. Wainwright*, 372 U.S. 335 (1963): Held that the Sixth Amendment right to counsel entitles indigent criminal defendants to court-appointed lawyers.

52. *Sherbert v. Verner*, 374 U.S. 398 (1963): Held that the Free Exercise of Religion Clause of the First Amendment requires government accommodation of individuals' religious beliefs when they conflict with government's usual rules, unless the law is narrowly tailored to serve a compelling governmental interest.

53. *New York Times Co. v. Sullivan*, 376 U.S. 254 (1964): Held that the First Amendment bars defamation suits by public officials absent strict proof that false statements were made intentionally or with reckless disregard for the truth.
54. *Heart of Atlanta Motel v. United States,* 379 U.S. 241 (1964): Unanimously upheld the Civil Rights Act of 1964's prohibition of racial discrimination in public hotels, restaurants, theaters, and sports arenas, as a valid exercise of Congress's power under the Commerce Clause.
55. *Griswold v. Connecticut*, 381 U.S. 479 (1965); *Eisenstadt v. Baird*, 405 U.S. 438 (1972): *Griswold* held that the use of contraceptives by married persons is protected by a constitutional right to privacy supported by the "penumbras" of other rights. *Eisenstadt* held that equal protection principles required extension of the right to unmarried persons.
56. *Harper v. Virginia Board of Elections*, 383 U.S. 663 (1966): Struck down a $1.50 "poll tax" for state elections as a violation of the Equal Protection Clause.
57. *Miranda v. Arizona*, 384 U.S. 436 (1966): Held that police must warn criminal suspects of their Fifth Amendment rights to remain silent and to have legal counsel.
58. *Loving v. Virginia*, 388 U.S. 1 (1967): Struck down state laws forbidding blacks and whites to marry one another as a violation of the Equal Protection Clause.
59. *Jones v. Alfred H. Mayer Co.*, 392 U.S. 409 (1968): Held that Congress's power to enforce the Thirteenth Amendment includes the power to prohibit certain forms of private discrimination in housing and in making commercial contracts.
60. *United States v. O'Brien*, 391 U.S. 367 (1968): Upheld a law prohibiting the burning of draft cards on the ground that the law regulated conduct for reasons unrelated to the suppression of expression.
61. *Brandenburg v. Ohio*, 395 U.S. 444 (1969): Free Speech Clause decision modifying the "clear and present danger" test and invalidating the conviction of a Ku Klux Klan leader for advocacy of unlawful acts, where speech was not "directed to inciting or producing imminent lawless action."
62. *Cohen v. California*, 403 U.S. 15 (1971): Upheld free speech

right to wear a jacket bearing a vulgar message in a public courthouse on the ground that the offensiveness of a speaker's message or manner of expression cannot justify its suppression.

63. *New York Times Co. v. United States* (*The Pentagon Papers Case*) 403 U.S. 713 (1971): Rejected, on First Amendment grounds, the Nixon administration's request for injunctions against newspapers publishing leaked, classified documents.

64. *Lemon v. Kurtzman*, 411 U.S. 192 (1971): Struck down laws providing direct state financial assistance to private religious schools as a violation of the Establishment Clause.

65. *Wisconsin v. Yoder*, 406 U.S. 205 (1972): Held that Wisconsin could not require Amish families to send their children to school beyond eighth grade, in contravention of the families' religious beliefs, under a general school attendance law.

66. *Furman v. Georgia*, 409 U.S. 902 (1972); *Gregg v. Georgia*, 428 U.S. 153 (1976): *Furman* held that the death penalty, as applied, was random and unpredictable, violating Due Process Clause and the Eighth Amendment ban on cruel and unusual punishments. *Gregg* upheld the constitutionality of the death penalty under certain conditions.

67. **Roe v. Wade**, 410 U.S. 113 (1973); *Doe v. Bolton*, 410 U.S. 179 (1973): Famous modern cases creating a "substantive due process" constitutional right to abortion throughout pregnancy.

68. **United States v. Nixon**, 418 U.S. 683 (1974): Significant case unanimously asserting judicial supremacy over the president, limiting presidential power over other executive branch officers, and rejecting a claim of plenary presidential privilege to refuse to produce evidence in a criminal prosecution by a special prosecutor.

69. *Buckley v. Valeo*, 424 U.S. 1 (1976): Leading case establishing constitutional framework for modern campaign-finance law under First Amendment.

70. **Craig v. Boren**, 429 U.S. 190 (1976): Struck down an Oklahoma law providing different legal drinking ages for men and women as a violation of the Equal Protection Clause of the Fourteenth Amendment, as applied to sex-based classifications.

71. *Regents of the University of California v. Bakke*, 438 U.S. 265 (1978): Held that the use of strict racial quotas in admissions

to public universities violated the Equal Protection Clause, but signaled the permissibility of using race as one factor among others when making decisions about individual applicants, in split decision joined in full by only one justice.

72. ***Widmar v. Vincent***, 454 U.S. 263 (1981): Held that First Amendment's Free Speech Clause requires that religious speakers and groups be granted equal access to a public forum for expression and that the Establishment Clause does not justify exclusion of such speakers because of the religious content of their expression.

73. *Immigration and Naturalization Service v. Chadha*, 462 U.S. 919 (1983): Struck down, as a violation of the separation of powers, "legislative veto" arrangements under which one or both houses of Congress might reserve the power to veto administrative actions of the executive branch pursuant to authority delegated by Congress.

74. *South Dakota v. Dole*, 483 U.S. 203 (1987): Embraced a broad view of Congress's spending power, including the power to attach substantive regulatory conditions to the receipt of federal funds by the states.

75. *Morrison v. Olson*, 487 U.S. 654 (1988): Important decision upholding the federal Independent Counsel Statute against constitutional separation-of-powers challenges.

76. *United States v. Mistretta*, 488 U.S. 361 (1989): Significant modern separation-of-powers case upholding broad delegation of federal lawmaking power to the U.S. Sentencing Commission, an "independent agency" composed of judges and executive appointees.

77. ***Texas v. Johnson***, 491 U.S. 397 (1989): Struck down state law prohibiting flag "desecration" as applied to the expressive conduct of burning a flag as an act of protest.

78. ***Employment Division v. Smith***, 494 U.S. 872 (1990): Established modern rule that Free Exercise Clause does not require the accommodation of religion where the law in question is neutral toward religion on its face and applies generally.

79. ***Planned Parenthood v. Casey***, 505 U.S. 803 (1992): Major case reaffirming *Roe v. Wade*'s creation of a substantive due process right to abortion, but on the basis of *"stare decisis"* rather than on the correctness of the original decision.

80. *United States v. Lopez*, 514 U.S. 549 (1995): Struck down the Gun-Free School Zones Act prohibiting gun possession near schools as beyond Congress's power to regulate commerce absent a demonstrated connection to interstate commercial activity.

81. *Hurley v. Irish-American Gay, Lesbian and Bisexual Group of Boston*, 515 U.S. 557 (1995): Unanimous decision holding that speakers, including groups, have First Amendment right to control the content of their own messages and membership.

82. *United States Term Limits, Inc. v. Thornton*, 514 U.S. 779 (1995): Held that the states may not limit the number of terms served by U.S. Representatives and Senators elected to represent them in Congress.

83. *Rosenberger v. Rector and Visitors of the University of Virginia*, 515 U.S. 819 (1995): Held that the Free Speech Clause requires that religious speakers and groups be granted access to government benefits and media for expression on the same terms as other private speakers and that the Establishment Clause does not forbid equal access to state funding on account of the religious nature of a group's expression or identity.

84. *Romer v. Evans*, 517 U.S. 620 (1996): Struck down, as a violation of the Equal Protection Clause, a Colorado state constitutional provision repealing local gay-rights ordinances.

85. *United States v. Virginia*, 518 U.S. 515 (1996): Held that a state military academy open only to men violated the Equal Protection Clause, employing a strict standard of review for sex-based classifications.

86. *City of Boerne v. Flores*, 521 U.S. 507 (1997): Held that Congress's power to enforce the provisions of the Fourteenth Amendment is limited to the enforcement of the Supreme Court's interpretations of the amendment. Struck down an act applying Congress's broader interpretation of the Free Exercise Clause against state governments.

87. *United States v. Morrison*, 529 U.S. 598 (2000): Struck down provisions of the federal Violence Against Women Act punishing certain intrastate violent acts as beyond Congress's powers either to regulate commerce or to enforce the Fourteenth Amendment's Equal Protection Clause prohibitions on state government action.

88. *Apprendi v. New Jersey*, 530 U.S. 466 (2000): Held that the Sixth Amendment right to a trial by jury in criminal cases requires proof, beyond a reasonable doubt, of every fact forming an element of the offense or that increases the allowable punishment.

89. *Stenberg v. Carhart*, 530 U.S. 914 (2000); *Gonzales v. Carhart*, 550 U.S. 124 (2007): *Stenberg* found a constitutional right to the "partial birth" abortion procedure, which involves initiating live-birth delivery and then puncturing the skull during the birth process. *Gonzales* upheld a federal law banning the procedure as long as abortion could be obtained by other means.

90. **Bush v. Gore**, 531 U.S. 98 (2000): Politically controversial decision striking down state recount procedures in a presidential election as a violation of "one person, one vote" principles under the Equal Protection Clause holdings of *Baker v. Carr* (1962) and *Reynolds v. Sims* (1964).

91. *Zelman v. Simmons-Harris*, 536 U.S. 639 (2002): Rejected an Establishment Clause challenge to inclusion of religious schools in school-choice "voucher" programs.

92. **Grutter v. Bollinger**, 539 U.S. 306 (2003); *Gratz v. Bollinger*, 539 U.S. 244 (2003): *Grutter* upheld the consideration of racial-minority status in state university admissions as justified by a compelling educational interest in racial diversity, but *Gratz* struck down overt racial quotas or flat numerical point awards based on race alone.

93. **Lawrence v. Texas**, 539 U.S. 558 (2003): Held that the Constitution creates a substantive due process right to engage in homosexual sexual conduct free from state interference.

94. **Hamdi v. Rumsfeld**, 542 U.S. 507 (2004): Held that the president's Commander-in-Chief Clause authority to conduct war includes the power to capture and hold American citizens caught fighting for the enemy, but that the Due Process Clause requires that U.S. citizens be given a hearing to contest their detention.

95. *Kelo v. New London*, 545 U.S. 469 (2005): Held that the Fifth Amendment permits government to take private property "for public use," in the form of transfer to a private development corporation.

96. *Hamdan v. Rumsfeld*, 548 U.S. 557 (2006): Held that neither the president's constitutional power as Commander-in-Chief nor Congress's "Authorization for Use of Military Force" of 2001 was sufficient to authorize use of military tribunals to try enemy combatants for violations of the law of war.

97. **Boumediene v. Bush**, 553 U.S. 723 (2008): Held that alien unlawful combatants captured abroad and held overseas at a U.S. naval base possess U.S. constitutional right to the writ of habeas corpus to challenge the legality of their detention.

98. *District of Columbia v. Heller*, 554 U.S. 570 (2008): Held that the Second Amendment protects an individual right to possess a firearm for self-defense in the home and not merely a right in connection with service in a state militia.

99. *Citizens United v. Federal Election Commission*, 130 S. Ct. 876 (2010): Struck down a provision of federal law limiting corporations' free speech rights to advance independent views concerning candidates, issues, and elections.

100. **McDonald v. City of Chicago**, 130 S. Ct. 3020 (2010): Held that the Fourteenth Amendment applies the Second Amendment right to keep and bear arms to the states in the same way that it applies it to the federal government.

101. **National Federation of Independent Business v. Sebelius**, ___ U.S. _____ (2012): Important case holding that provision of federal law mandating individual purchase of health insurance or pay a penalty is within Congress's power under the Taxing Clause but not under the Commerce or Necessary and Proper clauses. Also held that coercive conditions attached to federal funding of Medicaid, imposed on states, exceed Congress's spending power.

BIBLIOGRAPHY

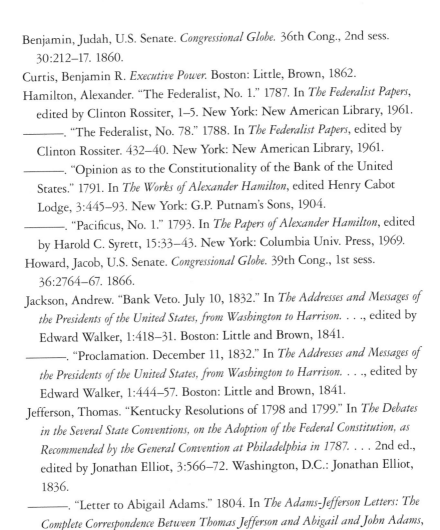

Benjamin, Judah, U.S. Senate. *Congressional Globe.* 36th Cong., 2nd sess. 30:212–17. 1860.

Curtis, Benjamin R. *Executive Power.* Boston: Little, Brown, 1862.

Hamilton, Alexander. "The Federalist, No. 1." 1787. In *The Federalist Papers,* edited by Clinton Rossiter, 1–5. New York: New American Library, 1961.

———. "The Federalist, No. 78." 1788. In *The Federalist Papers,* edited by Clinton Rossiter. 432–40. New York: New American Library, 1961.

———. "Opinion as to the Constitutionality of the Bank of the United States." 1791. In *The Works of Alexander Hamilton,* edited Henry Cabot Lodge, 3:445–93. New York: G.P. Putnam's Sons, 1904.

———. "Pacificus, No. 1." 1793. In *The Papers of Alexander Hamilton,* edited by Harold C. Syrett, 15:33–43. New York: Columbia Univ. Press, 1969.

Howard, Jacob, U.S. Senate. *Congressional Globe.* 39th Cong., 1st sess. 36:2764–67. 1866.

Jackson, Andrew. "Bank Veto. July 10, 1832." In *The Addresses and Messages of the Presidents of the United States, from Washington to Harrison. . . .,* edited by Edward Walker, 1:418–31. Boston: Little and Brown, 1841.

———. "Proclamation. December 11, 1832." In *The Addresses and Messages of the Presidents of the United States, from Washington to Harrison. . . .,* edited by Edward Walker, 1:444–57. Boston: Little and Brown, 1841.

Jefferson, Thomas. "Kentucky Resolutions of 1798 and 1799." In *The Debates in the Several State Conventions, on the Adoption of the Federal Constitution, as Recommended by the General Convention at Philadelphia in 1787. . . .* 2nd ed., edited by Jonathan Elliot, 3:566–72. Washington, D.C.: Jonathan Elliot, 1836.

———. "Letter to Abigail Adams." 1804. In *The Adams-Jefferson Letters: The Complete Correspondence Between Thomas Jefferson and Abigail and John Adams,* edited by Lester J. Cappon, 278–80. Chapel Hill: Univ. of North Carolina Press, 1959.

———. "Opinion on the Constitutionality of a National Bank." 1791. In *The Writings of Thomas Jefferson: Being His Autobiography, Correspondence, Reports, Messages, Addresses, and Other Writings, Official and Private.*, edited by H.A. Washington, 3:255–561. New York: Riker, Thorne, 1854.

———. "To Judge Spencer Roane." 1819. In *The Works of Thomas Jefferson*, edited by Paul Leicester Ford, 12:135–40. New York: G.P. Putnam's Sons, 1905.

Lincoln, Abraham. "Final Emancipation Proclamation." 1863. In *A Compilation of the Messages and Papers of the Presidents, 1789–1897*, edited by James D. Richardson, 6:157–59. Washington, D.C.: Government Printing Office, 1897.

———. "First Inaugural Address." 1861. In *A Compilation of the Messages and Papers of the Presidents, 1789–1897*, edited by James D. Richardson, 6:5–12. Washington, D.C.: Government Printing Office, 1897.

———. "Letter to Winfield Scott." 1861. In *A Compilation of the Messages and Papers of the Presidents, 1789–1897*, edited by James D. Richardson, 6:18. Washington, D.C.: Government Printing Office, 1897.

———. "Order of Retaliation." 1863. In *A Compilation of the Messages and Papers of the Presidents, 1789–1897*, edited by James D. Richardson, 6:177. Washington, D.C.: Government Printing Office, 1897.

———. "Proclamation Suspending the Writ of Habeas Corpus." 1862. In *A Compilation of the Messages and Papers of the Presidents, 1789–1897*, edited by James D. Richardson, 6:98–99. Washington, D.C.: Government Printing Office, 1897.

———. "Proclamation Suspending the Writ of Habeas Corpus Throughout the United States." 1863. In *A Compilation of the Messages and Papers of the Presidents, 1789–1897*, edited by James D. Richardson, 6:170–71. Washington, D.C.: Government Printing Office, 1897.

———. "Special Message to Congress." 1861. In *A Compilation of the Messages and Papers of the Presidents, 1789–1897*, edited by James D. Richardson, 6:20–31. Washington, D.C.: Government Printing Office, 1897.

———. "Speech on the Dred Scott Decision at Springfield, Illinois, June 26, 1857." In *Speeches and Writings, 1832–1858*, edited by Roy P. Basler and Don E. Fehrenbacher, 390–403. New York: Literary Classics of the United States, 1989.

————. "To Erastus Corning and Others." 1863. In *Speeches and Writings, 1859–1865*, edited by Roy P. Basler and Don E. Fehrenbacher, 454–63. New York: Literary Classics of the United States, 1989.

————. "To James C. Conkling." 1863. In *Speeches and Writings, 1859–1865*, edited by Roy P. Basler and Don E. Fehrenbacher, 495–99. New York: Literary Classics of the United States, 1989.

Madison, James. "The Federalist, No. 39." 1788. In *The Federalist Papers*, edited by Clinton Rossiter, 208–14. New York: New American Library, 1961.

————. "The Federalist, No. 47." 1788. In *The Federalist Papers*, edited by Clinton Rossiter, 268–76. New York: New American Library, 1961.

————. "The Federalist, No. 48." 1788. In *The Federalist Papers*, edited by Clinton Rossiter, 276–81. New York: New American Library, 1961.

————. "The Federalist, No. 51." 1788. In *The Federalist Papers*, edited by Clinton Rossiter, 288–93. New York: New American Library, 1961.

————. "Report on the Virginia Resolutions." 1800. In *The Debates in the Several State Conventions, on the Adoption of the Federal Constitution, as Recommended by the General Convention at Philadelphia in 1787. . . .* 2nd ed., edited by Jonathan Elliot, 3:572–608. Washington, D.C.: Jonathan Elliot, 1836.

————. "Virginia Resolutions of 1798." In *The Debates in the Several State Conventions, on the Adoption of the Federal Constitution, as Recommended by the General Convention at Philadelphia in 1787. . . .* 2nd ed., edited by Jonathan Elliot, 3:554–58. Washington, D.C.: Jonathan Elliot, 1836.

Nixon, Richard. "Veto of War Powers Resolution." 1973. In *Public Papers of the Presidents*, compiled by James B. Rhoads, 893–95. Washington D.C.: Office of the Federal Register, 1975.

Senate Joint Resolution 23, Pub. Law No. 107-40, 115 Stat. 224, 2001. http://www.gpo.gov/fdsys/pkg/BILLS-107sjres23enr/pdf/BILLS-107sjres23enr.pdf

INDEX

ﻋﻠﻰ